SPECIAL BRANCH

SPECIAL BRANCH

A HISTORY: 1883–2006

RAY WILSON & IAN ADAMS

Biteback Publishing

First published in Great Britain in 2015 by
Biteback Publishing Ltd
Westminster Tower
3 Albert Embankment
London SE1 7SP

ISBN 978-1-84954-910-3

10 9 8 7 6 5 4 3 2 1

A CIP catalogue record for this book is available from the British Library.

Set in Bulmer

Printed and bound in Great Britain by
CPI Group (UK) Ltd, Croydon CR0 4YY

To Ian

CONTENTS

ACKNOWLEDGEMENTS

I AM DEEPLY INDEBTED to my friend and former colleague, the late Ian Adams, who permitted me to share in his authorship of this history. He sadly died when the book was only half completed but he had so successfully infected me with his enthusiasm for researching and recording police, and more particularly Special Branch, history that I was able to finish a task which, until his untimely death, had been a most agreeable experience.

I am also profoundly grateful to two of my tutors at Birkbeck, University of London: to the late Professor Sally Ledger for encouraging me to appreciate the written word and to Mari Alderman for unravelling the mysteries of research. Thanks are also due to Biteback Publishing, and particularly their editor-at-large, Michael Smith, and assistant editor, Victoria Godden, for making publication a comparatively trouble-free process.

In the absence of any access to police records it would have been impossible to produce a meaningful history of the Branch without the many recollections of former colleagues readily supplied. Particularly helpful contributions were supplied by Lord Peter Imbert. Ben Gunn, David Waghorn, Peter Westcott, Dewi Jones, Matt Dwyer, Dave Yeadell, Geoff Craft, Steve Cracknell, Gerrard Hancock, Jim Dale, Colin Colson, Peter Smither, Peter Gardner, Malcolm MacLeod, Don Buchanan, John Howley, David Bicknell, Tony Greenslade, Paul Croydon,

Kevin Kindleysides and John Hague and there were others. If I have overlooked some names, I apologise, attributing my oversight to lack of secretarial support and rapidly failing memory!

Finally I should like to thank the staff at the National Archives and the British Library for their unfailing and cheerful assistance and patience.

PREFACE

I N THIS HISTORY of the Special Branch of the Metropolitan Police, Ray Wilson and the late Ian Adams have successfully produced, in a meticulously researched work, the first complete account of the formation, development and eventual demise of this unique branch of the Criminal Investigation Department. They illustrate how the bombings and other violent activities of a small group of terrorists, in an effort to change the political course and direction of a democratically elected government, brought about an extension of the Metropolitan Police remit to cover what we might describe as 'political crimes'.

The writers correct the misconception that in its earliest days the sole purpose of the Special 'Irish' Branch was to contain and bring to justice the Fenians and other politically extreme Irish groups. As the reader will discover, it was also tasked with the requirement to pass information to the government of the day about the activities of the many home-grown and foreign anarchist groups; the dubious activities of the Russian secret police directed against their own targets in London; and even the intentions and activities of the women's suffrage movement, the very nature and being of which became a huge embarrassment and threat to the government as its members adopted increasingly violent tactics.

This extensive and thoughtful story of the formation and development of the Special Branch of the Metropolitan Police will stand as a reference book, not just on its birth, life and amalgamation into the Counter-Terrorism Command of the Metropolitan Police Service, but will, without giving away any vital state secrets, add authenticity and detail to any account of the development of this country's security services. I recommend the book, not only to those with any connection to or who work within the security arena, but also to the wider public who have an interest in the defence of this country's interests. There is much knowledge to be gained from this excellent study.

Lord Peter Imbert CVO QPM DL
Commissioner of the Metropolitan Police 1987–93

HEADS OF SPECIAL BRANCH
FROM 1883 TO 2006

1883 Adolphus ('Dolly') Williamson

1887 John Littlechild

1893 William Melville

1903 Patrick Quinn

1918 James McBrien

1929 Edward Parker

1936 Albert Canning

1946 Leonard Burt

1958 Evan Jones

1966 Ferguson ('Fergie') Smith

1972 Victor Gilbert

1977 Robert Bryan

1981 Colin Hewett

1986 Simon Crawshaw

1987 Peter Phelan

1991 John Howley

1996 Barry Moss

1999 Roger Pearse

2003 Janet Williams

INTRODUCTION

O N 2 OCTOBER 2006, the Special Branch of the Metropolitan Police (MPSB) ceased to exist when, as part of a larger operation designed to modernise the Metropolitan Police and improve its efficiency, the Branch – which in 1986 had been renamed 'Special Operations 12' (SO12) – was merged with another unit, the Anti-Terrorist Branch (SO13), to become SO15.[1] The move was greeted with dismay by past and present members of the redundant department, who were proud of its fine traditions and felt that the knowledge and expertise that had been accumulated and honed for well over a century were to be diluted and allowed to disappear into thin air.

While numerous books published over the years describe particular aspects of Special Branch work, there is no comprehensive history covering the whole of its lifespan, not least because the confidential nature of its work has inhibited the disclosure of some of its more interesting, but covert, operations. However, in recent years, and particularly since the passing of the Freedom of Information Act in 2000, there has been a growing tendency for some security and other official organisations to be more forthcoming about their evolution, past

---

1   Throughout this book it will continue to be referred to as 'Special Branch' and SO13 as 'the Anti-Terrorist Branch'

RAY WILSON & IAN ADAMS

records and the way in which they operate. For example, in 1997, the Security Service (MI5) declassified a limited selection of its archives and shortly afterwards commissioned the publication of an authorised history of the Service.[2] The Secret Intelligence Service has also given access to some of its records.[3] In contrast, the greater part of Special Branch archives has remained closed, and much of its past and recent activity has continued to be unnecessarily shrouded in mystery.

There are of course valid reasons why certain matters should remain secret, and while each has to be judged on its merit, they can be summarised as those disclosures which might:

(a) prejudice ongoing enquiries;

(b) prejudice human or technological sources;

(c) damage the United Kingdom or its relations with another country; or

(d) be not financially viable due to lack of resources or manpower.

Most government papers on which a time restriction has been imposed are available after thirty, seventy or 100 years. The Metropolitan Police has resisted disclosing many documents even after the expiry of such periods and this has made the task of historians more difficult. The primary sources cited in this book are all within the public domain; they include the few Special Branch reports that have been released, contemporary news reports and documents sent by the Branch to the Security and Intelligence Services, the Cabinet Office, the Home Office and the Foreign Office, and subsequently released by them. Together they show the substantial contribution to the security of the state made by the Special Branch during its lifetime. We have also drawn on a number of interesting articles by writers on the internet and, inevitably, on the recollections of former members of the MPSB. No single book could adequately cover the vast

---

2   Christopher Andrew, *The Defence of the Realm: The Authorized History of MI5* (London: Allen Lane, 2009)

3   Keith Jeffery, *MI6: The History of the Secret Intelligence Service, 1909–1949* (London: Bloomsbury, 2010)

number of cases with which the Branch was involved, but we hope that the examples we have been able to give will illustrate how the Branch helped to enable the government to distinguish between those who sought to destroy the state and those who merely wished to express a different political view about how it should be governed.

In the early part of the book, we follow the fortunes of this unique part of the Criminal Investigation Department (CID) from its inauspicious birth in Queen Victoria's reign, describing the ever-widening range of its responsibilities and activities during the challenging times of the late nineteenth and twentieth centuries, and concluding in the later chapters with its loss of identity and eventual demise in the massive reorganisation of the Metropolitan Police to cope with a new type of terrorist threat at the beginning of the twenty-first century.

In the 1880s, political violence, a commonplace phenomenon in Ireland, spilled over into mainland Britain in a brief but bloodthirsty campaign, frequently referred to as the Dynamite War, which lasted from 1881 to 1885. The British police, especially those in the capital, were totally unprepared for this unprecedented development in the Irish struggle for self-determination. In particular, there appeared to be a total lack of police intelligence about the intentions of the Fenians, prompting the Home Secretary, Sir William Harcourt, to express his misgivings, in 1881, to the newly appointed Director of the CID at Scotland Yard, Howard Vincent: 'I am much disturbed at the absolute want of information in which we seem to be with regard to the Fenian organisation in London.' Vincent was instructed to direct all his efforts to 'get some light into these dark places'.[4]

By far the most significant of the measures taken by the Director to get some light into dark places was the creation of a 'Fenian Office' at Scotland Yard, which would liaise with the Home Office's Fenian adviser and its explosives officer; with British provincial police forces; and with an Irish police inspector on attachment. This was the forerunner of the Special Irish Branch (SIB), soon to become

---

4   S. H. Jeyes & F. D. How, *The Life of Sir Howard Vincent* (London: George Allen, 1912), p. 106

XVIII   RAY WILSON & IAN ADAMS

the Special Branch, the establishment of which was marked by a brief entry in Metropolitan Police Orders of 17 March 1883. From its humble beginnings (its original staff of twelve men didn't even have their own office), 'the Branch', as it became known, eventually boasted an establishment approaching 1,000 officers.

We have drawn extensively on the memoirs of a number of Special Branch officers; the styles of Herbert Fitch and Harold Brust reflect the genre of the popular adventure stories of their day, in which the writer is the hero, but that in itself is no reason to regard them as apocryphal. John Sweeney, Ralph Kitchener, George Wilkinson and Leonard Burt are more factual and expand our knowledge of many incidents that occurred during their service. We also quote from the memoirs of Sir Basil Thomson and Sir Wyndham Childs, two senior officers who had ultimate responsibility the Branch in turbulent times. All these writers, however, had their own agendas.

Of the most helpful secondary sources describing the origins and development of state security, Rupert Allason's *The Branch*, written in 1983 to mark the hundredth anniversary of its formation, relies on the memories of former officers, contemporary news reports and files released to the National Archives. It contains some minor errors and although Allason does not disclose his primary sources, the work provides a useful account of the challenging events of the first 100 years of the Branch's life. Christopher Andrew's excellently researched *Defence of the Realm* has been a valued source of information. Bernard Porter's *Plots and Paranoia*, his *The Origins of the Vigilant State* and Richard Thurlow's *The Secret State* cover the development of Special Branch, MI5 and MI6, but are handicapped by not having access to documents that at their time of writing were not declassified. Porter was misinformed by Special Branch that the documents he sought were pulped during the Second World War. Richard Thurlow, in a prestigious work, has pointed out that a number of documents, still covered by the Official Secrets Acts in this country, were forwarded to United States intelligence services and subsequently released to the American public. For fear of infringing the Act, he did not quote from them. Other works we have consulted, in a wide range of secondary sources, are listed in the Bibliography.

Our own requests for information from the Metropolitan Police have proved disappointing, although we have had access, during some sixty years of police service, to some of the most highly classified material and are perhaps even more aware than their present guardians of the special sensitivity of a few documents.

CHAPTER ONE

FENIAN TERRORISM

O N 12 FEBRUARY 1867, the citizens of Chester, alarmed by an unusually large influx of dubious-looking strangers into the city, were
aware that something untoward was afoot. Reports in *The Times* and
elsewhere graphically illustrate the citizens' concern, the Irishmen's crude preparations (for Irishmen they were) and the exaggerated reaction by the authorities:

Liverpool, Monday, Midnight.

In the course of the morning a large body of ruffians made their appearance in Chester. The city police were at once armed. [...] Mr Binger the
superintendent of the [railway] station, at once made arrangements to
pull up the rails at points on the Birkenhead line if necessary. At eleven
o'clock two companies of the 54th Regiment and the Volunteers mus-
tered in the Castle.[1]

The authorities, regularly briefed by an informant, John Joseph Corydon, were

---

[1]   *The Times*, 'Apprehended Riots at Chester', 12 & 13 February 1867

well aware of what was going on.[2] The 'ruffians', a group of Irish revolutionaries loosely termed 'Fenians',[3] were proposing to storm Chester Castle and seize arms and ammunition stored there in large quantities. These were to be rushed to Ireland on hijacked trains and boats for use in a Fenian uprising planned to take place throughout Ireland later the same day.[4] Confronted by the combined might of the police and army, the raiding party retired in disarray and the rising in Ireland was postponed. Although this was a relatively minor incident, it was significant for, although Fenian-inspired violence was a common occurrence in Ireland, this was the first occasion on which the nationalists had extended their activities to mainland Britain.

Centuries of what Robert Kee succinctly describes as 'London's claim to concern itself with Ireland'[5] had led to a situation whereby the nationalists' impassioned fight for self-determination could no longer be contained within the confines of the Emerald Isle. The Irish Catholics' anti-British hatred, fuelled over the centuries by the British government's repressive legislation, saw thousands of embittered Irishmen leaving their homeland for other countries, principally North America (1.5 million) and, paradoxically, England (300,000). It is estimated that by 1871, 5 per cent of the population of the United States was Irish-born.[6] It was inevitable that among these hordes of disaffected Irishmen there would be some who would seek revenge for what they saw as the cruel and calculated injustices that the British government had inflicted on them and their families. And so it was that in January 1867, a group of Irish-Americans set up headquarters in London where they formulated plans for what turned out to be the twin debacles of the following month, the uprising in Ireland and the raid on

---

2   Joseph Denieffe, *A Personal Narrative of the Irish Revolutionary Brotherhood* (Shannon: Irish University Press, 1969), p. 140

3   The term 'Fenian' was used to refer to the two main Irish republican movements: the Fenian Brotherhood in the USA and the Irish Republican Brotherhood (IRB) in Ireland, both formed in 1858

4   Robert Kee, *The Bold Fenian Men* (London: Penguin, 1989) pp. 34–5

5   Robert Kee, *Ireland: A History* (London: Sphere Books, 1982)

6   James H. Murphy, *Ireland: A Social, Cultural and Literary History, 1791–1891* (Dublin: Four Courts Press, 2003), p. 104

Chester Castle. Most of the cabal in London had seen action in the American Civil War, an experience upon which they drew in the subsequent terrorist campaign on mainland Britain.

THE MANCHESTER MARTYRS

Secure in their London base, they rearranged the aborted February uprising in Ireland for 5 March, but once again the authorities, regularly briefed by Corydon, thwarted their plans and arrested many of their ringleaders, though not the committee who had organised the two disastrous operations. Their ringleader was 'Colonel' Thomas J. Kelly, who had fought with distinction for the Republican Army during the American Civil War and was now chief of the main Fenian group, the Irish Republican Brotherhood (IRB). On 11 September, Kelly and a fellow member of the IRB, 'Captain' Timothy Deasy,[7] who were being urgently sought by police, were arrested in Manchester and remanded in custody. A rescue plan was immediately organised by Edward O'Meagher, with whom they had been staying.

A week later, Deasy and Kelly were rescued by an armed gang of about thirty Fenians, who attacked the prison van conveying them from the remand hearing. During the skirmish, a shot was fired through the door of the vehicle, killing the unarmed police sergeant Charles Brett inside. Of the many Irishmen subsequently arrested, three were later executed: William Allen, Philip Larkin and Michael O'Brien – 'the Manchester Martyrs'. Their memory has been perpetuated in the press, by chroniclers of Irish history, through numerous monuments sited in Manchester and throughout the Republic of Ireland, at annual memorial services and in songs such as 'God Save Ireland' and 'The Smashing of the Van'.[8] The whole tenor of the trial – the suggestion of perjured police evidence,

---

7 Veterans of the American Civil War frequently used their former ranks when joining the IRB

8 Murphy, *Ireland*, p. 112. Over the next forty years, seventeen monuments were erected and, thirty years after the executions, twenty-six annual memorial services were still being held throughout the country and elsewhere

the arrest of innocent men and the condemned men's final, patriotic statements from the dock – produced a remarkable transformation in Irish public opinion. Outrage at the executions was matched by a new sympathy for Fenianism that the 'risings' of 1865, '66 and '67 had failed to achieve.

THE CLERKENWELL EXPLOSION[9]

However, much of this sympathy turned to public condemnation following the IRB's next operation in England. This was the failed attempt to rescue one of their number from the Clerkenwell House of Detention. Among the IRB members who had settled in London in 1867 was the organisation's principal arms procurer, Richard Burke. On the evening of 20 November, acting on a tip-off from an informant, the Metropolitan Police arrested Burke and a confederate, Michael Casey, who were remanded in custody.

Burke's IRB colleagues immediately began making plans to effect his escape from prison. James Murphy, organiser of the IRB in Scotland, travelled to London with his aide, Michael Barrett, to take charge of the rescue attempt. Burke's sister, Mrs Barry, was allowed to visit him in prison and smuggled out a note from her brother which she passed to Murphy. It read:

Dear Friend,

You see the position I am in. If you exert yourself you can get ourselves out of it. There is a house called 'The Noted Stout House' opposite the yard where we go to exercise and there is a gateway at the wall. If you get a barrel of gunpowder and place it there it will drive it to hell. If you cannot do this you ought to be shot.

9   Ian Adams, *Fenian Folly: The Story of the Clerkenwell Explosion, Friday 13 December 1867* (Titchfield: Spiker Publications, 2006) gives full details of the incident with bibliography

By 11 December, sufficient gunpowder had been purchased and a meeting of IRB members agreed to carry out the rescue attempt the following day. Guns were distributed, during which delicate operation one of the conspirators managed to shoot himself in the foot. The plan was to blow a hole in a wall of the prison yard between 3 p.m. and 4 p.m. when the prisoners were exercising there. A white ball thrown over the wall would be a signal that the attempt was on.

Scotland Yard, however, was well aware of the conspirators' intentions, as up-to-the-minute, accurate intelligence was being transmitted from the police in Dublin through the Home Office. The elderly Commissioner, Sir Richard Mayne, was not in his office when the information was received, but his deputy, Captain Labalmondiere, took steps to ensure that the local police were aware of the precise details of the Fenians' plans. The local police superintendent was directed to 'have the external wall examined to ascertain that there has been no attempt to mine and arrange for an observation to be kept on it'.

An attempt was, in fact, made to blow up the wall on the 12th at about 3.45 p.m. Burke, who was being exercised, saw a white ball come over the wall and promptly fell out of line and pretended to take a stone out of his shoe. The incident aroused no suspicion at the time but a prison officer recalled it afterwards, as he pocketed the ball and took it home for his children. Murphy attempted to light the fuse but it went out, so the conspirators put the barrel of gunpowder back on the handcart that had been used to bring it to the prison and wheeled it away.

A further attempt was made the following day (Friday 13th) when the barrel containing gunpowder was again placed against the perimeter wall and ignited with a fuse. The resulting explosion caused the deaths of fifteen persons and another forty were removed to hospital, most of them disabled and affected for life. Many of the casualties were children. Six hundred families suffered loss or privation caused by damage to work, homes or property. A relief fund raised more than £10,000 to give temporary assistance to the victims and provide for those permanently disabled. The damage to property was met by a grant of £7,500 from the Exchequer, promoted by the Prime Minister Benjamin Disraeli in his capacity as First Lord of the Treasury. Predictably, the public was outraged and the police were put under considerable pressure to find the culprits. Why they failed to act more effectively, in view of the precise information they had received, resulted in severe and justified criticism. Their lame excuse was that they 'expected the wall to be blown up when in fact it was blown down'. They had anticipated a more sophisticated method to be employed for breaching the wall. Sir Richard Mayne, the elderly Commissioner, accepted responsibility for the shortcomings of his force and offered his resignation, which was declined. He died, a broken man, a year later on 26 December 1868. Ironically, Burke was not rescued, as the prisoners' exercise time had been changed as a precautionary measure. Had it not been, Burke and many other prisoners would probably have been killed or seriously injured.

In the immediate aftermath of the explosion, Inspector Adolphus ('Dolly') Williamson, of the Detective Branch, was appointed to take charge of the investigation. As a result of extensive police enquiries, six people were brought to trial at the Central Criminal Court on 20 April 1868 charged with murder. The trial lasted a week, but at the end of it only Michael Barrett was convicted.

The jury accepted the testimony of a co-defendant, Patrick Mullany, that Barrett claimed to have fired the gunpowder, although his evidence was riddled with inconsistencies: he was not at the scene of the explosion and the descriptions of the man who was seen to light the fuse, given by other witnesses, conflicted with his own description of Barrett. In the wake of the allegations of perjured evidence in both the Manchester and Old Bailey trials, the authorities set up a Special Commission to examine the evidence in the case of Barrett. It concluded that no miscarriage of justice had taken place and so the sentence of death was confirmed. Barrett was executed on 26 May 1868, the last man to suffer public execution in England. And so another name was added to the rapidly growing Fenian 'roll of honour'.

Burke was convicted and served out his sentence at Woking Prison before his release in 1872. He later emigrated to the United States, where he died in 1922 at the age of eighty-four.

In political terms, the Fenians of 1867 achieved little. The bombing of Clerkenwell Prison and the exploits of the 'Manchester Martyrs' were not premeditated acts of terrorism. The perpetrators had no political agenda; theirs were the actions of incompetent and inexperienced groups of men and women who made grave miscalculations that resulted in death, injury and serious damage to property. Unlike the terrorist bombing campaigns directed against England from 1881–85, their deeds were not designed to publicise the cause of Irish self-determination by murdering innocent citizens. The Clerkenwell explosion, although a total disaster for the Fenians, for the police and, most tragically, for the innocent victims, did illustrate one fact that the republicans were later to capitalise on – that one such act in England drew more attention to the Irish cause than ten in Ireland. It also accelerated the formation of the Metropolitan Police Special Branch.

THE POLICE

U p to this point in Irish history, direct confrontation with Westminster on the soil of mainland Britain had slowly become inevitable. But from this moment onwards, the demand for home rule gave the movement added impetus. Despite the Fenians' determination to show that they were not shy of operating on English soil, Whitehall did nothing to prepare for the coming onslaught; the authorities remained comparatively unperturbed so long as the various factions engaged in warfare within the confines of Ireland. In particular, Britain's police forces were totally unprepared for the type of terrorist warfare that was about to be directed at the country's principal cities, none more so than the Metropolitan Police Force.

Sir Robert Peel had faced considerable opposition in steering his Metropolitan Police Bill through Parliament in 1829. The public, too, were vociferous in their objections to anything resembling a martial organisation and, in an effort to stifle their protests, members of the new constabulary were dressed to resemble gentlemen of leisure rather than custodians of the law. Their smart blue tunics had swallow tails which concealed a short wooden truncheon and in the summer the blue trousers were exchanged for white; the whole ensemble completed with reinforced top hats. Only ranks above inspector could carry firearms, though in exceptional circumstances cutlasses would be issued.[10] Such a body of men was not likely to strike fear into the hearts of armed Fenian terrorists.

In the early years, officers were subjected to derision and animosity, and serious breaches of public order put the police under severe pressure, often exposing them to the risk of personal injury. Frequently, as reported by *The Times*, they displayed commendable courage,[11] but at other times, so David Goodway claims, 'during the Chartist turbulence of 1848 Metropolitan Police constables appear to have lost control and inflicted savage beatings on both Chartist demonstrators and anyone else who innocently got in the way'.[12]

When public disorder was anticipated, it was most important for the police to obtain advance intelligence about the demonstrators' likely mood, numbers, targets and other matters that would affect the police response. In those days, the two principal ways in that such intelligence could be obtained was either through informants, notoriously unreliable, or by the police themselves. Well before the Metropolitan Police Force came into existence, Sir Robert Peel had shown himself strongly opposed to any use of informants as *agents provocateurs*, a practice much used by the French and the Irish. Commenting on the Prime Minister's (the Duke of Wellington) robust views on a London police force, he remarked in Parliament, 'God forbid that he should mean to countenance a system of espionage.'[13] A *Times* editorial in 1845 encapsulated the general public's attitude to police officers deceiving the populace by abandoning their uniforms and donning civilian clothes: 'There was and always will be something repugnant to the English mind in the bare idea of espionage. It smacks too strongly

10   Clive Emsley, *The English Police: A Political and Social History* (Harlow, Essex: Addison Wesley Longman, 2nd edition 1996), p. 26

11   *The Times*, 2 November 1853

12   David Goodway, *London Chartism, 1838–1848* (Cambridge: Cambridge University Press, 1982), pp. 120–24

13   Parliamentary Debates, XXI, 803

of France and Austria; and the powers it entrusts often to unworthy hands are liable to great abuse.'[14]

Nevertheless, the joint police commissioners were well aware of the value of first-hand intelligence in preserving the peace in troubled times and officers in plain clothes, as well as informants, were sometimes used to infiltrate subversive groups who represented a threat to public order. These unsophisticated forays into the murky world of undercover police work did not always meet with success, and on occasion ended in disaster, as illustrated in the cases cited below.

In 1832, Sergeant William Popay was detailed to investigate a recently formed radical political group, the National Political Union (NPU). Masquerading as an unemployed coal merchant, he infiltrated the Walworth and Camberwell branch of the organisation and played an active and vociferous part in their meetings. A subsequent investigation by a parliamentary committee of the House of Commons into his conduct found that Popay had incited members of the organisation to commit offences which they would not otherwise have done. He was dismissed from the police and his senior officers were severely criticised, with the inevitable consequence that the police became even more circumspect in their attempts to collect intelligence.

Emsley comments that on another occasion, in 1840, two officers in plain clothes attended a Chartist committee meeting and, when challenged for their names and addresses, rather than give false particulars, left the hall to return later in uniform, requesting formal permission to attend the meeting. In the 1850s and 1860s it was not uncommon to see officers in uniform openly taking notes at political meetings.[15] Such was the futility of unprofessional attempts at intelligence-gathering. However, it was rapidly becoming obvious to Sir Richard Mayne and Sir Charles Rowan, the joint Commissioners of the Metropolitan Police, that despite the public's continued hostility to policemen operating in plain clothes, there were certain situations where anonymity was essential.

14   *The Times*, 2 December 1845

15   Emsley, *The English Police*, pp. 104–105

In the face of public outrage, a 'detective branch' (variously referred to under different titles) comprising eight dedicated investigators (two inspectors and six sergeants), was set up at Scotland Yard in 1842.[16] The satirical magazine *Punch* typically referred to it as the 'Defective Department', while even the Commissioner admitted that 'a detective system is viewed with the greatest suspicion and jealousy by the majority of Englishmen and is, in fact, entirely foreign to the habits and feelings of the nation'.[17]

It can be seen that any proposal at this time for a 'political' department of the police similar to the Special Irish Branch that came into existence forty-one years later would never have been entertained by the authorities and would have met with determined opposition from the public. But the detectives were not without their supporters, one of whom was Charles Dickens who, after meeting the entire department, wrote an article entitled 'The Detective Police', which appeared in his magazine *Household Words* and was subsequently reproduced in *The Uncommercial Traveller and Reprinted Pieces etc*. The piece is fulsome in its praise of the officers: 'The Detective Force organised since the establishment of the existing Police, […] does its business in such a workmanlike manner […] that the public really do not know enough of it, to know a tithe of its usefulness.'[18]

Whether Dickens's writing had any influence on the public is difficult to assess, but there is no doubt that by the 1850s there were signs that at least some of the press were more favourably disposed not only towards the detective branch, but towards the police in general, the normally critical *Punch* magazine grudgingly conceding that:

> The police are beginning to take that place in the affections of the
> people […] that the soldiers and sailors used to occupy. In the old war-time

16   Philip Thurmond Smith, *Policing Victorian London: Political Policing, Public Order and the London Metropolitan Police* (Connecticut: Greenwood Press, 1985), pp. 62–3

17   T. A. Critchley, *A History of Police in England and Wales, 900–1966* (London: Constable, 1967), p. 161

18   Charles Dickens, 'The Detective Police' in *The Uncommercial Traveller and Reprinted Pieces etc.*, (London: Oxford University Press, 1958), p. 485

there was a sort of enthusiasm for the 'blue jackets', the defenders of the country; but in these happier days of peace, the blue coats – the defenders of order – are becoming the national favourites.[19]

For a number of reasons, however, the small unit of detectives formed in 1842 had failed to make an impact in the fight against crime. Detectives were greatly hampered in their investigative work by the regulation forbidding them to associate with criminals, and there remained the perennial fear of officers working in plain clothes being less conducive to discipline and more susceptible to corruption.

The abject police mismanagement of the events at Clerkenwell led to a Home Office inquiry the following year, which recommended an enlargement of the Detective Branch; fortuitously the new Commissioner, Colonel Sir Edmund Henderson, was thinking along the same lines. So, in 1869, the penultimate step was taken on the rocky road towards the establishment of the Criminal Investigation Department, and ultimately Special Branch.[20] The establishment of the Detective Branch based at Scotland Yard was increased to twenty-seven men and, for the first time, 180 full-time plain-clothes detectives were allocated to the different divisions. It is true that from the early days of its establishment the Force had deployed divisional officers on an *ad hoc* basis for the purpose of surveillance or infiltration, as the unfortunate incident of Sergeant Popay all too graphically illustrated, but never before had each division been given the luxury of its own dedicated investigators.[21]

Over the next eight years, this new enlarged force of detectives achieved no outstanding successes to enhance its reputation, which had never been particularly high, but in 1877 it was rocked by a disaster of gargantuan proportions. Two of its four chief inspectors and one inspector were found guilty at the Central Criminal Court of conspiracy to pervert the course of justice and each was

---

19   *Punch*, July–December 1851

20   Clive Emsley, *Crime and Society in England, 1750–1900* (Harlow, Essex: Addison Wesley Longman, 2nd edition, 1996), p. 237

21   David Ascoli, *The Queen's Peace* (London: Hamish Hamilton, 1979), pp. 138–41

sentenced to two years' hard labour; another chief inspector was acquitted on a similar charge.[22]

Following this scandal, a departmental commission was set up to enquire into the 'state, discipline and organisation' of the Metropolitan Police Detective Branch; the commission's findings led to the formation, in April 1878, of a Criminal Investigation Department (the CID) based at New Scotland Yard under a director (later Assistant Commissioner), Howard Vincent, a barrister.[23] Although Vincent was nominally the head of the new department, its day-to-day management was in the experienced hands of the newly appointed Chief Superintendent Adolphus Frederick Williamson, who had joined the Metropolitan Police in 1852 and, after successfully negotiating the lower ranks, had been elevated to superintendent, in charge of the Detective Department in 1870. Initial establishment of the CID was about 250 men, but despite a modest increase in the number of arrests for crime it was not until the next century that the CID began to enjoy the esteemed reputation which earned 'Scotland Yard' worldwide acclaim.

The authorities still considered it was not necessary, or indeed desirable, to form a quasi-political section of the police force. Frequent disorderly demonstrations were seen as simply overt expressions of aggression and were dealt with in a low-key and diplomatic manner, as breaches of the peace and ordinary crime.[24] One possible exception to this was a special 'foreign' section of the old 'detective department', which, during the 1850s, monitored the activities of foreign refugees and reported directly to the Commissioner. Porter describes this unit as keeping 'an effective systematic watch' on foreign revolutionaries seeking asylum in this country from the more repressive regimes of their homelands. Low-key reports on their activities were sent through the Home Office to the Foreign Office for onward transmission to the appropriate foreign government, if this were considered necessary.[25]

---

22 Ibid., pp. 146–7

23 Philip Thurmond Smith, *Policing Victorian London*, Chapter 3

24 Bernard Porter, *The Origins of the Vigilant State* (London: Weidenfeld & Nicolson, 1987), p. 11

25 Ibid., pp. 8–9

However, a scenario was soon to unfold that would awaken police and government interest in visitors to our shores and lead to the establishment of a unique
'political' department of the police – the Metropolitan Police Special (Irish)
Branch – which, for more than 100 years, would share with other intelligence
agencies the responsibility for the defence of the realm. The circumstances leading to this remarkable shift in policy by a police hierarchy that, influenced as
it was by public opinion and the views of Parliament, had always endeavoured
to avoid any suggestion that it was a political watchdog, can be traced back to
the oppressive measures already referred to, which were imposed on the Irish
people from the time of Henry II. The compulsory surrender of all land to the
English monarch in 1534, the subsequent establishment of 'plantations' and many
other factors, created a canker which was to infect relations between England
and Ireland for over 400 years.

THE LULL BEFORE THE STORM

After the events of 1867 there followed a period of apparent outward calm
marked by increased political activity on both sides of the Irish Sea, of which
one of the dominant topics was the age-long problem of land tenure. But, despite
all the discussion over the land question by the various Irish political factions as
much as by their enemies in Westminster, what remained the major target for the
nationalists was independence from England. O'Brien asserts that in Fenian eyes
agrarian reform or agrarian revolution was merely a 'stepping stone to separation
from England',[26] while Charles Stewart Parnell, the newly elected MP for Meath and
an increasingly dominant figure in Irish nationalist politics, 'while publicly avoiding any commitment to the Fenian movement as such' had managed in private 'to
convince its leaders of his adherence to the principle of absolute independence'.[27]

---

26   R. Barry O'Brien, *The Life of Charles Stewart Parnell* (London: Smith, Elder & Co., 1898), p. 168

27   Paul Bew, *Land and the National Question in Ireland, 1858–82* (Dublin: Gill & Macmillan, 1978), p. 49

THE AMERICAN INFLUENCE

M eanwhile, in the United States, the large population of Irish republican activists had not been idle. In 1871, as a result of an amnesty granted by the British government to Fenian prisoners held in English jails, waning American Fenianism was given a shot in the arm when many of these hardened revolutionaries arrived in the States, their dreams of a Republic of Ireland undimmed by their enforced stay as guests of HM Government. Their numbers included many of the IRB's key members, such as: Jeremiah O'Donovan Rossa, one of the most celebrated Irish republicans of all time; Thomas J. Kelly, who was to become head of the IRB; Thomas Francis Bourke, who had been sentenced to life imprisonment for his part in the 1867 rising; and many others of similar calibre. All these were to become household names to the as-yet unformed Special Irish Branch.

In 1876, the two main Irish nationalist groupings in the States, Clan na Gael and the IRB, united to form a joint Revolutionary Directory (RD) with responsibility 'for striking the enemy'. The Irish revolutionaries were not lacking in manpower, but needed money if they were to carry out their intentions. To meet this requirement, a 'skirmishing fund' was set up by O'Donovan Rossa specifically to finance what became known as the 'Skirmishers', who were introduced to the American public on 4 December 1875, through the pages of the *Irish World*:

> A few active, intrepid and intelligent men can do so much to annoy and hurt England. The Irish cause requires Skirmishers. It requires a little band of heroes who will initiate and keep up without intermission guerrilla warfare – men who will fly over land and sea like invisible beings – now striking the enemy in Ireland, now in India, now in England itself, as occasion may present.[28]

---

28 *Irish World*, 4 December 1875

The fund soon exceeded its target of $5,000 and, by 1877, according to John Devoy, leader of Clan na Gael, it had raised $23,000, which had risen to $78,000 by 1880.

THE STORM BREAKS

As a result of internal bickering, O'Donovan Rossa was deposed as secretary of the fund and became *persona non grata* with the Clan; he set up his own fund, the United Irish Reserve Fund, and prepared to launch his Skirmishers against the British mainland. At the same time, Clan na Gael was secretly making its own plans for an attack on England. The man who was deputed to mastermind the operation was Captain William Mackey Lomasney, born in Ohio of Irish parents, whose family had an outstanding republican pedigree. Formerly in the IRB, he was now a leading member of the Clan and yet another of the prisoners released under the terms of the 1871 amnesty. But it was not Lomasney who was to strike the initial blow against the common enemy – that distinction went to O'Donovan Rossa and his Skirmishers.[29] The target chosen for their initial foray onto the mainland was the British Army's infantry barracks in Salford. The date: 14 January 1881. By modern standards it was a minor incident – only one innocent child was killed and a woman seriously injured – but the ramifications were considerable. This was the first step in an Irish republican campaign to terrorise Britain into granting Ireland home rule, a campaign that was to continue intermittently throughout the twentieth century and into the twenty-first.

The authorities acted promptly: mindful of the Clerkenwell bomb, a police patrol, later replaced by the military, was mounted at Strangeways Prison; a troop of cavalry was dispatched to the neighbourhood; 100 foot soldiers were deployed at St Helens, an important railway junction. In Whitehall, the Home

---

29   K. R. M. Short, *The Dynamite War* (Dublin: Gill & Macmillan, 1979), p. 48

Secretary, William Vernon Harcourt, wrote to Vincent, head of the Metropolitan Police CID, in the following terms:

> The reports that come into me as to the probability of explosions under the auspices of the 'Skirmishing Committee' become more and more alarming. I am much disturbed at the absolute want of information in which we seem to be with regard to Fenian organisation in London. All other objects should be postponed in our efforts to get some light into these dark places. If anything occurs there will be a terrible outcry.[30]

He further urged Vincent to 'devote himself exclusively for the next month to Irish and Anglo-Irish business'. Without delay, Vincent contacted all police forces, seeking any information they might have about Fenian activities in their area; arrangements were put in place for additional security to be set up at all of London's key buildings, particularly the Houses of Parliament, the Tower of London and the Royal Mint, and precautions were taken to strengthen the protection of armouries maintained by volunteer military organisations. Most significantly, in addressing himself to the Home Secretary's anxiety to focus on intelligence-gathering, he set up a 'Fenian Office' at Scotland Yard that would liaise with Robert Anderson, the Home Office Fenian specialist and American spymaster; with Colonel Vivian Majendie, Home Office explosives expert; with provincial police forces; and with an Irish police inspector posted to the Fenian Office on attachment.[31]

Two months were to elapse before the terrorists struck again, on 16 March, when their target was London's Mansion House. The device, consisting of 15 lbs of explosives in a wooden box, had been placed in a window recess in the outer wall of the banqueting hall, where it was discovered by a patrolling policeman who deposited it without delay at Bow Lane Police Station. The banqueting

---

30   Jeyes and How, *The Life of Sir Howard Vincent*, p. 106

31   Porter, *The Origins of the Vigilant State*, p. 41

hall was empty but the detonation of a bomb in the very heart of the City would have been a tremendous fillip to the perpetrators; numerous suggestions as to the identities of the members of the group were put forward by newspapers of the day. One thing they had in common: they were all members of O'Donovan Rossa's Skirmishers, and they were sought, not only by the police, but by the Revolutionary Directory, and, in particular, William Lomasney, who referred to them as 'a lot of fools and ignoramuses, men who do not understand the first principles of the art of war, the elements of chemistry, or even the amount of explosive material necessary to remove or destroy an ordinary brick or stone wall'.[32]

Two of O'Donovan Rossa's men, James McGrath, alias Robert William Barton, and James McKevitt, shared lodgings in Liverpool. With typical bravado, these two Skirmishers selected the police station as their first target, with the night of 16 May chosen as the time for the attack. The device was successfully detonated but, because of the bombers' ignorance in the art of bomb-making, only caused superficial damage to the adjacent police section house. Lomasney must have derived some satisfaction from his disparaging and accurate assessment of their bomb-making ability, though his satisfaction would have been short-lived as he blew himself up when planting a bomb under London Bridge in 1884.

The second Liverpool target was the Town Hall. Early in the morning of 10 June, the two men, armed with revolvers, planted a powerful explosive device at the door of the building. For the first time, the explosive used was commercial dynamite, but the bombers' intentions were thwarted by the timely arrival of a police constable who actually saw the fuse being lit. Other officers arrived on the scene but were not in time to prevent the bomb detonating; little damage was caused, although the officers were fortunate to escape without injury. McGrath and McKevitt were both arrested after a short chase and received sentences of life imprisonment and twelve years respectively.[33]

The bomb at Liverpool Town Hall marked the end of this flurry of Skirmishing

---

32   William O'Brien and Desmond Ryan (eds), *Devoy's Post Bag: 1871–1928*, vol. 2: *1880–1928* (Dublin: Irish Academy Press, 1953), pp. 51–52

33   *The Times*, 13 June 1881

activity in England, although rumours were circulating of shipments of explosives from America; indeed, a major cache of arms and ammunition, believed to be in transit from the continent to the IRB in Ireland, was discovered at 99 St John's Road, Clerkenwell on 16 May 1882. It was a considerable haul, consisting of 70,000–80,000 rounds of ammunition, 400 rifles adorned with shamrock motifs, sixty revolvers and a quantity of bayonets; a further 400 revolver cartridges and a number of old revolvers were later found at the home of John Walsh, who was charged in connection with his possession of the items.[34] In the same week a viable bomb, which failed to explode, was discovered against a window of the Mansion House in London. In the absence of any positive information as to the identity of the perpetrators, the incident was optimistically written off by the Home Secretary, acting on the police assessment of it, as 'a Fenian scare of the old clumsy kind [...] my police report very little Fenianism in London but of course it may be imported any day either from America or Ireland'.[35] These two incidents, although they received little publicity, were clear indications that the Fenians were intent on pursuing their business in London.

Of far more concern to the government was the assassination in Dublin on 6 May of Lord Frederick Cavendish, newly appointed chief secretary for Ireland, and Thomas Burke, permanent undersecretary for Ireland. The assailants, claiming to be members of the 'Irish Invincibles', who had hitherto kept a low profile, were eventually arrested, some being hanged and others sentenced to long periods of penal servitude. In the aftermath of this outrage, the Irish police forces came in for heavy criticism, particularly from Earl Spencer, Lord Lieutenant of Ireland, who constantly complained to the Prime Minister about the inefficiencies of the Irish police, in particular regarding intelligence-gathering that produced 'rumours ... of great plots coming to the boil, but never anything specific'.[36] As a result, Colonel Henry Brackenbury, essentially a military man, was

34   Short, *The Dynamite War*, pp. 94–5

35   Sir William Harcourt (Home Secretary) to Earl Spencer (Lord Lieutenant of Ireland), 14 May 1882, WVHP, p. 39

36   Ibid., p. 43

sent to Dublin to take up the newly created post of 'Assistant Under-Secretary
for Police and Crime'; he resigned after only two months but had already put
in place the framework for an 'intelligence network aimed to destroy Fenianism
at all its various sources, in America and mainland Britain as well as Ireland'.[37]

Brackenbury's replacement, Earl Spencer's private secretary Edward Jenkinson, lost no time in implementing his predecessor's plans. By March 1883 he was
able to report to the Home Secretary that in Ireland he had in place a system of
surveillance for monitoring the movements of Fenians and the operations of secret
societies; had a unit of specially selected police officers; had recruited informants; and was receiving regular information from the United States.[38] But, like
Brackenbury, his ultimate goal was to destroy Fenianism in Britain as well as in
Ireland and, as yet, little had been done to curb Fenian activity on the mainland.

THE DYNAMITE WAR

I ronically it was the Fenians themselves who stirred the authorities into action
when on 20 January 1883 they caused an explosion at Glasgow Corporation's
gasworks, followed by two further explosions on the same day. The prelude to
the so-called 'Dynamite War' had begun, and Jenkinson was ready for the forthcoming struggle. He did not have long to wait.

The evening of 15 March 1883 saw the start of a Fenian terrorist campaign in
London. The first target was the head office of *The Times* near Blackfriars Railway Bridge; the device was similar in make-up to the Glasgow aqueduct bomb,
nitroglycerine and dynamite contained in a hat box, and, like the Scottish
bomb, failed to detonate. Later the same evening the bombers successfully created
a tremendous explosion at the new Local Government Board offices in Parliament
Street, which destroyed a stone balustrade and caused a considerable amount

---

37   Ibid., p. 44

38   Jenkinson memorandum, 22 March 1883, WVHP, box 103, ff. 10–15.

of superficial damage, including countless shattered windows; again, mercifully, there were no human casualties, but worse was to come.[39] The next attack did not take place until October, by which time the Home Secretary, disillusioned by the continuing lack of intelligence about the Fenians' intentions in England, had decided to call Jenkinson to London to set up a new 'Irish Bureau' at Scotland Yard under the management of Chief Superintendent 'Dolly' Williamson who was already head of the CID and had been in charge of police investigations into the Clerkenwell bomb disaster, although he had escaped the general criticism of the Force's mishandling of the affair.

A memorandum, dated 17 March 1883, from Howard Vincent to Williamson informed him of his new role and the establishment of what, in effect, was the seed from which the Metropolitan Police Special Branch grew. Williamson lost no time in promoting one of his most trusted inspectors, John Littlechild, to chief inspector and appointed him operational commander of this new branch of the CID; its initial establishment was twelve officers (almost exclusively Irish), named in Police Orders as Inspectors Pope and Ahern, Sergeants Jenkins, Melville and Regan, Constables O'Sullivan, Walsh, McIntyre, Foy, Thorpe and two Enrights.[40] Williamson was to maintain daily contact with Vincent; with Anderson, the Fenian specialist at the Home Office; with Royal Irish Constabulary (RIC) officers in London maintaining a watch on known Irish extremists; and to report direct to the Home Secretary any information.

Meanwhile Jenkinson, still based in Ireland, was busy creating on the mainland a system similar to the one he had successfully established in Ireland, with a 'supremo' at the Home Office – similar to his own position in Dublin – who had control over the provincial chief constables and reported directly to the Home Secretary. Conscious of the risk of alienating chief constables if they saw their autonomy threatened by this arrangement, Jenkinson had chosen a man for this position whose tact and discretion he trusted and who had experience

---

39   *The Times*, 16 March 1883

40   Police Orders of 18 March 1883, TNA MEPO 7/45

in dealing with the Irish as a magistrate in Ireland.[41] This person was Major Nicholas Gosselin, who moved into his new office in May 1883. His principal responsibility was to manage the gathering of Fenian intelligence in Scotland and those centres in Northern England with large Irish populations. Initially, according to his reports to the Home Secretary, he seemed to be proving highly effective in this role, for he claimed not only to have new informants in Birmingham, Manchester and Liverpool[42] but also, in January 1884, that he knew 'every Fenian Leader of importance from the Tweed to Birmingham and could put my hand on them tomorrow'.[43] And yet, later that same month, he had to confess to the Home Secretary, 'I regret to say I have nothing but bad news, all my plans have failed so far.'[44]

By the time Jenkinson arrived in London to take up his new post, he had been instrumental in setting up, with Harcourt's blessing, a range of measures designed to thwart the terrorists' plans. He himself, in overall charge of all anti-Fenian operations worldwide, was established at the Home Office with access to the Home Secretary and a direct telephone connection to Williamson at the Yard. He ran three distinct counter-Fenian agencies; one for operations in Ireland, America and on the Continent, which he controlled himself; one for London, run by Williamson; and another for the rest of Britain, which was Gosselin's responsibility. There was one additional element in Harcourt's security set-up and this was Robert Anderson, a barrister by profession, who operated from the Home Office for fifteen years engaged in 'the monitoring of continuing Fenian activity'.[45] His main role was to handle the ace informant, Thomas Beach, alias Major Henri Le Caron, a prominent and trusted member of the Fenian hierarchy in America.

By June 1883 Harcourt felt able to tell HM the Queen, with some assurance,

---

41   Porter, *The Origins of the Vigilant State*, pp. 46–7

42   Gosselin to Harcourt, 26 August 1883, WVHP, box 105, f. 76

43   Ibid., ff. 109–10

44   Gosselin to Harcourt, 24 January 1884, WVHP, box 105, ff. 113–14

45   Short, *The Dynamite War*, p. 16

that the Fenians were now under control and that 'we have the enemy by the throat'.[46] Harcourt's confidence had been boosted by the arrests on 4 and 5 April 1883 of five members of a Fenian gang that was in Britain to carry out further attacks in the 'Dynamite War'. On 14 June all the arrested men with the exception of Thomas Lynch, yet another 'patriot' who betrayed his mates for personal gain, were sentenced to life imprisonment for conspiracy 'to depose the Queen; to levy war upon the Queen; to intimidate and overawe the Houses of Parliament'. Lynch was deported in early July.

While this team had been carrying out reconnaissance in London in preparation for further acts of terrorism, some of O'Donovan Rossa's men who had been engaged on a similar mission in Liverpool were arrested and sentenced to life imprisonment for treasonable felony.

It appeared that the new security arrangements were paying dividends, for the information leading to these timely arrests emanated from Jenkinson's network of informants. Moreover, Williamson and his newly created Special Irish Branch were actively involved in the police operations and it was Littlechild who arrested two of the terrorists. However, any satisfaction gained by Harcourt, Jenkinson and the police over the pre-emptive strikes in Birmingham and Liverpool was quickly dissipated when, on 30 October, bombs were detonated on two trains on the London Underground, injuring seventy-two people, none fatally.

The campaign resumed at the end of February 1884, when dynamite bombs were left at four London railway stations. On the twenty-sixth of the month an explosive device contained in a portmanteau exploded in the left luggage office at Victoria; searches at other London railway stations revealed three similar bombs, at Charing Cross, Ludgate Hill and Paddington, which fortunately had not detonated because of faulty mechanisms. No injuries were reported.[47]

As a result of these alarming developments, Jenkinson established his base in London in March, earlier than planned and much against his will. His first

---

46   Harcourt to HM Queen, 13 June 1883, WVHP, box 691, f. 209

47   Short, *The Dynamite War*, pp. 176–7

concern was to stop the importation of explosives from the Continent and America. A massive increase in police presence at ports was authorised by the Home Secretary, with some eighty police officers drawn from the RIC and Scotland Yard being drafted into a port police force. The Special Irish Branch was allocated extra men to cope with their loss of men to this unit and the additional work generated by the increased port detachments.

Throughout 1884 Clan na Gael were carrying out clandestine operations throughout the country in order to select suitable targets for their deadly operations. Two of these Fenian marauders, John Daly and James Francis Egan, were kept under surveillance by Birmingham police for some months at the beginning of 1884. When arrested, Egan was in possession of bomb-making equipment; at Warwick Assizes on 1 August both men were found guilty of treason-felony and sentenced to life imprisonment.

Satisfying though they were, the arrest and successful convictions of Daly and Egan were scant consolation for the Home Secretary compared with the disaster which befell the capital on 30 May, in a series of Fenian bombs which exploded in the very heart of Jenkinson's security empire. Three separate incidents occurred within a few minutes of each other just after 9 p.m., the first two in St James's Square and the third at Scotland Yard; a further device left at the foot of Nelson's Column failed to explode. Target number one was the Junior Carlton Club, where five people were slightly injured but only superficial damage was caused, mainly to the kitchen. The second bomb was detonated a few seconds later outside the London home of Sir Watkin Wynn, although other buildings in the vicinity seemed more likely targets; again, little damage was caused.[48]

It was the third device that marked the pinnacle of the 'Dynamite War' and plunged the authorities into a slough of despond. The explosion was undoubtedly the work of Clan na Gael and the kudos it achieved for the organisation contrasted sharply with the poorly executed efforts of O'Donovan Rossa's teams over the previous two years. The Special Irish Branch office was housed on the

48   *The Times*, 31 May 1884

first floor of the CID headquarters building in Great Scotland Yard directly facing a public house, The Rising Sun; the corner of the ground floor, immediately
underneath the Special Irish Branch office, was occupied by a public urinal
and it was there that the bomb was deposited. A constable on duty outside the
building, 'to see that there were no evil characters about',[49] received concussion
and four other people were injured, but miraculously none of the injuries was
serious. The damage caused on this occasion was considerably more than that
suffered by the buildings in St James's Square, demolishing the urinal, blowing out a large part of the outer structure of the Branch office, reducing much
of the remainder to rubble as well as destroying many of the records on Fenian
matters held there.[50]

The final month of this inauspicious year for British security ended on a less
depressing note for the government's anti-Fenian forces, although not through
any of their own efforts. William Lomasney, architect of the dynamite campaign,
was killed, together with his two accomplices, his own brother and John Fleming,
when the bomb they had placed underneath London Bridge on 13 December
exploded prematurely, blowing them to pieces. But the Fenians derived some
solace from their sacrifice, John Devoy remarking that they had not intended to
destroy the bridge, only to scare HM Government and England's ruling class.
'And that it did frighten them as all the other dynamite operations did, there can
be no doubt.'[51] (Small consolation for Lomasney and his accomplices.)

Once again a failed terrorist attack resulted in frantic measures by the authorities to bolster security arrangements, particularly in the vicinity of the Houses
of Parliament; haste was urged by Jenkinson in view of intelligence he had
received from a reliable source that an attack on the House of Commons was
imminent. But the team to carry out the next instalment of the Clan na Gael's
campaign was already on its way across the Atlantic: Henry Burton, aged thirty,

49   Ibid., 2 June 1884
50   Short, *The Dynamite War*, p. 184, 186
51   O'Brien and Ryan, *Devoy's Post Bag: 1871–1928*, vol. 2: *1880–1928*, pp. 8–9

who had masterminded the unsuccessful suitcase-bomb attacks on London stations in February, arrived from New York on 24 December, while James Gilbert Cunningham, using the aliases Gilbert or Dalton, carrying a trunk packed with American-manufactured dynamite and other bomb-making paraphernalia, had successfully negotiated the recently reinforced customs controls at Liverpool four days earlier. Burton was the leader of the group, which contained at least one other member, Luke Dillon.

On the second day of the New Year, Cunningham struck the first blow of this mini-campaign, which was to be the last chapter of the 'Dynamite War'. Posing as a workman, he boarded an early-morning train at Aldgate on the Metropolitan Line carrying a tool box containing a dynamite bomb. As the train approached Gower Street Station the bomb exploded, slightly injuring a few people and severely damaging the train, which was able to limp as far as the platform, where Cunningham and two other men with him hastily alighted and left the station.[52]

But the most prestigious targets of the Fenians in their struggle to establish their own independent Irish nation were saved till the end of their five-year campaign of terrorism in Britain. Two historic buildings, the Tower of London and the Palace of Westminster, were bombed on the same day, Saturday 24 January 1885. Cunningham was selected for the raid on the Tower but the identities of the perpetrators of the attack on the House of Commons have never been revealed; Short believes they were Luke Dillon and, possibly, Burton, who was certainly a key figure in the planning of the two raids.[53]

It was the bomb at the Tower of London that was the first to explode. Cunningham had smuggled in the device, which was strapped under the large coat he was wearing; it exploded in the banqueting room at 2 p.m., too quickly for Cunningham to get past the guards at the gate, who detained him. Apart from the gun carriage where the bomb had been concealed, little damage was caused, but two women and two children were seriously injured.

---

52   *The Times*, 12 May 1885

53   Short, *The Dynamite War*, p. 208

At the Palace of Westminster at least two bombers were involved, one to cause an explosion in the Commons chamber itself and the other to create a diversion with a bomb in a different part of the building. Like Cunningham, the bombers, one of whom may have been disguised as a woman, had their missiles concealed under their voluminous clothing. The decoy left his parcel of dynamite in the crypt, primed and with the fuse ignited; the unfortunate Constable Cole, alerted to the danger, bravely carried the smouldering device up the steps towards Westminster Hall, but it exploded while in transit. Cole and another constable suffered shock, while the former also received four broken ribs, the Albert Medal, £200 reward and promotion to the rank of sergeant. As the bombers had planned, the noise of this explosion caused the constable on duty in the Chamber to leave his post to investigate, whereupon the second bomber dropped his missile into the unguarded hall. Minutes later it exploded, causing extensive damage; since it was a Saturday, the House was not sitting and there were no casualties. The two bombers escaped in the confusion and were never captured.

Although no evidence could be produced to link Burton with the explosions on 24 January, he appeared with Cunningham at the Central Criminal Court on 11 May in relation to planting the bombs at Charing Cross and Paddington Stations, while his accomplice was further charged with the explosions at the Tower of London and Gower Street Station, both treason-felonies. *The Times* of 12 May gave a detailed account not only of the trial but of the two men's activities in the days leading up to their arrests. The actual wording of the charge makes interesting reading:

> That they with other persons whose names are unknown, did, within the United Kingdom and without, compass devise and intend to deprive and depose our Most Gracious Lady the Queen from the style and honour or Royal name of the Imperial Crown of the United Kingdom and to levy war against her in order to compel her to change her measures and councils, and in order to intimidate and overawe both Houses of

Parliament, and such intentions did utter and declare by divers overt acts and deeds.[54]

Both men were sentenced to life imprisonment.

Although, naturally, it was not appreciated at the time, that was the end of the 'Dynamite War' – not apparently the dynamiters' original intention, for a store of dynamite of American manufacture was discovered at a house on the Harrow Road in February 1885. Although the loss of so many key players in the terrorist campaign – Burton, Lomasney, Cunningham, Deasy, Daly, Egan and others – would have made it difficult for the Fenians to regroup, at least in the immediate future, it was for other reasons that mainland Britain enjoyed many years of freedom from Irish machinations, apart from (possibly) the 'Jubilee Plot' of 1887.

The Irish Republican Brotherhood had always maintained a firm line in opposing the terrorist tactics of Clan na Gael and O'Donovan Rossa's Skirmishers. They considered that the constitutional methods they favoured, rather than support for the dynamiters from across the Atlantic, put them in a better position to refuse supporting the terrorist campaign in Britain. Jenkinson himself adjudged that 'few IRB members were in favour of explosions and outrages [which] must do great harm to the Irish working population in Great Britain'. He considered that the IRB role was that of a reluctant partner of Clan na Gael at the very most.[55]

A PERIOD FOR REFLECTION

The government was concerned at the cost of implementing and maintaining the new security measures. The cost of renovating the cramped offices

54 *The Times*, 12 May 1885

55 Jenkinson, memorandum, 26 January 1885, WVHP, box 106

of the Special Irish Branch alone was put at £445, although no provision was made for rebuilding the outside toilet.[56]

But there were other factors to be taken into consideration, particularly the conflict of personalities. Soon after arriving at the Home Office, Jenkinson was complaining that there was 'not a man in Scotland Yard worth anything', though he conceded that Williamson was 'steady' and 'trustworthy' but 'without a trace of brilliancy or dash'.[57] In fact he seemed to find everyone in London against him; Porter alludes to the clash of personalities, invariably involving Jenkinson. Harcourt is described as an 'irritable' man and Jenkinson regarded him as 'unreasonable', 'impulsive' and even 'unscrupulous'; for his part Harcourt refers to Jenkinson's 'ungovernable temper and overbearing treatment of Scotland Yard'.[58] Vincent had been replaced as head of the CID in June 1884 by James Munro, who was himself a man of fiery temper. Not surprisingly he too incurred Jenkinson's wrath, not totally undeserved.

One of the main causes of disagreement between Jenkinson, on the one hand, and the police on the other, was the sensitive matter of informants and the handling of information. The police have traditionally treated informants with extreme caution in the knowledge that although they can be an invaluable commodity if handled properly, they can equally lead to disaster. Informants, or agents as the Security Service refers to them, may be motivated by any one of a number of reasons – jealousy, revenge, personal gain (usually money), excitement and many other stimuli, but rarely out of a sense of duty or patriotism. As a breed, they are notoriously unreliable and intelligence received from them has to be treated circumspectly; nevertheless they can be a priceless source of information in situations where other methods of investigation, such as surveillance or interception, are not possible.

Unlike the British police, Jenkinson derived the greater part of his intelligence

---

56   Short, *The Dynamite War*, p. 188

57   Porter, *The Origins of the Vigilant State*, pp. 51, 54, 55

58   Ibid., p. 56

from informants and in Ireland, working closely with the Dublin Metropolitan Police, operated a spy network of clandestine agents all over the country to warn of anti-British feelings.[59] When he took up his appointment at the Home Office he did not appreciate, or chose to ignore, the suspicion of informants that the British police and public had traditionally harboured. The informant too closely resembled the *agent provocateur*, anathema to the British sense of justice and fair play. John Littlechild, head of Special Branch from 1887 to '93, postulated this problem when he wrote in his memoirs: 'I have to confess that the "nark" is very apt to drift into an *agent provocateur* in his anxiety to secure a conviction, and therefore he requires to be carefully watched.'[60] Porter neatly explains the police attitude to detective work and, in particular, the use of informants which he claims, 'was rooted [...] in the Metropolitan Police's liberal and Peelite past'.

> Scotland Yard had come to accept the need for detectives ... but it saw their role as not very far removed from that of the uniformed police. So far as possible they should prevent crime, by acting on what they knew as soon as they knew it, even if that meant saving putative criminals from the retribution that would have followed if they had been allowed to mature their plans. They accepted disclosures from informants, but did not go out of their way to cultivate them, and certainly not by means of wholesale deception, like setting spies up in artificial or 'front' occupations. Hence Jenkinson's oft-repeated complaint about Scotland Yard's lack of informants, which he regarded as ineptitude, but for them was a matter of deliberate policy.[61]

However, the warring factions in the counter-terrorist programme were soon to move on, with a corresponding transformation in the role and fortunes of

---

59   Andrew Cook, *M: MI5's First Spymaster* (Stroud: Tempus, 2004), p. 33

60   John Littlechild, *The Reminiscences of Chief Inspector Littlechild* (London: Leadenhall Press, 1894), p. 96

61   Porter, *The Origins of the Vigilant State*, p. 59

the Special Irish Branch. First to go, in June 1885, was the Home Secretary, Sir William Vernon Harcourt, who had survived a turbulent five years at the Home Office and was succeeded by Richard Asherton Cross. In the same month Earl Spencer, the Lord Lieutenant of Ireland, who had consistently supported Jenkinson in his battles with Harcourt and the Metropolitan Police, also vacated his office, to become Lord President of the Council. Left without a patron, Jenkinson had no one to fight his battles in Parliament and resigned in January 1887; undoubtedly the diminished likelihood of terrorists from across the Atlantic striking again in the foreseeable future made ministers less inclined to support Jenkinson-style espionage in this country. A few months prior to his retirement, Harcourt encapsulated the popular attitude to this method of criminal investigation in a speech he made in Westminster Hall when presenting Sergeant Cole with the Albert Medal for bravery:

> I know that it is said sometimes that the English police are deficient as a 'detective force'. I am not prepared myself, according to my observation and my knowledge of other forces, to admit that that charge is altogether well founded. It ought always to be remembered that in a free country, as England is, the police work under restrictions in the detection of crime which do not apply to the police of other nations. There are very good reasons for that, reasons which I do not desire to alter, but it ought to be remembered, in considering the success of the police, that they have to labour under the disadvantages to which I have referred and, having regard to these circumstances, I do not believe that there is in this country or in this metropolis a greater amount of undetected or unpunished crime than is to be found in other states.

The speech was fully reported in *The Times* of 27 March 1885, which included a fulsome editorial comment, giving unstinting praise to the police and the British system of policing. Could Harcourt have been having a parting shot at Jenkinson? There were new faces at Scotland Yard as well. James Munro became

Commissioner in November 1888. He had been rapidly promoted from his position as Assistant Commissioner of the CID to be replaced, surprisingly, by Robert Anderson, who was resurrected from the backwater in the Home Office where he had spent the years of the 'Dynamite War' running his shadowy network of agents under the watchful eye of Jenkinson. The final member of the government's anti-Fenian team to depart was the veteran and popular Detective Chief Superintendent Adolphus Williamson, who had enjoyed a successful career in the Metropolitan Police, being involved in whatever political investigations required police attention. As overall head of the Special Irish Branch from 1883 to 1887, he managed to avoid serious criticism, was respected by his senior officers and even drew grudging praise from Jenkinson. The new head of the Special Branch was Chief Inspector John Littlechild, promoted from inspector in the Special Irish Branch, which in the dying years of the nineteenth century dropped the 'Irish' from its title.

Although the Special Irish Branch (SIB) had been established in 1883 as a vital cog in Harcourt's anti-Fenian machine, its participation in the government's lukewarm attempts to thwart the dynamite bombers was, it seemed, only marginal. Partly on account of police reluctance to arrest and convict not only terrorists but all types of law breakers on the evidence of informants, it was upon Jenkinson, Gosselin, Anderson and their team of agents that the work of uncovering Fenian plots fell. Once information had been received from the 'spy master', the SIB, working in conjunction with provincial forces and the RIC, would follow up these leads, through interrogations, surveillance and, hopefully, arrests. Their work, frequently repetitive and lacking in excitement was, for the most part, carried out unobtrusively and unheralded, but it played a not insignificant role in helping to contain the Fenian threat. The first anniversary of the SIB's formation was marked by the arrival at the Home Office of Jenkinson, who promptly dispatched three-quarters of their meagre staff to supplement watchers at ports, replacing them with inexperienced recruits whose role was confined to searching baggage at railway termini; only six men remained to carry out essential enquiries, surveillance and personal protection of VIPs. By August 1884, the establishment had increased to twenty-two but the unit was still grossly under-staffed; it is little wonder that the Branch found success and official recognition elusive commodities in the early years of its existence.

Contemporaneous official records provide only a sketchy picture of what Branch work was actually like when the section first became 'Special' in 1887.[62] Edward Jenkinson, in a fit of pique, had demolished all documents relating to his counter-terrorism work when he resigned from the Home Office in January 1887 and many of the SIB's files on the Fenians and their activities had perished in the 1884 explosion at their office in Old Scotland Yard. It is to an early member of the Special Branch, therefore, that we are indebted for an insight into what life as a nineteenth-century officer in that department entailed. John Sweeney, an Irishman born in County Kerry in 1857, joined the Metropolitan Police in 1876. For over eight years he was employed as a constable in uniform, but in 1884 he was promoted to sergeant and drafted with a number of other officers into the SIB. Nineteen years later he retired with the rank of inspector and wrote his memoirs; he frankly admits that his reminiscences are recorded entirely from memory, without recourse to notes, and that there may be 'some stray inaccuracies' but that 'nowhere have I been guilty of any misrepresentation of fact that should do harm or injustice to any one'. Where authenticated versions of the events he describes are available, they corroborate Sweeney's accounts.[63]

Sweeney was evidently endowed with the luck of the Irish, for on the day when a Clan na Gael bomb reduced his office to a pile of rubble, he had left it only shortly before the explosion took place; in dramatic terms he records that 'his desk was blown to pieces' and he himself 'escaped death by about a quarter

---

62   The term 'Special Branch' was regarded by some departments of the Metropolitan Police, particularly the CID, as an indication that SB officers considered themselves as superior beings. It was of course never intended as such, the title having been bestowed, unofficially, on the section when the Special Irish Branch ceased to be concerned exclusively with Irish affairs in 1887

63   John Sweeney, *At Scotland Yard: Being the Experiences During Twenty-Seven Years' Service of John Sweeney* (London: Grant Richards, 1904), p. vi

of an hour'.[64] Some months after this escape, William Lomasney, leader of the dynamiters, perished when the bomb he was planting under London Bridge detonated prematurely. No trace was ever found of his body or those of his accomplices. However, some three to four years later, Sweeney relates, he was detailed to follow up some information of dubious reliability which led him, after several weeks of alcohol-fuelled surveillance, to the sister of John Fleming, one of Lomasney's partners in crime. By pretending to be a friend of her brother, Sweeney induced her to virtually admit that he was dead; a subsequent search of Fleming's belongings produced evidence which satisfied the police that Fleming had been in London in 1884 to commit acts of terrorism and had indeed perished at London Bridge.

This case illustrates the type of work that members of the SIB were engaged in during the early years of its existence – following up leads, carrying out surveillance, questioning witnesses and exploiting other sources of information on Irish terrorism – but soon the Branch was to undergo radical changes in its structure and a dramatic widening in the scope of its work. With fewer demands on its anti-Fenian commitments, the unit was able to spend more time, for example, keeping an eye on the activities of anarchists.

A WIDENING OF THE SPECIAL BRANCH ROLE

The police were increasingly being called upon to deal with anarchists from other parts of Europe, who had traditionally seen Britain as a safe haven from the less liberal regimes of their own country. Their presence here posed a constant problem to the British, not only because they broke our laws, but because our government was constantly harassed by foreign states demanding the extradition of wanted men. Before the end of the '80s the Special Branch had officially assumed responsibility for monitoring the activities of these political

---

64   Ibid., pp. 21–22

extremists and Sweeney claims that he had 'done more work in connection with the anarchists than in connection with criminals of any other type. I have had more to do as an anarchist-hunter than as a bodyguard; and that is saying a good deal.'[65] Certainly his accounts of some of the anarchist cases in which he was involved are evidence of the extent to which the Branch was occupied with these revolutionaries.

Sweeney's reference to bodyguard duties is an indication of another important function entrusted to the section. He goes on to record that 'during my service at the Yard, no small element of my duties was represented by attendance on various august personages'.[66] According to Sweeney, and there is no reason to disbelieve him, he performed protection duties at various times with members of the British royal family, including HM Queen Victoria, King Edward VII, the Prince and Princess of Wales and foreign dignitaries such as the German Emperor, the Czar and Czarina of Russia and the Prince of Naples. Other early members of Special Branch, for example Detective Inspectors Harold Brust[67] and Herbert Fitch,[68] have likewise recorded their memories of protection duties with members of the British royal family as well as visiting dignitaries. It was not until well into the twentieth century that Special Branch ceased to be the main source of personal protection for our royal family.

Apart from creating a wider remit for the Special Irish Branch, Munro completely reorganised the section; Littlechild was chosen to take charge of an elite and highly secretive group (Section D) of three inspectors (Melville, Pope and Quinn), which would assume national responsibility for police work of a political nature and might be called upon to act in the provinces and abroad as well as in London.[69] According to Porter, this small section, financed from national funds, was the first to bear the title 'Special Branch'. The Special Irish

---

65   Ibid., p. 204

66   Ibid., p. 55

67   Harold Brust, *I Guarded Kings: The Memoirs of a Political Police Officer* (London: Stanley Paul & Co., 1935)

68   Herbert Fitch, *Memoirs of a Royal Detective* (London: Hurst & Blackett, 1933)

69   Andrew Cook, *M: MI5's First Spymaster*, pp. 64–5

Branch continued to operate within the CID, under Williamson, as Section B, distinguished from Section D only by the latter's wider sphere of operations and its source of finance; by 1911 the two sections had been assimilated, together with Section C (ports) into one unit, 'CID, Special Branch' (soon to be referred to simply as Special Branch), totally financed by the Metropolitan Police. A fourth division, Section A, dealt with serious crimes of a non-political nature and, as Special Branch assumed its own identity, so Section A became the CID.[70]

With the dilution of Jenkinson's spy network, Munro, who had never been an admirer of the former's special agents, looked to his own constables, both CID and uniform, to provide him with information that they might obtain while patrolling their beats, through diligent observation and the fostering of good relations with members of the public, particularly in areas frequented by Irish-Americans.[71]

THE JUBILEE PLOT

It was not long before Munro's new security set-up was put to the test, when he received intelligence of a plot to disrupt Queen Victoria's Golden Jubilee celebrations in June 1887. The information emanated from Henri Le Caron, who informed his handler, Robert Anderson, that General F. F. Millen, at one time a prominent Clan na Gael member and another of Anderson's informants, had been commissioned by Alexander Sullivan, head of Clan na Gael in America, to head a team of five Irish-American members of Clan na Gael to disrupt the Queen's jubilee celebrations with a sizeable explosion during the service of remembrance at Westminster Abbey. Special Branch was given the names of the group – John J. Moroney aka Joseph Melville, Thomas Callan, Michael

---

70   Letter from Home Secretary to Commissioner, dated 4 June 1911. TNA HO 148/17/519

71   Memo from Munro to all divisions, dated 17 March 1886. TNA MEPO 3

Harkins, Joseph Cohen and one other. They were all kept under surveillance from the moment they left America; the intended explosion never materialised. Callan and Harkins were arrested, Moroney escaped and Cohen, too, was never apprehended – he died before the police caught up with him.[72] Apparently Millen, who was in France, had been informed by Chief Superintendent Adolphus Williamson, in Boulogne, that he would be arrested if he came to England.[73] Callan and Harkins were convicted at the Central Criminal Court in February 1888, of conspiracy to cause explosions and were each sentenced to fifteen years' imprisonment.

This whole affair was shrouded in mystery and rumours were rife that the failure of the conspiracy was not such a resounding success for Munro's Special Branch as the public had been led to believe. In 1910, allegations were voiced in the House that the whole affair was a 'put-up job' engineered by the British secret service.[74] Anderson himself admitted as much when, over twenty years after the event, he wrote in his memoirs: 'Millen arrived in Britain to carry out his two-fold mission on behalf of Clan na Gael and the British Government' and later 'a detective superintendent was sent from Scotland Yard to notify him [Millen] the bargain was repudiated and not to cross the channel'.[75] The implication was that the Secret Service had been aware of the plot virtually from its inception and was waiting for it to develop, hoping to catch the dynamiters red-handed, but the more pragmatic Munro decided to prevent the conspiracy continuing. There were fears that, if arrested, Millen might reveal the government's complicity in the scheme, so he was induced to return to America; police feared that his fellow conspirators might pursue their original plans regardless, and accordingly they were kept under surveillance from August to November

---

72   Most of these details derive from a report in *The Times* of 20 April 1888 and are cited in Henri Le Caron, *Twenty-Five Years in the Secret Service: The Recollections of a Spy* (Wakefield: EP Publishing, 1972), Appendix, pp. 281–3. Correspondence between Devoy and Luke Dillon of Clan na Gael also throws some light on the conspiracy – O'Brien and Ryan, *Devoy's Post Bag: 1871–1928*, vol. 2: *1880–1928*, pp. 298–9

73   *Pall Mall Gazette*, 28 October 1887

74   Hansard, 5th series, vol. 16, cc. 1938, 2375

75   Robert Anderson, *The Lighter Side of My Official Life* (London: Hodder & Stoughton, 1910), pp. 109–10

in the hope that they would leave the country without having done any harm. Eventually dynamite was found dumped in a yard in Islington, resulting in the arrest of Callan and Harkins.[76]

---

76   Andrew Cook, *M: MI5's First Spymaster*, pp. 70–71

CHAPTER TWO

ANARCHISTS AND BOLSHEVIKS

THE OFFICERS OF the Special Branch, relatively untroubled by the depressing times that their colleagues in the CID were suffering, were not idle during the twilight years of the nineteenth century – the *fin de siècle*. While protection duties took up an increasing amount of their time, and they did not neglect to keep an eye on the Fenian scene, anarchists, both home-grown and foreign, who had been a constant source of trouble to the police for many years, had been added to the Special Branch's list of special responsibilities.

Anarchism is the political philosophy that holds the state to be undesirable, unnecessary and harmful. After the destruction of the Paris Commune in 1871, European countries found themselves increasingly the target of revolutionary refugees who, in line with anarchist thinking, advocated the destruction of the rulers and organs of states by violent means.

In order to counter this threat, Continental police, notably Italian, Russian and French, often deployed agents in other countries to keep a constant watch on dissidents and to liaise with the domestic police, in the case of Britain MPSB, who kept the Home Office and Foreign Office informed with regular intelligence bulletins on the subject.

The first anarchists to take up residence in England were Germans. Johann Most, who had been expelled from Berlin, arrived in London in December 1878 and made his headquarters in the Social Democratic Working Men's Club. In name, the club, which had several hundred members, was ostensibly a social democratic association, but soon after Most arrived it began to display pronounced anarchist leanings. On 3 January, just a month after his arrival, Most published *Freiheit*, the first number of a paper written in German, which was exceedingly violent in tone. The British authorities did not take any immediate action, possibly because being printed in a foreign language it was not monitored. In Germany, efforts were made to suppress the paper in view of its inflammatory contents, which included the following:

> Science at the present day places means at our disposal which allow us to proceed safely, commodiously, and on a large scale, with the destruction of the beasts of prey. Princes, ministers, statesmen, bishops, prelates, a good proportion of the officers of the army, the greater part of the higher officials, various journalists and lawyers, and, in fine, all the important representatives of the aristocrat and capitalist classes, are the personages on whose backs we have a stick to break.

Following the murder of Czar Alexander II, the issue of *Freiheit* for 19 March 1881 contained a particularly virulent article written by Most in which he extolled the murder of the Russian Emperor as 'a glorious and incomparable deed that would count among the most illustrious achievements of humanity'; the writer concluded his scandalous article with the hope that the outrage would not be the last of its kind. Most was tried on a charge of libelling the Czar and incitement to murder; he was found guilty, sentenced to sixteen months' hard labour and on release went to America.

Before his arrest, Most repeated his inflammatory remarks at a socialist meeting held on 23 March 1881. On reading an account of the meeting in the *Daily Telegraph*, Queen Victoria's secretary, Henry Ponsonby, expressed his concern to the Liberal Home Secretary William Harcourt who forwarded his letter to the Commissioner minuted, 'Tell the police to look after this.'

In the days before the formation of the CID it was Superintendent Williamson who was 'charged with [investigating] matters of the greatest importance to the government and of the most confidential character',[1] and he was sometimes assisted by Detective Inspectors Hagen and Von Turnow. At times these enquiries concerned anarchists who, according to the various reports of anarchist activities of the period, were divided into two distinct classes, the intellectual theorists, like Prince Peter Kropotkin, and the naked violence of the street practitioners. Williamson, by now (March 1881) in charge of the newly formed Fenian bureau, was the natural choice to 'look after this'.

Thus the Special Irish Branch of the CID became responsible for monitoring anarchist terrorism in this country, in addition to their Irish republican responsibilities; there was a continual demand from the police of other countries for information concerning anarchists here, and the Branch regularly kept track of their movements and reported back to the Foreign Office through the Home Office.[2]

Harold Brust illustrates clearly the demands placed on him and other members of the Branch following the assassination of the Czar, which encouraged anarchists abroad to carry out similar attacks against their governments, and it is hardly surprising that, following the atrocity, the Russians should be concerned that the United Kingdom was giving shelter to its enemies. Brust wrote:

> In those days the duties of the Special Branch detectives in regard to Russia were two-fold. We had to keep a close watch on the undesirable aliens, political refugees who had been driven from their own country for various reasons, and also, equally important, we had to keep a constant watch upon Imperial Russian spies working against the interests of Great Britain.

---

1   Pearson and Henderson, 5 January 1883. TNA HO 144/190/A46472, sub. 2

2   Porter, *The Origins of the Vigilant State*, p. 40

Scarcely a week passed but the Special Branch had an 'Urgent' message from the dreaded organisation 'The Third Section' (as the Russian secret police were called), advising us that some scoundrel or another was on his way to England. Sometimes a wholly false and dreadful catalogue of crimes would be tacked on to the refugee's record, with a view to earning him disfavour with the English police as soon as he landed. In time this habit of the Russian secret police defeated itself, for nobody attached the slightest importance to what they said.[3]

There was good reason for the Russians to fear anarchist terrorism, for their own secret police chief was assassinated in 1890 and, during the '90s, revolutionaries were responsible for riots and political killings throughout Europe, particularly in France. In 1893, the Paris Chamber of Deputies was bombed. In 1894, the French President, Carnot, was assassinated at Lyon, stabbed by an Italian anarchist, Sante Geronimo Caserio, who was executed on 14 August 1894. Other European dignitaries to meet similar fates were the Spanish Prime Minister, Canvas del Castillo (1897); Empress Elizabeth of Austria (1898); and King Humbert of Italy (1900).[4]

In England, after the departure of Most, the two most prominent anarchists were Josef Peukert, a German, and Victor Dave, a Belgian, the founder of *The Rebel*. The Dave faction regarded Peukert as a spy. The movement in London was centred on the anarchist clubs – Peukert founded the Autonomie Club at 6 Windmill Street while his rival, Dave, created the Communist Working Men's Club at 46 Whitfield Street, W1, with a branch at 49 Tottenham Street, W1, under the title of the Social Democratic Communist Club. In Cable Street, W2, there existed for some time a club known as The Dawn, but greater notoriety was attached to the anarchist club, originally known as the Nihilist Club, in Berner Street, E1, founded by

---

3   Brust, *I Guarded Kings*, p. 86. The Third Section of the Russian Imperial Chancellery (Tretiye Otdeleniye) was a secret department serving as the Imperial regime's secret police. It was disbanded in 1880 and replaced by the Okhrana, which continued to be referred to by that name

4   Porter, *The Origins of the Vigilant State*, pp. 101–102

Russian refugees. Its members were mainly recruited from the populous colony of foreign Jews who settled in the East End of London. Englishmen were not as interested in anarchism as the European refugees but efforts were made to recruit a small number who at this period professed anarchist opinions. An English section of the Autonomie Club was formed, and an English edition of *Freiheit* was produced, but the English section, together with its version of *Freiheit*, soon folded up. In the early days of agitation, an informal club was established at a public house in Sun Street, Finsbury, kept by a German named Daubenspeck.

A number of serious incidents in England achieved considerable publicity. They included: the Walsall Bomb conspiracy (1892); the Greenwich Park explosion (1894); Polti and Farnara's plot to bomb the Stock Exchange (1894); the Tottenham outrage (1909); and the siege of Sidney Street (1911).

THE WALSALL BOMB CONSPIRACY

Although they mixed in the same circles as the Eastern European émigrés, the Walsall bombers who captured public attention in 1892 were English, French and Italian. John Sweeney described how on 6 January 1892, a Special Branch team under Inspector Melville followed Joe Deakin, an anarchist living in Walsall, from Euston Railway Station to the Autonomie Club. Before he could enter the club, he was stopped and found to be in possession of a parcel containing chloroform. He was arrested and charged with the unlawful possession of the liquid. Following the arrest, Melville went to Walsall, where he assisted the Chief Constable of Walsall, Charles Taylor, to arrest a number of suspects, including French refugee Victor Cails, Fred Charles, William Ditchfield and John Westley. Their premises were searched and items relating to bomb-making were found. Subsequently Melville arrested a sixth man, an Italian, named Jean Battolla, in London.

Deakin was questioned by Melville and Taylor, and believing that Charles was a police informant, made a damning statement involving his co-conspirators. The prisoners appeared at Stafford Assizes on 30 March jointly charged with possession of bomb-making equipment and conspiracy to cause an explosion. Seven days later Cails, Charles, Battolla and Deakin were found guilty and sentenced to ten years' penal servitude. The jury made a recommendation for mercy in the case of Deakin, who was given five years; Westley and Ditchfield were found not guilty and discharged.[5]

It was claimed by the anarchist press that the Special Branch informant in the Walsall Bomb case, a man named Auguste Coulon, went too far and was guilty of entrapment, but the limited evidence before the trial court disclosed a clear willingness of the offenders to commit the crime. During the trial Melville was put under pressure by defending counsel to disclose the name of his informant, and asked whether he had ever paid Coulon, but his refusal to answer was upheld by the judge. Coulon was not called upon to give evidence.

In 1895 ex-Detective Sergeant MacIntyre wrote a series of articles in *Reynolds News* in which he alleged that Coulon had indeed become Melville's informant in the Walsall case. Among other things he alleged that: 'Special Branch special accounts show that he [Coulon] received his first payment from Melville as early as 18 July 1890 and continued on the payroll till 1904 under the alias of Pyatt. He got extra money during the Walsall Case, and briefly in 1894.'[6]

EXPLOSION IN TILNEY STREET, MAYFAIR

Mr Justice Hawkins, the judge in the Walsall case, had incurred the wrath of the anarchist movement and other revolutionaries by the harshness of the sentences he handed out. On 4 November 1894, there was an explosion in Tilney Street, Mayfair, on the doorstep of a house opposite His Lordship's address, which caused some damage but injured nobody. It was believed that the bomb was mistakenly left at No. 2 instead of No. 5. Nobody was arrested.

---

5   Sweeney, *At Scotland Yard*, pp. 209–211

6   Coulon never admitted that he had acted as an *agent provocateur*, but in a letter in *Reynolds News* on 21 April 1895, he admitted he had been paid by the police

R. v. NICHOLL

The Walsall case led to a subsequent prosecution of David Nicholl, the editor of a paper called *The Commonweal*. At a number of meetings in Hyde Park, shorthand notes were taken by John Sweeney and D. C. Powell of speeches in which Nicholl denounced the police and asked for contributions towards the defence of the Walsall prisoners. He then wrote an inflammatory article in *The Commonweal* in which he incited the murder of the Home Secretary Henry Matthews, Mr Justice Hawkins and Inspector Melville. *The Commonweal* offices were raided by Special Branch on 18 April 1894, and a quantity of evidential material seized. Nicholl was convicted at the Central Criminal Court of: 'Unlawfully encouraging divers unknown persons to murder.' On 6 May 1894, he was sentenced to eighteen months hard labour.[7]

THE GREENWICH PARK BOMB

On 15 February 1894, an anarchist bomb was detonated in Greenwich Park, London. Precisely what its objective was has never been entirely clear, for the bomber appears to have blown himself up accidentally and that is certainly the opinion postulated by Joseph Conrad in his novel *The Secret Agent*, which is based on the incident. Conrad, himself a Polish refugee, expresses his views on the futility of anarchy in general and of the Greenwich Park bomb in particular, 'that outrage could not be laid hold of mentally in any sort of way, so that one remained faced by the fact of a man blown to bits for nothing even most remotely resembling an idea, anarchist or other'.[8]

On the fateful afternoon, the park warden heard a loud explosion and found a man who, despite his massive injuries, was still alive and able to speak. He was taken

---

7   Sweeney, *Scotland Yard*, pp. 219–24

8   Joseph Conrad, *The Secret Agent* (London, Vintage Books, 2007), author's note, p. 9

to the nearby Seamen's Hospital and died there thirty minutes later, giving no expla-nation for his action. Special Branch established that the man's name was Martial Bourdin, a 26-year-old Frenchman living in Fitzroy Street, Westminster. He was in possession of a large sum of money, which may have indicated his intention to leave the country for France after the explosion. Bourdin was a member of the Autonomie Club. Later that day police raided the club and arrested a number of those present.

The funeral of the bomber evoked much sympathy from fellow anarchists in London and attracted large crowds. Anarchist writers subsequently claimed that Bourdin's brother-in-law was a police informant and had incited the vic-tim. In this connection it is interesting to note that in *The Secret Agent* it is the weak and mentally retarded brother-in-law of the 'secret agent', Mr Verloc, who blows himself up while carrying the bomb, an unwitting party to the proposed crime. The real-life bomber, Bourdin, is portrayed by *The Times* as an under-developed, effeminate man with blond, silky hair,[9] a description interpreted by some writers as 'a generalised trope for anarchism', an image that accords with the general view held by the cultural public of the era.[10]

R. *v.* POLTI AND FARNARA

In April 1894 Francis Polti and Guiseppe Farnara, Italian anarchists, aroused the suspicions of Thomas Smith, the manager of Cohen's, a metal dealer's, of 240 Blackfriars Road, London, when they arranged to purchase metal pipes and other parts suitable for bomb making. Polti had done the ordering because Farnara did not speak English. Smith reported the matter to police and Special Branch offic-ers DS Sweeney and DS Maguire took up observation in the vicinity of Cohen's shop; they saw Polti leave the premises with a parcel under his arm and after a short ride on an omnibus Sweeney arrested him and took him by cab to Scotland Yard.

---

9   *The Times*, 17 February 1894

10   Sally Ledger & Roger Luckhurst, *The Fin de Siècle: A Reader in Cultural History c. 1880–1900* (Oxford, Oxford University Press, 2000), p. 199

The prisoner was found to have four keys in his possession, a number of documents and a memorandum book. In that book there was the entry '9 April 1894 Carnot 3s', and underneath, 'Cohen 7s 6d paid 5s'. On the other side was an entry in Italian and two receipts from Cohen and Miller. Polti volunteered the information that the entries referred to another pipe that he had ordered in the name Carnot, from Norm's, near Waterloo Road, and that it was not finished.

A search of Polti's address, 33 Warner Street, revealed a box containing a bottle of sulphuric acid, a packet of white powder and a packet of yellow powder, a black manuscript book, a printed book on Alfred Nobel's dynamite and a pencil sketch of a bomb. When the prisoner was charged with having explosives in his possession, he alleged that the chemicals belonged to Emile Carnot, whom he had known for only three weeks. He then volunteered to make a statement in which he claimed to have been acting as messenger for Carnot, known as Piedmonte, living at an address in Back Hill, Clerkenwell Road. He added that he hated the anarchists and was afraid of Piedmonte.[11]

It was from an agent of an Italian police officer in London that information as to the whereabouts of Farnara was obtained.[12] This enabled DI Quinn to arrest the Italian at his east London address on 22 April 1894 and charge him. On 30 April, Giuseppe Farnara and Francis Polti were found guilty at the Central Criminal Court of possessing explosive substances with intent to endanger life and were sentenced to twenty and ten years' penal servitude respectively.[13] Farnara claimed that the target for the bombs was intended to be the Stock Exchange, as he had insufficient money to take the bombs abroad. He was not released at the end of his sentence, being certified mentally insane, and was transferred to Broadmoor Criminal Lunatic Asylum.[14]

11 Sweeney, *At Scotland Yard*, pp. 235–64

12 Pietro Dipaola, *Italian Anarchists in London, 1870–1914* (London: University of London, PhD Dissertation, 2004), pp. 121–5

13 Old Bailey proceedings online

14 TNA HO144/17/11/A55860D/14

EXPLOSION ON THE METROPOLITAN RAILWAY

O n 26 April 1897 there was a severe explosion on an Inner Circle train at
Aldersgate; one passenger was killed and another nine were taken to St
Bartholomew's Hospital. The explosion occurred within the jurisdiction of the
City Police, but Special Branch officers were deputed by the Commissioner to
assist. A Coroner's jury returned a verdict of unlawful killing of the dead man.
The identities of the perpetrators of this outrage were never discovered.[15]

THE TOTTENHAM OUTRAGE

T he prelude to this drama took place in Paris in 1907. Three Latvian anarchists, Peter and Jacob Lapidus and Paul Hefeld, had fled from their
homeland to Paris the previous year and, on May Day 1907, they made an abortive attempt to assassinate the President of France; unfortunately for them the
bomb they were carrying exploded prematurely, killing Peter Lapidus. The other
two were badly shaken but managed to evade capture.

In January 1909 a messenger from a Tottenham factory had just drawn the
staff's wages from the bank when the bag of money was snatched from him by a
stranger, the Latvian Jacob Lapidus. The chauffeur grappled with him but was
hit on the head with the butt of a heavy revolver. A hue and cry ensued in which
Lapidus fired at one of his pursuers, but the bullet passed harmlessly through
his jacket. The chase continued and Lapidus's accomplice, Hefeld, fired at and
disabled a following car. The sound of shots brought a policeman, PC Tyler,
into the chase and he then led the pack, who were closing on the two men when
Lapidus turned round and shot him through the neck. A fearless boy, Joseph
Joscelyne, closed in on Hefeld and was shot in the chest.

Jacob Lapidus ran on ahead and disappeared while Hefeld tried to climb a

15   Sweeney, *At Scotland Yard*, pp. 292–3

fence into a garden, slipped and fell. As he did so he turned his revolver on himself and fired. He was still alive when he reached hospital, but died the same night. That evening police traced Jacob Lapidus to a Walthamstow cottage, and on entry found his body in a crumpled heap.

THE SIEGE OF SIDNEY STREET

This famous incident took place in 1911 at a time when the nihilist and anarchist movements in Russia were again becoming extremely active. Large numbers of Russian secret police in London were employed in keeping watch on the movements and haunts of these ardent revolutionaries who, while ostensibly leading the lives of honest men, were working secretly and illegally in their underground movements. One group financed their revolutionary activities with the proceeds of crime.

On the night of 16 December 1910, their attempts to break into the premises of a jeweller's in Houndsditch aroused the attention of a neighbouring resident, who called the City of London Police, in whose district the address was situated. When the street door in Houndsditch was opened and they tried to enter, the police officers were met by a hail of bullets; three were shot and fatally wounded, and a fourth was left on the ground seriously injured. The gang, comprising several men and two women, were well armed with automatic pistols; one of their number, a man named Gardstein or Morin,[16] was accidentally shot by an accomplice and two of the men and a woman helped him escape to an address in Whitechapel, about a mile away, where one of them had a room. He was found there the next day fully dressed lying dead on a bed with a loaded automatic pistol under the pillow and a number of spare rounds nearby. The people who had left him had disappeared. The gang went into hiding in Whitechapel, occasionally moving from one house to another. A reward of £500 was offered for information leading to their arrest.

---

16   Many of the East European revolutionaries used aliases. Gardstein was no exception

Information was received that some of the men could be found at 100 Sidney Street, Whitechapel. Two of the group were believed to be Fritz Svaars and Jacob Peters, and it was thought for some time that a third man, known as 'Peter the Painter', was with them. All three were members of the Whitechapel Anarchist Club.

Ralph Kitchener described a meeting with an informant, a member of the Russian secret police, who told him, many years later, that he was the person who had informed the City Police of the gang's location. At any rate he was the one who drew the reward:

> When I was told I was going to have the reward and was asked how I would like the money, I said I would like it in gold; if I were asked now I should probably say I would have it in bills, but in those days I did not know anything about paper money, so I asked for gold, and I had a surprise when I did get it. I had to meet Mr Stark [of the City Police] at the Manchester Hotel in Aldersgate, and he gave me the money there. There was £250 in gold in a bag; did you ever handle that much gold at one time? You'd be surprised at how much it weighs. It's a pretty big lot naturally, and I felt very strange when I went walking out of the hotel with this bag of gold in my hand.[17]

The Houndsditch robbery and the siege of Sidney Street also involved one of the most important of the intellectual Italian anarchists, Enrico Malatesta, who was living in Islington at the time, and allowed his workshop to be used for making the tools for the robbery.

The Home Secretary, Winston Churchill, attended the scene and an armed company of the Scots Guards aided the police. Superintendent Quinn, who by that time had replaced Superintendent Melville as the head of the Branch, was also present and was hit by a ricochet bullet which tore his coat without harming him. The end came with the building on fire and two anarchists dead inside.

---

17   Ralph Kitchener, *The Memoirs of an Old Detective, 1910–37* (unpublished), p. 125

BOLSHEVIKS

In 1905, two years after he joined the Special Branch, Herbert Fitch was instructed to cover a meeting to be attended by Vladimir Ilyich Ulyanov (Lenin), apparently under the auspices of the 'Foreign Barbers of Islington', a pseudonym for the Bolsheviks. It was a closed meeting and Fitch covered it by hiding in a cupboard with the help of the landlord of the public house where it was held. During the course of it he heard Lenin say:

> It must be bloodshed – bloodshed on a colossal scale. My comrades here have advocated politics. I say politics are useless to us. We must revolt, and when we revolt there shall be no mercy. We shall think of our brothers shot and hanged at the caprice of the nobles, or sent to rot in Siberia. The Czar, princes, dukes, police, civil servants, shopkeepers – all must perish. In Russia first, and then from one side of Europe to the other. It is the bourgeoisie we must fear, in Russia, in Germany, in England. When the day comes, they must perish, down to the man who keeps a stall in the street![18]

Fitch was detailed to attend the next meeting, which took place on May Day – Labour Day. This time, in the absence of a convenient cupboard, the versatile detective covered proceedings in the guise of a waiter, with the help of a co-operative landlord. At the end of the meeting, Fitch managed to obtain the minutes by surreptitiously scooping them up in a napkin.

Some days later, Fitch covered another meeting at a public house in Great Portland Street. Lenin and Trotsky both made passionate speeches and a ballot was taken on the advisability of fomenting revolution in Russia. Twenty-one members voted for it and seven for postponement. After the results were announced, Lenin rose, during an impressive silence, and declared:

18   Herbert Fitch, *Traitors Within* (London: Hurst & Blackett, 1933), p. 24

Comrades of the Revolution, I have waited and served all my life for this hour. My brother died for it. Within the next few months, in Russia, we shall sweep out our oppressors on a tide of blood. And then Germany, Italy, France, England shall follow. In ten years from today, perhaps, the whole world shall be free, and the people shall possess the earth.[19]

Harold Brust described an important meeting of Russian émigrés he attended at about that time at the Jubilee Club in the East End of London, where the 'Third Section' had warned that practically every ruffian and regicide in Europe would foregather in London. He said he realised how much importance the Third Section attached to the affair when he saw Colonel Kharoff, one of the chiefs of the secret police of Russia, entering the Ritz Hotel, surrounded by a strong bodyguard. Special Branch officers were detailed to watch the Colonel. The meeting was soon in uproar, which SB officers tried to quell, arresting a number of people who were taken to the police station, where one of those arrested told Brust that he was an army officer on loan to the Third Section. He had visited the meeting on instructions, and was recognised; he and his colleagues were released from custody and escorted to the West End in taxi cabs. Another prisoner was Lenin but he also was released after Prince Kropotkin and other rich émigrés vouched for him.[20]

Around 1904 Lenin took up residence with his wife in Islington. At the same time the Bolshevik newspaper *Iskra* moved here and set up business at 37a Clerkenwell Green (now the Marx Memorial Library) – Harry Quelch, the editor of the British Social Democrat weekly *Justice*, made its printing press available, with *Iskra* just having to provide its own typesetters. In addition, the *Iskra* editorial board rented a five-roomed flat in Sidmouth Street, just off Gray's Inn Road, and this became a commune.[21] Lenin returned to Russia in 1905 to support the revolution. Apart from Lenin, well-known revolutionary Russians in London

19   Herbert Fitch, *Traitors Within*, p. 24–6

20   Brust, *I Guarded Kings*, p. 88–9

21   http://sarahjyoung.com/site/2011/01/16/russians-in-london-lenin/

between 1880 and 1914 were Joseph Stalin, Nadezhda Krupskaya (Lenin's partner) and Leon Trotsky.

It is difficult to say to what degree their movements were successfully monitored by Special Branch, which remained numerically small, provoking criticism
from other European states for not devoting sufficient coverage to their activities;
Brust's and Fitch's testimony, however, suggests that this was not so.

CHAPTER THREE

THE SUFFRAGETTE MOVEMENT

W HILE A LARGE part of Branch resources was devoted to personal protection and to monitoring the activities of revolutionary anarchists and Fenians, it was another group of militant activists that was to prove an unexpected and formidable adversary for Special Branch in the final decade of the nineteenth century and beyond.

Increasing support for women's rights was symptomatic of the late-Victorian emergence of a new feminist ideal, the 'New Woman', and nowhere was this revolution more marked than in women's clamour for suffrage. Successive Reform Acts of 1832, 1867 and 1884 failed to give women the vote and the struggle for women's enfranchisement became increasingly bitter and, at times, bloody. Moreover, the battle was fought not only by women, for John Stuart Mill was a vociferous supporter of women's rights and put their case in the Commons, though with little success.

Then, in 1903, Emmeline Pankhurst formed the militant Women's Social and Political Union (WSPU), which restricted membership to women. Emmeline Pankhurst and her daughters Christabel, Sylvia and Adela were influential leaders. Up until this time, women generally pursued their aims within the restrictions imposed by law, but from 1905 the WSPU adopted a policy of civil disobedience and by 1910, antagonised further by the delaying tactics of the government, they embarked on a policy of direct action. Its members smashed windows, did wide-spread damage to public property and were frequently in physical confrontations with the police.

Special Branch officers were employed to cover meetings and demonstra-tions in order to pre-empt offences, provide public order intelligence for their uniformed colleagues and, where possible, to record inflammatory speeches. As the campaign escalated, meetings became increasingly rowdy and many arrests were made. At first the women did not resist when taken into custody, but many refused to pay fines and were sentenced to imprisonment. The Commissioner, Edward Henry, prompted by the head of Special Branch, Superintendent Quinn, appealed to the Home Secretary for an augmentation to the hard-pressed Branch, slyly pointing out that 'the question of preventing annoyance to Cabinet ministers by Suffragettes has been engaging the attention of the Commissioner'. His letter went on to suggest that 'the Special Branch of the CID be assigned the duty [of protecting ministers] as members of this Branch have already been engaged in making enquiries regarding members of several Suffragette organisations'. The Commissioner concluded by requesting an augmentation of sixteen officers to undertake work, in the Provinces if necessary, and to obtain intelligence about their leaders' designs. The application was approved.[1]

In 1910 the government attempted to cool the situation by introducing the Conciliation Bill, which granted women very limited enfranchisement; but the Bill failed to get through Parliament.[2] This provoked reaction from Mrs Pankhurst and her cohorts and a meeting of the WSPU was held at Caxton Hall on Friday 18 November 1910, which unanimously agreed to send a message to the Prime Minister protesting at 'the policy of shuffling and delay with which the agitation for women's enfranchisement has been met by the government'.

---

1   Letter from Henry to Home Secretary dated 15 September 1909. TNA MEPO 2/1310

2   The Parliamentary Franchise (Women) Bill was given a second reading by the large majority of 299 to 190 on 12 July 1910. Before the Bill could be given a third reading, the government refused to allow time and when a general election was called the Bill was dropped.

A deputation about 300-strong took it to the House of Commons. The first twenty ladies were allowed to stand at the entrance to the House but as more and more suffragettes arrived the police forced them back to Bridge Street. A number of women broke through the police cordon, rushed at the wall of Palace Yard, and tried to climb over; they were restrained and forced back. In the ensuing skirmishes, some officers lost their helmets and others sustained minor injuries but, despite this, according to *The Times*, the police remained good tempered, although 'their method of shoving back the raiders lacked nothing in vigour. They were at any rate kept warm by the exercise, and so were the ladies who flung themselves at the defending lines.'[3]

On being told that the Prime Minister was engaged, Mrs Pankhurst reluctantly agreed to go in with two companions to see his private secretary, Mr Nash. When she returned to the waiting ladies stating that the situation was unchanged, they all sat down on the pavement until the House rose. Meanwhile, the police in front of the entrance to Palace Yard continued to be kept busy repelling women trying to break through the cordon –

> some of whom came up smiling every time to the attack, while a few scolded like viragoes and most were simply stolid. They were in every case seized and pushed, sometimes carried, to the other side of Bridge Street. The horse and motor traffic there was not stopped, but was somewhat hindered.[4]

By the time the House rose, at about 6 p.m., 119 arrests had been made. At that point the police were withdrawn and those women who had not been arrested returned to Caxton Hall, where Mrs Pankhurst announced that demonstrations would be repeated on Monday at 2 p.m., and every day until the Dissolution of Parliament.

---

3   *The Times*, 19 November 1910

4   Ibid.

Ralph Kitchener, who, in 1910, was a newly appointed uniformed constable in the Metropolitan Police, described the situation as he experienced it at that time:

> On 21 November 1910, a 'Women's Parliament' was called to meet at Cax-
> ton Hall, Westminster. From that meeting deputations were sent out to call
> on Members of Parliament and the government, and to press the women's
> claim for the vote. They attended in such numbers that very soon there
> was congestion in Parliament Square; the Police tried to move them on
> but they would not be moved. Finally the situation became so bad that
> arrests had to be made, but as one lot of women was arrested another took
> its place, and before the day ended 220 women and three men sympathis-
> ers had been arrested. On another occasion during the same period 285
> women were arrested in three days.[5]

The following day, *The Times* reported that Caxton Hall was filled once again with suffragettes who were awaiting Mr Asquith's statement in answer to Mr Keir Hardie's question as to 'what action the government proposed to take in connection with a measure for the enfranchisement of women'. When it was received, Mr Asquith's answer was considered so unsatisfactory that hostilities were resumed and a column of militant suffragettes, over 100-strong, left Caxton Hall for Downing Street. They reached Downing Street untroubled by the police; the single line of police there could not withstand the impact of the attacking force, and there was soon a seething mass of spectators, struggling police and suffragettes. Police reinforcements arrived, and the process of clearing the street began. The fight lasted only ten minutes.

When the Prime Minister left the Palace of Westminster he was mobbed by the suffragettes in Parliament Square and escaped in a motorcar, the window of which was broken before he got away. The homes of other ministers were attacked. The women broke windows at the Home Office with metal weights

---

5   Kitchener, *The Memoirs of an Old Detective*, p. 27

and other missiles; several were charged with malicious damage. The police were said by *The Times* correspondent to have behaved with self-control and good humour under the greatest provocation. It was evident, he said, that 'the women's conduct alienated the sympathy of the crowd'.[6]

The government found itself faced with another problem when women prisoners went on hunger strike and had to be forcibly fed, which caused a public outcry. Women's suffrage had become a national issue. New legislation meant that women had to be released on licence as soon as they went on hunger strike. The licences were generally for fourteen days, and the suffragette, after spending the greater part of that period at home, would leave unobtrusively and move to another address where she could not be found. Special Branch officers then had to trace and re-arrest her to complete her sentence. In a few cases where they could not get away from their address, owing to police observation, they remained indoors, for although the Act gave police power of arrest, it gave no right of entry. The Act soon became known as the 'Cat and Mouse Act'.

Twelve months after the scenes of mayhem in and around Whitehall, the situation remained unresolved. On 21 November 1911, the WSPU held another meeting at Caxton Hall. A resolution was passed condemning the Manhood Suffrage Bill and demanding that new legislation be passed giving equal franchise rights to men and women. The meeting was followed by rioting in the vicinity of Parliament Square, with window-smashing and other incidents of malicious damage. Some 220 arrests were made, including a number of well-known ladies and some men; they were released on bail after the House had risen.[7]

There followed a period when the WSPU held packed meetings in the Pavilion Theatre, Piccadilly every Monday afternoon. A handful of male supporters was allowed in, which made it possible for one or two Special Branch officers to infiltrate and take shorthand notes of the speeches. As a result, Mrs Pankhurst was arrested and charged, and at the Central Criminal Court sentenced to three years'

---

6   *The Times*, 23 November 1910

7   Ibid., 22 November 1911

imprisonment; she immediately went on hunger strike and was soon released on licence.

On 5 March 1912, Mr and Mrs Pethwick Lawrence, Mrs Pankhurst and Mrs Tike were arrested for conspiracy to incite persons to commit malicious damage to property. Christabel Pankhurst avoided arrest by escaping to France, where she remained, organising the campaign from Paris. The others each received nine months' imprisonment.

Kitchener, by now a Special Branch officer, described events in March 1912 when the WSPU called on supporters to assemble in Parliament Square on 4 March. The suffragettes defeated police plans to forestall trouble when on 1 March they went on a window-smashing rampage in the West End of London.

> ...they started in several streets simultaneously, and completely wrecked most of the windows in Regent Street, Oxford Street, Piccadilly, Bond Street, Coventry Street, the Strand, Trafalgar Square, Whitehall and Parliament Street. Every available police officer was rushed to the Strand; in all on this day 219 were arrested.[8]

In her memoirs, Sylvia Pankhurst reflected on the methodology. 'There is nothing like a hammer for smashing plate glass; stones, even flints, are apt to glance off harmlessly.' Damage amounting to thousands of pounds occurred. She recalled that police stations were inundated with complaints, museums and picture galleries in central London were closed and shop windows covered with hoardings or wire screens.[9]

Sentences on the offenders ranged from seven days to two months, but those committed to the sessions received sentences from four to eight months. Mrs Pankhurst went on hunger strike and soon had to be released for health reasons. On her release, she was taken by her friends to a flat in Great Smith Street, Westminster, on which Special Branch officers kept constant surveillance. One evening

8   Kitchener, *The Memoirs of an Old Detective*, p. 27–8

9   Sylvia Pankhurst, *The Suffragette Movement: An Intimate Account of Persons and Ideals* (London: Virago, 1977), pp. 372–4

two officers noticed numbers of women entering the flat; suddenly the door of the building burst open and some forty or fifty women surrounded the officers, preventing them from moving. Meanwhile, Mrs Pankhurst slipped out and drove off in a taxi. Some days later she was located at an address in Notting Hill Square, where observation was resumed. This was continued for several days, when the suffragettes announced that their leader was going to speak from the balcony of the house. A crowd of several hundred women was briefly addressed by Mrs Pankhurst, who announced that she would shortly leave the house under the protection of her 'bodyguard'. A strong contingent of uniformed police, as well as a number of detectives, was present. Kitchener described the scene:

> The 'Bodyguard' ... had been formed from among the younger and athletic members of the suffragettes to protect their leader, and for a time they had been meeting indoors to practise Indian club swinging and other exercises; whenever it was thought that their services might be called for they carried their clubs suspended and hidden under their skirts, ready to be produced if the need arose. On this occasion when the time came for Mrs Pankhurst to leave, the assembled suffragettes gathered thickly in front of the house to act as a screen against the police and the bodyguard rushed out from the building with a veiled woman in their midst. The crowd of supporters outside at once commenced a fight to prevent the police from getting at the woman and there was considerable disorder, during which several arrests were made for assault and obstruction. Eventually the veiled woman was reached, and in spite of the efforts of her escort, was arrested and taken to the nearby police station of Notting Hill. Here, however, in a better lighted place than had been that of the street, there was soon consternation, for it was found that the arrested woman, although of the same physical appearance as Mrs Pankhurst and wearing similar – if not the same – clothes as Mrs Pankhurst had worn, was not, in fact, that lady. In the meantime Mrs Pankhurst, taking advantage of the disorder in the Square had quietly, like the Arabs, 'folded her tent and slipped away'.

Mrs Pankhurst was traced to a house in Glebe Place, Chelsea, and another siege began. When a veiled woman left the house, another fight with the police began, and some of the 'bodyguard' were soon using their Indian clubs. Unfortunately they were not expert in the management of their weapons and one of the women was accidentally hit on the head by a fellow bodyguard's truncheon; she later had to receive medical attention. This time the subterfuge of the veiled woman had been expected, and after it was made certain that she was not Mrs Pankhurst, she was not arrested, and her leader remained indoors.[10]

The violent actions of the WSPU were becoming counter-productive. Fighting with the police, setting fire to houses, destroying golf courses and sports pavilions, breaking windows and street lamps, setting fire to the contents of letter boxes, cutting telephone wires and destroying valuable, publicly owned art works did their cause little good. The more militant the WSPU's actions, the less inclined Parliament was to meet its demands.

Kitchener described an amusing incident following the discovery of a suffragette incendiary bomb at Piccadilly Circus. Superintendent Quinn called him into the corridor outside his office:

'Now,' said the Superintendent to me. 'I want you to go with Sergeant Lenehan, and walk beside him to see that no one bumps into him,' then turning to the sergeant added, 'Very well sergeant you can go,' and he then returned to his office outside which the incident had taken place, and Lenehan and I turned away. 'It's alright, boy,' he said. 'I've only got a bomb in my pocket, to take over to the duck pond in the Park,' where at the time, there was a small office used by bomb experts.

He then went on to explain matters in this way:

The old man sent for me a while ago, and told me to go to Piccadilly Circus

---

10   Kitchener, *The Memoirs of an Old Detective*, p. 32

Underground Station, where a bomb had been found in a lavatory. I have been there, and sure enough, there was one and I took possession of it. Then I came back here and knocked on the Super's door and opened it. 'Oh, Sergeant Lenehan,' he said. 'Come in. And was it a bomb?' 'Yes sir,' I said. 'Oh, was it?' he asked. 'And where is it now?' 'I've got it here in my pocket,' I said, 'if you want to see it.' 'No, no, no, take it out of my office,' he said. 'I don't want it here.' And then he dashed off for you. And now we'll take it across the road – I expect it's only an incendiary after all.

And that is what it turned out to be. The Superintendent was rather proud of a photograph that was hanging in his office, showing the damage that had been caused in an earlier office at the Yard by a Fenian bomb, but he obviously had no desire to experience at first hand any in his own office.[11]

Meanwhile, the Women's Freedom League, led by Charlotte Despard, the sister of General French, found a less destructive means of demonstration. A detective sergeant called at its office in Adelphi to make an enquiry. The women present accused him of being an impostor, and prevented him from leaving their premises 'til someone comes from Scotland Yard to vouch for you – if you are as you claim to be a police officer'. They telephoned to Scotland Yard. The sergeant felt his humiliation very keenly when a colleague called to rescue him.[12]

By 1912, the activities of the suffragettes had escalated beyond mere militancy and had assumed a far more serious aspect. In December 1911 two members of the movement, Emily Davison and Nurse Pitfield, carried out arson attacks and were imprisoned. In July 1912, a well-organised series of secretly planned arson attacks took place under the direction of Christabel Pankhurst, in which churches and historic buildings were targeted. In 1913 Emily Davison threw herself under the King's horse, 'Anmer', at the Derby and was fatally injured. On 10 March 1914, the famous Rokeby Venus painting by Diego Velásquez, on display

11   Ibid., pp. 28–9

12   Ibid., p. 34

in the National Gallery, was mutilated by a prominent suffragist, Mary Richardson, who said that she had tried to destroy the picture as a protest against the government destroying Mrs Pankhurst.[13]

But worse was to come. In 1913, a number of bomb outrages were perpetrated. On 19 February a bomb seriously damaged a cottage being constructed for David Lloyd George at Walton-on-the-Hill, near Dorking. It was thought to have contained 5 lbs of gunpowder, as a similar device which had not exploded was found nearby. On 7 May, a dynamite bomb was planted near the Bishop's throne in the Chancel of St Paul's Cathedral, but failed to detonate. On 14 April, a bomb was found attached to railings outside the Bank of England. One final act of defiance in this mini bombing campaign took place on 11 June 1914, during a House of Commons debate on the suffrage issue. A loud explosion was heard when a bomb hidden behind the coronation chair in Westminster Abbey erupted, causing minor damage.[14]

Superintendent Quinn had taken personal control of the suffragette investigations; his intentions were made clear in a report appearing in *The Times* on 1 May 1913:

> Shortly after eleven o'clock yesterday morning the police entered the
> offices of the Women's Social and Political Union in Kingsway and made
> six arrests. The defendants, who are charged with conspiracy, were afterwards brought up before Mr Curtis Bennett at Bow Street Police Court
> and remanded in custody, bail being refused. Mr Bodkin, who appeared
> for the prosecution, made an important statement. He said that the *Suffragette* newspaper must be put a stop to, and he gave public warning that
> if any printer after that warning printed and published the literature of
> the union he might find himself in a very awkward position. Proceedings
> would be taken immediately against any person who made a speech in

13   *The Times*, 11 March 1914

14   Pankhurst, *The Suffragette Movement*, p. 569

encouragement of the union's course of conduct, and any persons who sub-
scribed to the union's funds might also find themselves in a very awkward
position ... He said that the proceedings were taken with a view to putting
down what had become a danger to the civilised community. The defendants were among the ringleaders of the organisation, which had continued
to carry on its nefarious practices notwithstanding repeated warnings.[15]

Early in 1914, Sylvia Pankhurst broke away from the WSPU and formed the
East London Federation of Suffragettes, which combined suffragette militancy
with left-wing socialism, and it was not long before she appeared in court. She
was given a term of imprisonment and went on hunger strike. Given the usual
short period of freedom on licence, she made no effort to escape but at the end
of the period she announced she would attend a mass demonstration in Victoria
Park. The authorities regarded this threat as open defiance, and said that if she
was able to attend open-air meetings she was sufficiently recovered to go back
to prison. Kitchener described what happened:

> When the time of the demonstration came, a long procession was assem-
> bled in front of the house where Sylvia had been residing and she was
> brought out lying on a stretcher and given a place in the middle of the pro-
> cession. On the police side a car had been placed in a strategic spot on
> the route the procession was to take, and as soon as the marchers reached
> this point, the procession was cut in two by mounted men, and the dele-
> gated party of us young detectives stepped in and quickly transferred the
> stretcher and its burden to the car and drove off with them to the wom-
> en's prison at Holloway.[16]

Shortly after the outbreak of war in August 1914, information was received in

---

15   *The Times*, 1 May 1913

16   Kitchener, *The Memoirs of an Old Detective*, p. 35

Special Branch that many women were assembling outside 10 Downing Street. All available officers were hurriedly sent there and about thirty demonstrators were arrested. A truce was called in this long-running battle of attrition on the understanding that after the 'real' war was over the question of votes for women would be resolved. 'It was, and for all practical purposes, that was the end of the suffragette movement.'[17]

The patriotism and war-work of women during the First World War may have had more to do with them achieving the franchise than the criminal conduct in which many of them took part at the height of their campaign. The Representation of the People Act (1918) enfranchised women over the age of thirty years whose names were on the Local Government Register, or who were married to men on that register. Women over twenty-one years of age were eventually allowed to vote on the same terms as men, as a result of the Representation of the People Act of 1928.

---

17   Ibid., p. 37

CHAPTER FOUR

ESTABLISHMENT

T HE SPECIAL IRISH Branch in its original form comprised a mere twelve officers (two inspectors, three sergeants and seven constables), which was augmented the following year by the addition of ten constables, the majority of whom hailed from Ireland. By the time the Dynamite War was over, the SIB boasted an establishment of twenty-six officers (two inspectors, four sergeants and twenty constables) who, according to the new Commissioner, Charles Warren, were all 'employed on Fenianism'.[1] However, he neglected to mention the calls made on the services of Special Branch to provide personal protection to British royalty and other dignitaries.

After the 'Jubilee Plot' of 1887, the Branch enjoyed a few years of comparative calm disturbed only by the constant rumblings of the anarchists and continual demands for the services of protection officers. By the end of 1891, the Commissioner, Edward Bradford, considered that the terrorist situation was sufficiently settled for the strength of Special Branch to be reduced by four officers, a suggestion to which the Home Secretary readily agreed.[2] This proposal was never

---

1 Letter from Warren to Home Secretary, dated 22 December 1886. TNA HO 144/133/A34848B sub. 12

2 Letters from Bradford to Lushington, and vice versa, dated 17 November 1891 & 31 December 1891. TNA HO 151/5

put into effect as the Walsall bomb plot was a stark reminder of the ever-present anarchist threat, but despite this and with the violent activities of the militant suffragettes a continuing drain on their resources, over the next seventeen years the establishment of SB had only increased by eight, to thirty-four.

Patrick Quinn took over as head of the Branch after the retirement of William Melville in 1903 and throughout his tenure of office made strenuous efforts to raise the establishment to realistic proportions. In 1909 he was successful in gaining an augmentation of twenty officers because of the threat posed by Indian nationalists, an increasingly volatile anarchist community, and the escalating scale of suffragette activity. He also restructured the Branch, amalgamating the former sections B, C and D into one unit to be known as the Special Branch, while Section A, now referred to simply as the CID, would continue to deal with serious crimes of a non-political nature.[3]

By 1914, because of the unwelcome attention of the suffragettes, it was felt necessary 'to increase the level of personal protection to members of the government ... to include all Cabinet ministers'. As a result, fifteen more men joined the Branch, which, after the restructuring mentioned above, brought its strength up to seventy-three, not including those serving at port.[4] Just after the outbreak of World War One, a steep rise in naturalisation applications and enquiries regarding 'alien matters', including investigation of espionage cases, stretched the resources of the Branch to breaking point and Quinn again appealed to the Commissioner for more men. At that time the authorised establishment of the Branch was 114, although the actual strength was eighty-six, deployed as follows:

Thirty-four – port; five – Aliens Registry; five – called up to serve in the Reserve Force; eleven – temporarily serving with the Intelligence Corps of the British Expeditionary Force in France; twelve – detailed daily to locate suspects from the Continent for interrogation; ten – engaged daily on protection duty with royalty or Cabinet ministers; four – at Victoria Station every day searching

---

3   Letter from the Home Secretary to the Commissioner, dated 14 June 1911. TNA HO 148/17 f. 519

4   Letter from the Commissioner to the Home Secretary, dated 16 April 1913. TNA HO 45/10932/163556

baggage and passengers from the Continent; five – performing duty outside the MPD for the Admiralty investigating alleged cases of espionage.

In support of his case, Quinn stated that his whole staff had been working overtime since the outbreak of war in August, with no leave, either annual or weekly. As a result, officers' health was suffering and two were unable to work because of illness.[5] He was given twenty-five more men.[6]

Quinn's efforts were largely neutralised by the demands of the war. In addition to the eleven officers conscripted to serve with the Intelligence Corps in the British Expeditionary Force in France,[7] some enlisted voluntarily and others were wholly employed by government departments. Fresh demands were continuously being made on the department's resources, particularly to man south coast ports; promotions were made 'in the field' without the normal requirement to pass the promotion examination and staff were constantly being shuffled around to cope with the needs of the moment.

After the war all public bodies, including the police, were required to cut back on expenditure. As a result, a massive reorganisation of the Metropolitan Police took place, although in Special Branch it was only at senior level that any change in establishment took place. From 1 April 1919, Special Branch and the CID were to be under the overall command of one Assistant Commissioner (Colonel Sir Wyndham Childs), a reversion to the pre-war organisation. Each department would have its own Deputy Assistant Commissioner with Lieutenant Colonel J. F. C. Carter appointed as the nominal head of Special Branch, although Detective Superintendent James McBrien continued to be responsible for the day-to-day running of the section. It was recognised that the work of Special Branch, 'for reasons which are obvious, has greatly increased in volume' (since 1914). It was therefore proposed to transfer to the Foreign Office

---

5   Memo from Quinn to Henry, dated 20 November 1914. TNA MEPO 2/1643

6   Letter from Henry to Home Secretary Blackwell, dated 2 December 1914, and reply, dated 23 December 1914. TNA MEPO 2/1643

7   Edwin Woodhall in *Spies of the Great War* (London: John Long, 1936), p. 15, names these officers as Dan McLaughlin, Leo Gough, Martin Clancy, Ernest Hill, Canning, Palmer, Bannon, Frost, Kirchner, Cox, Trevit-Reid, Worth, Smith, Warner, Kite, Geater, Selby, Parkes, Hansen, Phelps, Brattle, Albers and Woodhall himself

a 'portion of work relating to foreign affairs', although a 'large volume of work
relating to Bolshevist, Communist and Revolutionary matters generally' would
remain with the Branch. It was accepted that this 'will involve a large reduc-
tion in the number of senior police officers now performing duty in the Special
Branch and their absorption ... will be an extremely difficult matter owing to
the numbers involved'.

The Commissioner cynically noted that 'there are several senior officers in the
Special Branch above the numbers authorised for that Department'. To rectify
the error it was intended that a number of senior officers should be transferred
into the Force as a whole as vacancies arose – and yet, over the next ten years,
the establishment of the Branch remained virtually unchanged.[8]

At the beginning of the '30s the Branch underwent a major transformation.
In October 1929, McBrien had retired as head of the Branch, to be replaced by
Acting Superintendent Edward 'Teddy' Parker,[9] who was soon to assume total
control when Carter was suddenly transferred. Parker was quickly promoted to
superintendent and briefly remained as head of Special Branch until his retirement in 1936. At about the same time the Branch was stripped of its lead role in
countering communist subversion, which was taken over by the Security Service,
who simultaneously inherited some of SB's experts on subversion and many of
its relevant files. Ironically, the move did not reduce SB's workload; in fact, the
reverse was the case, for MI5, formed in 1909, had no executive powers and no
additional staff to cope with the extra work. It was on Special Branch that they
relied to carry out their time-consuming enquiries.

When Parker departed, his place was taken by Chief Inspector Albert Canning,
who was soon promoted to superintendent and by the time of his retirement in
1946 held the rank of Chief Constable. One of Canning's chief concerns was his
lack of adequate manpower to deal with the increasing work load (in 1933), caused
principally by the emergence of fascism as a political threat and the consequent

---

8   Letter from Commissioner to Home Secretary, dated 1 March 1922. TNA MEPO 10/3
9   *The Times*, 30 October 1929

reaction of (mainly) communist and Semitic groups. MI5's continuing demands for information were also a great drain on resources.[10]

Three state occasions that occurred between 1934 and 1937 added to these manpower problems. These were the wedding of HRH the Duke of York (1934), the Silver Jubilee of HM King George V and HM Queen Mary (1935) and the coronation of HM King George VI and HM Queen Elizabeth (1937). Two substantial augmentations were approved; in 1934 fifty officers were transferred on a temporary basis (of which number, thirty-five became permanent) and in 1937 a further fifty were drafted in.[11] On all such state occasions security considerations are paramount and Canning's problems were no different from those of his predecessors and are equally applicable today. In applying for these increases, Canning explained to the ACC that:

(i) All political suspects, British and alien, in addition to those already regularly reported on, must be checked.

(ii) A survey to be carried out of 200 or more mentally unstable individuals and those with fixations on royalty or grievances against the state.

(iii) Vetting of lines of route.

(iv) Increased supervision of aliens arriving at ports.

(v) Personal protection for visiting royalty and other VIPs.[12]

In 1937, to cope with a marked increase in the activities of political extremists, particularly fascists, a further twelve officers were transferred to the Branch, bringing its permanent establishment up to 180.[13]

---

10   Letter from Commissioner to the Home Secretary, dated 12 December 1933. TNA MEPO 2/3826

11   Dealt with on TNA MEPO 2/3827, which shows that the augmentation comprised two DIs, twelve DSs and thirty-six DCs.

12   Memo from Canning to ACC, dated 14 September 1937. TNA MEPO 2/5385. The augmentation was four DIs, eight DSs and thirty-eight DCs.

13   Police Orders, 27 November 1936 and 1 January 1937

CHAPTER FIVE

PROTECTION

A LTHOUGH IT WAS Fenian terrorism that led to the formation of the Metropolitan Police Special Branch, another aspect of its work, the personal protection of VIPs, has always featured prominently in its day-to-day activities. Vital operational duties have frequently suffered when officers have been called away to perform a task that was, in the early days, little more than that of a part-time chaperone. Corroboration of this is provided by John Sweeney, who testified that, 'During my service at the Yard, no small element of my duties was represented by attendance on various august personages.'[1]

ROYALTY PROTECTION

S oon after the establishment of the Metropolitan Police Force, it assumed responsibility for the personal protection of the sovereign, a task that had previously been performed by such military formations as 'The Yeomen of the Guard' and

---

1   Sweeney, *At Scotland Yard*, p. 55

'The Gentlemen at Arms'.[2] In 1837, it was the officers of A Division, the police division in which the Queen's new home, Buckingham Palace, was situated, who were given the role of royalty protection officers. After the formation of Special Branch, it became the practice for its officers to provide extra security when required – an arrangement that remained in place until the creation of the Protection Command of the Specialist Operations Branch of the Metropolitan Police in 2006.

Over the years, 'additional protection' from Special Branch was frequently called for, particularly when senior members of the royal family were travelling outside the Metropolitan Police District and when information was received of specific threats to their security. Sweeney describes his first experience of being involved in the protection of a royal sovereign, Queen Victoria, when she was staying at Balmoral. The detective claims that 'whenever the Queen went out, a detective was within reach' and 'that all strangers in the neighbourhood were carefully watched' without their knowledge.[3] (Most unlikely!)

Sweeney's narrative is typically bombastic, but it gives a far clearer impression than bald statistics of what Special Branch protection to royalty entailed in those early days. In 1885 information was received of an attempt to be made on the life 'of a certain royal personage, in Pall Mall'. Sweeney's account runs:

> I found it a rather ticklish job, as of course it was advisable that the Prince should not know that anything of this unpleasant nature was in the air. I had to put myself in touch with the right persons in order to keep acquainted with his intended movements, and to take care that he should not observe my attentions. When he drove anywhere in his carriage I followed at a discreet distance in a hansom; when he came out of any house he had been visiting of an evening, I was on the kerb hard by, carefully keeping in shadow; and I saw him return to Marlborough House, myself unseen.[4]

---

2   Originally known as 'The King's Bodyguard of the Yeoman of the Guard' and 'His Majesty's Bodyguard of the Honourable Corps of the Gentlemen at Arms' respectively

3   Sweeney, *At Scotland Yard*, p. 57

4   Ibid., pp. 55–7

The menial nature of royalty protection in days gone by is clearly illustrated by the experiences of the Special Branch sergeant who used to accompany the Prince of Wales during his frequent visits to France in the 1920s and '30s, to attend private functions, play golf, participate in drag hunts and, occasionally, act in his official capacity. It is open to conjecture whether the sergeant was there to act as a bodyguard or as an additional lackey, as he was expected to travel separately from the prince in order to supervise the safe conveyance of the heavy luggage, which could not be transported in the aircraft carrying the royal party.[5] It was not only the lower ranks who performed these onerous duties; on several occasions King George V was escorted abroad by very senior officers, Patrick Quinn, the head of Special Branch, acting as bodyguard when he visited the troops on the front line in 1914;[6] the Commissioner himself accompanied His Majesty to India in 1911, assisted by Constable Tibbenham from Special Branch (presumably looking after the heavy baggage!).[7]

PROTECTION OF CABINET MINISTERS, FOREIGN DIGNITARIES AND OTHER VIPS

However, the main role of Special Branch in the field of protection was initially to safeguard the security of the Prime Minister and certain Cabinet ministers. This role was gradually expanded to include visiting foreign dignitaries and other high-profile figures whose personal security was considered to be at risk.

An insight into the early days of police protection duty is provided by a police memorandum sent to the Home Office in 1884 during a dispute between police and Home Office over expenses:

---

5   Details of protection for the Prince of Wales on his European trips are contained in TNA MEPO 38/151

6   Letter from Henry to Home Office, dated 17 December 1914. TNA HO 46/181

7   Referred to in TNA HO 45/10651/211757

> They [the police] parade on duty daily at the hour Parliament assembles
> and are posted in communication with each other at various points on the
> lines of route taken by the several Cabinet ministers on their way to
> the Palace of Westminster, escorting them to and, more importantly, from
> the House to their respective destinations.[8]

Special Branch officers became involved in the protection of Cabinet ministers
during the 1880s, though in truth it was little more than a form of surveillance. It
was feared that the Fenians might seek to further their evil intentions by attacking prominent public figures, particularly those associated with Irish politics.
Sweeney, who was frequently employed on this duty, describes how Lord Aber-
deen 'used to drive about in one hired cab with me following in another'.[9]

Another politician whom Sweeney protected was Arthur Balfour when he
was Chief Secretary for Ireland. Sweeney narrates how Balfour and his private
secretary used to run to the House from his office in Queen Street, which was
only a short distance away. Sweeney 'used to run behind with a colleague, the
people encouraging us with ironical cheers and bidding us take care of him and
not let him get shot'.[10]

The outbreak of World War One saw an end of suffragette militancy, but
the extra men who had been recruited to ensure ministers' security were soon
required in another field. The age-old 'Irish Problem' once more reared its ugly
head when the Easter Rising of 1916 abruptly shattered the uneasy calm that
Ireland had been enjoying since the beginning of the century. Towards the end
of 1920, murder and general lawlessness spilled over into mainland Britain and
continued until 1923. Arguably the most dramatic of the terrorists' murderous
actions here was the assassination in London on 22 June 1922 of Field Marshal
Sir Henry Wilson, Security Adviser to Sir James Craig's government in Northern

---

8   Letter from the Commissioner to the Home Office, dated 11 June 1884. TNA HO 45/9643/A35121. The men
    were asking for an increase in their 1s 11d weekly expenses (about 10p)

9   Sweeney, *At Scotland Yard*, p. 115

10   Ibid., p. 121

Ireland. Ironically, Special Branch protection for the Field Marshal had been discontinued when he retired from the army not long before his assassination, which is described fully in Chapter 10.

Once the Anglo-Irish Treaty had been signed in December 1921, the Home Secretary, after consultation with the Commissioner, removed from nineteen ministers and other officials considered to be less vulnerable the personal protection that had been afforded to them during the Irish campaign of violence. Fourteen individuals, including the Prime Minister Bonar Law, the former PM David Lloyd George, Winston Churchill and Lady Wilson, widow of the late Sir Henry Wilson, continued to receive Special Branch protection. In addition, similar facilities would be provided in London for Ulster government members if their government requested it. At the same time as making these decisions the Home Secretary decreed that, other than the Prime Minister, government ministers should not receive protection 'in the absence of any personal reason to the contrary'. He did not propose to have protection for himself.[11]

In succeeding years the allocation of personal protection continued to be made according to the current threat assessments provided by Special Branch to the Home Secretary. Protection for the Prime Minister remained constant but otherwise the list of those protected fluctuated considerably: in February 1924, for example, only six individuals had protection[12] but by the end of the year, because of the general election in October, this number had risen to nineteen – election time tending to bring out the worst in the electorate.[13] The following year, with the election over, the figure had reduced to eleven, which would continue to go down as the Fenian threat diminished.[14]

By 1925, personal protection methods employed by Special Branch officers were still very basic considering that they had been performing this work for

11   Memo from Home Office to Commissioner, dated 25 October 1922, and letter from Commissioner to Home Office, dated 27 October 1922. TNA MEPO 38/126

12   Special Branch memorandum, dated 1 February 1924. TNA MEPO 38/126

13   Letter and attachment from Commissioner to Home Office, dated 8 December 1924. TNA MEPO 3/557

14   Commissioner's report to the Secret Service Committee. TNA CAB 127/366

over forty years, but at least the bodyguard would travel in the same vehicle as his principal and not, as in Sweeney's day, independently – as this officer amusingly illustrates, such a practice could have disastrous results.

> Mr Balfour [then Chief Secretary for Ireland] had been staying with Lord Rothschild at Tring; and a colleague and myself travelled up to Euston in the same train. On these journeys Mr Balfour had but to walk out of the station, step in to his brougham, and be whisked off. We had to drag out our bags, take the first cab we saw, and follow him as best we could. In those days Mr Balfour had a particularly speedy mare, which bustled every cab horse that had to follow near it. Well, that day we got in to a hansom drawn by a horse which had been a hunter, and had never before been between the shafts in the London traffic. The driver whipped it up to keep Mr Balfour's carriage in sight. He was making for the Irish Office, Westminster. As we crossed the Euston Road our beast took fright at something and bolted. We dashed along Gower Street at a furious pace. We all but ran down the brougham, but I shouted to Mr Balfour's coachman and he just managed to pull out in time to avert an awful smash. As we came into Bedford Square our driver thought he would tire his horse out by driving it round and round the square. Round we flew about twelve times, a circus drive which I never want repeated. Every window had faces pressed against its panes; crowds of people watched us from the pavements. The pace was far too hot for us to think of jumping out of the cab; while no one dared to spring at the horse's head. Meanwhile the driver, being an elderly man, began to tire and lose his control over the reins. Finally the animal, guided no longer, made a wild dash at some area railings. Over went cab and horse with a crash.[15]

Mr Balfour continued his journey without 'protection' and arrived unharmed at his destination.

---

15   Sweeney, *At Scotland Yard*, pp. 119–20

Other early Special Branch officers have shown in their memoirs that VIP protection was not the exacting and sophisticated task that it was to become later in the twentieth century, and it was more a matter of good fortune than professional ability that in the formative years of its performance by Special Branch officers none of their protégés came to harm. Men such as Herbert Fitch and Harold Brust as well as John Sweeney basked in the perceived glamour that protection duty offered. Typical is Brust's claim that 'The duty of guarding royalty is a "peak" job for the Special Branch officer, a pinnacle in his career.'[16] Fitch epitomises the obsequiousness displayed by the other two when he declares:

> I have met officially a good many of the royal visitors to this country, I have shown them the sights of London, travelling by bus and tube incognito and unrecognised, and I have met them occasionally when I have been abroad guarding our own royalties in foreign visits. Nearly all these personages were exceedingly nice to me; some of them pressed rewards and decorations on me, as when the Kaiser presented me with the Order of the Red Eagle for attending him when he was over here before the war.[17]

It was not only VIPs who were afforded protection; in special cases protection was afforded to persons who were 'thought likely to attract unwelcome attention'. One such person was the public executioner, John Ellis, who had taken up hanging in 1907 after running a hairdresser's and newsagent's business in Rochdale. In 1922 he was called upon to carry out the execution of Reginald Dunne and Joseph O'Sullivan, the IRA murderers of Sir Henry Wilson. The impending execution provoked massive protests from republican extremists and Ellis received many threatening letters, which prompted the Home Secretary to recommend Special Branch protection 'as it would make it difficult to find another man who would readily take his place' if anything happened to him.

---

16   Brust, *I Guarded Kings*, p. 40
17   Fitch, *Traitors Within*, p. 55

In the event, a Special Branch officer, DS Davies, was dispatched to Rochdale to provide personal protection until after the execution had taken place, as the Chief Constable stated that the executioner was 'in a state of funk'.[18] The following year, after the particularly unpleasant execution of Edith Thompson, Ellis became an alcoholic and unsuccessfully attempted suicide by shooting himself in the mouth, a crime for which he was charged and bound over for twelve months. However, on 20 September 1932, he achieved more success with a razor and cut his throat.

Every protection has to be treated on the circumstances of the particular case, and some of the more unusual visitors to these shores, such as the Grand Mufti of Palestine, Mahatma Gandhi and the Pope, presented their protection officers with unique problems. Some of our own residents too provided their bodyguards with particular problems; men like Edward Heath with his predilection for ocean-going yachting, and Salman Rushdie, the controversial author who was given police protection after becoming the target of a *fatwa*, proclaimed by the Iranian religious leader Ayatollah Khomeini. In his personal account of surviving a *fatwa*, Rushdie paid tribute to his protection team:

> If it had not been for the efforts of ... Special Branch, the Metropolitan Police and their colleagues in the Special Intelligence Services of the United Kingdom, I might not have been in a position to write this – or indeed any other book.[19]

Rushdie was not the only individual to be grateful to Special Branch for the protection its officers provided. It is a fact that only one individual has been killed while receiving Special Branch protection. This was Field Marshal Lord Kitchener, the Secretary of State for War, who on 5 June 1916 lost his life when HMS *Hampshire*, the Royal Navy cruiser on which he was travelling to Russia,

18   Details of correspondence between the Home Office, the Commissioner and the Chief Constable of Rochdale Borough Police appear on TNA MEPO 38/157

19   Salman Rushdie, *Joseph Anton: A Memoir* (London: Jonathan Cape, 2012), Acknowledgements

is believed to have struck a German mine and sank with heavy loss of life. DS Matthew McLoughlin, the Special Branch officer accompanying Lord Kitchener, also perished in the disaster – his name appears on the Metropolitan Police roll of honour. McLoughlin was not the only protection officer to die while on duty; DS Harry Battley was killed while on his way to the Yalta Peace Conference on 1 February 1945, to take up protection with the Foreign Secretary, who had gone ahead on a RN warship carrying the Prime Minister. Battley was travelling in a RAF 'York' aircraft, which crashed into the sea after experiencing navigational problems.[20]

---

20   Hilary St. George Saunders and Denis Richards, *Royal Air Force 1939–45, Vol. III: The Fight is Won* (London: Her Majesty's Stationery Office, 1955), p. 187

CHAPTER SIX

NATURALISATION
AND PORT CONTROLS

SOON AFTER THE formation of Special Branch, it took on the responsibility for checking the bona fides of applicants for naturalisation. In those days enquiries would normally be confined to confirming the applicant's place of employment and address, that he was of good character, establishing the reasons for the application and ensuring that the referees were suitable. A typical report for the Home Office would take up no more than one side of a sheet of foolscap but, in the days before technology ruled, this was a time-consuming and frustrating distraction from the task of catching Fenian bombers.

As time went on, the attraction of British citizenship flourished, despite the first faint signs of weakening in Britannia's control over her hitherto ever-expanding Empire, to such an extent that in 1909 and again in 1914 the Commissioner cited naturalisation enquiries as a reason for seeking to increase the establishment of Special Branch.[1]

After the war, applications for British naturalisation continued to increase, with 686 cases being dealt with in the first six months of 1925. Enquiries were now

---

1   Letter from Commissioner to Home Secretary, dated 7 December 1909. TNA MEPO 2/1297

more thorough than hitherto and, according to the Commissioner, entailed 'an enormous amount of enquiry, which is done by officers in between performing such duties as lines of route, attending meetings and making special enquiries';[2] little changed in this respect during the next eighty years. The advent of World War Two saw an acceleration in the rate of applications to 140 a month but, thankfully for the hard-pressed officers of Special Branch, no fresh applications were accepted by the Home Office during the course of the war.

PORT CONTROLS

In 1884, in an attempt to plug the gaps through which the Fenians were importing explosives, Edward Jenkinson dispatched droves of police officers to ports all round the country, and on the Continent, to supplement the efforts of local customs officers. The initial draft of eighty-four included thirty officers from the Royal Irish Constabulary, withdrawn in 1886, and nine from the Metropolitan Police Special Irish Branch (whose places in the Branch were filled by less experienced officers); five of the original force were deployed to cities on the Continent (Antwerp, Rotterdam, Paris and Hamburg).[3]

Gradually, men from local forces took over from the 'outsiders' and by 1888 only about forty-five Met officers, including a mere handful from Section C, the new SIB ports section, comprised the 'port police' unit, with officers stationed at the following ports: Gravesend, Dover, Southampton, Harwich, Newhaven, Plymouth, Weymouth, Folkestone, Queensborough, Le Havre, Bremerhaven, Antwerp, Rotterdam, Amsterdam, Cherbourg, Copenhagen, Hamburg, Christiansand.[4]

As Special Branch grew, ports were increasingly staffed by Section C personnel;

---

2   Commissioner's report to the Secret Service Committee in 1925. TNA CAB 127/366

3   Assorted correspondence on TNA HO 144/133/A34848B, subs. 1–12

4   Letter from the Commissioner to the Home Secretary, dated 20 November 1888. TNA HO 144/222/A49500M, sub. 3

by the early 1900s the initial threat from the Fenians was considered to be over
and the watch at ports had been relaxed to such an extent that in 1909 Superintendent Quinn reported to the Commissioner that there were nine vacancies in
Section C which he was not proposing to fill for the time being.[5]

At the outbreak of World War One, thirty-four of the Special Branch establishment of 114 officers were employed at port; during the course of the conflict,
however, frequent changes of personnel took place, according to the exigencies
of the moment. For example, Folkestone rapidly became the chief British port
for passenger services to and from the Continent and its pre-war establishment
of a sergeant and a constable had been raised to one inspector, five sergeants
and two constables.[6]

After the war was over, the Special Branch presence at ports became more
settled and by 1925 remained virtually unchanged from the 1914 figure; of its
establishment of thirty-five men, five were stationed on the Continent. Officers performed duty at the following ports: Newcastle, Hull, Grimsby, Harwich,
Gravesend, Dover, Folkestone, Newhaven, Southampton, Port of London, Paris,
Brussels and Rotterdam.

In that year the Commissioner outlined the work performed by SB officers
at air and sea ports, which remained virtually unchanged until 2006:

Liaison with Home Office immigration officers – recording arrivals and
departures of British and foreign criminals and revolutionaries – preventing the
importation of revolutionary propaganda – pointing out suspected persons to
the Customs for search – recording the arrival and addresses to which proceeding of criminal deportees – searching passenger lists and examining passports
for the purpose of arresting individuals circulated as wanted for crime (many
criminals have been arrested by port officers) – facilitating the arrival and departure of British and foreign royalties and notabilities.

The Commissioner, in describing the duties of those officers serving abroad,

5   Memorandum from Quinn to Commissioner, dated 7 July 1909. TNA MEPO 2/1297

6   Memo from Quinn to A.C.C., dated 5 January 1915, and letter from Home Office to Commissioner, dated 24
     February 1915. TNA MEPO 2/1643

stated that they acted as liaison officers between the Metropolitan and foreign police forces, monitored the activities of revolutionaries, smugglers and 'dope' traffickers and made enquiries for ambassadors and consular officials.[7]

By 1934, holidays abroad had become so popular that extra men were required in the summer to perform what became known as 'summer relief'. In 1934, for example, nine men were so employed but every year this number increased, which put an additional burden on those remaining at Scotland Yard. After the war, the Ports Unit assumed a not inconsiderable section of Special Branch, both in size and functions, with a commander in charge and its own training section.

---

7   Report compiled for the Secret Service Committee by the Commissioner in 1925. TNA CAB 127/366.

CHAPTER SEVEN

GERMAN ESPIONAGE
AND SUBVERSIVE PACIFISM
IN GREAT BRITAIN

B Y THE END of the nineteenth century, Germany had developed from a small group of loosely joined states into a nation dominated by Prussian militarism. Britain regarded Germany's intentions with mistrust and suspicion, especially when it started to expand its navy with large battleships.

Stimulated by fictional works such as *The Riddle of the Sands* by Erskine Childers and William Le Queux's *The Invasion of 1910*, the public shared the government's misgivings and a spy fever developed. There was, nevertheless, a small number of genuine cases of espionage which were dealt with in the courts, and the Committee for Imperial Defence began to question whether Britain was adequately defended against espionage.

In fact, two tiny departments of the War Office with responsibilities for foreign intelligence (MO2 – later MI6) and counter-espionage (MO3 – later MI5) did exist. They were run discreetly from premises in Victoria Street, Westminster, under the cover name of W. Morgan, General Agent. Their investigations were carried out clandestinely by William Melville, who had quietly resigned as head of Special Branch in 1903 to be recruited by the War Department. Over the next few years he created a small investigative group of former police officers which, in 1909, was formally established as the Secret Service Bureau; however, they were given no statutory powers of arrest or search, and had to rely on the police for any executive action that was necessary.

Between August 1911 and July 1914, MO3, now headed by Vernon Kell, provided Special Branch with information gathered from a number of technical and human resources, which led to the arrest of some ten suspected spies, most of whom were inept amateurs. During the following period of hostilities, thirty-one spies were arrested, nineteen of whom were sentenced to death and ten imprisoned.

The principal target of German espionage was the Royal Navy, so it followed that the German Intelligence Service should seek potential spies in naval bases such as Devonport, Portsmouth and Chatham. Prior to the war they recruited people of German origin but, later, nationals of neutral countries were frequently chosen as persons whom they believed would loyally assist the Fatherland.

In 1910, a Special Branch operation discovered what turned out to be an invaluable asset in the struggle to combat German espionage. When the Kaiser came to England for the funeral of King Edward VII, MPSB mounted a surveillance operation on one of his staff, Captain von Rebeur-Paschwitz, known to them as a naval officer attached to the Nachrichten Abteilung (Naval Intelligence Department).[1] One evening after the funeral he was followed by DIs Drury and Seal to a barber's shop at 402a Caledonian Road, Islington. This was the business address of Karl Gustav Ernst, a British subject of German descent. A Home Office warrant was obtained by MO5 which revealed that it was a 'cut-out' address through which the Nachrichten Abteilung received information from other agents in the United Kingdom and passed it on to Germany. For the next four years MO5 shared the product with Special Branch, examined and recorded it. The monitoring of suspect addresses, as in the Ernst case, was extremely productive and resulted in the identification of a number of agents

1   German Naval Intelligence, known in security circles as 'N'

and the addresses they used. Special Branch played a major part in bringing the spies to justice, making arrests, carrying out interrogations and giving evidence in court. At every stage there was excellent cooperation between the Special Branch and MI5, although in his history of MI5 Christopher Andrew makes no mention of the not insignificant part played by the Branch.

One of those using the Caledonian Road address was Gustav Steinhauer, the head of the Nachrichten Abteilung. In 1909 he recruited an agent called Karl Hentschel and sent him to Chatham, where he taught German to Royal Navy officers. Hentschel recruited a Royal Navy Warrant Officer, George Parrott, an expert in naval gunnery, who was stationed at Sheerness. The two worked successfully together until Parrott decided to deal directly with the Nachrichten Abteilung and retain all the profits for himself. Hentschel denounced Parrott to the British authorities and, in June 1912, the monitoring of Ernst's 'drop address' revealed that he (Parrott) was travelling to Ostend to meet a German contact. He was followed by Special Branch and, on his return, questioned. He was dismissed from the service for a disciplinary offence, 'travelling abroad without permission', but continued to receive correspondence from Ernst addressed to a 'Mr G. Couch, 136 King's Road, Chelsea'. He was arrested there by DIs Riley and Parker from Special Branch when he collected an intercepted letter which contained a £5 note and an intelligence questionnaire signed 'Richard'. Parrott's bank account showed a large number of deposits of £5; he was sentenced to four years' penal servitude. Hentschel was given immunity from prosecution and an assisted passage to Australia.[2]

In 1911, William Salter, a former naval rating, advertised his services as a private detective in Portsmouth and was contacted by a German agent, Heinrich Grosse, posing as Captain Hugh Grant. Salter was not convinced of his cover story and informed the Admiral Superintendent of the Dockyard, who passed the case to Special Branch. Grosse was found in possession of compromising

---

2   James Morton, *Spies of the First World War* (London: National Archives, 2010), p. 51; Christopher Andrew, *The Defence of the Realm*, pp. 44–6

documents, arrested and sentenced to three years' imprisonment. On completion of his sentence he was interned and died while still in custody.

In 1911, DI Fitch liaised with local police in Plymouth who had received
information from a solicitor, Samuel Duff, indicating that one of his clients was
a spy. Fitch described how a German named Max Schultz, posing as a journalist,
attempted to obtain information about the Royal Navy's state of readiness. He
set himself up in a houseboat on the River Yealm just outside Plymouth, where
he entertained British naval officers. Duff reported the matter and Fitch, with
the aid of Vernon Kell, arranged for false information to be supplied to Schultz
and his mail monitored. His controller was identified as an officer of the Nachrichten Abteilung. Schultz was prosecuted under the newly passed Official
Secrets Act and sentenced at Exeter Assizes to twenty-one months' imprisonment on 4 November 1911.[3]

Some spies were trapped through their own carelessness; Frederick Adolphus
Schroeder, alias Gould, was a case in point. He had been a successful German
agent for ten years when he retired as landlord of the Queen's Head public house
in Rochester in 1913. When he vacated the pub, the new landlord discovered
two Admiralty charts and a letter indicating that he had worked for the German
Secret Service since 1903. These were passed to Special Branch. Gould and his
wife Maud, who had moved to Wandsworth, were kept under observation and
their mail was intercepted. When it was learned that Mrs Schroeder was to travel
to Brussels to hand over some documents to one 'Schmidt', she was followed to
Charing Cross Station, where DI Hester arrested her in a railway carriage. She
endeavoured to conceal three sealed envelopes, which were recovered by DS Passmore; they were found to contain a number of Admiralty documents, some marked
'restricted'. She was taken to Bow Street Police Station, where she was detained.

Once Mrs Schroeder was in custody, the officers arrested her husband at
the Wandsworth address, where they found further incriminating documents.
The couple was charged with offences against the Official Secrets Act 1911 and

---

3   Fitch, *Traitors Within*, pp. 106–11

appeared before the Central Criminal Court on 3 April 1914. Mrs Schroeder was acquitted, as the police were unable to prove that she knew what the sealed envelopes contained, but Frederick Schroeder was convicted and sentenced to six years' penal servitude.

The addresses of Steinhauer's agents in Britain and on the Continent were carefully recorded in a suspect index. Steinhauer claimed in his memoirs that the Germans were aware that the mail was being read by the British but this seems unlikely, as so many of his agents were detained before they could leave the country when war was declared. Kitchener described the rounding up of espionage suspects:

> Most of the German agents were known, and marked down for action should war be declared. When the actual moment came, therefore, the word was given for immediate action. All available Special Branch officers were called together, and when 'P.Q.' (Detective Superintendent Patrick Quinn) walked into the general office, we saw a most unusual sight, for with him, he had not one warrant but a whole handful which were for the arrest of all the known German agents within the district. The efficiency of the steps which had been taken previously could scarcely have been improved upon, for out of the thirty known German agents not more than two or three escaped through the net.[4]

Karl Gustav Ernst was arrested by DCI Ward and charged under the Official Secrets Act with illegally communicating information to Steinhauer. On conviction he was sentenced to seven years' penal servitude. In the initial round up of spies who were identified through Ernst's postal service, a total of twenty-one were arrested and interned. A twenty-second, Otto Weigals, avoided arrest and returned to Germany.[5]

---

4   Kitchener, *The Memoirs of an Old Detective*, p. 39

5   Leonard Sellers, *Shot in the Tower: The Story of the Spies Executed in the Tower of London During the First World War* (London: Leo Cooper, 1997), p. 6

Once war commenced in August 1914, espionage in Britain proved fatal for those German agents who were caught in the act. The Defence of the Realm Act carried the death penalty for communication with the enemy. Although espionage remained primarily the responsibility of MO5, Special Branch also played a major part in bringing spies to justice. Questioning of suspects was often carried out by Basil Thomson, the Assistant Commissioner in charge of Special Branch, at his office in New Scotland Yard.

The censorship of letters and cables to neutral countries bordering Germany continued to be a most valuable tool in uncovering cases of espionage. Techniques evolved within the Post Office facilitated the detection of letters containing secret messages written between the lines in invisible ink. Special Branch instituted the enquiries to identify the enemy agents responsible for this correspondence and arrests were made.

The first German agent to be arrested in the United Kingdom after the war commenced was Carl Hans Lody, a reserve officer in the German Navy who volunteered to spy in England. He travelled to Edinburgh on a United States passport and sent reports to Germany about the Royal Navy's strength there. As a result, a British cruiser, HMS *Pathfinder*, was sunk by a German submarine. He continued to send reports to Germany written in German, which brought him under the notice of the British censors. He was identified and followed by a Special Branch officer, Jeremiah Lynch, to Killarney, where he was arrested by the Royal Irish Constabulary and brought back to England. He was tried, convicted and executed by firing squad in the Tower of London on 6 November 1914.[6]

Over the next year ten more individuals were convicted of espionage and executed by shooting at the Tower of London. They were: Carl Frederick Muller, Haicke Petrus Marinus Janssen, Willem Johannes Roos, Augusto Alfredo Roggen, Ernest Waldemar Melin, Fernando Buschman, George Traugott Breeckhow, Irving Guy Ries, Ludovico Hurwitz-y-Zender and Albert Meyer. The

6   TNA WO 71/1236

eleventh spy, Peter Hahn, was sentenced to seven years' imprisonment.[7] Lizzie
Wertheim, a confederate of Breeckhow, was also convicted and sentenced at the
Central Criminal Court to ten years' imprisonment, but she died in Broadmoor
of pulmonary tuberculosis on 29 June 1920. In every case it was the interception
of letters, parcels or telegrams that led to their downfall. Special Branch officers
were involved in the arrest and prosecution of all the enemy agents.

ROGER CASEMENT

A case of a totally different complexion was that of Sir Roger Casement, a
former British Consul who was executed for his part in a failed insurrection in Ireland. The plot was discovered due to the interception by the Royal
Navy of German signals and the work of 'Room 40' at the Admiralty, where German diplomatic codes were broken. After the outbreak of war, Casement offered
his services to the German ambassador in the United States and his Irish-American allies. He then made his way to Berlin, where he had conversations with
German intelligence officials and addressed Irish prisoners of war at a camp at
Lossen, but his attempt to recruit them to fight in Ireland against Britain succeeded in enlisting only fifty-six.

The uprising in Ireland was fixed for Easter Saturday 1916. The Germans
had agreed to disembark weapons shortly beforehand, followed by an aerial
raid to distract the attention of the British on the night preceding the landing;
Casement and two companions were to be landed by submarine. As the supply
ship, carrying the arms and flying the Norwegian flag, approached the coast,
it was stopped by HMS *Bluebell* and ordered to follow it to Queenstown. The
crew, however, scuttled the ship with its compromising cargo. The same week,
Casement was arrested and sent to London to be interrogated by Basil Thomson. Thomson commented on the affair:

7   TNA WO141/2/2

The rising was a failure; instead of the 5,000 men promised by the Irish, only some 500 arrived in Dublin; [...] One or two public buildings were captured and were held for some hours, but, long before nightfall, the rising was over and many of the participants in jail. Casement was tried for high treason and was executed; the danger had passed for the moment but the harm had been done. From that moment, the movement that hoped to take advantage of the war in order to stab Britain in the back engaged continually in secret political activities involving subversion and murder. Loyal Irishmen who had fought for the Allied cause were often the victims.[8]

Casement was charged with treason, convicted at the Central Criminal Court and hanged. His supporters alleged that diaries recording his homosexual activities, which were found during a search of his property, had been forged in order to discredit him. This was untrue. Photographic plates of disputed entries were retained in Special Branch for many years.

'MATA HARI'

Less successful was Thomson's interrogation, in November 1916, of Margaretha MacLeod, alias Mata Hari, a Dutch 'exotic dancer' suspected of espionage.[9] She was arrested by DS George Grant, of MPSB, when the ship on which she was travelling to Holland put into Falmouth. It seems that when Thomson interrogated her, she 'spun him a yarn' about being a French double agent and Thomson lodged her in a room at the Savoy Hotel then let her go.[10] She returned to Spain, where she was arrested by French Deuxième Bureau

8   Preface by Sir Basil Thomson in Edward M. Brady's *The Irish Secret Service in England, 1919–21* (Paris: Payot, 1933)

9   TNA MEPO 3/2444

10 Bernard Porter, *Plots and Paranoia* (London: Unwin, 1986), p. 140

officers, tried, and executed on the indisputable evidence contained in intercepted German signals that she was a German double agent, 'H21'.[11]

SUBVERSIVE PACIFISM

D uring the war some revolutionary and pacifist groups caused concern to the government because of their extreme anti-war views. In 1917, Thomson submitted a report to the Cabinet on such groups revealing that a number had been the subject of surveillance by Special Branch, but of all the groups he mentioned, only the Union of Democratic Control and the Independent Labour Party could be described as remotely subversive.

Included in Thomson's report were the names of a number of minor agents in whom Special Branch showed some interest but only one gave any real cause for alarm. This was Baron Louis von Horst, whom Thomson claimed was a German. He was in correspondence with the socialist trade unionist Ben Tillett,[12] and, at the time of the transport workers' strike in 1912, gave free meals to the strikers' children and attended their meetings on Tower Hill. In 1913 von Horst stood bail for the suffragette Flora Drummond, and in 1914 he was in touch with Jim Larkin (misspelt Larking), an IRA member in Dublin. Thomson claimed that the Baron had also enquired about the cost of purchasing 500 Mauser rifles and ammunition from a gunsmith in the Strand, the implication being that they were intended for Irish nationalists, and that he had also been in touch with Sir Roger Casement.[13]

During the early weeks of the war, von Horst proposed to the Home Office the setting up of a Committee for the Relief of Distressed Germans who had been left in Britain without any means of subsistence. Shortly afterwards he was

---

11   Morton, *Spies of the First World War*, p. 160–61

12   Ben Tillett was a socialist Member of Parliament and trade union leader

13   Memorandum entitled *Pacifism* by Basil Thomson, dated 24 November 1917. TNA CAB 24/34/9

interned and remained in custody until 1919, when he was expelled from Britain. Since the discovery of von Horst's papers, doubt has been cast on Thomson's interpretation of his behaviour; undoubtedly there were grounds for suspicion about his activities and his associates but there is no evidence to confirm that he was ever a German agent. Special Branch officers spent a lot of time in establishing organisations' real *raisons d'être*; frequently, as in this case, there were found to be no ulterior motives in their activities.

CHAPTER EIGHT

THE RISE AND FALL
OF THE DIRECTORATE
OF INTELLIGENCE

E ARLY IN 1919, concerned by reports that the secret services were not operating effectively,[1] the Prime Minister, David Lloyd George, appointed a Secret Service Committee chaired by Lord Curzon, Foreign Secretary in waiting, and consisting of five other Cabinet ministers, to enquire into what was being done by the branches of the Secret Services, and to consider how best their work could be improved.[2] Papers were submitted by the relevant ministries and further information was received from, among others, Sir Basil Thomson, Assistant Commissioner of the Metropolitan Police; Captain Mansfield Smith-Cumming, RN, Chief of the Secret Intelligence Service; and Colonel Vernon Kell, Director of MI5.

The committee met in February 1919 and reviewed the history and performance of the secret services, noting that MI5 and MI6 (formed in 1909) were responsible for military intelligence at home and abroad respectively, that there

---

1   Memo by Walter Long, Secretary of State for the Colonies, dated 16 January 1919. TNA CAB 127/356

2   Cabinet minutes, 24 January 1919. TNA CAB 23/9/WC 519

was a small department of the Home Office dealing with Irish extremism in America, and that the Special Branch of the Metropolitan Police dealt with Irish, anarchist and other dangerous political criminals in this country.

The committee noted that during the war the secret services had expanded in every direction and that valuable intelligence on industrial and political matters, much of which had been gathered by the Special Branch, had taken on a new importance. In reaching its conclusions, the committee focused particularly on the civilian side of the secret services, and the machinery for collecting information about persons engaged in revolutionary or anarchical movements in the United Kingdom. It also considered the ways in which such information was used by the government.

In April 1919, Cabinet approval was given to the committee's recommendations that a Directorate of Intelligence should be created without delay, and that Sir Basil Thomson, in overall charge of Special Branch, should be relieved of all other police duties to lead it. The Home Secretary and the Commissioner, Sir Nevil Macready, agreed to Thomson's request that he should retain his rank of Assistant Commissioner and that his staff should retain their status as Metropolitan Police officers. Special Branch was to be separated from the Criminal Investigation Department and moved from New Scotland Yard to the new Directorate's headquarters at Scotland House.

For just under three years the Directorate of Intelligence supplied the Cabinet with fortnightly reports on the political, industrial and security situation. These are sometimes alleged to have been overstated and Thomson's flamboyant character invited criticism. His access to the Cabinet (he reported directly to the Home Secretary) and his new title were sources of irritation to Sir Eric Holt-Wilson, the Deputy Head of MI5, who wrote to his Director, Vernon Kell:

> Despite statements to the contrary in the press and elsewhere, Sir Basil
> Thomson's organisation has never actually detected a case of espionage,
> but has merely arrested and questioned spies at the request of MI5, when
> the latter organisation, which had detected them, considered that the time

for arrest had arrived. The Army Council are in favour of entrusting the work to an experienced, tried and successful organisation rather than to one which has yet to win its spurs. Sir Basil Thomson's existing higher staff consists mainly of ex-officers of MI5 not considered sufficiently able for retention by that Department. The Army Council are not satisfied with their ability to perform the necessary duties under Sir Basil Thomson's direction, and they are satisfied that detective officers alone, without direction from above, are unfitted for the work.[3]

Holt-Wilson's views reflected the frustration and irritation felt by MI5, whose staff, since the end of the war, had been much reduced in size and had been left with responsibility only for counter-espionage and for subversion within the armed services. Kell was anxious to extend his responsibilities to include the subversive activities of the civil population and saw the new Directorate as a threat to that ambition. Holt-Wilson's criticism was no doubt directed at Captain Hugh Miller, a civilian member of Thomson's staff who had recently left MI5, but it is interesting to note that Captain Guy Liddell, another civilian member of Thomson's 'insufficiently able staff', was later to become Deputy Director General of the Security Service, the post occupied by Holt-Wilson.

THE DIRECTORATE OF INTELLIGENCE (SPECIAL BRANCH) 1921

Director of Intelligence: Sir Basil Thomson
Assistant Director of Intelligence: Lieutenant Colonel J. F. C. Carter
Detective Superintendent: Edward James McBrien
Detective Chief Inspector: Edward Parker
Ex-Detective Superintendent: J. McCarthy CID

---

3   Security Service Archives, cited in Andrew's *The Defence of the Realm*, p. 117

DETECTIVE INSPECTORS:

P. Byrne	Roddy Cosgrove	E. Hallett
Joseph Clarkson	Lionel Kirchner	Bob Brown
Joe Sandercock	Charles H. Frost	I. J. Bannon
Fred Norish	E. Cox	Thomas Haines
Herbert Fitch	George Wood	Harold Brust
Ernest Moyle	H. Ashley	H. Norwood
Albert Warrell	A. Randall	

DETECTIVE SERGEANTS:

John Philpott	Victor H. Auger	Ralph Kitchener
W. Leonard	John Durkin	W. Montgomery
Bert Sumpton	W. Hay	C. Renshaw
Otto Albers	M. McCarthy	T. Stephenson
John Bonstred	Frank Hansford	Cecil Scutchey
Ernest Bowden	J. W. Taunford	George Grant
Thomas Worth	Thomas Clancy	Alfred Waldram
James Tansley	John Painter	John T. Probert
William Sange	John O'Sullivan	Albert Howard
P. Barrett	V. Twomey	Arthur Potter
Walter Dew	A. G. Foster	Percy Phillips
William Dear	Frank Clinker	W. H. Thomson
W. Palmer	W. Smith	G. McLeod
Harvey Hawkins	Edward Billett	Michael Delany
Martin Clancy	Emest Passmore	James Curry
A. Canning	Frank E. Bickers	Harold Keeble
Albert Geater	J. Cummins	Charles Gill
John Fitzgerald	Dan O'Connor	R. M. Lewis

A. Goodman	James R. Cross	Charlie Wilson
H. Poupard	C. Atkinson	Harold Williams
W. Evans	William Flood	Timothy Barr

DETECTIVE CONSTABLES:

Arthur Twyan	William Gagen	G. Hatherill
C. Percy Park	Robert Cooper	George Butson
Cecil Pavey	Eric Brown	Leonard Watson
John Carr	A. Stopley	William East
T. Aitchison	Ernest C. Oliver	Charles Allen
E. Stone	L. D. Gorman	Ernest Tansley
Alfred J. Relf	J. Mulholland	Arthur Newton
Arthur Allum	William Porter	Chester Smith
S. G. Young	J. H. Connor	C. Harvey
Joseph de Mora	John O'Reilly	Doug Bowson
Arthur Davies	Patrick J. Phelan	W. Thompson
H. R. Morse	T. Gorman	Stan Corder
John Redmore	Leon C. Peel	H. J. Willey
W. Shute	W. A. Haybittle	Sydney Barnes
Fred Jempson	R. Groombridge	Ed Sanders

The newly appointed Commissioner of the Metropolitan Police, Brigadier General Sir William Horwood, who had been an Assistant Commissioner, junior to Thomson, felt that once he was Commissioner, Thomson should be accountable to him. He complained in a letter to the Prime Minister that 'the independence of the Special Branch was a menace to the discipline of the force' and concurred with Holt-Wilson 'that in no instance had intelligence from Thomson ever led to a successful prosecution for political crime'.

This delicate situation became increasingly so in the autumn of 1921 when Thomson unexpectedly resigned, allegedly over a breach of security at Chequers in which four Irishmen painted pro-Irish republican slogans on a greenhouse, although the real reason for the resignation was more complex. In March 1921, a new Secret Service Committee (made up of permanent under secretaries as opposed to ministers) recommended to the Home Secretary that the Special Branch should be returned to the direct control of the new Commissioner, a proposal that Horwood wholeheartedly supported. He saw no advantage in it retaining its quasi-independent status and the proposed move would save money.[4]

Thomson threatened to resign if the committee's plan went ahead. It did and he carried out his threat. In a letter to *The Times* the following week, Sir Basil explained his version of what had happened. In this letter he outlined the reasons for the formation of the Directorate and the part he had played in it, all of which met with the approval of the Commissioner, General Macready. The letter goes on to say that all went well until March 1920, when General Horwood was appointed Commissioner. Realising he would not be able to work with the new Commissioner, who was 'not fitted by temperament or experience to have control of the Directorate', Thomson told the Home Secretary that rather than have the friction that he knew must result, he would ask leave to retire. In July 1921 he was informed that the committee, having received evidence from General Horwood that reflected badly on the Directorate, had decided to merge it once more with the Metropolitan Police. On 27 October the Home Secretary informed him that the merger was to take place and on the following day he was told he would be given leave of absence until the end of November, and be retired on pension on 30 November.[5]

The Labour Party and Bolsheviks were delighted with his departure and revolutionaries of other persuasions also celebrated his retirement. The Irish had

---

4   Report of the fifth meeting of the Secret Service Committee held on 30 June 1921. TNA CAB 127/359.

5   *The Times*, 7 November 1921

particular cause to rejoice. The *Irish Exile* of December 1921 carried a 'tongue in cheek' valedictory on his departure:

> Such a man must have many enemies and few friends. However, for spe-
> cial reasons, he was an object of interest to the Irish exile in London. In
> person or through some of his well paid, but not too intelligent proxies,
> he was on visiting terms with many of us in London, feeling free to call at
> any time of the day or night and so familiar was he that he assumed the
> right of an honoured guest, helping himself freely to anything he might
> fancy. It is no exaggeration to say that his visits, seldom unexpected, proved
> interesting and often amusing, if also occasionally inconvenient. So anx-
> ious was he to extend his acquaintance among the Irish in London that
> he often borrowed address-books, card index-boxes, and similar things
> from Irish offices and homes. [...] If he finds one pamphlet of this kind
> he seizes it with avidity and carefully advertises the fact in the well known
> phrase: 'A mass of seditious literature was taken away and is being care-
> fully examined.' Occasionally he did not return the documents, etc., that
> he had borrowed. Some people might have seen in this a sort of official
> kleptomania, but we who understood him so well, knew that he never
> made his actions subject to honour or dishonour. We always accepted his
> excuses knowing that his motto was a free translation of noblesse oblige.

The article added that it was not concerned with Sir Basil's private life as the writers 'only had the honour of his acquaintance' in his public capacity. It concluded:

> It is apparently certain that Sir Basil has retired. The flexibility of the Eng-
> lish language permits us to ask: Did he resign or was he resigned? In any
> case he will be wise if he resigned, and might later be made a great official
> Master of the Bed Chamber.[6]

---

6   *Irish Exile*, December 1921

Sir Basil's reputation as a serial philanderer was well known in Irish circles in London. An IRA team, sent to assassinate him in 1920, found that their task was made difficult by the fact that he never slept in the same bed twice in any week. That aspect of his character remained concealed from the public in 1921, but five years later it received some notoriety when he was prosecuted following an incident in Hyde Park with a young woman. It has been suggested that the prosecution was 'set up' to prevent him being considered for the Commissionership of the Metropolitan Police, which was likely to become vacant. However, the evidence was convincing and his conviction was upheld on appeal. He spent the next two decades writing authoritatively on police matters, and was the author of a number of fictional detective stories.

With Sir Basil's resignation, the Special Branch was returned to its original place as a branch of the Criminal Investigation Department under the command of the Commissioner of the Metropolitan Police. On 5 December 1921, Sir Wyndham Childs was appointed to succeed him and, from 1 April 1922, took on the additional role of Assistant Commissioner, Criminal Investigation Department, holding the dual posts until his retirement on 8 November 1928. The Branch, however, retained its critics and those elements within the intelligence community who envied its responsibilities, and wished to extend their own. As with Thomson, Childs's tenure of office was not without difficulties.[7]

The Directorate of Intelligence has been described by some historians as a failure.[8] The criticism levelled by the Commissioner, Sir William Horwood, that no criminal prosecution had arisen from the intelligence it gathered, was untrue. Another allegation that the Directorate was spying on the Labour Party is also misleading. In the Bolshevik and Irish republican fields there were a number of successful prosecutions for which the Directorate was responsible. Its reports to the Cabinet enabled the government to discriminate between those

7   Sir Wyndham Childs, *Episodes and Reflections: being some records from the life of Major-General Sir Wyndham Childs, K.C.M.G., K.B.E., C.B.* (London: Cassell & Co., 1930)

8   Gill Bennett, *History Notes: A Most Extraordinary and Mysterious Business: The Zinoviev Letter of 1924* (London: Foreign and Commonwealth Office, 1999)

who intended harm, and those who did not. It is evident from these reports that the Special Branch had exceptional human and technical sources of information, from paid informants within organisations, intercepted communications, local police, press and other sources, as well as the Government Code and Cypher School (GC&CS), MI5 and MI6. With certain exceptions,[9] the legal powers of Special Branch officers did not extend outside the Metropolitan Police District. The prosecution of offences was, therefore, a matter for local Chief Constables, although MPSB officers were often deployed to assist other forces. Intelligence was passed freely between police forces and a great deal of the information provided by Chief Constables was included in the fortnightly reports to the Cabinet.

9   Exceptions were at ports; within a mile of Royal palaces; until 1922, in HM Dockyards

CHAPTER NINE

THE SECRET SERVICE COMMITTEE 1925

D ESPITE THE SECRET Service Committee's overhaul of the secret services in 1921, it became apparent that the system was still not working effectively and the committee was reconvened in 1925. It commissioned an investigation to be carried out by Sir Russell Scott of HM Treasury 'into all Branches of Scotland Yard, as more light is required on the internal workings of Scotland Yard than has hitherto been available'.[1] Sir Russell based his subsequent report on material supplied by Sir Wyndham Childs in a detailed breakdown of the work carried out by the three bureaux at Scotland Yard, dealing with what is loosely referred to as 'secret service' work. This document also served as a useful reference point for police historians endeavouring to penetrate the largely uncharted territory of Special Branch. The following is an abridged version of Sir Russell's report to the committee.[2]

In April 1922, when Sir Wyndham Childs took command of Special Branch,

1   Letter from Secret Service Committee to Prime Minister, dated 19 June 1925. TNA CAB 127/361

2   Report by Sir Wyndham Childs (for the information of Sir Russell Scott), dated 30 June 1925. TNA CAB 127/366

it was being run by Lieutenant Colonel Carter who, to quote Childs, 'was not a police officer and had no power of command over the personnel of the Special Branch'. His position was regularised on 24 October, when he was appointed a Deputy Assistant Commissioner responsible for the management of the Branch, which remained under the direction of the ACC. (Note: Carter himself was merely a figurehead; the *de facto* head of the Branch, as he had been since 1918, was Superintendent James McBrien.)

Childs was highly critical of his predecessor and the manner in which he ran Special Branch, commenting, 'It was obvious to me before I had been here more than a few weeks that the staff had been working in the dark and had no knowledge of the activities of their Chief.' The ACC had inherited:

(i) SS1, the four civilian members of which (two officers, two clerks) dealt with the study and investigation, through the SIS, of revolutionary movements abroad and the monitoring of communist and other revolutionary aliens and literature entering the United Kingdom from the Colonies.

(ii) SS2, comprising only two female officers and a clerk, all civilians, who dealt with 'all matters relating to revolutionary movements and organisations in this country other than of alien or Irish origination'. This included, among other things, the weekly submission of intelligence reports to Chief Constables, government departments and intelligence branches on revolutionary activity (political and industrial) taking place in England, Scotland and Wales; informing MI5 and appropriate military authorities of communist activity likely to affect them; and keeping the Deputy Assistant Commissioner of Special Branch informed of political activities that might call for police action.

Both these sections were financed by Secret Service funds, but expenses of the third were chargeable to the vote for the police.

(iii) Special Branch itself, under the overall administration of the ACC and a Deputy Assistant Commissioner, with an establishment of 134 police officers of all ranks – the superintendent in charge supported by one chief inspector; seventeen inspectors; sixty-nine sergeants; forty-five male and one female constable. In very general terms its functions were:

To do such police work in regard to revolutionary activities as may be necessary within the Metropolitan area and at certain ports [and to deal with] all phases of the Irish revolutionary movement within this country. It also provides the necessary staff for the protection of members of the royal family [not strictly true], Cabinet ministers and other persons.

The term 'revolutionary' was applied to a surprisingly wide range of organisations and included such groupings as the Communist Party of Great Britain, Young Communist League, Irish Workers' League, Irish Self Determination League of Great Britain, Irish Republican Army, Egyptian Association of Great Britain, Union of Chinese Associations in Great Britain, East West Circle, various anti-fascist organisations and a host of less well-known groups.

Childs emphasised that not all revolutionary activity in the country was monitored by Special Branch. 'A special section of the Directorate of Military Intelligence at the War Office [MI5]' dealt with such activity directed at the armed forces. Furthermore, outside the Metropolitan Police District (MPD), the local police authorities concerned themselves with such matters, while maintaining close contact with Scotland Yard. The Assistant Commissioner condemned the system that had been in operation before he took up his current post, whereby nine Special Branch men were 'out in the Provinces poaching in the preserves of Chief Constables' in order to obtain information for the Cabinet on industrial unrest. Childs wasted no time in withdrawing these men, thereby reducing any friction with provincial forces, and setting up better lines of communication with the county forces, of which he declared with pride:

Today there is an absolute and complete liaison between all Chief Constables in the United Kingdom and myself and the exchange of information can I think be justly termed colossal, and I think I can safely say that there is no Chief Constable in the United Kingdom who will not today do anything for me.

In order to protect the confidentiality of Special Branch work, Childs set up what he referred to as a 'barrier' which would prevent 'rank and file policemen' being privy to secret service work. Documents relating to secret work filed in SB registry, an adjunct of the Scotland Yard general registry, would be stamped with the letter 'Y' and be accessible only to Lieutenant Colonel Carter. There was also a 'secret registry' closely supervised by a trusted civilian, in which highly sensitive documents would be stored.

Childs observed that: 'The Special Branch is entirely distinct from the CID and has a separate establishment. The only connecting link is that the personnel of the Special Branch is recruited from the CID but when once permanently allocated to the Special Branch all connection with the CID is severed.'

One of its main functions was to act as an 'intelligence department' for the rest of the Metropolitan Police and, to a lesser extent, for provincial forces. From various sources, intelligence would be obtained relating to public order problems (strikes, demonstrations etc); this would be submitted to the appropriate department or police force so that the necessary police arrangements could be made. One such source was meetings, both indoor and open air, at which revolutionary and other subversive organisations would broadcast their views and sometimes give details of future activities. Such events were, and always have been, covered by SB officers, who have frequently been required to use their shorthand skills to record actionable speeches.

The use of informants was essential for obtaining information to prevent and detect crimes against the state. Strict control was exercised in managing the money allocated for the payment of these individuals; an informants' fund was maintained by the Receiver for the Metropolitan Police, who once a fortnight disbursed payments on receipt of accounts countersigned by the AC or DACSB.

Other work performed by members of Special Branch was referred to in Sir Russell's report. Many officers were fluent in foreign languages and were frequently called upon to act as interpreters or carry out translations in police cases. On occasions, they were employed in this capacity for other government departments. Naturalisation enquiries occupied many hours of police time and were constantly increasing in number. Officers were frequently engaged out of London on port work, while others were employed full time protecting ministers and other dignitaries, both British and foreign.

Scott's report, quoting Childs verbatim, concluded with favourable comments on the Branch.

> The work of Special Branch is of a highly specialised character. Officers in this Department, besides having a full knowledge of the powers and duties of the Uniform Police and CID, have to possess an intimate knowledge of world-wide revolutionary politics. The inquiry staff is recruited from serving Metropolitan Police Officers who are of good appearance and address, of good education, and possessing knowledge of foreign languages or the ability to write shorthand at a high speed in order to submit a verbatim report and give evidence on their notes in a Court of Law.
>
> The Officers, although usually specialising in one section of the work, are engaged in the general work of the Branch, as the principle is inculcated that an all-round knowledge of Special Branch work is necessary for promotion.
>
> It is, of course, realised that the work performed is of an especially secret nature. Many matters are dealt with between DACSB and the superintendent which are unknown to subordinates, such as dealing with informants, where frequently a man's life is at stake if his identity were to become known.

In his report, Scott concluded that he had 'no reason to think that the present arrangement by which the Assistant Commissioner at Scotland Yard keeps in touch with local police authorities throughout the country [or indeed with other agencies] is unsatisfactory'. However, he did express misgivings about the relationship between SS1, SS2 and Special Branch, which appeared to lack 'adequate control and direction'.[3]

---

3   Sir Russell Scott's report of October 1925 to the Secret Service Committee. TNA FO 1093/68

When publishing the result of its deliberations on 1 December 1925,[4] the committee also examined the roles of the other four sections of the secret service – GC&CS, MI5, MI6 and the Indian Political Intelligence Service.

Eventually, after the collection of wisdom from a vast array of security experts, the committee noted that with one exception, Rear Admiral Hugh Sinclair, the Chief of SIS, those consulted expressed general satisfaction with existing arrangements.[5] However, it was not until several years had elapsed that any changes suggested by him were forthcoming.

The committee remained in being and produced other reports up until 1931; in the final year of its existence it made a number of recommendations, which the government approved. SS1 was taken over by MI5 and SS2 by the Home Office. MI5 was renamed the Security Service, and its responsibilities extended to cover the collation and dissemination of intelligence concerning espionage and civil subversion throughout the Commonwealth. It ceased to be a department of the War Office. It was brought under the control of the Home Secretary, but remained independent of the Home Office. The gathering of intelligence concerning espionage remained its prime responsibility. The main change, however, was that the Security Service took over responsibility for assessing all threats to the United Kingdom, except for those posed by anarchists and Irish republicans. The staff of SS1, Captain Guy Liddell, Miss Bunty Saunders and Miss Millicent Bagot, were transferred to the Security Service offices in Cromwell Road, Kensington. The committee was no doubt influenced in its recommendations by the Zinoviev Letter affair, the ARCOS raid and the scandal of the Ewer Spy Ring, which led to the sacking of Detective Inspector Van Ginhoven and Detective Sergeant Jane.[6] The Special Branch retained responsibility for extreme Irish republicanism, anarchists, gun-runners, personal protection of ministers and others at risk, and port controls.

---

4   The Secret Service Committee's report, dated 1 December 1925. TNA FO 1093/67

5   Undated note by Sinclair to Secret Service Committee. TNA CAB 127/364 & FO 1093/67

6   See Chapters 11 and 12

Sir Vernon Kell was jubilant about the expansion of his empire, but was given few additional resources with which to fulfil his new remit. MI5 continued to rely on the support of the police, the armed forces and the civil service for supplying information and making enquiries, and on the GPO and GC&CS for the interception of communications. While it was able to employ agents of its own to penetrate suspect organisations, it had only thirty case officers, most of whom were former officers in the armed services or the police. In addition, it had six watchers to carry out surveillance and a secretarial and registry staff. In fact it was reliant on the good will of other organisations and powerless to order them to do anything. Decisions to prosecute remained the prerogative of the Attorney General.

The diminishing of Special Branch's responsibilities must have been a blow to their pride, which was exacerbated by the knowledge that in future they would be saddled with helping the understaffed Security Service to cope with its increased workload, a situation that was not calculated to improve the already fractious relations between the two services.

CHAPTER TEN

THE IRISH TROUBLES 1919–23

A FTER THE FIRST World War, Lloyd George's coalition government still optimistically believed that Irish nationalist aspirations
could be satisfied by some form of Home Rule, which would also
be acceptable to the Unionists of North East Ulster. The futility of such aspirations became apparent when in the general election of December 1918 Sinn
Féin candidates won seventy-three of the 106 Irish seats in the Westminster
Parliament, but refused to take them. In January 1919, they formed a Parliament
in Dublin, the Dáil, but the Unionists refused to recognise it, so the Sinn Féin
members formed their own government and declared Ireland to be an independent republic; their writ, however, did not run to the six counties of North East
Ulster, where the Unionists still enjoyed a majority. Southern Ireland now had
two competing administrations, the British in Dublin Castle and the republicans in the Dublin Mansion House. Sinn Féin's manifesto pledged to withdraw
representation from Westminster and create a new Irish assembly but, although
it had a mandate from the electorate for Irish independence, the mandate did
not sanction the use of violence to achieve that aim.

The Irish Volunteers now assumed the role of an Irish Republican Army,
and embarked on a violent campaign against the officers of the Royal Irish

Constabulary, who were regarded by them as the principal means by which British rule in Ireland was imposed. In January 1919, two police officers were shot dead and the explosives they were escorting stolen; Cathal Brugha, the acting head of the republican government, circulated the following statement in the republican paper *An tÓglách* on 31 January:

> Every volunteer is entitled legally and morally when in the execution of his military duties, to use all legitimate methods of warfare against the soldiers and policemen of the English usurper, and to slay them if it is necessary to do so to overcome their resistance. He is not only entitled but bound to resist all attempts to disarm him. In this position he has the authority of the nation behind him, now constituted in concrete form.[1]

In December 1919, following an assassination attempt on Lord French, Lord Lieutenant of Ireland, the British government decided that future intelligence-gathering in Ireland would be controlled from London by Sir Basil Thomson, head of the Metropolitan Police Special Branch (the Directorate of Intelligence). A Special Branch officer was attached to British Army GHQ in Dublin, for liaison purposes. After a year the system was declared to be inoperable and the collecting of intelligence in Ireland was placed in the hands of a new organisation in Dublin, under the command of Brigadier-General Sir Ormonde de l'Épée Winter.

In the spring of 1920, with the political situation in Ireland worsening, 800 special constables from Britain were sent to reinforce the dispirited ranks of the Royal Irish Constabulary. Many of these men were unemployed ex-soldiers, and paid ten shillings a day, with all found. They had no formal training as police officers and no police experience. They became known as the Black and Tans, from the colour of their original uniforms; they were, and still are, despised by republicans. The following July, 200 former army officers were recruited to form an Auxiliary Police Service. They were given a short course in police duties and a

---

1   *An t'Óglách*, 31 January 1919

rank equivalent to sergeant in the Royal Irish Constabulary. Both groups became targets for IRA murder squads and suffered heavy casualties. They reacted predictably to these murderous attacks and, being unable to identify their attackers, struck out blindly at the nationalist population, burning homes and businesses. Thus the situation degenerated into a bloody conflict.

In December 1920, two Parliaments were established in Ireland, one in the north and one in the south, but the whole island was to remain part of the United Kingdom. When informing Parliament, Lloyd George declared, 'No party in Ireland is prepared to accept anything but the impossible. But that is no excuse for British government inaction.' In the absence of Irish republicans at Westminster, there was no opposition to counter this proposal.

Cathal Brugha responded by calling upon Irishmen living in mainland Britain to help with arms and money and to take the war directly into the enemy's camp. Units of the Irish Volunteers had existed in England and Scotland since 1911; they now took on the mantle of an Irish Republican Army of the kind that already operated in Ireland.

Detailed summaries of intelligence were regularly forwarded by Sir Basil Thomson through the Home Secretary to the Cabinet.[2] One such report showed that in March 1920, an inaugural meeting of the Irish Self-Determination League (ISDL) was held in Manchester. The name 'Sinn Féin' had been discarded because of its association with the violence in Ireland. The title, Sinn Féin, was retained in Scotland. At a meeting in Manchester in November 1920, the ISDL gave approval to its constitution:

> To band together the Irish residents in Great Britain in order they shall
> as a body support their compatriots in Ireland, and use every means in
> their power to secure the application of the Irish Republic, proclaimed in
> Dublin in 1916, [...] and further, in the meanwhile to render all and every

---

2   The information on the following pages has been largely extracted from the regular fortnightly reports sent by the Directorate of Intelligence (Special Branch) to the Cabinet (TNA CAB/24) and from contemporaneous issues of *The Times*

assistance to any Irish subject imprisoned in Great Britain, and do all
other acts which will further the cause of an independent Irish Republic.

The League became a fertile recruiting ground from which suitable young men
were drawn into the ranks of the Irish Republican Army units that had been
formed in the centres of Irish population in England and Scotland. IRA officers from Dublin were sent over to the units on the mainland to induct the newly
recruited members into the secretive, oath-bound Irish Republican Brotherhood. Thus the IRB became the controlling inner circle of the IRA in Britain
directing violent activities.

To be an ordinary member of the ISDL or Sinn Féin, or a Volunteer in the
IRA, it was not necessary to be a member of the Irish Republican Brotherhood,
although many were. Theoretically, the IRA owed its allegiance to the Dáil Éire-
ann, composed of the elected representatives of the Irish people, but in reality it
was controlled by Michael Collins as President of the Supreme Council of the
IRB. Éamon de Valera, the President of Sinn Féin, and Cathal Brugha, the Sinn
Féin Minister of Defence, did not belong to the IRB; they feared and detested
the power and influence which it gave to Collins.

The ISDL established its headquarters at 182 Shaftesbury Avenue, in London, and appointed Art O'Brien, the London representative of the Sinn Féin
government, as its first President, with Sean McGrath its General Secretary. The
organisation was self-financing and its officials were paid out of the subscrip-
tions of its members of one shilling per quarter. The General Secretary received
£6.6s per week and six organisers were each paid £6 per week. There were also
a few paid clerks.

Regular reports from the Directorate of Intelligence (SB) to the Cabinet show
that it was well aware of the relationship between the ISDL, the IRA, the IRB
and the Sinn Féin government. It covered meetings addressed by Sean McGrath
and Art O'Brien, who spoke regularly in Hyde Park. O'Brien, in his capacity
as the London representative of the Sinn Féin government, also had an office at
3 John Adam Street, where he carried on his work under the cover of running

an Irish press office. The expenses of this office and his salary and that of his staff were paid directly from the funds of the Sinn Féin government in Dublin.

As well as its political work, the ISDL had a social and cultural side. Regular dances were held, which provided a useful cover to hide its more sinister work from the prying eyes of the police. One venue for these functions was behind Bolger's tailor shop at 5 Queens Road, Peckham, in south London, where both amateur and professional musicians played the kind of music that enticed patriotic young Irish men and women to 'the cause'; there is no doubt that Special Branch officers attended such functions as they continued to do in more recent times – a lighter side of Special Branch work. Similar establishments existed in the other centres of Irish population, notably in Paddington, Kilburn, Manchester, Liverpool and Newcastle.

The ISDL also raised money for the procurement of arms through the sale of bonds. Most of the Sinn Féin clubs in England that were in existence before the formation of ISDL were incorporated into the League, but three clubs (two in Liverpool and one in Maiden Lane, London) continued to use the name Sinn Féin, and were used to introduce suitable candidates to the IRA. A Special Branch report recorded that Art O'Brien was President of this English Sinn Féin organisation, Nicholas Keogh of 17 City Road, Hulme, Manchester, was its treasurer and Michael O'Leary of 9 Milfods Street, Liverpool, its secretary.

In Scotland, where Sinn Féin continued to use that name, the organisation was reputed to be more militant than branches in England. In 1920, Scottish membership of some forty clubs, mainly in the Glasgow area, was reported to be as high as 15,000, with an annual income in the region of £5,600. The IRA found Sinn Féin in Scotland a fertile recruiting ground; the IRA in Scotland was a separate entity. The Chief Constable of Glasgow kept the Branch informed of developments there.

A republican intelligence network existed in England, of which a vital member was Sam Maguire, an old friend of Michael Collins. In 1921 he was employed in a key position in the Mount Pleasant Sorting Office in London and relayed messages to Michael Collins in Dublin. He liaised closely with Art O'Brien and

Sean McGrath, both of whom had intelligence functions in addition to their other duties in the ISDL, and were assisted from time to time by women couriers and by active service units sent over from Ireland by Collins.

Rory O'Connor, the IRA's Director of Engineering, commanded the IRA in England but was not resident there. He operated through the commandants of the IRA units formed in London, Liverpool, Manchester and Tyne and Tees. By the end of 1920 the IRA in Great Britain had evolved into a small but substantial terrorist organisation with three distinct functions: the procurement of arms, the gathering of local intelligence and the planning and execution of attacks on specified targets. The leaders were often former soldiers who had served in the British Army during the First World War.

Towards the end of 1920, as a reaction to alleged atrocities committed by the Royal Irish Constabulary and the British Army in Ireland, the IRA Command in Dublin decided upon reprisals in Britain. O'Connor drew up plans for incendiary attacks on farms, public buildings, the telephone network, and the families and private houses of the British Army commanders in Ireland, and also on the families and homes of soldiers and RIC auxiliaries in England.

Intelligence received by MPSB from the Irish police suggested that IRA headquarters in Dublin had a poor opinion of their units on mainland Britain. It was considered that, because of lack of training, volunteers could not be expected to carry out large-scale operations in this country, with the possible exceptions of Liverpool, London, Glasgow and Newcastle.

Despite these shortcomings, O'Connor was able to introduce an element of cohesion into IRA operations in England and Scotland, by timing them to take place simultaneously, and so create the impression of a large force capable of striking on a broad front. In most cases the targets were suggested by members of the units themselves but in other instances, such as the attacks on telephone lines and on the homes of former RIC officers and their families, they were intelligence-based.

The London Battalion of the IRA was formed in 1919, at a meeting at St Anne's Hall, Underwood Street, in the East End of London. Art O'Brien and

Sean McGrath were present at the meeting, but it was Reginald Dunne who was elected to command the new unit. Dunne had served in the Irish Guards in France, was wounded in April 1918, discharged, and returned to civilian life to become a student teacher at a Jesuit College in Stamford Hill. Pat Sullivan was vice commandant, Jim O'Carroll adjutant and Sean Golden quartermaster. Later the battalion was split into four companies, each with a separate zone of operations within the Greater London area. O'Carroll subsequently resigned and Pat Sullivan moved on to other duties and was replaced by Denis Kelleher.[3]

Edward Brady, a member of the Birkenhead unit of the IRA, later wrote a book about his experiences in the movement, which gives an illuminating insight into life as a Volunteer.[4] He followed a typical path into the IRA, via Sinn Féin and the ISDL, and gives a detailed description of his induction, which took place in the basement of a house in Birkenhead, reached through a series of dark alleys.

> Only twelve men were present. It was the total strength of the secret army of Birkenhead. Some minutes after my arrival, the instructor shouted attention, like an old non-commissioned officer. A part of the instruction was about launching grenades and was followed by a conference on what we could be called upon to do. The exits to the basement were concealed, and conversation about the IRA was not allowed between Volunteers. These training sessions and conferences took place twice a week, under the noses of the police. The discipline was rigid although not severe, because it was a voluntary service, strictly obedient to Irish republicanism. My second meeting was more exciting because the instructor showed us a box of different calibre revolvers and ammunition and told us how to use them.

Four hundred and twenty-two IRA operations are known to have taken place in mainland Britain between November 1920 and June 1922. There were attacks on

3   Richard Bennett, *The Black and Tans* (London: Hulton, 1959)

4   Brady, *The Irish Secret Service in England, 1919–21.* The narrative on the following pages is largely drawn from this book

members and relatives of RIC officers living in England, resulting in murder and
serious injury. Other operations involved the theft and smuggling of arms and
explosives to Ireland, setting fire to buildings and crops and the destruction of
telegraph and telephone cables. The IRA GHQ in Dublin was anxious to stop
recruits to the IRA in Ireland from emigrating and joining units in England, as
they were robbed of their money and travel documents when in transit through
English ports. It must be said that although the calibre of many of the Volunteers was poor, the campaign was well planned and, from the IRA point of view,
was partially successful in terrorising the British public, disrupting communications, causing damage and wreaking revenge for alleged atrocities committed
by British troops and the Irish police. Whether it achieved its ultimate objective
of furthering the cause of an independent Irish republic, however, is doubtful.

The Metropolitan Police Special Branch continued to fulfil its original role
of gathering, collating and disseminating information concerning Irish republican extremism in Great Britain and although many of the events described in
the following pages took place outside the Metropolitan Police District, SB was
still very much involved in them, whether by collating the information received
from Chief Constables or disseminating to them intelligence about possible IRA
activity in their area. Special Branch frequently sent officers to incidents in other
force areas to run the investigation, to act in a liaison capacity or to give advice.
During this period its resources were stretched to the limit.

The campaign began early in November 1920, when some 150 Volunteers of the
Liverpool IRA were addressed by Rory O'Connor, who outlined a plan to destroy
a large number of Liverpool warehouses. Special Branch in Liverpool and London was aware that Liverpool Docks were a target; Liverpool had its own Special
Branch and there was close co-operation between it and the Metropolitan Police.

The anticipated action commenced on 20 November, when a massive attack
in the city saw twenty warehouses set on fire and destroyed. Wire-cutters, paraffin oil, firearms and ammunition had been distributed to each group taking
part. Brady described being in a unit of five, armed with a revolver and twenty
rounds of ammunition.

Liverpool police made numerous raids in succeeding days, mostly on private houses. Several men were detained under the Defence of the Realm Regulations, and numerous documents were seized. Three members of the IRA were convicted on 14 February 1921 at Liverpool Assizes. Neil Fowler and James McCaughey were each sentenced to ten years' penal servitude for conspiracy to murder, and Matthew Fowler to two years' imprisonment for conspiracy to commit arson. Some twenty other suspects were arrested and deported to Ireland. The cost of the damage ran to many thousands of pounds.[5] Liverpool was again the target in March and in May when farms in the neighbouring countryside were attacked and haystacks burned. From Brady's descriptions, these operations achieved their objective but were chaotic in their execution due to the inexperience of the participants. Other accounts suggest that the idealistic young men of the IRA were more frightened than those they were trying to terrorise.

The first incident in London was on the Vacuum Oil Works in Wandsworth. At the Old Bailey on 18 February 1921, three youths were convicted of the attempted arson and shooting at the police.[6] But, compared with other areas, the IRA at first maintained a low profile in the metropolis.

However, in May 1921, events took a more sinister turn when the IRA began to terrorise the men and families of RIC officers in England.[7] Five armed men called at 33 Stowe Road, Shepherd's Bush, and asked for Mr Birthwright, a former member of the RIC. They claimed that they were there to arrest him, forced their way into the house, smashed bottles of paraffin on the floor, set the house on fire and made off. Soon afterwards seven men visited another house in the same area where they forced an entry and set the house on fire. At 42 Bloemfontein Road, Shepherd's Bush, an elderly man, Horace McNeil, answered a knock on the front door. Four men on the doorstep asked to speak to Mr Cornes, McNeil's son-in-law, who was serving in the RIC. Mr McNeil pointed out

---

5   *The Times*, 15 January 1921

6   Bennett, *The Black and Tans*, p. 141

7   The authors are indebted to *The Times*, which gave extensive coverage to all the campaign

that Cornes didn't live at the address. Two of the men forced their way in and when McNeil tried to close the door he was shot in the stomach; he was taken to West London Hospital, where he died a few days later. The men ran off, leaving behind two bottles of paraffin wrapped in brown paper and a revolver; one suspect was detained but subsequently released. No other arrests were made.

At about the same time a similar outrage occurred at an address in St Albans, where an RIC auxiliary was lodging with his wife. They were both shot in the head but survived. Special Branch was informed and DI Everest and DS Waldram travelled from London by car to commence the investigation. Similar attacks took place in Liverpool and south London, where an elderly man and his wife were shot. In some cases the raiders travelled by car and on several occasions they abandoned their weapons and bottles of paraffin after the attacks. Special Branch responded with arrests of ISDL officials and raids on the organisation's branches and offices, from which valuable information was obtained. On 19 May it was reported that twelve men and four women had been detained and that six men had been deported to Ireland under the Defence of the Realm Regulations.[8]

In Manchester, following attempts to burn down a warehouse, a number of hotels and a café, armed police raided the Irish Club in Hulme, where a gun fight ensued and twelve men were arrested; others followed. A subsequent search of the premises located high explosives, a large quantity of revolver and rifle ammunition and several jars of paraffin. Continuing police surveillance resulted in the discovery of a cache of arms, ammunition and explosives and the arrest of three further suspects. Nineteen prisoners were charged with various offences including treason-felony, contravention of the Firearms Act and Explosives Substances Act and arson. Sixteen were convicted and three acquitted.

Communications remained a prime target and attacks were carried out on telephone and telegraph systems, particularly in the Liverpool area; telephone routes connecting the north with the south of England were disrupted.[9] In the

8   *The Times* carried reports of all these attacks in its May editions

9   *The Times*, 4 June 1921

south similar targets were attacked; communication between London, Cardiff, Swansea and Bristol was disrupted and on the night of 7 June 1921 two 40-foot telegraph poles were cut down on Banstead Downs in Surrey. Three hundred circuits were affected. Once again, although the damage was quickly repaired, the attacks severely disrupted services.

To counter such activities in the outskirts of London, the police set up road blocks manned by armed officers. As a result of these measures, four men were arrested, after firing at police, while on a foray to cut telephone lines in the Bromley area of Kent. The prisoners, named Affection, Minihane, Tangley and Robinson, were charged with shooting with intent to cause grievous bodily harm and convicted at Kent Assizes, at Maidstone, on 3 July 1921. Robinson, described as the ringleader, was sentenced to twelve years' penal servitude, the other three to ten years' penal servitude each. A fifth man with them was never traced.

The campaign was not confined to those areas mentioned above. In 1920 Gilbert Barrington, a leading member of the ISDL in the north-east of England, arranged with the IRA high command in Dublin for all members of the ISDL in the Tyneside District to be recruited into a Brigade of the IRA. Barrington himself, who was appointed quartermaster of the Brigade, later wrote a detailed account of their considerable activities in the area in which he mentioned the presence of two Special Branch officers deployed there.[10]

On 22 July 1921, an uneasy truce was established between the British forces and the Sinn Féin government, during which extremist elements of the IRA made it plain that they were still intent on prolonging the violence, and the IRA leadership continued to organise the procurement of arms and explosives in south Wales, Merseyside, Manchester, and Tyneside. On 23 November, Cathal Brugha, the Sinn Féin Minister of Defence, gave £1,000 to Michael Brennan, Commandant of the IRA's 1st Western (Ireland) Division, to buy weapons. Brennan contacted Michael Hogan and Ned Lynch in London, but instead of buying the weapons,

---

10   Barrington's account was later edited by his daughter, Mary A. Barrington, and published as *The Irish Independence Movement on Tyneside, 1919–1921*

they stole them from Chelsea and Windsor Barracks with the assistance of a sergeant in the Irish Guards, Michael John Roche.

DS Kitchener describes the bizarre circumstances that enabled Hogan, Lynch and a third IRA member, Ned Cooley, to gain possession of the firearms through a combination of luck, bravado and alcohol during the evening of Saturday 21 November 1921.[11] By chance the three men met Roche, off duty but in uniform, in a West End bar and, while plying the soldier with alcohol, began running down the new Irish government. 'Indeed, after a time they showed clearly that they were now as bitterly opposed to the new powers as they had been to the British, and were working for its overthrow through the ranks of the Irish Republican Army.' They explained that one of the difficulties in carrying on this fight was in obtaining arms and ammunition. Eventually the sergeant, by now suffering from the effects of the liquor gratuitously supplied, was prevailed upon to help them overcome this difficulty. They took a cab to the Sergeant's Mess in Chelsea Barracks, where he was the NCO in charge of the armoury. After more drink, he went to the armoury, removed two Lewis guns and two rifles and left the barracks with the three Irishmen in the waiting cab. They were waved through the gate by the sentry and drove to an address in Forest Gate, in east London.

Fired with their success, they drove to Windsor to carry out a similar operation at the barracks there. The IRA men waited in their borrowed car while Roche went into Combermere Barracks. He made his way through a dormitory of sleeping men to the armoury at the end of the room and emerged with three machine guns and several rifles. He passed these through the iron railings of the barracks to the Irishmen, then walked out of the gate and rejoined them.

Next morning the army became aware of the loss of its weapons and the absence of Sergeant Roche. Special Branch was informed and a description of Roche was circulated. On 23 November he was arrested as he attempted to board the Irish boat train at Euston. He was questioned by DS Kitchener. Faced with the prospect of seven years' imprisonment, Roche turned King's evidence. Early next morning

---

11   Kitchener, *The Memoirs of an Old Detective*, pp. 90–94

the three Irishmen were arrested at a lodging house in Star Street, Paddington, and the arms were recovered from a railway goods depot in Shepherd's Bush.

THE ANGLO-IRISH TREATY

D espite stalling on both sides, the Anglo-Irish Treaty was eventually signed on 6 December 1921, an event that split the nationalist movement, led to civil war in Ireland and has divided the country ever since. It was a compromise agreement signed in the face of Britain's threat to resume hostilities if the Irish delegates did not sign. It permitted the Unionists of the north to create a state in which sectarian discrimination flourished. It was hailed as a solution but in reality the Treaty gave little to Sinn Féin that was not on offer before the Anglo-Irish War. The Irish delegation failed to achieve an independent Irish Republic and left a large nationalist population abandoned in the six counties of Ulster. Any hope that the intransigent Northern Unionists would join a Council of Ireland quickly faded and it was perhaps this, more than anything else, that led to subsequent feuding.

In Great Britain, a majority of the IRA opposed the Treaty and the Special Branch continued to monitor its activities. In Ireland de Valera rejected the Treaty but it was accepted by the Dáil by the slimmest of majorities. The pro-Treaty IRA became the Free State Army, the Royal Irish Constabulary was disbanded and the Garda Siochana became the Irish Free State's police force. The dissident element in the IRA fought on. Within weeks, 'contumely, vilification and death' were once again the order of the day as the Irish Civil War was fought to a bloody conclusion.

ASSASSINATION OF FIELD MARSHAL
SIR HENRY WILSON

T he continued deployment of Special Branch officers to protect government ministers and others who were thought to be at risk from the IRA was a contentious area. The measures of heightened protection, by both uniformed police and Special Branch, were brought to an end in January 1922. Field Marshal Sir Henry Wilson, formerly Chief of the Imperial General Staff, had his personal protection by Special Branch withdrawn after his retirement. Shortly afterwards, on 22 June 1922, he was murdered on the steps of his London home at 38 Eaton Place, returning there after unveiling a war memorial at Liverpool Street Station. The killers were Reggie Dunne, Commandant of the London Brigade of the IRA, and Volunteer Joseph O'Sullivan. They were captured after they had shot and wounded two pursuing police officers, PCs Sayers and Marsh, and a civilian. They were convicted of murder and hanged at Wandsworth Prison in August 1922.

The Field Marshal, a staunch Unionist, was Member of Parliament for North Down. He openly expressed antipathy towards the Irish Nationalists, and his name was on an IRA death list. Both Dunne and O'Sullivan had served in the British Army in France. O'Sullivan, a lance-corporal, had lost a leg in the Battle of Ypres while Dunne had served as a corporal in the Irish Guards. Unsubstantiated claims said that O'Sullivan had previously executed a police informant, Vincent Forvargue,[12] on 2 April 1921, and dumped his body on Ashford golf course in Middlesex, bearing a note claiming that the IRA had executed him as a spy. Kitchener described two searches he made of suspects' addresses. The first, on 23 June, the day following the murder, was that of Mrs Elizabeth Eadie, the sister of James Connolly, in Notting Hill. On top of a wardrobe he found a box of incendiary bombs. She was subsequently sentenced to two years' imprisonment at the Central Criminal Court. The second address he visited was in Aynhoe Road, West Kensington, the lodgings of Herbert Leo Wrigley, a clerk in the Post Office Savings Bank. Wrigley immediately surrendered an unloaded revolver. Kitchener found written notes which indicated that he had been gathering intelligence concerning RIC officers, and locating targets, including timber yards, petrol

---

12   Forvargue was a Britsh agent employed by Ormonde Winter, in charge of British intelligence-gathering in Dublin

pumps, power stations, a margarine factory and an acetylene plant. He was sentenced to twelve months' imprisonment.[13]

UNLAWFUL DEPORTATIONS OF IRA SUSPECTS

I n the civil war in Ireland that followed the signing of the Anglo-Irish Treaty, it is believed that between 700 and 2,000 people perished, including most prominent leaders of the Nationalist movement, among them Collins, Brugha, Erskine Childers and Rory O'Connor. The fatalities also included seventy-seven men executed by the government, while between 11,000 and 12,000 were detained in government prisons.[14] At the end of the war, the IRA dumped its arms but it did not surrender them. Thus it continued to be a threat to both governments of Ireland and to the United Kingdom – and a continuing problem to Metropolitan Police Special Branch.

In March 1923, correspondence addressed to a known IRA activist in London, referred to as 'Officer Commanding Britain', was intercepted. It indicated that there were plans afoot to overthrow the Free State government and to engage in outrages in Great Britain. The Home Secretary ordered the deportation of a large number of IRA suspects.[15] Kitchener relates that the deportations were carried out at the request of the Free State government following the visit of the Irish Prime Minister, Liam Cosgrave.[16]

On 11 March, 110 suspects, including thirty-three in London, were arrested throughout the United Kingdom and shipped to the Free State on the destroyers HMS *Castor* and HMS *Wolfhound*. There they were detained in Mountjoy

---

13   Kitchener, *The Memoirs of an Old Detective*, pp. 85–8

14   Tony Gray, *Ireland This Century* (London: Little, Brown, 1994), pp. 83–90; F. S. L. Lyons, *Ireland since the Famine* (London: Weidenfeld & Nicolson, 1971), p. 467

15   Hansard, HC Debate, 12 March 1923

16   Kitchener, *The Memoirs of an Old Detective*, p. 90

Prison.[17] The legality of orders deporting British subjects from this country to another state, without a preliminary hearing in the British courts, was immediately questioned, and the action raised an outcry, both in and out of Parliament. On appeal to the House of Lords it was held that expulsion, under the Restoration of Order (Ireland) Act, was unlawful, since following the ratification of the Anglo-Irish Treaty, the Free State was a sovereign power and the Act no longer applied to it. On 17 May, ninety of the deportees were returned to England and the Home Office was obliged to pay £43,000 in compensation. According to Allason, when they returned, seven who were found to be armed were arrested and their weapons impounded. A Restoration of Order Ireland (Indemnity) Act was passed later in 1923, under which an Irish Deportees Compensation Tribunal was set up and the amount of compensation paid to the deportees was limited. Special Branch officers were obliged to issue the returning deportees with travel warrants to return home.[18] ('A policeman's lot is not a happy one.')[19]

Between 1924 and 1938 there was little IRA activity in Great Britain but Special Branch continued to monitor Irish republican meetings here.

17   Allason, *The Branch*, p. 86

18   Ibid., p. 8

19   W. S. Gilbert, *The Pirates of Penzance*

CHAPTER ELEVEN

THE COMMUNIST THREAT

URING THE 1920S, one of the principal responsibilities of the Special
Branch became the gathering of intelligence concerning Bolshevik subversion. The Communist Party of Great Britain (CPGB) had evolved
in August 1920 from a number of pro-Bolshevik groups influenced, but not
controlled, by the Comintern, and included the Socialist Labour Party, the Communist Unity Group and the Workers Socialist Federation. It represented a threat
that the security agencies could not ignore.

By 1920, the CPGB had its first MP in the unlikely figure of Lt Colonel Cecil
John L'Estrange Malone who, not unnaturally, attracted considerable Special Branch attention; but his early career contained no hint of his subsequent
espousal of the communist cause. Indeed, in the general election in November
1918, he stood as a Coalition Liberal and won the East Leyton seat, although he
subsequently claimed that he never actually joined the Liberal Party. Later he
became a member of the executive committee of the virulently anti-communist
Reconstruction Society and wrote a number of articles strongly criticising left-
wing activists.

He was born in 1890, in Yorkshire, the youngest child of Savile Richard William L'Estrange Malone, rector of Dalton Holme, and Frances Mary Foljambe. He

was related to the sisters Constance, Countess Markievicz, and Eva Gore-Booth, both Irish nationalists and suffragettes; Constance, moreover, was a member of James Connolly's Irish Citizens' Army, and took part in the 1916 rising in Dublin. She was imprisoned for treason but was released under the amnesty in 1917, and in 1918 was the first woman to be elected to the Westminster Parliament. So it can be seen that Cecil Malone's eventual conversion to communism, though not permanent, was not totally inconsistent with his family's unconventional background.

Cecil Malone also had a distinguished career in the armed forces, initially in the Royal Navy in which he commanded an aircraft carrier but later, having turned to flying, was appointed Assistant Director of the Air Department at the Admiralty. Towards the end of his career he represented the United Kingdom at the Supreme War Council at Versailles. He was awarded the Order of the British Empire.

It was not until 1919 that Malone first came under the notice of Special Branch when his conversion to communism, already suspected, became apparent after he visited Russia as a guest of the Communist Party. During the next five years he featured regularly in Directorate of Intelligence and Special Branch reports to the Cabinet on 'Revolutionary Organisations in the United Kingdom'.[1] In November 1919, Special Branch, in its Directorate of Intelligence role, reported that:

> Lieutenant-Colonel Cecil L'Estrange Malone, MP for Leyton, returned to the United Kingdom on the 28 October, after visiting Moscow and Petrograd. He went immediately to the office of the *Daily Express*, which has continued to publish his articles, though it is understood that some of them were refused as being too openly Bolshevist propaganda. The following note of Colonel Malone's earlier activities may be of interest: He held, and still holds, a Commission in the Navy, and he was known among his brother officers as a person of extreme views. In April last a meeting of

---

1   Numerous documents in the TNA CAB 24 series

the Sailors', Soldiers' and Airmen's Union was held at 10a Heddon Street, attended by Commander Kenworthy, Mr Neil Maclean MP, and Colonel Malone. This was the preface to a meeting at the Abbotsford Hotel, Russell Square, where Colonel Malone met Mr Robert Williams, of the Transport Workers' Federation and Mr W. F. Watson, now undergoing a term of imprisonment for a revolutionary speech. Plans were discussed for seizing Whitehall and Westminster and for feeding the troops who were expected to join the revolutionaries. It is to be remembered that both Colonel Malone and Commander Kenworthy were commissioned officers at the time. Colonel Malone appears to have got into Russia in the following way: He had asked in the House of Commons whether a Commission could be sent to Russia, and was told that it was not considered necessary. He then applied for a passport for himself, which was refused. After this, he appears to have obtained a passport on the pretence that he was attached to the Military Mission in Finland. He arrived at Helsingfors on 20 September, and went to Viborg, where arrangements were made for his journey by Sulo Vulijoki, a Finnish Senator of communist sympathies. He then made his way, with the help of Bolshevist agents, to Lake Ladoga, which was crossed in a sailing vessel. In Russia he was the guest of the Communist Party, and he accompanied Trotsky to a review of troops near Moscow in the same motor car; the Bolsheviks naturally regarding him as a first-rate medium for propaganda.[2]

(The report is quoted in its entirety, as it is a typical example of the thoroughness, the quality and style of SB reporting which contrasted favourably with the stilted police terminology, reminiscent of the Victorian era, still being used in the 1920s.)

Special Branch interest in Malone became more acute when, on 27 October 1920, Erkki Veltheim, a communist courier under surveillance by Special Branch

---

2   Directorate of Intelligence report No. 28, dated 6 November 1919. TNA CAB 24/92/71

officers, was seen to emerge from Malone's home at 4 Wellington House, College Road, Chalk Farm, with a Miss Gilbertson. The surveillance continued and the next day Veltheim was arrested in possession of a number of documents. He was charged with failing to register as an alien and to answer reasonable questions put to him by a police officer under the Aliens Order of 1920. After Veltheim's arrest, Sir Basil Thomson wrote to the Home Secretary informing him of Veltheim's impending trial, in which Malone would be appearing as a witness. Thomson enclosed with his letter to the Home Secretary an article from *The Communist* entitled 'From the Gasworks', in which Malone expressed cynical views of 'parliamentary democracy'. Sir Basil suggested that the Speaker of the House of Commons should be informed.[3]

The information leading to Veltheim's arrest had been supplied to Thomson by Jacob Nosovitsky, the Comintern's principal courier operating between Russia and the United States. Thomson had taken the opportunity to recruit him as an informant when he was detained in Liverpool in June 1919. Nosovitsky also worked for the United States Department of Justice as Agent N-100 and was used by them to spy on US communists.

At his trial at Bow Street Police Court, extracts from Veltheim's documents, including the following passage from a letter to Grigori Zinoviev, head of the Comintern, from Sylvia Pankhurst, were read out by Counsel for the prosecution:

> The Communist Parties are not large enough, nor intelligent enough, to make capital out of the situation. We are talking of a Communist Council of Action. Colonel Malone with whom I have been speaking, and who is a member of the Executive of the Communist Party (BSP[4]) tells me his Executive does not wish to join with us but to absorb us. However he will try.

There was also, said counsel, a postscript which referred to an amount of £3,522,

---

3   Letter from Sir Basil Thomson to the Home Secretary, dated 1 November 1920. TNA HO 144/22952
4   The British Socialist Party faction of the Communist Party

said to have been promised to Sylvia Pankhurst on behalf of the Third International in Moscow. Another document in code was deciphered by the Government Communications and Cypher School. This read:

> Rothstein or his deputy not here yet. Impossible go successfully Ireland to start party, etc., or negotiate Republican Mission without money. Present using £300 sent to Irish unions while waiting news. Lent Tanner £70 to run his paper. Instruct us how to obtain money by our note from Kobietsky, or instruct representatives here help us immediately. Consult Rosenberg, Foreign Office and send news re exchange Larkin. Reply J. Cowper, 28 Little St., St Andrew Street, London, WC, 20 October.

Sergeant Foster of Special Branch in his evidence to the court stated that the Rosenberg mentioned in the document was an East End Jew who held a high position in the Foreign Office in Moscow. Counsel questioned him concerning a 56-page typewritten document addressed to Louis Fraina, International Secretary of the Communist Party of America. Foster said that Fraina was a well-known revolutionary and that he believed the document to have been written by Jacob Nosovitsky, a member of the Russian Revolutionary Party.

Cecil Malone in his evidence denied knowing Veltheim and was unaware that he had called at his house. He said that as a Member of Parliament many people called at his home to see him even when he was in the House of Commons. Veltheim pleaded guilty and was sentenced to six months' imprisonment with hard labour and fined £10 on each of the two remaining charges. He was also recommended for deportation.

In the summer of 1920, Special Branch learned that during discussions taking place between the government and the Russian trade mission over a proposed trade agreement between the two countries, the Russians were clandestinely financing the Hands Off Russia Committee, of which Malone was an active supporter, and were funding the *Daily Herald*. After a short break in July, for consultations with his government, the head of the trade mission, Leonid Krasin, returned to London to resume negotiations. He was accompanied by Lev Kamenev and brought with him a large consignment of diamonds. Within weeks the *Daily Herald* was supplied with £75,000 from the proceeds of their sale, and smaller sums were given to other left-wing periodicals and to the CPGB. Special Branch monitored this laundering operation with increasing interest.

It was felt in government circles that these clandestine activities were exerting undue influence on sections of the Labour movement in an attempt to bring the government down by strike action. These were matters that could not be ignored by any democratic government. But Lloyd George was reluctant to expel the whole trade mission, thereby abandoning the hope of solving the unemployment problem. At the same time he had to appease those anti-Bolshevik members of the Cabinet, and the intelligence community, who were demanding action. So when Lev Kamenev returned to Moscow in September 1920, the Prime Minister told the trade mission that Kamenev had been guilty of a breach of faith in secretly financing the *Daily Herald* and would not be permitted to return to this country but the mission could remain. This solved nothing.

On Sunday 7 November 1920, Malone made a speech at a meeting held jointly under the auspices of the Hands Off Russia Committee and the Communist Party of Great Britain at the Royal Albert Hall, celebrating the anniversary of the Russian Revolution. The authorities took particular exception to one part of Malone's speech, in which he said:

> We are out to change the present constitution and if it is necessary to save bloodshed, to save atrocities, we shall have to use the lampposts or the walls. What, my friends, are a few Churchills or Curzons on lampposts compared to the massacre of thousands of human beings? What are a few Churchills or Curzons against the wall, compared to the bombing of harmless Egyptians in Egypt – compared with the reprisals in Ireland?

As a consequence, DI Fitch was instructed by Sir Basil Thomson to obtain a warrant for the arrest of Malone and to search his home. By the time Fitch visited his address, Malone was in Dublin on business, so his property was searched in his absence. On the premises police found a number of items of interest, including two railway cloakroom tickets, a copy of Malone's speech at the Albert Hall, two loaded automatic pistols and ammunition and an Underwood typewriter. In his memoirs Fitch describes visiting the cloakroom and collecting parcels that contained bundles of typed sheets, making up twelve copies of a booklet entitled 'Red Officers' Course'. Subsequent examination by an expert from the Underwood Company revealed that these booklets had been typed on the typewriter found in Malone's home. The booklets were instructions in sabotage and subversion to be carried out by a 'British Red Army'.

The purpose of Malone's visit to Ireland was to deliver a lecture on Bolshevism to a meeting of Trinity College History Society. Fitch obtained the authority of the Director of Public Prosecutions to request the Dublin Metropolitan Police to detain him for an offence under Regulation 42 of the Defence of the Realm Act. As a result, at about 7.30 p.m. on 10 November when Malone and other guests of the Trinity College History Society were taking tea in the College, the police called to arrest him. He was escorted back to England by the officers and, at Euston Station, placed in the custody of DI Fitch.[5]

On 12 November 1920, Malone appeared at Bow Street Police Court charged with 'using words calculated to cause sedition or disaffection among the civil population', contrary to Regulation 42 of the Defence of the Realm Act. He was remanded on bail for one week in his own surety of £1,000 and those of Mr Neil Maclean MP and Commander Grenfell RN (retired) of £500 each. He appeared again at Bow Street Court on 19 November 1920, when he was additionally charged that he 'was an evil disposed person and not of good fame and a disturber of the peace and inciter to others to commit breaches of the peace'.

At his trial, extracts from Malone's Albert Hall speech, which were said to be deliberate and considered utterances, were read to the court. Evidence was

5   Fitch, *Traitors Within*, pp. 87–9

given of the items found during the search of his flat and of the pamphlets entitled 'Red Officers' Course' recovered by police from the railway cloakroom.

An introduction to this pamphlet said:

> We are soldiers of the International Red Army, that army of proletarians
> and workers led by the communists who fight – or soon will fight – in every
> country over the five continents of the Earth. We shall not lay down arms
> before the world is ours and the dark night of oppression and the blood
> red stormy dawn of revolution have changed it into the glorious day of
> freedom and communism. A grim struggle lies before us on our section of
> the international front. Down with our enemies, the Churchills, the impe-
> rialists, and all their lackeys. Long live the Red Army.

After that came a syllabus of lectures which made it clear that the book was intended
for the use of persons in an armed insurrection. The course was designed for 'comrades of a determined revolutionary spirit' and its object was to train communists
and give them sufficient knowledge of military work to enable them, in the near
future, to carry out duties as officers of a British Red Army. When trained, they
were to be at the disposal of a Communist Revolutionary Authority at the time
of an actual revolution, when the order for mobilisation would be issued. That
authority, said the pamphlet, could not at present be defined and, for the present,
the work must be carried out underground and in strict secrecy. It referred to the
British Army as 'the enemy' whose skill and discipline could be 'broken by propaganda, and parts of it may be got over to our side'. Cadets were warned to treat
the course as secret and it concluded with the ominous warning that those 'who
betray their comrades must be punished with death'.

DC Brown, Special Branch, who had taken shorthand notes of the defendant's speech in the Royal Albert Hall, gave evidence of what he had heard and
recorded, and of the mood and composition of the meeting. In the witness box
DI Fitch gave evidence of searching the defendant's flat, where he broke open an
office door and found a typed draft of the Albert Hall speech, the firearms already

mentioned by Counsel and a typewriter. Two days later, on 11 November, he arrested the defendant at Euston Station on his arrival under escort from Ireland.

> Malone was sentenced to six months' imprisonment which, having regard to his character as a soldier in the past and for that reason only ... would be in the second division. In addition he was bound over in his own recognisance of £2,000 to be of good behaviour and keep the peace for months and ordered to find two sureties of £1,000 each – Lt. Cdr. Grenville RN (retd.) and Miss Ann Withers were accepted as sureties. His appeal against conviction and sentence failed. He was released from Pentonville on 1 June 1921, having been granted a remission of one month.

The *Globe* newspaper saw the Malone trial as a worrying manifestation of the threat posed by Leninists and other revolutionary organisations. An article published in the newspaper after the trial warned that revolutionary organisations were being quietly and efficiently perfected and that 'persistent propaganda is being carried out not only among the industrial classes, but in the army and the fleet, and hardly anything appears to be done to counteract its malignant effects'.

On his release from prison, Malone was stripped of his Order of the British Empire but remained a member of the House of Commons. He continued to work in politics but left the Communist Party to join the Independent Labour Party. He subsequently moved to the right wing of the Labour Party and in a by-election in 1928 was elected by a small majority for the Northampton constituency.[6] But gradually this fascinating character, who had loomed large on the Special Branch horizon for a few years, faded into relative obscurity. In 1940 he wrote to Winston Churchill offering his services in the war effort; his offer was declined. He died on 8 June 1965, aged seventy-four.

---

6   The Conservative Fritz Forbes was expected to win, and might well have done so had his mistress not been on the platform at a public meeting. His mother turned up to support him but, on seeing the mistress, she mounted the platform and publicly berated the candidate, who subsequently lost the seat by some 200 votes.

THE MISFORTUNES OF THE FIRST
SOCIALIST GOVERNMENT

I n January 1924, for the first time, a socialist government, with Ramsay Mac-
Donald as Prime Minister, came to power. His Cabinet had modest objectives
and was anxious to demonstrate that Labour was fit to run the country; but fate
conspired against him. He immediately alienated the right-wing press by entering into trade negotiations with the Soviet Union.

This section of the press was further antagonised when the Attorney General refused his fiat over an article that appeared in the CPGB's official organ,
Workers' Weekly, on 25 July 1924. Entitled 'An Open Letter to Fighting Forces',
the piece called on the armed forces to

> Unite to form the nucleus of an organisation that will prepare the whole
> of the soldiers, sailors and airmen, not merely to refuse to go to war, or to
> refuse to shoot strikers during industrial conflicts, but will make it pos-
> sible for the workers, peasants and soldiers and airmen to go forward in
> a common attack upon the capitalists and smash capitalism forever, and
> institute the reign of the whole working class.

John Ross Campbell, the acting editor of Workers' Weekly, was arrested by Special Branch and charged under the Incitement to Mutiny Act of 1797.[7] The
Conservatives and Liberals were outraged at the Attorney General's decision
and on 8 October tabled a vote of censure on the government. The government
was defeated and a general election was called.

---

7   Report of Cabinet meeting held on 6 August 1924. TNA CAB 23/48/23

THE ZINOVIEV LETTER

B efore the election could be held, however, the government was to face further censure over the 'affair of the Zinoviev letter'. The letter purported to be a communication from the head of the Comintern, Grigori Zinoviev, to the Communist Party of Great Britain, instructing it to persuade the British proletariat to support the ratification of the Anglo-Soviet trade treaties. It also contained an incitement 'to prepare for future armed insurrection and a class war'. This letter was not very different from other intercepted communications from Zinoviev to the Communist Party of Great Britain. Its authenticity was confirmed to the Foreign Office by the Secret Intelligence Service, who had received a copy from an agent in Riga.

On 10 October 1924, the permanent undersecretary at the Foreign Office was shown an English translation of the letter but decided not to inform the Prime Minister until corroboration that it was genuine was received. When the Prime Minister did see it and was assured of its authenticity, he stated that he was in favour of publication. A letter of protest, which the Prime Minister had only seen in draft form, was sent to M. Rakovsky, the head of the Anglo-Soviet Trade Delegation, on 24 October. He refuted the allegations the following day and described the Zinoviev letter as a gross forgery. A further letter from Rakovsky on 27 October, on the instructions of the Soviet government, offered to co-operate in proving that it was a forgery intended to disrupt relations between the two governments. The Prime Minister believed that the official who signed the note on his behalf had misunderstood his instructions.

The publicity surrounding the publication of the Zinoviev letter, which had been leaked to the *Daily Mail* and the Conservative Party on the eve of the election, probably did not damage the Labour Party as much as has been claimed, for the Conservative Party had a landslide victory. Controversy over what was undoubtedly a forgery has continued to rumble on over the years without resolution. Various culprits have been suggested as being involved in publicising the letter, including SIS and Security Service members.[8] There has not, however,

---

8   Andrew, *The Defence of the Realm*, pp. 149–50

been any suggestion that Special Branch had any part in the leakage of the letter to the *Daily Mail*. Wyndham Childs believed the letter to be genuine, as it was similar in content to other intercepted letters from Zinoviev already in the possession of Special Branch, who watched the scandal unfold with interest and collected a vast number of press cuttings from the case.

All the evidence points to the letter being a White Russian forgery intended to prejudice the trade agreements. Whether officers of the Security Service and SIS, who were consulted about its probity, were involved in an opportunistic conspiracy with Conservative Party officials and the *Daily Mail* remains a mystery.

THE RAID ON THE CPGB

Early in 1925, intercepted mail from Moscow to the CPGB indicated that the Comintern had decided to establish a 'Lenin School' in Moscow, for the political education of Communist Party members. Five worker-students from Britain were selected to attend for a period of eighteen months, with a view to full-time work for the party on their return. A similar central school was proposed in Britain to accommodate twenty students for a six-month course. Fears were expressed in Whitehall that this might foreshadow Russian attempts to undermine the discipline of the armed forces.

On 14 October 1925 Special Branch officers arrested eight Communist Party officials on warrants alleging the publication of seditious libels. The party's headquarters in King Street and other premises were searched, resulting in the seizure of large quantities of literature, which were taken to New Scotland Yard for examination. At King Street, DCI Parker, deputy head of Special Branch, arrested Albert Inkpen, the general secretary, and Ernest Cant, the London organiser, of the CPGB. DS Foster arrested Tom Winteringham and John Ross Campbell, the assistant editors of *Workers' Weekly*, at Dr Johnson's Buildings in the Temple. DI Norwood arrested William Rust, the secretary of the Young Communist League, and Harry Pollitt, the secretary of the National Minority

League, was arrested at 38 Great Ormond Street. William Gallacher and Tom Bell were detained at their homes in Scotland. On 22 October, Special Branch officers arrested a further four officials; DCI Parker arrested Arthur McManus and John Murphy at King Street and DS Foster arrested Wal Hannington at Paddington Station, while DS Van Ginhoven searched his rooms in Hampstead. Robin Page Arnot, the head of the Labour Research Department, was detained at his office in Mecklenburgh Square. Thorough searches of all the prisoners' homes and offices were carried out and further items were seized and taken to New Scotland Yard. The prisoners were all charged with conspiracy to publish seditious libels and to incite mutiny in the armed forces.

They appeared initially at Bow Street Court and were granted bail; George Bernard Shaw and the Countess of Warwick were among those who offered themselves as sureties. The case was subsequently tried at the Central Criminal Court, in a trial lasting eight days, with the Attorney General, Sir Douglas Hogg, leading for the Crown. All twelve defendants denied the charges but were convicted on 25 November 1925; Inkpen, Pollitt, Hannington, Rust and Gallacher, who had previous convictions, were each sentenced to twelve months' imprisonment. The remaining seven had the option of being bound over to be of good behaviour, but declined, and were each sentenced to six months' imprisonment.

THE GENERAL STRIKE

In 1926 a long, drawn-out miners' strike took place when the mine owners told their employees that they would have to accept a cut in their wages. When the miners' representatives refused, there was a lock-out. In sympathy with the miners, the TUC called a general strike on 4 May. Although the CPGB was involved in supporting the strike it did not cause it, nor was it able to exploit its full revolutionary potential. Individual CPGB leaders played a part, as did many of the rank and file. Robin Page Arnot, for instance, who was released from prison on the eve of the strike, helped to form the Northumberland and Durham Joint Strike

Committee. Just how much communist involvement there was during the few days of the strike is difficult to say, although the Comintern encouraged revolutionary situations wherever they occurred. However, the TUC capitulated on 12 May, leaving the miners bitter and betrayed. There was little public support for the strikers and because volunteers from all walks of life manned the essential services it was very quickly over. In the absence of any concerted involvement in the strike by the CPGB or other revolutionary movements, Special Branch interest in it was confined to a watching brief. However, the Branch was very much involved in the political furore that followed.

On 16 June 1926, the Home Secretary, William Joynson-Hicks, submitted a memorandum to the Cabinet in which he raised two issues. The first was whether the staff of the All Russian Co-operative Society (ARCOS) and other Russian state institutions in London, including the Russian embassy, should be expelled from the country, in view of the fact that Russian money had been contributed to the miners' strike fund during their stoppage. He said that he and the Foreign Secretary took the position that the Soviet government could not escape responsibility for the actions of the Comintern run by Zinoviev, whose objective was to capture the British trade unions through the National Minority Movement. The second question was whether he should invoke his powers to stop the influx of foreign money, whether from Russia or some other foreign source.

He added that he was aware, as the result of intercepted telegrams, that ARCOS had sent £25,000 in May to the Trades Union Congress. This gift from the All Russian Central Council of Trades Unions and the International Workers' Aid Society to support the strikers was returned by the TUC. This was followed a few days later by the transfer of £200,000 and then by a further £300,000 through the banking system, for the aid of the strikers. The Home Secretary used his powers under emergency legislation to stop some of these transfers.[9] While the government was deliberating on what further action should be taken, events were taking place elsewhere which were to have an influence on their decision.

---

9   Foreign Office Memorandum, dated 16 June 1926. TNA CAB 24/180/50

WILFRED MACARTNEY AND THE RAID ON ARCOS

In 1927, Wilfred Francis Remington Macartney, a former intelligence officer in the British Army, was working as a Soviet agent. After leaving the army he had inherited, and squandered through high living, a considerable sum of money; he resorted to petty crime but was imprisoned and afterwards was converted to communism, which he claimed to see as a 'clear burning light in a corrupt society'. He was a flamboyant, undisciplined character who lacked the tradecraft of a spy and, in his early months as a Soviet agent, was arrested twice for being drunk and disorderly.[10]

In March 1927, Admiral Sir Reginald Hall MP, the former Director of Naval Intelligence, was informed by a reliable contact, George Monkland, a former army officer, that Macartney had approached him and asked whether he could supply him with details of arms shipments to countries bordering the Soviet Union. Monkland was put in touch with Freddie Browning, the former Deputy Chief of SIS, and handed him a questionnaire that Macartney had given him concerning the Royal Air Force, which bore the hallmarks of having been compiled by an intelligence expert. Monkland was interviewed by Desmond Morton, a senior SIS officer, who introduced himself as Peter Hamilton. Both Monkland and Macartney were put under surveillance and their letters and telephone calls intercepted. This involved bringing Special Branch and MI5 into the operation.

By now it had been decided that the offices of ARCOS should be raided, but the picture of events leading up to the raid on ARCOS at this point becomes blurred. One version suggests that a fake 'secret document' was given to Macartney by Monkland in order to entrap him when he passed it on to his Soviet contact in ARCOS; information was received, by SIS, from a British member of the ARCOS staff that a 'military code book' had indeed been copied in the ARCOS office. As this was a case of espionage, it fell within the province of MI5

---

10   Christopher Andrew, *Secret Service: The Making of the British Intelligence Community* (London: Hodder & Stoughton, 1986), pp. 467–9

and was passed to them to continue the investigation. Desmond Morton (SIS) claimed that Kell and Holt-Wilson took a month to check the information before preparing a case for the Director of Public Prosecutions. More prevarication followed but eventually the story reached the ears of the Home Secretary, Foreign Secretary and the Prime Minister, who agreed that the offices of ARCOS must be raided by Special Branch to recover the 'fake document'.[11]

Preparations for the raid on the morning of 12 May 1927 took place in great secrecy. It was hoped this would put an end to Russian espionage and other subversive activities which the government knew were being carried on by ARCOS. The police raiding party was not aware of the actual target until it arrived at the premises. ARCOS shared its offices in Soviet House, Moorgate, with the Russian trade mission, which enjoyed diplomatic privilege; as the premises were situated in the City, the City of London Police executed the search warrant and then handed over the search to Wyndham Childs and his team of fifty SB officers; they had not been briefed about what documents were to be seized and none of them could read Russian. After an exhaustive three-day search, and the seizure of numerous documents, the military code manual remained undiscovered. It is believed to have been spirited off to Berlin some three weeks earlier. The Russians tried to destroy some documents but were physically restrained. A government statement after the raid suggested that the persons responsible for the theft of the code book had already been prosecuted.

Although no sign was found of the elusive code book, a vast number of documents relating to Russian espionage was discovered, sufficient for the government to demand the closure of ARCOS and expulsion of the Russian trade mission; at the same time, diplomatic relations with the Soviet Union were severed.

Rumours that the Russians had been forewarned of the raid were difficult to support. Apart from unsubstantiated claims from the unreliable Macartney that he had received foreknowledge of the raid from a police clerk, there was no evidence to show that the police had leaked information about the operation;

---

11   Andrew, *The Defence of the Realm*, p. 154

indeed, even Sir Wyndham Childs had not been put fully in the picture until the morning of the raid. The only other agencies who were known to be privy to the operation were MI5 and SIS. It must be said, however, that the following year two SB officers, Jane and Van Ginhoven, were dismissed for allegedly supplying information to a Soviet spy ring, although no evidence was produced to suggest that, in this instance, either of the officers leaked the information (see Chapter 12). In fact, MI5 was later told by a renegade member of the same spy ring that the head of the group only learned of it after it had taken place.

MI5 dropped their interest in Macartney but Special Branch continued to maintain constant observation on him for another six months and his mail was still intercepted. As a result, it was known that he was to meet an important contact in Hampstead on 16 November 1927. He was followed and met a man known only to the police as 'Johnson' in a café opposite Hampstead Underground Station. Detective Superintendent James McBrien and DCI Edward Parker, the Branch's most senior detectives, followed him from the café to the station, where they arrested him. Meanwhile DIs Patrick Byrne and Roddy Cosgrove arrested 'Johnson' in the café where the meeting had taken place. 'Johnson' was identified as Georg Hansen, a German, who was Macartney's Soviet controller. Both men were charged with offences against the Official Secrets Acts and were tried at the Central Criminal Court in January 1928. Each received a sentence of ten years' penal servitude. Hansen was deported to Russia in 1935.

The Secret Service Committee enquired into the circumstances of the ARCOS raid and interviewed the heads of the services separately. Their main criticism was directed at Kell, who had bypassed the civil service by directly approaching ministers.

CHAPTER TWELVE

THE REDS IN THE
SPECIAL BRANCH BED

TOWARDS THE END of the First World War, pay and conditions in the police service were so bad that many officers joined the National Union of Police and Prison Officers, contrary to their terms of employment. The General Secretary of the Union, Jack Hayes, was a former Metropolitan Police sergeant and he led the union in strikes in 1918 and 1919. Although Special Branch officers did not strike, a number of them refused to leave their office on the day the strike was called. In response to this, the government set up the Desborough inquiry, which recommended an increase in pay and pensions and the creation of a Police Federation to represent the interests of the officers. Members of the NUPPO were dismissed and had to find other employment. Jack Hayes opened the Vigilance Detective Agency and later became a Member of Parliament for a Liverpool constituency.

In November 1924, an advertisement in the *Daily Herald* announced that a Labour Group, carrying out an investigation, would be glad to receive information and details from anyone who had ever had an association with any Secret Service department or operation. It gave a PO Box number for replies. As a consequence, MI5, under cover, set up a meeting with the advertiser, who was

later identified as William Norman Ewer. An MI5 surveillance team under John
Ottaway was deployed to cover the meeting but the advertiser did not show up.
They noticed that they were themselves being kept under observation by a man,
subsequently identified as Walter Dale, a former police officer who had been
dismissed for striking. Dale worked for Hayes in the Vigilance Detective Agency.

In February 1925, another meeting under cover was successfully arranged
between Ewer and an MI5 agent, 'D', in which Ewer disclosed that a Labour
Group was setting up its own 'secret service' to defend itself against the government. The surveillance team followed Ewer to the ARCOS office in Moorgate
and then to the Federated Press of America (FPA) office in the Temple. As a
result of telephone and mail intercepts at these premises it was learned that Ewer,
using the name Kenneth Milton, was in receipt of secret French diplomatic correspondence used by George Slocombe, the Paris correspondent of the *Daily
Herald*, for his articles in the newspaper.[1]

As MI5 continued their enquiries they began to uncover a complex and dis-
turbing network of communist agents run by William Norman Ewer. Ewer was
born on 22 October 1885; he lived with his parents in Hornsey and attended
Merchant Taylors' School, from which he won a scholarship to Trinity College,
Cambridge. He graduated in 1907 with first-class honours in mathematics and
history. Following an introduction to George Lansbury MP, in 1912, he joined
the staff of the *Daily Herald*. In that year he was married. His wife, Monica, was
a writer and theatrical producer and shared his interest in Fabian Socialism.
Ewer was a poet, a pacifist and a conscientious objector. In 1917 he published
an anthology of socialist and anti-war poetry entitled *Five Souls and Other War-
time Verses*, containing the memorable lines:

> *I gave my life for freedom – This I know*
> *For those who bade me fight had told me so.*[2]

---

1   Andrew, *The Defence of the Realm*, p. 152, 158

2   *Five Souls and Other War-Time Verses* (London: The Herald, 1917)

In 1918 he was the *Daily Herald* correspondent in Russia. Early in 1919 he was appointed foreign editor. Ewer was an advocate of workers' control in industry and joined the Communist Party of Great Britain shortly after its formation in 1919. It was he who had set up the London Office of the Federated Press of America.

At some time after the police strike Jack Hayes introduced Ewer to Detective Sergeant Van Ginhoven of Special Branch as someone who might be able to assist in regard to a story concerning Menshevik attempts to discredit the Bolsheviks with forged copies of the newspaper, *Pravda*; the British government was suspected of aiding them.

Hubertus Cornelis van Ginhoven was a Dutch immigrant born in 1882. In 1902 he was married to Martha Riminton at Brentford and the couple moved to Windsor. In 1903 Martha died in childbirth. A son, Martinus, survived. In 1905, when van Ginhoven was living in Isleworth, he applied for, and was granted, British nationality. In 1906 he was married to Martha's younger sister, Frances Riminton; they had three children. In 1909 van Ginhoven joined the Metropolitan Police and served in south London. The following year he was selected for duty in Special Branch. During the First World War he was recommended for secondment to the War Office Department of Military Intelligence and is reported to have gathered intelligence behind the German, Austrian and Turkish lines. Holland was a neutral country and, being fluent in Dutch and German, he could pass himself off as a friendly alien. After the war he returned to the Metropolitan Police Special Branch.

Jack Hayes also introduced Ewer to Arthur Francis Lakey. Lakey was born in 1886 at Chatham, and was brought up in Devonport by his sister, Matilda, after his mother died. He joined the Royal Navy as a boy seaman in 1900 and was trained at HMS *Ganges* at Shotley in Suffolk. In 1911 he bought himself out of the navy in order to join the Metropolitan Police. He was a sergeant in 1918 when he was sacked for taking part in the strike. Ewer gave Lakey a job with the Federated Press of America and, shortly afterwards, asked him to take charge of its London office. He introduced him to Nikolai Klishko, a Russian diplomat. Klishko instructed him to rent a flat at 51 Ridgmount Gardens, Bloomsbury, and Lakey lived and worked there until the FPA office moved to the Outer Temple in 1923.

Nikolai Klimentovich Klishko, an engineer, settled in Britain before 1910 and was married to an Englishwoman, Phyllis Frood. In 1919 Klishko, who at that time was employed by Vickers Armstrong, brought himself to the notice of the authorities as a Bolshevist involved in the International Socialist Bureau and was expelled to Russia together with Maxim Litvinov, subsequently the Soviet Foreign Minister, with whom he shared a house in London. In May 1920 Klishko returned to Britain with diplomatic status as the Secretary of the Russian Trade Delegation. In addition to his other duties, Klishko was a Cheka officer engaged in espionage and subversion.

In Special Branch, van Ginhoven was promoted to detective inspector in 1928. Over the intervening years he had continued his liaison with Ewer and his group through another sacked former police officer, Walter Dale, the chief investigator of the Vigilance Detective Agency. From time to time Van Ginhoven was engaged in protection or other duties away from London and when this happened his colleague, DS Charles Jane, maintained the liaison.

The MI5 investigation continued and Lakey was approached by them and agreed to co-operate under the pseudonym 'Albert Allen'. He caused considerable consternation when he revealed that the two Special Branch officers had supplied Ewer with the addresses of the Secret Intelligence Service in Adam Street and Melbury Road, and the MI5 office at 35 Cromwell Road, which enabled the members of the Vigilance Detective Agency to identify and follow officers of those services. The Agency operations on behalf of Ewer, who was supplying information to the Russians, were described in a diary kept by Walter Dale and included:

(i) To observe the offices of British intelligence, their staff, and persons with whom they were in contact.

(ii) To observe Russians resident in this country who were looked upon with suspicion by the Soviets.

(iii) To investigate prominent political or social personages about whom the Soviet government required information and

(iv) To make sure that Ewer and others were not observed or shadowed by MI5 or the police.

Lakey at first did not name van Ginhoven or Jane, but after they were detained he confirmed their involvement. He alleged that they had supplied information from the Special Branch registry, port circulation lists, intercept warrants, and acquired other information of interest to the Russians and to the Communist Party, as and when required. He said he had been told the officers gained access to the registry at night, as van Ginhoven often worked late on translations. Lakey claimed DS Jane had warned Rose Edwardes, another employee of the detective agency, about an impending raid on the Communist Party's King Street office in 1924, but apparently Jane was so guarded on the telephone that Edwardes failed to grasp the significance of the message, and didn't pass the warning on.[3]

Van Ginhoven, Jane and Dale were arrested on 11 April 1929. Dale's office was searched and his diary seized. This revealed that he had acted as an intelligence agent under Ewer's directions between January 1922 and May 1927 and as a 'cut out' between Ewer and the Special Branch officers until his arrest in 1929. *The Times* reported that there was a high-level investigation before they were arrested and the case was referred to the Attorney General for his fiat, which he declined to issue. The information against them provided by Lakey, initially, was largely hearsay and whether it would have been admitted as evidence in court is a matter for conjecture. Van Ginhoven and Jane appeared before a disciplinary board on 2 May 1929, presided over by the Deputy Commissioner Rear Admiral Sir Charles Royds (a hero of Scott's *Discovery* Expedition). They were found guilty. No further action was taken against Dale. Details of the hearing were made public in a report appearing in *The Times* the following day:

> The two Special Branch officers of Scotland Yard who were suspended from duty some time ago while inquiries were being made into allegations against them appeared before a Disciplinary Board at Scotland Yard

3   TNA KV 2/990

yesterday. At the time the allegations were made Scotland Yard, in an official statement, said that the matter concerned 'internal discipline', and was associated with the leakage of information from the Yard. Rear-Admiral C. W. Royds, Assistant Commissioner [sic], presided over the board. At the conclusion of the sitting last night, it was stated that two officers of the Special Political Branch at Scotland Yard were dismissed the force. An official statement issued by Scotland Yard last night was as follows: Reasons for the dismissal of Inspector [van] Ginhoven are:

(1) Breach of confidence. Without proper authority communicating to an unauthorised person matters connected with the force – namely, communicating to W. E. Dale, a dismissed police officer, information contained in Special Branch records, such information being found in a diary in Dale's possession;

(2) falsehood or prevarication. Wilfully or negligently making an inaccurate statement in an official CID diary – namely, making the following entry in his diary for 3 April 1929: 'Then to office ... until 3 p.m., thus engaged till 5 p.m.,' whereas he was in the said W. E. Dale's company at 19 Walbrook from approximately 3.40 p.m. to 4 p.m. that day.

(3) Neglect of duty. Failing to report a matter which it was his duty to report – namely, failing to enter in his official CID diary dates and times of his meetings with an informant and to report any information obtained from him.

Reasons for dismissal of Sergeant Jane are:

(1) Breach of confidence. Identical with No. 1 in Ginhoven's case;

(2) Neglect of duty. Failing to make any entry in his official diary of his meeting with an informant in the City on 21 March 1929.

When it first came to the notice of the Yard authorities that information
had been disclosed, the Commissioner (Lord Byng) was informed, and
immediately a special conference was called. The matter was regarded as
being of such urgency that senior officers of the force met late one night,
and did not complete their deliberations until early the following morning. Following this, two officers were suspended and inquiries have been
in progress. It is understood that a considerable amount of evidence was
placed before the Disciplinary Board yesterday.[4]

There can be little doubt that the activities of the two officers damaged the reputation of the Branch and were instrumental in the appointment of MI5 in 1931
as the lead organisation in countering espionage and subversion.

---

4   *The Times*, 3 May 1929

CHAPTER THIRTEEN

SEDITION, THE INVERGORDON MUTINY AND ELIAS VERSUS PASSMORE

T HE SPECIAL BRANCH agenda was nothing if not varied. There follow just three examples of the type of work that the Branch was frequently called upon to deal with, generally with a successful outcome.

THE INVERGORDON MUTINY

D uring the economic crisis of September 1931, the national government, without due consideration of the fairness and possible effects, cut the pay of the Royal Navy. The result: the ratings of the Home Fleet at Invergordon on the Cromarty Firth held a meeting at the local naval canteen and refused to sail until the matter was resolved. Technically it was mutinous conduct; Len Wincott from HMS *Norfolk* addressed the meeting and afterwards prepared a petition which read: 'We the loyal subjects of His Majesty the King, do hereby present to my lords the Commissioners of the Admiralty our representative, to implore them to amend the drastic cuts in pay which have been inflicted on the lowest paid men of the lower deck…'

Admiralty policy in regard to mutiny was to persuade the sailors back to work by promising concessions, and delaying the punishment of the ringleaders until discipline was restored. After two days the Admiralty agreed to review the position and the crews returned to their ships. Mistaking lower-deck reaction for Bolshevism, the Naval Intelligence Department and the Security Service informed the Cabinet that the position was grave, that 'the mutiny' was organised and further trouble could be expected when some of the ships reached Portsmouth on 22 September. This turned out to be totally untrue. Publicity concerning the Fleet's action alerted the CPGB to the possibilities of the exploitation of the discontent and they hurriedly dispatched their agents to the principal naval ports, Devonport, Portsmouth, Chatham and Sheerness.

The *Daily Worker* was taken by surprise, since 'the mutiny' was not communist-inspired, and on 17 September intimated that strikes were likely to occur throughout the navy. The next day it published the petition from HMS *Norfolk* and suggested that when the ships reached their home ports the crews should be greeted by workers and demand answers to the questions raised at Invergordon. It called for all sections of the armed forces to rally round the slogan: 'Not a penny off the pay'. On 21 September the newspaper reported interviews with sailors from HMS *Valiant* and HMS *Repulse*, which had arrived at Sheerness. Special Branch officers raided the *Daily Worker* offices the next day and seized documents; the premises of the Utopia Press, the paper's printers, were also raided and the printer H. T. Wilkinson arrested and charged with incitement to mutiny.[1]

The Royal Navy had alerted its crews to the possibility of communist exploitation by the time Able Seaman Bateman from HMS *Horizon*, recently returned from Invergordon to Portsmouth, went into a café on the Hard to purchase his supper and found himself engaged in conversation by a civilian. The stranger, who introduced himself as 'Shorty' Hutchings, told Bateman he was a journalist and was seeking information about the mutiny at Invergordon. Bateman, who

1   Andrew, *The Defence of the Realm*, pp. 163–4; and contemporaneous issues of *The Times*

knew nothing of the affair, reported the approach to senior officers and it was agreed that Hutchings should meet a 'telegraphist named Bousefield' who knew more about the matter. Who precisely Bousefield was is not entirely clear, but he was certainly acting under the instructions of naval officers. Hutchings told Bousefield that he was a freelance writer but admitted he was a member of the Communist Party and was hoping to see the Fleet come out on strike. He suggested that they should arrange a small meeting at the Sailors' Rest to carry their propaganda to other sailors. He said to Bousefield: 'You are a telegraphist, and in Russia they want specialists like you. I will see that you get a job in Russia and get very well paid for it. You will be very well looked after.'

'That's all very well,' said Bousefield, 'but what about the time I am serving in prison? And what about my wife?'

It was agreed that if Hutchings could obtain sanction for the payment of £100 he would send Bousefield a telegram saying that his mother was ill.

Two days later Bousefield received the telegram and with his commanding officer's approval met Hutchings's superiors at a house in Hampstead, where he was introduced to William Shepherd, an unemployed woodworker who lived in Camden Road. It was agreed that the £100 should be paid to Bousefield's wife at the rate of £2 per week for twelve months. Bousefield was asked to draft a pamphlet suitable for distribution among the sailors, which would be collected by a third man. This was another communist, George Allison, a trade union organiser, who met Bateman and Bousefield in Portsmouth and collected the draft. He promised to have 15,000 copies printed, to be distributed among other men in the Fleet. Allison then returned to London and on the following morning Special Branch officers followed him to the headquarters of the Communist Party in King Street. Two days later he returned to Portsmouth, met the two sailors in a public house, and was arrested by the Portsmouth Police.

Meanwhile, DI Waldram of Special Branch arrested Shepherd in Camden Town. Hutchings had disappeared but it was learned that he had gone to an address in Southend. Southend Police went to the address and arrested a man there named Hutchings. He was taken to New Scotland Yard, where he was handed over to an escort from Portsmouth. When he was about to be charged by the Portsmouth Police, he disclosed that 'Shorty' Hutchings was his brother, who had now disappeared. Subsequently it was learned that he had fled to Russia. Allison and Shepherd were committed for trial, charged with maliciously endeavouring to seduce sailors serving in His Majesty's Navy from their allegiance to the King and to induce them to commit acts of mutiny. In November 1931, at Winchester Assizes, Allison was sentenced to three years' imprisonment and Shepherd to twenty months' hard labour. In 1932 Hutchings returned from Russia. He attempted to surrender to the Special Branch officer at Harwich and was surprised to hear that the police no longer wanted him. In the aftermath of the Invergordon Mutiny, thirty-six ratings alleged to be ringleaders were discharged from the Royal Navy. Two of them, Len Wincott and Fred Copeman, later joined the Communist Party.[2]

ELIAS VERSUS PASSMORE

Kitchener refers to marches organised by the National Unemployed Workers' Union (NUWU) and in particular to one held on 30 October 1932, demanding the abolition of the means test. Marchers from Scotland, Wales, Tyneside and Lancashire, together with groups from London and the Home Counties, converged on Hyde Park, where at Speakers' Corner there was trouble resulting in some eighty people being injured. The demonstration then marched on to Trafalgar Square. The square was packed and speakers addressed the marchers from three sides of the plinth. DS Oliver, a Special Branch shorthand writer, took notes.

The national organiser of the NUWM, Wal Hannington, and the main speaker, said in his speech:

---

2   Kitchener, *The Memoirs of an Old Detective*, pp. 127–31

A word to the policemen at this moment. Who are the police? They are drawn from the ranks of the working class. They organise their Blackleg Police Force, ready to take the jobs of the men in uniform if these men [pointing to the regular policemen there on duty] do as they did in 1919. We ask the policemen to understand that what we have marched for is in their interests. These men who are on point duty today – these Specials – should be spurned by the men. There is nothing meaner, there is nothing fouler than those who stand on point duty ready to take the place of the uniformed men...

The Trafalgar Square meeting passed off fairly quietly, but during the proceedings it was announced that a further demonstration would be held at the Houses of Parliament on the following Tuesday when, one of the speakers implied, there might be violence:

I want to advise every London unemployed and employed worker who comes on that demonstration on Tuesday to come prepared to meet the batons of the police and all the forces that are to be put against them. I want you to come into the struggle on Tuesday night, to bring this fight to its logical conclusion and force this government to its knees.

In view of this and the violence at Speakers' Corner, it was decided to forestall any further disorder with a pre-emptive strike – Wal Hannington was arrested for unlawfully attempting to cause disaffection among members of the Metropolitan Police Force. The arrest was carried out by DI Kitchener at the headquarters of the NUWM in Great Russell Street, Bloomsbury, where a thorough search of the offices was made. The following week Hannington was sentenced to three months' imprisonment.[3]

During the search of the NUWM premises, letters written from Profitern

---

3   Ibid., pp. 130–37

in Moscow by the chairman of the NUWM, Sidney Job Elias, to Hannington, were found. These left no doubt that Profitern was inciting disorder. A passage from one of the letters read: 'On previous marches the end of the march meant the end of agitation. Under the favourable conditions existing today to allow such would be criminal and tantamount to a failure to understand the fighting mood of the masses.'

The papers were referred to the Director of Public Prosecutions, who authorised DIs Passmore and Kitchener to arrest Elias, now in London, and charge him 'that in September 1932, you did unlawfully solicit and incite Emrhys Llewelyn and Walter Hannington, to cause discontent, disaffection and ill-will between different classes of His Majesty's subjects, and to create public disturbance against the peace'.

At the Central Criminal Court on 15 November 1932, he was found guilty and sentenced to two years' imprisonment. The case, however, did not end there. A writ was issued in the High Court in April 1933 against the Commissioner and the Receiver of the Metropolitan Police, Inspectors Passmore and Kitchener, in the names of Emrhys Glanf Llewellyn, George James and Walter Hannington. The action was to claim damages for alleged trespass on the premises and the seizure and detention of the documents which were taken away for examination.

The case centred on the right of police to search the premises where the arrest of Hannington took place. The search was held to be lawful and it was ruled that the exhibits used at the trial of Elias had been lawfully seized, but that this did not apply to other documents that had been taken away and afterwards returned because they were not the subject of proceedings. The judge said the police were not actuated by improper motives in seizing them and there was no evidence that the plaintiffs had suffered any special damages. Judgment was given for the plaintiffs with £20 damages for the trespass, and £10 for the detention of the documents used in the case against Elias and which had been retained by the police after the case was completed. An order was made for their return and the plaintiffs were awarded costs. The letters Elias had written, and were held by the trial court to be seditious, were thus ordered to be returned to him although he was still serving his two years' imprisonment.[4]

4   Ibid., p. 137

CHAPTER FOURTEEN

THE BUSINESS OF INFORMING: HENRI LE CARON, WILLIAM FOSTER WATSON AND THE *MORNING POST*

S PECIAL BRANCH'S SOURCES of information have always been many and various. Some it controlled itself, others were acquired through other police forces, MI5, MI6, newspapers and groups opposed to the target organisations. Information derived from agencies over which there was no control was sometimes problematic.

Much reliance was placed on the secret interception of communications and while officers regularly covered public meetings it was also necessary to use informants to penetrate the more secretive aspects of subversive organisations, in order to establish the 'who, what, why, when, where and how' of their activities and to assess their character by what they did, what they said, and what other people said about them. The honesty of these agents was paramount and it was imperative that they should not provoke the activities they reported.

It wasn't only Munro who had an aversion to informants, with their affinity with *agents provocateurs*. Anything resembling the methods employed by the

Irish and Continental police to obtain evidence through such means was anathema, both to the British public and to many of the police hierarchy (see p. 8). The cases outlined below illustrate not only the asset of a good informant, but also the liability of a bad one.

HENRI LE CARON

Henri Le Caron, who provided his handler, Robert Anderson, with a wealth of invaluable intelligence, was a remarkable man. Born Thomas Beach in Colchester on 26 September 1841, of English parents, he left home at the age of thirteen and settled in France for some years before emigrating to the United States, where he enlisted in the Northern Army and later joined the veterans' organisation, the Grand Army of the Republic. He relinquished his British citizenship and changed his name to Le Caron 'to avoid worrying his parents'.[1] While serving in the army, he became friendly with a prominent Fenian, who told him in confidence in 1865 of Fenian conspiracies against the British. Le Caron, who still retained his loyalty to Britain, passed the information to his father, who relayed it to his MP and thence to the Home Secretary. Le Caron was requested to pass on any further information which might come his way and so began his 'career' as an informant; it ended in 1889 when he voluntarily gave evidence before a Special Commission convened to enquire into allegations made in the *Times* newspaper that Charles Parnell had been implicated in Fenian malpractices. His undercover role exposed, he was provided with Special Branch protection until his death, for without it he would obviously have been a sitting duck for the Fenians, who would have loved to (in their own picturesque language cited by Sweeney) 'put his lights out'.[2]

---

1   Le Caron, *Twenty-Five Years in the Secret Service* (Wakefield: EP Publishing, 1972), pp. 1, 10, 13

2   Sweeney, *At Scotland Yard*, p. 150

Le Caron possessed that rare commodity in informants: patriotism, which so many of Jenkinson's spies lacked. The majority of them – Corydon, Millen, 'Red Jim' MacDermott and many others – supplied the government with information as and when it suited them and although much of it was valuable, it could never be relied upon as the truth. Le Caron, on the other hand, never knowingly misled his handler.

WILLIAM FOSTER WATSON

The same glowing terms of commendation could never have been applied to William Foster Watson, who revealed his role as a police informant in the course of a libel action he brought against the Duke of Northumberland and Howell Gwynne, the editor of the *Morning Post*, in 1921. The alleged libel was contained in an article written by the Duke, which was published in Gwynne's newspaper on 5 August 1921, and stated, among other things, that on his own admission Watson had 'acted as a spy for the government in Bolshevik circles'.

In Court, Watson denied having been a spy but admitted under cross examination that in 1918 he had assisted the CID, who had approached him for information regarding the Hands Off Russia Movement. He claimed to have been paid £3 a week for a weekly report on fourteen occasions. When asked by the judge whether his reports were true or not, he replied that they were not always true and some were taken from newspaper articles. He objected to being labelled a spy because from the start he had intended to supply false information. Later in the same year Special Branch officers, unaware of his arrangement with the CID, also started paying him £3 a week for information. When they became aware of his duplicity they stopped paying him and Chief Inspector McBrien took him down an alley and threatened to beat him (he said). In fact it was the Special Branch who had their noses bloodied, having paid out money for worthless information.

THE *MORNING POST*

D uring World War One the Special Branch received domestic intelligence concerning industrial relations from a number of right-wing organisations and the liaison continued after the war. One such source was the British Empire Union (formerly the anti-German Union), which was anti-communist and anti-Semitic. In 1918 the BEU claimed to have 10,000 members. It feared that the Labour Party, which was gradually gaining strength, would Bolshevise Britain. President of the BEU was Lady Bathurst, who was also one of the owners of the *Morning Post*, and Sir George Makgill was its secretary. The *Morning Post* frequently acted as a mouthpiece for the BEU.

Makgill built up an active intelligence organisation, the Industrial Intelligence Bureau, which provided much information concerning communist penetration of the trade unions, strikes and subversive activities, which the Secret Services (MI5 and Special Branch) reported to the Cabinet. A number of Makgill's people were subsequently employed in MI5 and by SIS. These included a group known as the 'Casuals', a controversial section whose sometimes illegal activities led to conflict between Sir Wyndham Childs and Sir Hugh Sinclair, head of SIS.[3] One of their number contended that the Branch sometimes supplied the BEU with funds and officers to carry out enquiries.

There was a common interest shared by such agencies, by right-wing newspapers and official intelligence organisations (including Special Branch) and there is little doubt that information was exchanged between them. The CPGB certainly thought so. On 25 April 1925 an article appeared in its official organ, the *Weekly Worker*, alleging that 'Scotland Yard' had obtained a copy of a privately circulated Communist Party Commission's report, and inferred that this had been passed on to the *Morning Post*. The article concluded: 'Indications of an intimate association between the *Morning Post* and the political secret

---

3   Gill Bennett, *Churchill's Man of Mystery: Desmond Morton and the World of Intelligence* (London: Routledge, 2007), pp. 106, 117, 127–34

service have long been evident to observant people [now] there is no longer a mere suspicion that the Special Branch provides reports for the *Morning Post*; the evidence is plain to see.'

The police, particularly Special Branch, have always been wary of relationships with the press, and their obvious connections with Makgill's organisation and its voice, the *Morning Post* were, to say the least, inadvisable. It is debatable whether the undoubtedly good information derived from these sources compensated for the stain that such associations left on the Branch's reputation.

CHAPTER FIFTEEN

FASCISM

FASCISM IS A political ideology that has three principal elements: ethnic-nationalism, totalitarianism (i.e. state control of social life) and messianic leadership.

This concept of fascism had been developing in Italy well before World War One but the cessation of hostilities saw the fascists' paramilitary leadership adopt a more aggressive policy. In 1922 the King, Victor Emmanuel III, appointed Benito Mussolini as Prime Minister. Without a majority in Parliament, he succeeded in forming a coalition government and proceeded to stamp his authority on the country with repressive domestic measures coupled with an aggressive foreign policy.

THE BRITISH FASCISTI

In Britain, early fascism gained momentum in the mid-1920s but, unlike the Italian version, as a counter-revolutionary rather than a revolutionary force. The British Fascisti (BF), the first fascist party in Britain, was ultra-conservative. It did not advocate change of government by revolution, was not overtly anti-Semitic and was intensely patriotic. Although the Special Branch monitored the movement as a paramilitary organisation that might threaten public order, it did not consider it subversive. Certainly MI5 did not regard it as such; indeed, according to Andrew, 'until 1933, MI5 "paid practically no attention" to Nazism – nor did Whitehall expect that it should'.[1]

BF's founder, Rotha Lintorn-Orman, was brought up with those values that fashioned the imperialist and anti-socialist attitudes of sections of the English middle class. She was a feminist with a strong sense of patriotic duty. She was opposed to trade unionism, and socialism, which she considered was endangering the British way of life. Although she admired Mussolini, she appeared to be unaware of the violence used by the Fascists in Italy against communists and socialists opposed to their regime.

Special Branch regarded the friction between BF and left-wing activists as a possible threat to public order and in 1923 reported to the Cabinet:

> On 7 October about 500 people attended the inaugural meeting of the London Branch of the British Fascisti. Miss Bennett, a former suffragette, opened the meeting but she and two subsequent speakers were interrupted to such an extent by extremists that the meeting became pandemonium and ended with the singing (by the opposing factions) of the National Anthem and 'The Red Flag'.[2]

By the end of 1924, with hundreds of new recruits enrolling each week, the British Fascisti opened an office at 71 Elm Park Gardens, London, SW10. In 1926 they were reliably reported to boast a membership of 185,000.[3]

Once the movement was up and running, Lintorn-Orman surrendered the leadership to Brigadier R. B. D. Blakeney, who became President of the Grand Council. Lintorn-Orman assumed the role of president of the women's units.

1   Andrew, *The Defence of the Realm*, p. 188

2   Special Branch report 226 of 11 October 1923, TNA CAB/24/162, p. 9

3   Report by Maxwell Knight, an agent – later an employee – of the Security Service, dated 22 August 1933. TNA KV 4/331

The Grand Council included some very senior former military officers and the BF could hardly be described as a subversive force. Other active members included Arnold Leese and Henry Simpson, the first fascists to be elected, in 1924, to a local council, and William Joyce, executed for treason at the end of the Second World War. Maxwell Knight, who later became a valued member of the Security Service, joined the movement in 1924 at the request of the Service, for whom he claimed to have served as an agent until 1930.[4]

Although (or maybe because) Blakeney was determined to build the organisation into an effective and disciplined body, membership began to decline and by 1930 was virtually moribund. Members continued to leave and by 1934 the movement, now called the British Fascists Ltd., was also in serious financial trouble. Special Branch continued to maintain a watching brief on its activities and in July reported that its leader, Henry Christopher Bruce Wilson, had met Oswald Mosley at the Grosvenor Hotel to discuss a possible merger of the BF with the British Union of Fascists (BUF), but Lintorn-Orman, still a force in the organisation, albeit a spent one, vetoed the move.[5]

As with many extreme right-wing organisations, break-away groups formed, and by the time of Lintorn-Orman's death in 1935, the BF had been consigned to history, amidst rumours that its founder was addicted to drugs and alcohol, which caused her death, and that she had formed a lesbian relationship, leading to a breach between herself and her mother.[6]

THE IMPERIAL FASCIST LEAGUE

One of the several fascist groups that took its place was the Imperial Fascist League, set up in 1929 by Arnold Leese, a veterinary surgeon from

---

4   L. Harrison Matthews and Maxwell Knight, *The Senses of Animals* (London: Methuen, 1963), p. 13

5   Special Branch report, dated 16 July 1934. TNA HO 144/20142, pp. 110–11.

6   Stephen Dorril, *Blackshirt: Sir Oswald Mosley and British Fascism* (London: Penguin, 2007), p. 198

Stamford in Lincolnshire. Leese, a eugenicist and an anti-Semite, was a disillusioned member of the BF. He was prosecuted for seditious libel when he wrote
that the Jews engaged in the ritual murder of Christians, and was imprisoned
for six months when he refused to pay the fine imposed by the court. On his
release he campaigned against war with Germany. The Imperial Fascist League
tended to be, as Roger Eatwell has pointed out, 'a talking shop for cranks',[7] and
was of little interest to Special Branch.

SIR OSWALD MOSLEY AND THE
BRITISH UNION OF FASCISTS

The same could not be said of the British Union of Fascists (BUF) and its
leader, Sir Oswald Mosley, who posed a problem, not only to the Special
Branch, but to the British Police in general for many years to come.

Oswald Mosley, born 16 November 1896, came from an aristocratic family
of landowners and was distantly related to HM Queen Elizabeth. He entered
Parliament in 1918 as the Conservative MP for Harrow, a seat he held until 1924
(the last two years as an Independent). He switched his allegiance in 1924 and
joined the Labour Party as well as the Independent Labour Party, winning the
Smethwick seat for Labour in a 1926 by-election.

Yet again his restless temperament prompted him to seek new political pas-
tures and in 1931 he left the Labour Party to create his own movement, the New
Party, which only survived for one year (1931–32). However, during its short life
Mosley demonstrated quite clearly that he had now embraced the fascist cause
and henceforth he deployed his undoubted charisma and powers of oratory to
creating a viable British fascist movement.

In 1932 he travelled to Italy and studied first-hand the activities of Mussolini and his fellow Fascists; on his return later that year, he set about uniting the

---

7   Roger Eatwell, *Fascism: A History* (London: Chatto & Windus, 1995), p. 179

various fascist factions in Britain and formed the BUF. MI5 continued to dis-
count fascism as a threat to the country's security and it was not until June 1934
that they saw fit to send the first of a series of reports to the Home Office on
'The Fascist Movement in the United Kingdom'.

But the Special Branch was well aware of the fascist threat – to public order
– and its officers were kept busy supplying their uniformed colleagues with
intelligence regarding Mosley's intentions; reporting to the Home Office on the
frequent violent confrontations between the BUF and its communist and Jewish
opponents and taking shorthand notes of the inflammatory speeches that were a
feature of BUF meetings. The merging of Jewish and communist elements that
characterised these hostile clashes is explained by Henry Srebrnik: 'In the face
of these [fascist] and other provocations it is not surprising that Jews increasingly regarded the Communist Party as their only form of self-defence. Disgusted
with both the Labour Party and the Irish they turned to the only Party in which
they constituted an ethnic majority.'[8]

It was a particularly unruly BUF rally held at Olympia on 7 June 1934 that
finally convinced MI5 of the threat they posed. Mosley, the sole speaker, was
constantly heckled by the hostile groups which were present in large numbers
despite the fascists' stringent security precautions. When the hardline fascist
stewards, commonly referred to as 'Blackshirts' (on account of their black uniforms), moved in to eject the hecklers, widespread brawling ensued and the
meeting developed into chaos.

Nineteen men and two women appeared at West London Police Court the
following day, charged with a variety of offences, including obstructing police,
possession of offensive weapons, insulting words and malicious damage. Sentences ranging from one month's imprisonment for possession of an offensive
weapon, to a fine of ten shillings for using insulting words and behaviour, were
imposed.[9]

---

8   Henry Felix Srebrnik, *London Jews and British Communism* (Ilford: Vallentine Mitchell, 1995), pp. 32–4
9   *The Times*, 9 June 1934

MI5, now fully alert to the threat posed by Mosley and his henchmen, sent a second bulletin to the Home Office drawing attention to the recent growth of the party.[10] This report drew heavily on information supplied by Special Branch, particularly in a detailed breakdown of the organisation's set-up at their offices at 55 King's Road, Chelsea, including the names of officials, numbers of staff, positions held and salaries.[11]

The adverse publicity he received following the Olympia rally did not deter Mosley from pursuing his policy of staging confrontational meetings and marches, particularly in areas with a predominantly Jewish population. In October 1936, the East End of London witnessed one of the most dramatic exhibitions of racial bigotry ever enacted on its streets up to that time. Subsequently referred to as 'The Battle of Cable Street', this was yet another attempt by Mosley to parade through an area populated predominantly by Jews, specifically to provoke his sworn enemies, the extreme left. His plan was for four separate contingents of Blackshirts to march to meetings in Shoreditch, Stepney, Bethnal Green and Limehouse, but the anti-fascists pre-empted the Blackshirts' intentions by blocking their path with a barricade in Cable Street. Scuffles ensued between the two factions and with the police; consequently the Metropolitan Police Commissioner, Sir Philip Game, banned the march from proceeding and the fascist demonstrators were diverted to the Embankment.

Special Branch reported to the Home Office that Mosley's opponents mounted what was 'undoubtedly the largest anti-fascist demonstration yet seen in London' and the government feared that even worse violence would occur if Mosley was allowed to pursue his devious campaign unchecked.[12] It was as a direct result of this confrontation that a Public Order Bill was hastily passed by Parliament (the Public Order Act, 1936). Among other things it prohibited the wearing of political uniforms, which effectively put an end to the life of the Blackshirts, many of

---

10   TNA HO 144/20142, ff. 110 et seq.

11   Special Branch report, dated 18 July 1934. TNA HO 144/20142, ff. 10–22

12   Andrew, *The Defence of the Realm*, p. 194

whom left the movement. Nevertheless the BUF continued to disturb the peace in the East End of London with their late-night marches, usually accompanied by drummers. Tension was again mounting, with escalating violence displayed on both sides. The local police commander feared that the situation was likely to get out of control. He proposed that demonstrations in the area should be prohibited, but the Commissioner, with Home Office approval, compromised by agreeing to a ban on evening gatherings.[13]

As war with Germany inexorably approached, the BUF adopted a lower profile and public opinion of Mosley became noticeably more hostile. On 23 May 1940 he was detained under Section 18B of the Defence Regulations, soon to be joined by hundreds of his erstwhile supporters; later the same year the BUF was proscribed and ceased to be a viable organisation. It was Special Branch who had the doubtful distinction of effecting the detentions.

THE RIGHT CLUB

Some of the BUF members joined the Right Club, which had been formed in 1939 by Archibald Ramsay, a Scottish Conservative MP. This organisation, comprising some 235 members, was, like the BUF, extremely anti-Semitic and pro-German but, unlike Mosley's group, not in favour of public confrontations with its enemies. As its name implies, the club was decidedly right wing and its activities were cloaked in secrecy; its members were reported to be in favour of 'appeasement'.[14]

Although the club did not present the police with public order problems, it attracted the attention of Special Branch and the Security Service on account of the treasonable activities of some of its members. According to Christopher

---

13   Letter from Home Secretary to Commissioner, dated 23 April 1937. TNA MEPO 2/3110

14   Richard Griffiths, *Patriotism Perverted: Captain Ramsay, the Right Club and British Anti-Semitism, 1939–1940* (London: Constable, 1998); Robin Saikia (ed.), *The Red Book: The Membership List of the Right Club, 1939* (London: Foxley Books, 2010) and Andrew, *The Defence of the Realm*, p. 224

Andrew, three MI5 agents had penetrated the Right Club and it was information from one of these, Joan Miller, codenamed 'M'/'Y', that led to the arrest
and subsequent conviction of one of the club's members, Anna Wolkoff, and
her confederate, Tyler Kent, an American employed as a cipher clerk at the US
embassy in London. On 7 November 1940 Wolkoff was sentenced to ten years'
imprisonment and Kent to seven years for offences under the Official Secrets
Act. Ramsay was not charged with any specific criminal offence but was interned
under Defence Regulation 18B, as were a number of other members. Special
Branch was involved in the prosecutions. Another member, William Joyce, better known as Lord Haw Haw, was later to be convicted and executed for treason
– an event which will be described later (see pp. 225–6).[15]

THE LINK AND ANGLO-GERMAN FELLOWSHIP

These two associations initially attracted the attention of Special Branch after
their foundation in 1935 and 1937 respectively, but were not considered to
pose a threat either to security or to public order.

THE NORDIC LEAGUE

In the years leading up to the war, the only domestic fascist organisation to
arouse the interest of Special Branch apart from those mentioned above was
the Nordic League. A Special Branch report to the Home Office in 1939 indicated that the 'League' had been established at the end of 1937 by a group of
extreme anti-Semitic individuals who had close ties with other fascist groups,
such as the Imperial Fascist League and the National Socialist League. Initially
the group held meetings behind closed doors at which they aired their extreme

---

15   Andrew, *Defence of the Realm*, pp. 224–2

fascist and pro-Nazi views. In 1939 they held a number of public meetings and reports of these, in addition to details of their closed meetings, were regularly sent by Special Branch to the Home Office and MI5.[16] But by October 1939, Albert Canning, head of Special Branch, who now held the rank of Chief Constable, was able to report to the Home Office that the Nordic League 'has to all intents and purpose ceased to function'.[17]

THE NATIONAL-SOZIALISTISCHE DEUTSCHE ARBEITERPARTEI (NSDAP) AND OTHER NAZI ACTIVITY IN ENGLAND

In 1930, when the Nazi Party became, for the first time, the second largest group in the German Parliament, it sent an official correspondent to London to write articles for its newspaper, *Völkischer Beobachter*. Hans Wilhelm Thost's mission was three-fold – to describe what was 'really going on in Britain; to promote peace between the two nations and to secure justice for the fatherland.'[18] The Foreign Office saw no reason to interfere with his activities.

In 1931 the London 'Ortsgruppe' (London Nazi group) was founded, with Thost the leader. Gatherings of a social nature were initially held by the group in a Soho café, but from January 1932, meetings became more formal and were held in private rooms – there were now about fifty members and during the next year this number doubled. By 1933 a Special Branch detective sergeant, William East, a fluent German speaker, had been accepted as a 'sympathetic observer' and sent regular reports to the Home and Foreign Offices on the Nazis' activities in London. Later, DI Hubert Morse was also accepted at the German meetings and the two officers' detailed and well-written accounts satisfied the authorities

---

16   Special Branch reports, dated 23 May 1939 et seq. TNA HO 144/22454

17   Report from Canning to Home Office, dated October 1939. TNA HO 144/22454

18   James J. Barnes and Patience B. Barnes, *Nazis in Pre-War London 1930–1939: The Fate and Role of German Party Members and British Sympathizers* (Brighton: Sussex Academic Press, 2005), p. 2

that the Germans were not using their 'Ortsgruppe' meetings to plan illegal activities in this country. What their reports did demonstrate, however, was the intensely patriotic nature of the meetings and the Nazis' fervent desire not to upset their hosts, the British; the following extracts from an early contribution by Sergeant East illustrate this: 'British politics were to be avoided, especially such questions as the political situation in India and Ireland' and 'They were to be courteous in all things as the new Germany would be judged by its representatives in this country.'

Later in the same report, East describes the proceedings, intensely nationalistic in tone, which invariably followed the same pattern. Both the Foreign and Home Offices received copies of East's work, which was also forwarded to the British embassy in Berlin minuted 'a clever feat of Sergeant East to be present at this meeting'.[19]

It was not until May 1935 that MI5 sent their first report on the NSDAP to the Foreign Office although, in an exchange of memoranda between MI5, the Prime Minister and the Foreign Office, it became clear that by 1937 'only MI5 was keeping surveillance on the Nazis'.[20]

The Nazis in London were still receiving attention from Special Branch, however. In 1938, the Home Office received a number of reports of interference by German embassy officials with 'the liberty of action' of individual Germans and Austrians living here. At the request of the Home Office, Special Branch officers interviewed a number of German and Austrian nationals, which revealed that the German embassy's action did not warrant intervention by the British authorities.[21]

---

19   Special Branch report of a Nazi meeting at 102 Westbourne Terrace, W2, dated 9 November 1933. TNA FO 371/16751 C10434, ff. 67–71

20   Barnes and Barnes, *Nazis in Pre-War London 1930–1939*, p. 187

21   TNA FO 371/12607, ff. 127 et seq.

CHAPTER SIXTEEN

THE 1939–40 IRA BOMBING CAMPAIGN

THE ANGLO-IRISH WAR was followed by a civil war when the IRA
refused to accept the terms of the Anglo-Irish Treaty of 1921; this campaign ended with the defeat of the IRA by the Cosgrave government
forces.

There ensued several years of political infighting in Ireland from which
the former republican leader Éamon de Valera and his new party, Fianna Fáil,
emerged triumphant, with its opposition coming from another new group,
Fine Gael. De Valera abolished the oath of allegiance and introduced a new
constitution, which claimed sovereignty over the whole island of Ireland.
The United Kingdom government reacted swiftly to these developments by
assuring the government of Northern Ireland that there would be no constitutional change in the province without the consent of a majority of its
people. Thus Britain ensured that the sectarian province would endure and
that reunification of Ireland would remain an increasingly unlikely prospect
for the foreseeable future.

In 1935 and 1936, Ireland was shocked by three brutal murders committed by
the IRA and once again the organisation was declared illegal; this drove the IRA

underground, but it was not destroyed.[1] The lawyer, Sean McBride, became the IRA's new chief of staff. He was opposed to violence and caused Sean Russell, a leading exponent of physical force, to be dismissed from the organisation for misappropriation of funds. McBride tried to steer the IRA towards acceptance of the constitutional status quo, but Russell, with the help and support of J.J. McGarrity, a Tyrone-born American businessman, managed to depose him as chief of staff and take his place. McGarrity had emigrated to the USA in 1892 at the age of eighteen. From 1893 until his death in 1940 he was a leading member of Clan na Gael and founded the republican newspaper the *Irish Press*; for many years after his death the IRA issued its communiqués over his signature. Russell had a long record of involvement at the top level with the IRA and, with him at the helm and McGarrity as financier, the way became clear for the IRA to mount a bombing campaign in England.[2]

THE SABOTAGE PLAN[3]

Russell persuaded Jim O'Donovan, a veteran republican, to draft a plan to sabotage British industry to such an extent that sovereignty would be surrendered to Northern Ireland. Within a matter of weeks he produced the 'Sabotage Plan' (the 'S Plan'), which was tactically sophisticated but strategically and politically naive, and far too ambitious for the resources available to him. O'Donovan believed that, to be successful, the guerrilla campaign should be carried out under cover of darkness in the moonless period from October to November 1938. He also thought that, from a propaganda perspective, it would be most advantageous to commence when no other major conflict was attracting the public's attention.

---

1   Lyons, *Ireland Since the Famine*, p. 533

2   Ian Adams, *The Sabotage Plan* (Titchfield: Spiker Publications, 2011), p. 11

3   A much fuller account of the 'Sabotage Plan' is contained in Ian Adams's *The Sabotage Plan*

Ideally O'Donovan favoured military, air or naval targets but realising that success against such well guarded places would be uncertain, felt that secondary targets such as public services, key industries, commerce, banking, transport and shipping would be more vulnerable. The aim of the plan was to do the maximum physical damage to the British economy while avoiding personal injury to the public, but O'Donovan and Russell seemed blind to the fact that a bombing campaign cannot take place without risking serious injury to and deaths of their own Volunteers and the public at large. They also underestimated the response of the police, which led to many arrests in the first few weeks of the campaign.

Once in control, Russell visited England to purchase explosives, set up 'arms dumps' and safe houses and recruit Volunteers, while O'Donovan trained young Volunteers, including the writer Brendan Behan, at Killiney Castle.[4] Neither Russell nor O'Donovan appeared to contemplate that the majority of English and Irish people living in England would view them as murderous cranks or that the British, Northern Irish and Eire governments might take effective measures to inhibit their activities.

Before the campaign started it received a grievous setback late in 1938 when police in Ilford stopped a car containing three senior officers of the IRA who appeared to be acting suspiciously. A large quantity of potassium chlorate was discovered in the boot of their car. The significance of the discovery was not immediately apparent, but the station officer informed Special Branch, as he was aware that the IRA used explosives made from weed-killer.

Special Branch wasted no time in searching the lodgings in Dagenham occupied by one of those stopped; a notebook was found which contained a number of names and addresses. These included several known activists, including the Commander of the IRA in Britain, Jimmy Joe Reynolds. By the time the significance of the notebook was realised, Reynolds had returned to Ireland on a mission to blow up British customs posts and was killed when a

4 Adams, *The Sabotage Plan*, p. 13

landmine he and two fellow terrorists were priming exploded prematurely. It was reported that Reynold's last words were: 'Stand back, John, James, there's been a wee mistake.'

On 27 December a specially selected team of would-be saboteurs travelled to Britain with false identities: Charles Casey, Seamus McGuinness and Eoin McNamee to London; Rory Campbell and Patrick Fleming to Manchester; Joe Deighan, Gerard Quigley and Michael Clear to Liverpool; Jackie Kearns and Sean Fuller to Birmingham and Peter Walsh to Glasgow.[5] Locally recruited battalions[6] of the IRA were placed on stand-by.

On 13 January an 'ultimatum' signed by Patrick Fleming and addressed to the British Foreign Secretary was delivered to the Foreign Office in London. It read:

> I have the honour to inform you that the government of the Irish Republic, as having its first duty towards the people, the establishment and maintenance of peace and order, herewith demand the withdrawal of all British armed forces stationed in Ireland. These forces are an active incitement to turmoil and civil strife not only in being a symbol of hostile occupation but in their effect and potentialities as an invading army. It is secondly the duty of the government to establish relations of friendship between the Irish and all other peoples. We must insist on the withdrawal of British troops from our country and a declaration from your government renouncing all claims to interfere in our domestic policy. We shall regret if this fundamental feeling is ignored and we are compelled to intervene actively in the military and commercial life of your country as your government is now intervening in ours. The government of the Irish Republic believes that a period of four days is sufficient for

5   T. P. Coogan, *The IRA* (London: Fontana Books, 1980), pp. 164–5. In his book, Coogan relies upon Eoin McNamee for his detailed description of the campaign

6   Note: the use of the word 'battalion' is an Irish exaggeration; battalions in Britain normally contained no more than twenty men

your government to signify its intention in the matter of military evac-
uation and for the issue of your declaration of abdication in respect of
our country. Our government reserves the right of appropriate action
without further notice if on expiration of the period of grace these conditions remain unfulfilled.[7]

Copies of the ultimatum were sent simultaneously to the Prime Ministers of the
United Kingdom, Northern Ireland and Eire, and to the Vatican, the Presidents
of the USA and France. The German and Italian ambassadors were also sent
copies, as were the Scottish and Welsh Nationalist parties and English, American and Irish councils for civil liberty. Walter Tricker, the Foreign Office clerk
who opened the mail, saw no significance in it and, treating it with some levity,
filed it. He was, after all, well used to foreign secretaries receiving all sorts of
ridiculous correspondence from the mentally deranged![8]

Three days later, 1,000 copies of a 'Proclamation of an Irish Republic' were
distributed throughout Ireland. In this the IRA claimed to be the *de jure* government of Ireland; a republic was proclaimed in Ireland and the allegiance of
all 'Irish Subjects' demanded.

True to their word, the IRA commenced their campaign on 16 January. At
5 a.m., at an isolated spot near Alnwick, in Northumberland, a bomb exploded
under a pylon of the electricity grid, causing it to tilt. The bang was heard five
miles away but the electricity supply was not cut off. At 6 a.m. there were three
serious explosions at electricity undertakings in the London area, at Willesden,
Harlesden and Southwark. In Manchester, a bomb placed in a manhole exploded,
killing Albert Ross, a fish porter, who was blown into the air and died instantly.
Another bomb exploded outside a bank in nearby Whitworth Street.[9] The violence of the explosions shook the centre of the city and power and lighting

---

7   *The Times*, 17 January 1939

8   Viscount Templewood, *Nine Troubled Years* (London: Collins, 1954)

9   *The Times*, 17 January 1939

were cut off, dislocating the postal and transport services and bringing work in the city to a standstill.

At a power station at Windle, in Lancashire, a bomb failed to explode and a fingerprint examination revealed the impression of a thumb print on the alarm clock which was used as a timing device. It was later identified as that of Michael Mason, alias Cleary. An unexploded bomb was found in Birmingham in one of the cooling towers of the Hans Hall Power Station and another at Clarence Dock in Liverpool.

In London, when the news broke, Walter Tricker, reflecting on his hasty decision to file the ultimatum received a few days earlier, rapidly retrieved it for dispatch to the Home Office for the information of Special Branch. In the light of the explosions, the Irish port controls were alerted and strengthened and Special Branch officers were put on full alert. A number of experienced CID officers were drafted in to aid the Branch's Irish Squad, virtually doubling it in size. Senior officers were sent to liaise with local police forces in areas of Irish settlement.

Early on the morning of 18 January 1939, Special Branch officers, rein-forced by CID and provincial police officers, raided the homes of many of the people whose names and addresses appeared in the address book found in the Dagenham lodging house. In London, the raids were particularly suc-cessful. Jack Logue, Francis Burns and Daniel Fitzpatrick were arrested by DI Keeble and DS Colin McDougall at an address in Mornington Crescent, Camden Town. They were in possession of eighty-eight sticks of gelignite, detonators and fuse wire. McDougall asked Fitzpatrick about the whereabouts of a weapon from an empty shoulder holster. He replied: 'If I'd had it in bed with me you'd all have been unlucky.' The raiding parties knew that alacrity between a suspect's bedroom door and his bed could be critical. There were no casualties that morning. James Lyons was arrested at his lodgings in Pether-ton Street, Islington, in possession of four drums of aluminium powder. At the home of Lawrence Lyons, DI William Rodgers and DS Coveney found a rifle and twenty rounds of ammunition. DI Newton arrested Brendan Kane at his home in Sutton in possession of a Mauser automatic pistol. DI Frank Bridges found Joseph Casey in possession of a Mauser automatic and seventy rounds of ammunition and a letter from a Gerald Wharton who lived in Camden Road. As a result, DI Thompson and DS Evan Jones raided Wharton's address and recovered a large quantity of potassium chlorate, iron oxide and more than a hundred balloons.

In Manchester, where Superintendent Page was in charge, the raids were also highly successful. At a house in Alexandra Road, he arrested Michael Rory Campbell and Patrick O'Connell. When told he was being arrested, Campbell said: 'What I did I did for Ireland.' O'Connell said: 'That goes for me too.' Police seized IRA literature and maps of Manchester and Salford on which were marked police stations, fire stations, military barracks and railway stations. At Parkfield Street, Rusholme, officers arrested Patrick Deviney and Jack Glenn. There they found copies of IRA Battalion Orders and other useful information. On 21 January, DI Foster and other officers searched a shop in Dryden Street, Chorlton-on-Medlock, where they found a barrel of potassium chlorate, forty-nine sticks of gelignite, two Mills bombs, ten electric detonators and an alarm clock concealed under the floor boards. Mary Glenn, aged twenty-two, who returned to the shop while the search was in progress, was arrested; other arrests followed, including that of a fifteen-year-old girl. A police surgeon, Dr T. H. Blench, worked through the night of the arrests in the police laboratory, testing for explosives on the clothing of the suspects. At Patrick Walsh's home in Ogalvie Street, the officers discovered several sealed barrels of potassium chlorate concealed under a bed.

The searches continued. On 25 January, DI Sidney Barnes searched the house of Michael O'Shea at Clewer Crescent, Harrow Weald, and arrested him for the unlawful possession of firearms. The police also found a quantity of IRA correspondence, including a copy of the 'Sabotage Plan' which, when read in conjunction with other documents in O'Shea's possession, left no doubt that there was a conspiracy to cause explosions on a massive scale throughout the country; the Home Office set about framing legislation to give the police more powers to contain the violence. That same day DI Baker arrested John Mitchell, a 24-year-old garage mechanic at Whiteside Road, Brentford, for conspiracy to cause explosions.

When Patrick Fleming, the OC of the London Battalion, who was using the name Michael Preston, was arrested at his lodgings in Cambridge Street, Pimlico, by DI Tansley and DS Cooper, they found papers indicating that he was collecting information about senior officials of the Defence Staff, and the location of aerodromes and factories; a notebook giving information about the strengths of explosives and three cipher keys labelled 'GHQ only', 'OC Britain only' and 'For Units in Britain'. With these they decoded some of the other correspondence in Fleming's possession. One message read: 'Send immediately a report of all explosives and material in your area, i.e. potash, fuses, detonators (electrical and commercial), gelignite and galvanometers.' Another document contained details of a plan to blow up the power station at Brimsdown in north London and further searches led to the discovery by DI Buckle of two tons of potassium chlorate and a ton of iron oxide at Fordington Road, West Hampstead, the home of John Healy, proprietor of the Irish Club in Kilburn.

On 28 January, Peter Walsh, the IRA operations officer, was arrested by DI Whitehead. His room in New Oxford Street contained a large quantity of bomb-making material and a Royal Air Force uniform. When asked why he had the explosives, he simply said: 'We want an Irish Republic.' In his possession were instructions signed by Michael Mason, Commander of the IRA in Great Britain, directing the IRA in London to 'abort operations if they could not be carried out without men being arrested, or civilians killed'. Liverpool Special Branch raided the address on the papers and detained Michael Cleary, and his flatmate Joseph Walker. More bomb-making material was found.

Other arrests in Liverpool included Thomas Edward Kelly, who had in his possession four barrels of potassium chlorate, and four other men, three of whom were acquitted. Kelly was also acquitted, as the jury believed his story that he had been paid five shillings by two strangers who came into his shop and asked him to store four barrels.[10] While records of court proceedings indicate that a few like Kelly used this defence successfully, the majority of juries were unconvinced by it.

The documents found at Fleming's address led to more explosives being discovered at a cycle shop run by Timothy Dacey in Cardiff; he was arrested. In London more arrests followed after thorough Special Branch examination of prisoners' correspondence. On 10 February, when the lodgings of Molly Gallagher in Thornhill Square were searched, police found two rucksacks of potassium chlorate and receipts for the purchase of a wide range of materials for causing explosions. Her address book contained the name of Peter Walsh, the London Operations Officer.

On 18 February, DS Fretwell and another officer went to an address in Tufnell Park, north London, with a warrant to search for explosives. In a bedroom occupied by James Patrick Connolly and Francis McGowan, as Fretwell went to lift a fibre suitcase, Connolly said: 'Go steady with that case.' He said that it belonged to Francis McGowan. It held nine brown paper parcels containing white and grey powder and a hot water bottle containing turpentine. Four of the parcels also contained lengths of magnesium tape. The two men were subsequently sentenced to six and a half years, and seven years' penal servitude respectively.

The first phase of the police response was at an end and their immediate concern was with collating the evidence and preparing the prosecutions against those they had detained.[11]

Any hopes entertained that the arrests would contain the IRA's offensive, however, were shattered on 2 March when there were explosions on the Grand Union Canal at Harlesden, and in a culvert under a canal at Wensbury, Staffordshire. Other incidents continued throughout the month, including a successful attempt to bomb Hammersmith Bridge on the 28th. Edward John Connell and William

---

10 Coogan suggests that many of those who stored explosives for the IRA did not know what they were doing or for whom they were doing it. *The IRA*, p. 160

11 Details of all the incidents in this first part of the 'S Plan' and the resulting trials were reported in contemporaneous editions of the *Times* newspaper

Browne hired a car to pick them up at Hammersmith and drive them to Ewell. The driver, named Moffatt, collected them at about 11.30 p.m. together with two other men. When they reached Tolworth, he was told to stop and threatened with what appeared to be a gun. He was put on the floor in the back of the car and driven to somewhere near Hammersmith, where two of the men got out and returned soon after carrying two suitcases. On arriving at Hammersmith Bridge, two of the men got out carrying the suitcases. They returned after a short while and stopped the car in Hammersmith Broadway when they heard one explosion. It transpired that a passer-by called Childs saw sparks coming from a suitcase near the bridge. He climbed through railings on to the footpath and threw the suitcase into the river, where it exploded, sending a spurt of water sixty feet into the air.

Surprisingly, the men paid Moffat his fare and allowed him to leave the car at Putney Bridge. He ran towards a telephone box to call the police, but a patrolling police officer appeared before he reached it. Together they caught up with two of the Irishmen and the officer arrested them. The suitcases had each contained about 30 lbs of explosive. The bridge was damaged and was closed for repairs costing £1,000. Connell was sentenced to twenty years and Browne to ten years' penal servitude for causing the explosions.

At the Old Bailey, the trial of the first nine prisoners arrested in police raids commenced on 23 March 1939, before Mr Justice Travers Humphreys, a judge with an outstanding reputation.

This first group consisted of: Michael Mason, alias Cleary, twenty-nine; Joseph Walker, twenty-six; Peter Walsh, alias Stuart, twenty-five; Patrick Fleming, alias Preston, twenty-three; Charles James Casey, twenty-three; John Healy, forty; James Michael Lyons, twenty-six; and Michael O'Shea, twenty-four; George Brendan Kane, twenty-three, all of whose arrests are dealt with above. The indictment against them contained fifteen counts, collectively and individually, the principal one being that they 'did conspire with other persons in Manchester, Liverpool, Cardiff and Dublin, and elsewhere in the United Kingdom and in Ireland to cause explosions of a nature likely to endanger life or to cause injury to property'. Other counts against them individually were that they had conspired to commit arson and that they possessed explosive substances or firearms with intent to endanger life.

Casey was led into the dock struggling but Mr Justice Humphreys, apparently unmoved by his antics, said to the officers, 'Let him stand or sit or lie, whichever he prefers.' Casey lay panting on the floor of the dock but eventually, when joined by the other prisoners, sat in a chair. Casey, Cleary, Walsh and Fleming each declared that he was: 'A soldier of the Irish Republican Army.' The judge ordered that pleas of not guilty should be entered. Walker, Healy, O'Shea and Kane pleaded not guilty.

Sir Donald Somervell, the Attorney General, referred to 'the ultimatum' delivered to the Foreign Office on 13 January and outlined the 'S Plan', which he described as an elaborate and carefully thought-out plan for an attack by criminal methods on all services and institutions essential to the life of the country.

The first witness for the Crown was DI Barnes, who described the search of Michael O'Shea's address at Clewer Crescent, Harrow Weald, where he found a copy of the Sabotage Plan and four copies of a proclamation of the Irish Republic which called for support of 'The effort we are about to make in God's name to enthrone the Republic of Ireland.' He gave evidence that another document he found included directions for the manufacture of 'Irish Cheddar' and stated that it was no longer a practicable explosive because of the difficulty of obtaining one of the ingredients. 'They don't recommend Irish Cheddar,' the judge commented.

On succeeding days the officers concerned gave their evidence of the arrests and property found, which included documents leading to further arrests. Typical of the responses made by the prisoners was that of Walsh, whose rooms contained a vast amount of incriminating material. When asked how he had obtained it, he simply replied, 'We want an Irish Republic.' The next day Chief Inspector Cherrill of the fingerprint department at New Scotland Yard gave evidence that a thumbprint found on an alarm clock attached to an unexploded bomb at Windle was Michael Mason's.

When the defence opened on 27 March, George Brendan Kane pleaded guilty to counts charging him with conspiring to cause explosions and with conspiring to commit arson. The jury returned a verdict of guilty against him on these counts. A verdict of not guilty was returned on another count charging Kane with having a pistol in his possession with intent to endanger life.

Walsh (Stuart), Patrick Fleming (Michael Preston), Casey and Lyons, who with Mason (Cleary) refused to plead, said they did not wish to give evidence or call witnesses. Mr Justice Humphreys told Mason he would have an opportunity of addressing the jury later. Joseph Walker denied that he had conspired with Mason or any other person to commit the crimes with which he was charged. He said that he was not a member of the IRA, he had not been convicted before and he was a man of good character.

Healy in evidence said that he had been in the country for twenty years, during which time he had never been in trouble and had never been a member of the IRA. He had purchased the chlorate of potash in England at the request of a pharmacist he knew in Dublin called Godfrey Burke, who would then transport it to Ireland without having to pay duty on it. He denied having at any time conspired with anyone in the dock or anyone else to cause explosions. He did not know in September when the chemicals were purchased that they were for explosives, because none of the explosions had occurred.

O'Shea said that on the day before he was arrested two men knocked at his door, and one of them said, 'We have got to leave some stuff with you.' The man told him he must not know what the stuff was and if he said anything to anybody about it they would see him later. When the police officers came to his house, he showed them the drums and an inspector said: 'This is the dump.' He had never before seen the rifle that was found in his house and had never seen any of the men in the dock before.

Mr Justice Humphreys asked Mason if he wished to make a statement in his defence. Mason first said that although Walker lived in the same house as he did in Liverpool, Walker knew nothing of his affairs. He said: 'I am not a criminal. I am fighting for the freedom of my country. For hundreds of years Irishmen have fought for freedom, and will continue to fight as long as any part of the country is occupied by the British.'

When it came to his turn, Walsh said in a loud voice:

> I am not a criminal. What I did was my duty as a soldier of the Irish Repub-
> lic to protest against the coercion of the Irish people by the British and
> the suppression of the Irish people. I don't care what sentence I get in this
> Court, I know the fight will go on. I shall take part in it again.

Looking thoughtfully at him, Mr Justice Humphreys asked the prisoner to repeat what he had said. Holding his head high and looking at the judge, Walsh said: 'If Ireland is not free when I come out I shall carry on the fight again. Ireland will be free and I shall set it free, I know.'

Next the judge called on Preston. Turning towards the jury box, Preston began to berate the British government, saying 'England's policy towards the Irish people has always been one of shooting, hanging or gaoling. We have stood up to that and we can stand up to it still.'

Mr Justice Humphreys said, 'That will do, Preston, I have listened to enough of this nonsense.' Preston went on to say that he took full responsibility for purchases of acid and aluminium powder, saying Healy had no way of knowing he was connected with the Irish Republican Army.

Casey and Lyons both declared their commitment to the republican cause and their determination to rid Ireland of the British presence. After submissions on behalf of Walker and O'Shea, the Attorney General made his final address to the jury.

In his summing up, Mr Justice Humphreys said that five of the men had made statements to the effect that they regretted nothing and that they gloried in what they had done. He pointed out that when a person ceased to employ constitutional methods of altering the position of part of a British Dominion and employed methods of terrorism, incendiarism, causing explosions and rendering life for respectable law-abiding citizens impossible, it was for the Crown and those who administered the law to suppress illegal and dangerous acts. He said the men in the dock were there not because they advocated a Republic of

Ireland but because it was alleged they used methods which could not be toler-
ated in a civilised country. After deliberating for an hour and fifty minutes the
jury found all eight men guilty of conspiring to cause explosions and conspiring
to cause arson. Walker was found not guilty of being in possession of bomb-
making equipment.

Dealing with antecedents, DI Thompson told the court that Mason had
refused to give particulars of himself, other than those which had been elic-
ited during the case. He arrived in England in December 1938 and took over
the post of officer commanding the IRA in Great Britain. Likewise Stuart had
refused to give any information about himself, but it was known that his correct name was Peter Joseph Walsh, he was born in Glasgow and was the son of
a pensioned police constable. When he was in Glasgow he was the secretary of
the Irish Nationalist Association there.

When asked whether he wished to put any questions to the officer, Mason
said, 'My real name is not Mason, it is Cleary.' Preston then said, 'My correct
name is not Preston it is Fleming.' Casey, Healy and Lyons all predictably
protested their innocence in the eyes of God. Thompson told the court that
O'Shea had been in England since 1936 and was unemployed at the time of
his arrest.

At the conclusion of the trial on 28 March, Michael Joseph Mason, alias Cleary,
received seventeen years' penal servitude, Peter Walsh, alias Stuart: fifteen years,
Charles James Casey: fourteen years, Patrick Fleming, alias Preston: twelve
years, John Healy: ten years, James Michael Lyons: ten years, George Brendan
Kane: seven years, and Michael O'Shea: five years. Joseph Walker was sentenced
to eighteen months' imprisonment with hard labour. At the conclusion of the
case Mr Justice Humphreys told the Attorney General that he thought that the
police had shown great acumen and celerity in making the arrests. Many Special Branch officers had taken part in them and in producing the evidence and
carrying out the investigations that led to them. During this period and for the
remainder of the campaign, which extended until March of the following year,
despite the infusion of CID officers, the Branch resources were stretched to

the limit but were blessed with good luck in that other matters which normally demanded their attention were at a low ebb.

During the trial of the second group of Irish bombers, which followed the pattern of the first, the judge remarked to Gerald Wharton, in front of the jury. 'You were a member of that gang which committed murders of British officers and others up to 1922.' On appeal, the conviction against Wharton was quashed and a guilty man walked free. Following the trial, Mr Justice Humphries was the subject of threatening letters; as a precaution, all trial judges in IRA cases were given police protection and an armed guard was placed on their homes. Clearly the IRA operation was not going according to plan and Russell blamed others for his own ineptitude, but the campaign continued. According to McNamee's account,[12] Russell was furious about the loss of explosives dumps.

Hardly had the first trials finished than the violence recommenced, but the bombers were becoming increasingly accident-prone. On 30 March, there was an explosion in a house in Trafalgar Road, Birmingham. Gerard Anthony Lyons, alias Dunlop, escaped, but police recovered 200 sticks of gelignite and 76 lbs of potassium chlorate. On 2 May there was another explosion, this time in a house in Rednal, Birmingham. Police arrested Martin Clarke and three women: Mary, Evelyn and Emily Higgins.[13]

Special Branch officers continued to act on every scrap of information. On the night of 3/4 May two women officers, Marjorie Urquart and Anne Winterbottom, followed suspects Patrick Dower and Joseph McAleer from an address in Sidmouth Street, Marylebone. At Great Portland Street Station they were joined by Gerard Kirk, alias Bradford, and at Baker Street Station, by Timothy Murray and two other men. Bradford appeared to be giving instructions to the others. They split up, and Winterbottom followed Dower, Murray and another man. At 11.35 p.m. she saw Dower put his hand in the letterbox at the premises of George Newman & Co., motor dealers, in Euston Road, and a little later saw Murray put

12   Coogan, *The IRA*, p. 170

13   Allason, *The Branch*, p. 106

his hand in the letterbox of Com-Motors, Ltd., also in Euston Road. The officer continued to follow Murray, whose identity she did not know, and at 1 a.m. he was seen to enter premises in St Mary's Terrace, Paddington.

Meanwhile, the second officer, Urquart, followed Bradford and Lyons. She observed Bradford take something from his pocket in the Aldwych and both men looked at it for about five minutes. They turned into Kingsway, and Bradford cautiously went to the door of Gestetner's. The two then hurried up Kingsway to High Holborn, where the officer saw them walking away from the premises of the Crittall Manufacturing Company. She continued to keep them under surveillance until they entered a house in Acton Street, Bloomsbury, at about 2 a.m.

At 5.15 a.m. Police Constable Ernest Hayward found a brown paper parcel, measuring about ten inches by three inches, lying on a window ledge at Heal and Son's premises in Tottenham Court Road. He unwrapped it and found inside a rubber balloon, a stick of gelignite and a fuse. After separating the gelignite from the balloon he put them into a bucket of water. At 8.45 a.m. a bomb exploded at Com-Motors. PC William Marshall reported the incident, in which a young woman at an adjoining tobacconist's kiosk was taken to hospital in a dazed and hysterical condition. At Gestetner's, PC Blake found a paper parcel, six inches by three inches in size, which contained two balloons, one inside the other, filled with acid, a stick of gelignite and a detonator. He also placed them in a bucket of water. At the premises of Henri Selmer & Co., Ltd., in Holborn, the time-keeper discovered a parcel inside the shop and placed it on a desk. Later on he picked it up again and it exploded in his hand. He threw it on to the floor and it burst into flames. He flung some curtains on to it and, while he was trying to stamp out the flames, there was a second explosion and he and a salesman were thrown to the floor. He suffered leg injuries and was taken to hospital.

By 9 a.m. six bombs had exploded along the route taken the previous night. Two more failed to explode. The rooms at Sidmouth Street and Acton Street were raided and four men were arrested. The men at the Acton Street address were Gerard Kirk, alias Bradford, and Gerard Lyons, who had escaped from the bomb factory in Trafalgar Road, Birmingham. Timothy Murray, who had been followed by one of the women officers to his lodgings at St Mary's Terrace, Paddington, was also arrested there.

Meanwhile, Sean Russell had travelled to the United States on a fundraising expedition and was arrested in Detroit for a technical immigration offence.[14] He described himself as John Russell and not Sean Russell. His visit to the United States coincided with the visit of King George VI and Queen Elizabeth.

In May, police in Liverpool discovered a suitcase full of gelignite which had been abandoned by a contact of Michael James O'Hara, who had handed it to him for safekeeping. In it was a piece of paper on which were written the words 'Miss J. Gardner, 37 Duke Street'. Painstaking enquiries by a Liverpool officer identified it as O'Hara's address in Glasgow. Liverpool police passed this information to their colleagues in Glasgow and on Sunday 14 May the police raided the Assembly Hall at 132 Trongate, where they arrested a number of men, including O'Hara, Edward Gill and John Carson. A further 500 detonators and 160 feet of fast-burning fuse were found at the prisoners' address.[15] O'Hara, Gill and Carson were each sentenced to ten years' penal servitude.

Shortly before 10 p.m. on Saturday 24 June 1939, the West End of London was rocked by a series of explosions which damaged branches of the Midland, Lloyds and Westminster Banks and injured some seventeen pedestrians in the vicinity. Three bombs were left at Madame Tussauds, two of which exploded, damaging several wax models. The bombings were condemned in a statement by Cardinal Hinsley, the Roman Catholic Archbishop of Westminster. The same evening, Thomas Hawkett, the attendant at a public lavatory in Oxford Street, spotted a suspicious parcel in one of the cubicles. He dumped the parcel in a bucket of water and called the police. Meanwhile DI Robert Fabian, attending an explosion in Piccadilly, was called to another suspicious packet. He picked it up, carried it to the yard of the nearby police station and dunked it in a bucket of water, burning his hands in the process. For this valiant act the inspector was

14   Gray, *Ireland This Century*, p. 139

15   Percy Sillitoe, *Cloak Without Dagger* (London: Cassell & Co., 1955), p. 143-4

awarded the King's Police Medal for Gallantry and £15 from the Bow Street award fund. The lavatory attendant received £5! The day ended with Thomas Nelson and Patrick Donaghy being arrested in the act of dropping incendiaries into pillar boxes, the result of police surveillance. Both were subsequently sentenced to twenty years' imprisonment.

A conference was hurriedly called at New Scotland Yard, chaired by the Commissioner, who described the night's events to the Home Secretary and led a discussion on possible measures that could be taken to curb the Irish atrocities.[16]

THE NEED FOR PREVENTIVE LEGISLATION

On 5 July the Cabinet met to consider a memorandum by the Home Secretary, Sir Samuel Hoare, in which he urged further legislation to deal with the IRA's criminal conspiracy. He pointed out that the police in Ireland, both north and south, had sweeping powers which were not available to their counterparts on mainland Britain. (The Northern Ireland Special Powers Act and, in Eire, the Offences Against the State Act.) In England, the Explosives Substances (Temporary Provisions) Act of 1883 related only to bombers found in possession of explosives; it was more difficult to pre-empt the activities of others who were merely suspected of being involved in acts of terrorism.

Cabinet minutes show that the Home Secretary stressed that the police were finding it increasingly difficult to secure convictions under the present legislation and that prompt action was needed before more outrages took place. He recommended that legislation should be introduced before the end of the current parliamentary session.

After prolonged discussion in the Cabinet, the Prevention of Violence Bill was presented to Parliament on 24 July. It gave the police additional powers of search and of detention for a period of up to five days. It also gave the Home

16   *The Times*, 26 June 1939

Secretary powers to exclude and deport persons whom he was satisfied were connected with the IRA, or cause them to register with the police. Sir Samuel Hoare was a skilful politician and he used the statistical evidence of IRA activity to advantage.[17] He outlined the campaign to date and referred to it being watched by 'foreign organisations'. Though he did not specify who, there is no doubt that the Germans had followed developments with interest and that the Irish-American lobby in the United States had financed it.

The necessity for the bill was largely accepted by the House of Commons. When it came to the division, only nineteen left-wing members voted against it. Between July 1939, when the act came into force, and 22 March 1940, 119 suspects were expelled, thirteen were prohibited from entering the United Kingdom and twenty-one were required to register with the police.

The onus to prove their bona fides had shifted to the suspects but the act was not to apply to persons born in Ireland who had lived in Great Britain for more than twenty years. There was an appeal system, which scrutinised the intelligence information, while protecting its sources. The appeal procedure did not allow the suspects to be given details of the specific allegations against them, however, making it difficult for them to rebut them. To deal with this problem independent advisers, nominated by the Home Secretary, were permitted to interview them and make submissions on their behalf.

BOMBS IN RAILWAY CLOAKROOMS AND AT COVENTRY

While the Cabinet deliberated, the IRA continued its murderous campaign. On 2 July, a bomb exploded in the left-luggage area of the LMS Railway

---

17   The Home Secretary relied on the following statistics relating to the period between January and July 1939 to support his case: No. of IRA attacks – 127; persons killed – one; persons injured – fifty-five; IRA terrorists convicted – sixty-six; sticks of gelignite seized by police – 1,500; detonators seized – 1,000; sulphuric acid seized – seven gallons; aluminium powder seized – four cwts

Station in London Road, Birmingham, causing extensive damage to the station concourse. The railway cloakrooms at Derby, Leicester, Leamington, Stafford, Coventry and Nottingham were also attacked. On 17 July, a bomb exploded in the parcels office of Wolverhampton Railway Station.

Elsewhere, in London on 22 July police arrested Gary Jones, John O'Regan, Herbert Moore, Edward Stapleton, Rose Conway and Charles Wood and his wife in possession of explosives. On 26 July, as if in defiant answer to the proposed legislation, a bomb in the left-luggage office at King's Cross Station blew off both legs of an academic, Dr Donald Campbell, and killed him. Twelve other people were injured including Dr Campbell's wife. Five members of the station staff at Victoria Station were injured in a similar, but non-fatal, bombing.[18] These savage attacks had the effect of speeding up the passage of the Prevention of Violence Bill and on 28 July it successfully passed through the second and third readings.

Throughout the rest of July and into August further outrages were committed, the principal target being the communication system. In London, bombs exploded in three pillar-boxes and one in a post box at the sorting office at Mount Pleasant. The following day telephone wires were cut in London, at Piccadilly. The Post Office continued to be the subject of incendiary attacks throughout the early part of August and mail was destroyed at Bradford, Halifax, Derby, Huddersfield, Preston, Blackburn and Blackpool.

On 13 August, an explosive dump on an allotment in Coventry was accidentally blown up and a shed destroyed. Two men were seen running away. But this was merely the precursor to the most traumatic incident of the whole campaign. On Friday 25 August, at about 1.30 p.m., an IRA Volunteer left a messenger's bicycle outside Burton's in Broadgate, in the centre of Coventry. In the cycle's basket was a bomb containing 5 lbs of high explosive. The timing mechanism attached to the detonator was set to fire at 2.30 p.m. It exploded and a mighty boom echoed across the city. Five people were killed instantly and many more were injured. Elsie Ansell, aged twenty-one years, was choosing her wedding

ring in Astley's the jewellers, next door to Burton's. She was hurled through
the plate-glass window. All that could be identified of her was her engagement
ring. This was only one of several such unspeakable horrors.

On 28 August, a combined team of Coventry City Police and Metropolitan
Police Special Branch officers, led by DCI Boneham of Coventry City Police and
DI Barnes of MPSB, acting on information they had received from a member
of the public, raided 25 Clara Street, Coventry. They arrested Brigid O'Hara,
her daughter and son-in-law Mary and Joseph Hewitt, and James McCormick,
who was lodging there under the name of Jim Richards. They found traces of
explosives and a number of items similar to those used in the Broadgate bomb.
In a sideboard was Mrs Hewitt's handbag, which contained an Irish republican poem and a three-year-old wedding card from the Betsy Gray Branch of
Cumann na mBan.[19]

The person who planted the bomb was not arrested. It was subsequently
reported that he fled the country and died, years later, in a mental home. Dominic Adams, mentioned by the women as being concerned in the purchase of the
bicycle used to carry the bomb, also escaped prosecution, returned to Northern Ireland and subsequently became a member of the Irish Republican Army
Council. His nephew was Gerry Adams who later became President of Sinn
Féin, but steadfastly denied membership of the IRA.

Joseph Hewitt was the tenant of 25 Clara Street, where he had lived with his wife
and mother-in-law for only a few months. About a week before they moved there, an
Irishman, who called himself Jim Richards, but whose real name was McCormick,
came to lodge with them in Meadow Street. When they moved, Richards moved
with them. He agreed to pay twenty-three shillings a week for bed and board. Joseph
Hewitt says he did not know Richards before he came to stay with the family.

In the days following the bomb, both Mrs O'Hara and her daughter made
long and detailed statements to the police. From these the following picture

---

19   Betsy Gray was a Presbyterian heroine of the United Irishmen's uprising in 1798, in which she was butchered,
     along with her brother and lover, by the Hillsborough Yeomanry

emerged of the unprofessional manner in which the IRA had gone about making preparations for the atrocity, displaying absolute disregard for security. Mrs
O'Hara related how Irishmen had frequently called at the house to see Richards, who always took them to his room out of earshot; he dug a pit under the
stairs and lined it with concrete slabs; he told an inquisitive neighbour 'This is
for a bit of a dump'; he told Mrs O'Hara that one of his visitors was 'Halfpenny'
Jones[20] and another 'Mr Barnes'.[21] Barnes frequently called to see Richards and
got Mary Hewitt to run errands for him, on one occasion to buy two sacks and
on another to purchase a suitcase. Once Richards told Mrs O'Hara he had
been with Dominic Adams to buy a bicycle (the one used as a conveyance for
the bomb). Another time she saw Richards in the kitchen opening a parcel
containing white powder, which he later told her was chlorate. All these grave
lapses of security on McCormick's part provided the prosecution with vital evidence and helped to bring about the downfall of Barnes and McCormick, whose
names were to join those of other 'illustrious' patriots who gave their lives for
'the cause'. Mary Hewitt's statement substantiated what her mother had said;
moreover she admitted that she thought the white powder was explosives and
that they were making bombs.

Barnes, when questioned, denied that he had any part in the affair. The evidence against him was overwhelming, however, particularly when an incriminating
letter found in his pocket was produced. His explanations were unconvincing.
McCormick, on the other hand, admitted his part in the preparations for the
bombing attack but claimed the bomb was to be set to explode at night. The
felony-murder rule at that time was that all persons jointly engaged in a common felonious purpose resulting in murder were equally guilty as principals
in the first degree. Consequently, the two women as well as Hewitt were also
charged with murder.

Mary Hewitt, Brigid O'Hara and, on appeal, her husband Joseph were

---

20 Gary Jones became the O.C. of the IRA in London after the initial arrests of the leaders of the campaign

21 Peter Barnes, who was hanged, with Richards (McCormick), on 7 February

acquitted by the jury. They accepted that the two women did not share a common purpose with the bombers.[22] Barnes and McCormick were convicted and, on 7 February 1940, were hanged at Winson Green Prison, despite a last-minute appeal from the Lord Mayor of Dublin for the Home Secretary to reprieve them. Thirty years later the bodies of Barnes and McCormick were returned to the Republic of Ireland, where they were interred in Ballyglass cemetery. As Professor Hogan put it: 'More thought might have been given to those they had murdered than to the incompetent fools who were being buried as martyrs.'[23]

Meanwhile, Special Branch officers in London had not been idle; a few hours before the Coventry explosion, police searched premises at 32 Leinster Gardens, Kensington. They had been keeping round-the-clock observation on the house, which was divided into flats. Five men were arrested loading 5 lb bombs into two tricycles and a carrier cycle. The men were Daniel Crotty, John Evans, John Gibson, Daniel Jordan and James O'Regan. The bombs were intended for the Bank of England, Westminster Abbey and New Scotland Yard. The explosives for the Coventry and Leinster Gardens bombs were supplied by Peter Barnes, who was traced to an attic room on the fourth floor of a lodging house at 176 Westbourne Terrace. When he returned there from Coventry after the explosion he found DS Hughes from MPSB waiting to arrest him. Three small packets of explosives were found in his possession. Barnes claimed they were shampoos. When he was told he was being arrested in connection with the Coventry explosion, he replied, 'Yes, I've been to Coventry, but coincidences can happen, can't they?'

On the eve of the executions of Barnes and McCormick, the IRA continued its offensive. Explosions occurred simultaneously in parcel offices in Manchester, Euston and Birmingham but by now the campaign had lost its momentum.

---

22   The details of the trial of Barnes and his fellow conspirators is based on a work entitled *The Trial of Peter Barnes and Others: The IRA Coventry Explosion of 1939* (London: Hodge, 1953) by Letitia Fairfield, who had access to the trial transcript and other official documents concerning the case. A doctor, barrister and criminologist, she was the sister of Rebecca West

23   'Funeral in Dublin', *Criminal Law Review*, 1970

Throughout February and into March a series of comparatively minor explosions occurred in Birmingham; in Oxford Street, London, when seven people were injured; in Salford; in Bayswater; in Park Lane, London, and finally in Paddington. This was the final act of the Sabotage Plan, appropriately it was on St Patrick's Day.[24]

THE GERMAN CONNECTION

W hen he presented the Prevention of Violence Bill to Parliament, Sir Samuel Hoare pointed out that the 'S Plan' was 'the kind of plan which might be worked out by a General Staff'. He went on to comment on the interest shown in the plan by 'foreign organisations' and questioned whether, in the event of war, 'would not the danger of serious sabotage be immeasurably increased by these terrorist outrages?' Clearly, he had in mind the likelihood of the imminent war with Germany and may well have been induced to make these remarks after reading an MI5 assessment which suggested that the 'S Plan' may have been written with German help, as it read like a German General Staff plan.

There were other indications of collusion between the IRA and the German intelligence services. A German agent, Oscar Phaus, had been in contact with the IRA; Jim O'Donovan had met Abwehr officials in Germany on at least three occasions; on 29 December 1939 Dublin police seized a radio transmitter supplied to the IRA by the Abwehr. In May 1940, Sean Russell underwent a course in Germany in the use of high explosives but died from a gastric ulcer before he could make use of the knowledge he had gained.

●   ●   ●

24   The authors are again indebted to the editors of *The Times*, which continued to report in detail all the incidents in the second phase of the 'S Plan'

S ome of the most militant activists mellow with age and their violence gives way to reason. In the 1960s even Jim O'Donovan, the author of the 'S Plan', expressed the view that the 1939 bombing campaign 'brought nothing but harm to Ireland and the IRA'.[25] He might also have reflected on the deaths of the seven innocent men and women who died because of his plan: Albert Ross, Donald Campbell, Elsie Ansell, James Clay, John Arnott, Gwilym Rowlands and Rex Gentle.

CHAPTER SEVENTEEN

SOVIET ESPIONAGE IN THE 1930S

ALTHOUGH THE MPSB had its functions reduced in 1931 when MI5 became the lead organisation for protecting the security of the state, it still retained its responsibilities for prosecuting cases of espionage within its jurisdiction.

The Communist Party of Great Britain continued attempts to foster discontent in the British armed forces, as it had been doing since its formation in 1920, prompting Parliament to pass the Incitement to Disaffection Act in 1934. The communists also infiltrated the trade unions to incite industrial unrest and many communists travelled to Russia in order to be schooled in these matters. All these activities were monitored by the Branch and the Security Service. Between 1934 and 1938 a secret radio link between an address in Wimbledon and Moscow was monitored by Special Branch, on behalf of the Security Service. This was codenamed 'Operation Mask'.

The Security Service could only request police action and not order it, and it still lacked powers of arrest and search of its own. Operational decisions remained with senior police officers. With only between twelve and twenty-six officers during the 1930s to carry out its many tasks, the Security Service relied increasingly on the good will of senior police officers for any executive action that was necessary. With the outbreak of IRA violence in mainland Britain at the end of the decade, the resources available to cover all aspects of the security of the state were seriously stretched. Nevertheless, the Branch still contrived to render valuable assistance to the Security Service in its constant probing of communist activities.

In 1939, Sir Vernon Kell, the Director General of MI5, boasted to the French foreign intelligence service, 'Soviet activity in England is non-existent, in terms of both intelligence and political subversion.'[1] He was wrong, but the scale of Russian penetration of the British establishment was certainly not apparent as we now know, with the benefit of hindsight. This was partly due to the Security Service's inability to cope with their task, given the resources available to them. Churchill regarded them as inefficient and by the end of the decade, when he became Prime Minister, he dismissed an ageing and ailing Kell.

Soviet espionage was organised in three different ways:

(a) through legal residents with diplomatic status in the Russian embassy,

(b) by illegal residents working independently with false identities,

(c) through a secret group within the CPGB.

In fact, far from being non-existent, Soviet activity in this country was considerable, as the following cases will show. And all of them, to a greater or lesser degree, required Special Branch involvement, whether through surveillance, interrogations, arrests or prosecutions.

In 1929, a Foreign Office cipher clerk employed in Geneva, Ernest Holloway Oldham, ran into financial difficulties through heavy drinking and offered his services to the Russians. He was handled by an NKVD agent, Dimitri Bystrolyotov. In 1933 Oldham was sacked by the Foreign Office for drunkenness, and committed suicide. Despite information from two Soviet defectors in 1929 and 1930, his betrayal was not fully appreciated by the authorities, who believed he was leaking information to the French, rather than the Russians. Before his death he put his Russian handler in touch with another cipher clerk, Raymond Oake,

1   Andrew, *The Defence of the Realm*, p. 185

who introduced him to his colleague, Captain John Herbert King, who was to assume an important role in Soviet espionage activity here.

In 1930, a series of articles in the *Daily Mail* by Sava Popovitch, a Serbian living in London, revealed that he had been approached by a Soviet agent, using the name Staal, to obtain British military secrets. Staal was identified as Ludwik Poretsky, alias Ignace Reiss, operating from Amsterdam, who became a Soviet illegal resident in Paris. Popovitch was interviewed by MI5, but nothing came of it at the time, although Poretsky was later to become the handler, together with Walter Krivitsky, of Henri Pieck, both of whom were to play prominent roles in the complex case narrated in the following pages.[2]

Throughout the 1930s, Special Branch was the public face of the Security Service and initially dealt with any approach from the public. As a result of one such approach, DI Kitchener was given information, in 1937, by one Conrad Parlanti. Parlanti was a young businessman who lived in Herne Bay and commuted to London, where he worked for a firm of shop-fitters. One day Raymond Oake, who had recently returned to this country from abroad to work at the Foreign Office, and was a fellow commuter, introduced Parlanti to a Dutchman. As the relationship developed, the Dutchman, Henri Christian Pieck, who described himself as a surveyor and artist, suggested they set up together in the shop-fitting business; he generously offered to provide all the capital for the proposed venture.

Parlanti accepted the offer and they acquired a suite of offices near Victoria Station at 34a Buckingham Gate, SW1. Pieck left the day-to-day running of the business to Parlanti, as he apparently had other business interests, but he retained one of the rooms in their premises for his exclusive use and always kept it locked. Although Pieck usually lodged in Herne Bay or stayed at the Lancaster Gate Hotel, he had a permanent home at 3 Emma Park in The Hague and occasionally returned there for short visits. Parlanti became curious about the contents of the locked room and one day, during Pieck's absence, had a look inside. He found a Leica camera fixed about three feet over a table arranged for photographing material that was placed under it.

Their friendship developed and Parlanti was invited to his partner's home in The Hague, where his wife lived. Mrs Pieck seemed overly friendly towards the Englishman and one day when her husband was suddenly called away to do some work in Germany, she attempted to seduce Parlanti; she told him that she and her husband worked for a large organisation and that they were borrowing confidential documents from a man in the code section of the British Foreign Office, which would help their company bring off financial coups. Parlanti was inclined to believe her at first, being unaware of the communist tactic of using 'honeypot' methods in order to ensnare people they wished to use. As time went by, Parlanti became suspicious of Pieck's activities and questioned his partner, who admitted that he was a Soviet agent and that the source of his Foreign Office information was Sir Robert Vansittart, the permanent undersecretary, who had a mistress called Helen Wilkie. Thoroughly alarmed, Parlanti sought other employment, the business was wound up and Pieck returned to Holland.

On reflection, Parlanti decided to inform the police of his misgivings and was seen by Kitchener, who in turn reported the matter to the Security Service. In particular, Parlanti was most suspicious about a meeting he had witnessed between Pieck and a stranger, who had handed the Dutchman some papers. Shortly afterwards Pieck left the hotel, where he had been drinking with Parlanti, ostensibly to return home, but when the latter walked round to their office in Buckingham Gate he noticed that a light was on in the room where Pieck kept his camera. Presented with this narrative, the Security Service decided to take no further action, as Pieck had not previously come under their notice and they could not believe that Sir Robert Vansittart was a spy.[3]

The story did not end there, however. In the autumn of 1939, the *Saturday Evening Post* in New York ran a series of articles by a Soviet defector named Walter Krivitsky; they were ghosted by a Russian émigré journalist, Isaac Don

3   Kitchener, *The Memoirs of an Old Detective*, Chapter 12

Levine. As the head of the Soviet Military Intelligence organisation in Western Europe, Krivitsky had been Pieck's controller. Krivitsky told Levine about John Herbert King, a Russian spy within the British Foreign Office's Communications Department, and another unnamed Soviet mole in the Cabinet Office. Levine informed the British ambassador, who passed the information immediately to Sir Robert Vansittart's replacement at the Foreign Office, Sir Alexander Cadogan, on 3 September 1939. King was easily identified but the identity of the Cabinet Office source remained a mystery. The Foreign Secretary instructed Brigadier Jasper Harker, the head of the Security Service's counter-espionage division, and Colonel Valentine Vivian, the head of SIS counter-intelligence division, to conduct a joint inquiry into Krivitsky's revelations. Arrangements were made to keep King under surveillance and to monitor his mail and telephone calls.[4]

From this point on, accounts of the joint investigation are confusing. According to Nigel West, a confession was extracted from King by two MI5 officers after he had been plied with drink and his office burgled to obtain evidence of his guilt.[5] Christopher Andrew, however, tells a different story. Both Raymond Oake and John Herbert King were interviewed on 25 September in the Foreign Office by DI William Rogers of Special Branch in the presence of Harker and Vivian. Oake was questioned first and described how he had introduced Pieck to King in the International Club in Geneva, probably in 1934. He denied having passed any official information to him. King was interviewed next and, apparently not realising how little real evidence there was against him, made a number of damaging admissions. He verified that he had first been introduced to Pieck by Raymond Oake in 1933 or 1934 at the International Club in Geneva. He admitted that he had accepted money from Pieck and, having given him information, was then blackmailed. His flat at 9 St Leonard's Mansions, Smith Street, Chelsea was searched by DI Ernest Tansley and he was arrested by Rogers. In October 1939 he was sentenced at the Central Criminal Court to ten years' imprisonment.

4   Andrew, *The Defence of the Realm*, pp. 263–8

5   Nigel West, *MI5: British Security Service Operations, 1909–45* (London: The Bodley Head, 1981), p. 73

Two other members of the Foreign Office Communications staff, Helen Wilkie and James Russell, were also suspected and the home of the former, at 218 Hamlet Gardens, Ravenscourt Park, in west London, was searched; it was discovered that she had a safe deposit box at 63 Chancery Lane, in which DI Rogers and DS Evan Jones found £1,300 that Wilkie said she was looking after for Captain King. She had been on holidays in France and Spain with King as the guest of the Piecks (she was not, as Parlanti had been led to believe, the mistress of Vansittart, but of King). She was arrested and charged with offences against the Official Secrets Acts but was discharged when King made a written statement exonerating her. Both Wilkie and James Russell were later sacked for what was euphemistically described by the Foreign Office as 'irregularities'.

The notes found in Wilkie's safe deposit box were traced to a bank account operated by Teodor Maly[6] in the name Paul Hardt at the Midland Bank, Russell Square. Some £4,700 had passed through the account between January 1936 and June 1937. Official documents retained by a Major Quarry, another Foreign Office official, were also found in Wilkie's safe deposit box. The explanation for this was more mundane. Helen Wilkie's sister, Ellen, had been Major Quarry's mistress since 1932 and he had retained the documents that dated from his service in Germany, just after World War One, for sentimental reasons; he had given them to Helen for safe keeping. As a result of the inquiry and King's conviction, Cadogan recommended to Lord Halifax, the Foreign Secretary, that the whole of the staff of the Foreign Office Communications Department be replaced. This was done.[7]

After the conviction of King, the spy in the Cabinet Office who had access to the Committee of Imperial Defence had still not been identified. By January 1940, the MI5 case officer was Mrs Jane Archer, née Sissimore, a former barrister, who over the course of the next two months led a team that interviewed Krivitsky in his room at the Langham Hotel in London. In a wide-ranging series

6   In 1936, Maly, an NKVD illegal, was posted to London to take over the running of King from Pieck

7   Andrew, *The Defence of the Realm*, p. 264

of interviews, Krivitsky disclosed information concerning some sixty Soviet agents over whom he had exercised some control. Their identities were not all known to him but he was able to provide clues about who they were, such as 'a Scotsman of very good family working for the Foreign Office who wore a cloak' and 'a journalist who was educated at Cambridge University who fought for Franco in the Spanish Civil War'. With hindsight they can be identified as Donald Maclean and Kim Philby. Later he provided other information about the Cambridge spy ring.

In 1935, when the Soviet intelligence service was setting up its agents in Britain, MI5 infiltrated a nineteen-year-old girl, Olga Gray, into the Communist Party. Eventually she was enlisted by the party as a courier of funds to India. By 1937 she had developed a relationship with Percy Glading, a communist who had also visited India on party business. At Glading's request, Gray rented a flat at 82 Holland Road, Kensington, to use as a 'safe house' for meetings with his Soviet contacts. Glading provided Olga with the cash for the rent of £100 a year and agreed to pay her £5 a week to do some photographic work for him. Soon Glading introduced her to one of his visitors, who called himself Peters but was in fact Teodor Maly. In August 1937, after Maly had returned to the Soviet Union, a couple calling themselves Mr and Mrs Stephens arrived at the flat and Olga Gray assisted Mrs Stephens in photographing plans that Glading brought there. Gray memorised a reference number on one of the plans and subsequent enquiries by the Security Service disclosed that it related to a gun being developed for the Royal Navy at Woolwich Arsenal. The Security Service decided to let the case run and in September Mr and Mrs Stephens were reported to have left the country for Paris en route to Moscow, travelling on false Canadian passports in the names Wily and Mary Brandes, showing that they were born in Romania.

On 12 January Glading told Gray that he had to photograph a book of about 200 pages at his home in South Harrow over the following weekend. He was seen to enter his home on 15 January 1938 with a parcel and leave the next day with a similar package. He was followed to Charing Cross Station where he met a young man and handed the package to him in the public lavatory. The young man was followed to his home in Plumstead and identified as Charles Munday, who worked in the War Chemists Department at Woolwich Arsenal. On 20 January Glading told Gray that he had information stored all over London waiting to be passed on to his Soviet masters and he asked her to prepare for an urgent photographic job. She believed that another meeting was due to take place between Glading and a Soviet agent at Charing Cross the next day and told Maxwell Knight, her MI5 handler. At this stage Special Branch was informed.

At Charing Cross Station Glading was approached by a man who handed over a parcel to him. DI Tommy Thompson arrested him and the second man was detained by DS Sidney Barnes. Inside the package there were four blueprints marked 'secret', but Gray was wrong, the meeting was not with a Soviet agent. The second man was an employee of Woolwich Arsenal called Albert Williams. The photographic session was not to prepare films for a visiting courier to take away but to photograph secret documents removed from Woolwich Arsenal. The Security Service was aware of Glading's association with George Whomack, who was also employed at the Arsenal where Glading had once worked himself. DS Evan Jones searched Glading's house and DIs Frank Bridges and Peel searched the home of Williams. A few days later George Whomack and Charles Munday were arrested. All four were charged with offences under the Official Secrets Acts. The police investigation was thorough and scientific examination, including fingerprint evidence, left little doubt about the guilt of the accused. The trial took place in March 1938, at the Central Criminal Court. The Crown offered no evidence against Charles Munday, who had been charged with Glading with obtaining information concerning explosives. The evidence against the other three was overwhelming and they were convicted. Glading was sentenced to six years' penal servitude, Williams to four years and Whomack to three years' imprisonment. Press reports at the time described Glading as an important member of the Communist International and disclosed information concerning his activities in India. It was also revealed that during 1932 he had been concerned with the production and distribution of the seditious newspaper the *Soldiers' Voice*, and in 1933 with the establishment of communist cells in factories in east London.

Although the prosecution of Glading was considered to be a textbook operation, it was one that failed to uncover the principal Soviet agents and to stop secret drawings being removed from the country. A much more serious failure, as it turned out, was that in examining Glading's documents, the investigators failed to discover the significance of an entry in his notebook regarding Melita Norwood, née Sernis, who was later discovered to have been one of the Russians' most productive atomic spies.

CHAPTER EIGHTEEN

THE WAR YEARS

ACCOMMODATION AND ESTABLISHMENT

Shortly after the outbreak of World War Two, the Special Branch of the Metropolitan Police was saddled with the time-consuming task of vetting over 70,000 alien refugees registered with the police and of supervising the Home Office programme of mass internment. To assist in this mammoth assignment, a number of CID officers was temporarily attached to the Branch. More spacious accommodation was required to cater for the newcomers and the whole Branch was moved into the 'North Extension', a most unattractive concrete construction adjacent to its previous home in the elegant turreted Norman Shaw building on the Victoria Embankment. Another raid on the ranks of the regular CID was carried out when, in the face of persistent demands by the Security Service to be given powers of arrest, and despite opposition from some of his senior officers, the Commissioner, Sir Philip Game, agreed to the temporary transfer of a few CID officers to MI5. This small detachment, headed by DCI Leonard Burt, who was later to become head of Special Branch, was commissioned into the Intelligence Corps but the members retained their status as police officers with powers of arrest. Among the group accompanying Burt were Chief Inspector Reg

Spooner, who later achieved fame as an outstanding detective, and DS Jim Skardon, who stayed on in the Security Service to become their 'ace' interrogator.[1]

More changes in the Branch's establishment were soon to follow. In the early days of the war, police officers were forbidden to enlist in the armed forces but by 1941 this embargo on Special Branch officers was lifted and a number volunteered for active service, with the majority opting for the Royal Air Force. A dramatic easing of the Special Branch workload had led to this change in policy, for by now the suspect alien population was either interned or detained under the defence regulations; the leading British fascists had been detained and their organisations proscribed; and naturalisation had been suspended for the duration of the war. Regrettably, of the number who had temporarily left the Branch to serve in the armed forces, fourteen failed to return; a plaque bearing their names was at one time proudly displayed in the head of Special Branch's office but its whereabouts since the dissolution of Special Branch remains a mystery.

Despite the Branch's reduced workload, however, its officers were heavily committed to dealing with fresh problems arising from the war.

RAID ON THE *DAILY WORKER* OFFICES

The *Daily Worker*, the official organ of the Communist Party of Great Britain (CPGB), had, almost from the outbreak of hostilities, been filling its pages with 'matter calculated to foment opposition to the prosecution of the war to a successful issue'. In July 1940 the Home Secretary, Sir John Anderson, had written to the editor of the paper expressing his disquiet at the tone of the articles; for some time there was some improvement but, by January 1941, the newspaper was again carrying anti-war articles, prompting Anderson to resort to more extreme measures. The head of Special Branch, Albert Canning, was directed to

---

1   Rupert Allason, *The Branch*, p. 116

bring the printing presses to a halt and ensure that the *Daily Worker* would not be published until further notice (the ban would not be lifted until August 1942).

Accordingly, early on 21 January 1941, a team of Special Branch officers led by DI Whitehead raided the *Daily Worker* premises in Clerkenwell, stopped all preparation of the paper, put a guard on the presses and confiscated the newsprint that had already been prepared for the next edition. Members of the management staff and other employees were interviewed but no arrests were made since, as explained in *The Times*, proceeding under Section 2D of the Defence Regulations (as had been done) effectively and immediately prevented further publications without the consent of the Court. After the premises had been secured, the Special Branch officers withdrew, leaving a uniformed presence to guard the building. Similar measures were taken against a second communist publication, *The Week*.[2]

INTERROGATION OF FOREIGN NATIONALS

The Branch was fully occupied in another field. As fans of the television programme *Dad's Army* well know, the English Channel presented the main barrier between the enemy and English soil; consequently security at the channel ports assumed an increasingly important role in the country's determination to exclude potential enemy agents. Extra Special Branch officers were posted to the principal south-coast ports and these were reinforced with men from the resurrected Intelligence Corps. British subjects returning from the Continent were closely questioned about conditions in Europe, while the large numbers of foreign nationals arriving at ports, particularly on the south coast, were directed to various 'reception centres' for intensive interrogation. Principal of these was the Royal Victorian Patriotic School situated on Wandsworth Common, where it is estimated that some 30,000 immigrants were 'grilled' before being allowed

2   *The Times*, 22 January 1941

to proceed, passed on for further interrogation or interned.[3] Special Branch officers were heavily involved in these operations. They also played a major part in the government's plans to have the 71,553 German and Austrian nationals resident here personally examined before special tribunals, which divided them into three categories:

Category A – 572 considered to be the most dangerous or unreliable were interned. The task of serving the internment orders at the outbreak of war fell to DI Gagen, a single man who often used to spend evenings in his office playing the violin (much to the alarm of younger officers working late who were unaware that Sherlock Holmes had risen from the grave!).

Category B – 6,690, posing no immediate threat, but with questionable backgrounds. They were permitted limited freedom, but their movements were strictly regulated.

Category C – 64,290, including 35,000 refugees from Nazi oppression, were considered to represent no threat and had no restrictions placed on them.[4]

However, Special Branch took little part, as it had done in World War One, in the arrest and interrogation of enemy agents. The Security Service, with its newly acquired team of CID officers, complete with power of arrest and expertise in interrogation, was now competent to deal with espionage cases unaided. Special Branch was merely required to play a subsidiary role, such as providing escorts for prisoners and executing warrants of arrest; the Security Service even had its own interrogation centre at Latchmere House on Ham Common in Surrey. They were successful in securing convictions against seventeen persons tried under the Treachery Act 1940, who were all executed, sixteen by hanging and one by the firing squad at the Tower of London. Of this total, three were British subjects.[5]

Special Branch also had little involvement in MI5's highly successful

---

3   Allason, *The Branch*, p. 121

4   Barnes and Barnes, *Nazis in Pre-War London 1930–1939*, p. 252

5   Stephen Stratford, British Criminal and Military History 1939–1949, www.stephen-stratford.co.uk/treachery, accessed on 11 January 2014

'Double-Cross System', which involved the turning of German agents into double agents and using them to send back false information to their controllers in Germany. By these means the German High Command was deceived by a constant supply of disinformation and our own codebreakers were enabled to break Abwehr ciphers. However, SB was able to render a little assistance; they provided the handcuffs when some of the more reluctant double agents were transported to a new base.[6]

Throughout the war, the task of VIP protection, whether of vulnerable resident or visiting dignitaries, remained at a high level and one of the most vulnerable of our own politicians was unquestionably the Prime Minister, Winston Churchill. His principal protection officer throughout the period of hostilities was Walter Thompson, whose account of his service with the country's leader gives some indication of how Special Branch protection duty had changed since the days of Sweeney, Brust and Fitch who, like him, committed to paper their recollections of protecting VIPs.[7] By the beginning of World War Two it had been accepted that personal protection as practised by these earlier members of the Branch could not be effectively carried out at long range. In his narrative, Thompson clearly illustrates that he, at least, and, one presumes, his colleagues, saw the job of protection as securing the personal safety of his protégé, and not as a general factotum to open doors, look after luggage and perform the duties of a lackey. He is the first Special Branch officer to talk openly, and lovingly, about his firearm,[8] for which he had a special holster designed to fit snugly inside his jacket; unlike his predecessors, Thompson used to travel in the passenger seat beside the driver, something that became established practice for subsequent protection officers. Another innovation, retained after the war, was the provision of a back-up police car as part of the Prime Minister's protection team.

In 1921 he became a permanent protection officer with Winston Churchill,

6   TNA KV 4/211, s.19a.

7   W. H. Thompson, *I Was Churchill's Shadow* (London: C. Johnson, 1951)

8   A .32 Webley & Scott self-loading pistol, adopted by the Metropolitan Police after the Sidney Street siege

the Secretary of State for War and the Air, and remained in this post until 1931 after the Conservative government had been defeated in 1929 and Churchill no longer held a ministerial post. Thompson retired from the police in 1936 and that would normally have been the end of his connection with Special Branch, but on 22 August 1939, now running a grocery business in Norwood, he received a brief telegram from Churchill: 'Meet me Croydon aerodrome 4.30 p.m. Wednesday.' In the final paragraph of *The Gathering Storm: The Second World War, Vol. 1*, Churchill explains the reason that prompted him to send this cryptic message:

> There were known to be 20,000 organised Nazis in England at this time, and it would have been only in accord with their procedure in other friendly countries that the outbreak of war should be preceded by a sharp prelude of sabotage and murder. I had at that time no official protection, and I did not wish to ask for any; but I thought myself sufficiently prominent to take precautions. I had enough information to convince me that Hitler recognised me as a foe. My former Scotland Yard detective, Inspector Thompson, was in retirement. I told him to come along and bring his pistol with him. I got out my own weapons which were good. While one slept the other watched. Thus nobody would have had a walkover.[9]

Thompson agreed to act in a private capacity as his personal protection officer for £4 a week, but Churchill soon persuaded Sir Philip Game, the Commissioner, to reinstate him as a Special Branch officer, a position he filled to the end of the war. During his career Thompson had the dubious distinction of meeting Benito Mussolini, but DS Lobb, bodyguard of the former Prime Minister, Neville Chamberlain, bettered this, having met Adolf Hitler during Chamberlain's ill-fated attempts to avert the war.

The subject of personal protection has always presented the police with special problems, and none more so than the complex situation arising from the

---

9   Winston Churchill, *The Gathering Storm: The Second World War, Vol. 1* (London: Cassell, 1948), p. 356

relationship between HRH King Edward VIII and Wallis Simpson, a divorcée, to whom he was married in June 1937 following her second divorce and his abdication on 10 December 1936. According to normal practice, the reigning monarch had been protected by an 'A' Division officer, Chief Inspector Storrier, but the decision to relinquish the throne resulted in a change to the composition of his protection unit; by 1938, Storrier, promoted to superintendent in January, now had a Special Branch officer, DS Attfield, in his team, at the request of the Prime Minister. The marriage put a strain on the security arrangements for the couple, who made little secret of their admiration for the Nazi regime; indeed, during a holiday in Germany in 1937 they met Adolf Hitler, which endeared them to the fascists in the UK, but at the same time alienated the communists and Jews, raising the prospect of clashes between the two factions. The Duke's marriage to a twice-divorced woman also enraged religious factions in Britain and there were fears of religious zealots venting their feelings in attempts on the personal wellbeing of the couple.[10]

It must have been with considerable relief that those responsible for the couple's protection in Britain were informed in 1940 that the Duke had been appointed as the Governor of the Bahamas, a post he filled, apparently with success, until after the war. It was again a Special Branch officer, DI Harry Holder, who was entrusted with responsibility for the Duke's continued protection on the island.

The six years of the war represented a comparatively uneventful period for the Branch – no suffragettes, no IRA, no naturalisation, and espionage cases were dealt with almost exclusively by the Security Service, assisted by their small team of CID officers. This is not to say that Special Branch officers were idle; as previously mentioned, a considerable number enlisted in the armed forces and those remaining were fully occupied with less exciting work at ports, with protection and with the more mundane aspects of counter-espionage such as arrests, serving warrants and escort duty.

---

10   TNA MEPO 10/35 deals with personal protection of HRH King Edward VIII

CHAPTER NINETEEN

THE RETURN OF PEACE

THE CESSATION OF hostilities saw major changes in the higher echelons of the Metropolitan Police; the ten-year reign of Albert Canning
(now a Chief Constable) came to an end when he retired in 1946, and
the newly appointed Commissioner, Sir Harold Scott, was thus confronted with
an early problem – choosing a new head of Special Branch. To widespread surprise, and not a little pique among the ranks of senior Special Branch officers, he
selected Leonard Burt, who had retained his status as a police officer despite his
six-year stint in the Security Service. Although an investigator of proven ability,
whose services had been much appreciated by MI5, Burt's knowledge of Special
Branch work was strictly limited and probably distorted by the years he had spent
working with MI5's senior officers, particularly Guy Liddell, a Director and an
outspoken critic of his former colleagues in Special Branch. The appointment
of Burt, with the rank of Detective Superintendent, was unexpected, since it
had been the practice from the beginning of the century for the deputy head to
take over from the outgoing leader. So Tommy Thompson, who had been Canning's right-hand man for many years, continued as bridesmaid.

Lieutenant Colonel Burt's final days as a member of the Security Service
were not without excitement. In May 1945, he was tasked with escorting William

Joyce ('Lord Haw Haw') back to England for his execution; vital evidence, with-out which Joyce may not have been successfully prosecuted, was provided by DI 'Mick' Hunt who, like so many of his Special Branch colleagues, had spent many boring hours listening to, and noting, the ranting of Joyce and his fascist pals. It was Hunt who was able to convince the jury that he recognised the voice of the man in the dock as that of the rabble rouser whom he had heard address-ing countless fascist meetings before the war and later, as 'Lord Haw Haw', delivering his notorious propaganda broadcasts. Burt's career as an MI5 officer was brought to a successful conclusion in February 1946, with the arrest, by DCI Whitehead of Special Branch, of Alan Nunn May for offences under the Official Secrets Act of 1911. Together with Reg Spooner, Burt had been investi-gating the activities of this nuclear scientist since October 1945 and it was largely due to his painstaking and professional conduct of the case that Nunn May was convicted and sentenced to ten years' penal servitude.[1]

The cessation of hostilities with Germany saw the beginning of another war – the Cold War – only this time the adversary was Russia. The government decreed that all communists and fascists should be excluded from work 'vital to the Security of the State', an edict that led the Security Service to conclude in October 1948: 'Our ultimate aim must be the keeping of accurate records of all members of the [CPGB].' The Service set up a series of operations, known collectively as STILL LIFE, which enabled them to have covert access to all CP offices in Britain and Northern Ireland. Over the years thousands of documents were copied by means of these clandestine operations and by 1952 the Security Service was able to report proudly that 90 per cent of the 35,000 membership of the CPGB had been identified.[2] However, this success was not achieved by MI5 unaided. A stream of STILL LIFE enquiries continued to arrive at New Scotland Yard well into the '60s and were farmed out to junior officers 'to cut their teeth on'. The information contained in many of these letters was extremely

---

1   The reference to Nunn May is from Burt's memoirs, *Commander Burt of Scotland Yard* (Pan Books: London, 1962), pp. 16–48

2   Security Service Archives cited in Andrew's *The Defence of the Realm*, pp. 400–402

sketchy, frequently inaccurate and on occasion bizarre as, for example, a request for identifying particulars of one E. Bear of an address in east London; this was quickly resolved by reference to the electoral roll, which showed that E. Bear shared his home with M. Mouse and J. Spratt. However, the majority of enquiries were satisfactorily answered and proved useful training exercises for new recruits to the Branch.

NATURALISATION

O n arrival at the Yard to take up his new appointment as head of the Metropolitan Police Special Branch, Burt was faced with more mundane problems than catching spies. Throughout the duration of the war there had been an embargo on new applications for naturalisation, but in September 1945, the Home Office focused its attention on the arrears of cases that had been gathering dust in its repositories for the past six years. Dealing with this vast backlog represented a considerable drain on Branch resources and as a first step an inspector was deputed to carry out preliminary arrangements. On his recommendation, the establishment of the Branch was increased by nineteen (three DIs, six DSs and ten DCs) and in December 1947 the unusual step was taken of drafting in reinforcements from the provinces. In total, thirteen officers from different constabularies were brought in and, with their help, the backlog of outstanding cases had been sufficiently reduced by early 1950 for these provincial officers to be returned to their home forces. When at full strength, this naturalisation section was dealing with 1,000 applications a month.[3]

Naturalisation enquiries remained a staple and necessary diet for Special Branch until the end of its days; some officers regarded the section as a dull backwater, but this was not so, as learning the most intimate secrets of famous (and not so famous) individuals could provide a most interesting insight into

---

3   Correspondence regarding these matters is dealt with on TNA MEPO 3/1945

human nature. Special Branch has always taken pride in the presentation of its work and naturalisation reports sent to the Home Office were no exception. Gone were the days when two or three paragraphs of handwritten notes would suffice to satisfy the naturalisation department of an applicant's worthiness to become British. Immediately prior to World War Two, reports were running to many pages of beautifully produced copperplate writing (without illuminated capital letters!) and the applicant was still quaintly referred to as 'the memorialist'. It was not until after the war that typewriters became available to the lowly constables (very few of whom had typing skills). A further labour-saving introduction to the officers' armoury was the photocopier, which blissfully replaced the messy and inefficient carbon paper. By 1960, an average naturalisation case would represent about three days of work, culminating in a well-presented report of some four to five typewritten pages. Naturally some of the more complicated cases would take much longer and run to twenty or more pages, as in the case of Mohamed Al-Fayed who, exceptionally, was twice refused British citizenship.

PROTECTION

As with naturalisation, VIP protection always featured in the duties performed by Special Branch. Reference has already been made to the improvements in protection techniques introduced since the days of Sweeney, Brust and Fitch. Burt throws further light on VIP protection as performed by Special Branch officers after the war. His first experience of a 'difficult' VIP visit was that of Marshal Tito, President of Yugoslavia, in 1953; naturally Burt was not part of the protection team, but as head of the Branch he was responsible for the safety of the Marshal while in this country. For the first time, five senior officers under a superintendent, in this case Bill Hughes, formed a close protection team that accompanied the President wherever he went; they were supplemented by seven Yugoslav security officers, who, after some initial reticence, seemed quite prepared to 'play second fiddle' to their British counterparts. This was not always the case with visitors from abroad, notably the American Secret Service and, to a lesser extent, the Russians, who were adamant that they should be allowed to carry firearms. The British were equally insistent that they should not and invariably won the day, though in 1956, prior to the visit of the Russian President Bulganin and the powerful secretary of the Communist Party, Nikita Khrushchev, Burt relented and issued four firearms certificates for their bodyguards.

The Russians were not so fortunate on the occasion of their next important visit to Britain in February 1967, that of the chairman of the Council of Ministers of the USSR, A. N. Kosygin. An advance party headed by Major General Sverchkov arrived a few days prior to the visit to discuss security arrangements. The initial meeting at New Scotland Yard proceeded smoothly until the question of firearms arose; on this occasion, after an extremely heated discussion, it was the British who stuck to their guns and the Russians who lost theirs. This was no surprise as the man in charge of Special Branch protection for Kosygin was Detective Chief Superintendent Victor Gilbert, not the easiest man to beat in an argument, as surviving contemporaries will confirm.

This visit incorporated many of the features that had become a routine part of VIP protection procedures. Most obvious to the public, and invaluable from a security standpoint, was the provision of a posse of motorcycle escorts from the Special Escort Group, who not only created a physical barrier in congested areas by closing up on the principal's vehicle but, like a knife through butter, could cut a swathe through seemingly impenetrable traffic jams. Up to a dozen motorcyclists would escort the more controversial personalities and, given suitable conditions, liked nothing better than to spread their wings and go into 'arrow formation' round the cavalcade. In the case of more important visits, it became standard practice for not only a back-up car but an advance vehicle to form part of the protection team; this ensured that the route was clear of obstructions and also that a member of the team was already in place when the VIP arrived at his or her destination. A dramatic improvement in communication came with the introduction of personal radios, and security was vastly improved with the provision of armoured cars (see Chapter 27 on protection).

But while all these close protection measures were being taken, other Special Branch officers would be fully engaged behind the scenes checking buildings overlooking the lines of route to be taken, vetting their occupants and establishing the movements of likely troublemakers. But as with the case of close protection, everything would be done as discreetly as possible; the Russians were astounded that demonstrators were allowed outside Claridges Hotel when Kosygin arrived there. In the Soviet Union they would all have been sent to Siberia for the duration of the visit (and maybe longer). The British way is to allow the professionalism of the personal protection team, backed by the vigilance, common sense and good humour of their uniformed colleagues, to provide an efficient, yet proportionate, level of protection; in a nutshell – to quote Burt – 'The Special Branch goes about its job quietly and unostentatiously.'[4] This method has rarely failed.

ZIONIST EXTREMISM

I n the years immediately following the war, Zionist extremists intent on creating an independent Jewish state were resorting increasingly to terrorist tactics to press their claims, and, in 1946, MI5 received a number of reports indicating that Irgun Zvai Leumi and the Stern Gang, the two most militant groups, were contemplating attacks on targets in Britain.[5] All three security services, MI5, MI6 and Special Branch, were now involved in monitoring the terrorists' intentions, justifiably so, as on 15 April 1947 a Stern Gang member, later identified as Betty Knout(h), aka Elizabeth Lazarus, charmed her way into the Colonial Office by persuading the doorman to let her use the ladies' cloakroom as one of her stockings was falling down. Fortunately the bomb she left behind failed to detonate, as the timing device jammed. The fact that the gelignite in the bomb was of French manufacture and that the girl spoke

---

4   Burt, *Commander Burt of Scotland Yard*, p. 106

5   Andrew, *The Defence of the Realm*, pp. 352–5

with a French accent pointed to a French connection and Special Branch's DCI E. W. Jones was promptly dispatched to Paris to liaise with the French police.[6] A thumbprint found on the unexploded bomb proved to be that of a known Stern Gang terrorist, Yaacov Levstein (aka Eliav), but neither he nor Knout was in France, for they had fled to Belgium, where they were arrested in possession of explosives and letter bombs. The Belgian police regarded their offences as political, which meant they could not be extradited to Britain, but they permitted a Special Branch officer, in the person of Superintendent Wilkinson, to sit in on interrogations of the couple.

Although Wilkinson was not able to have the pair charged with the attempt to cause the explosion at the Colonial Office, his collaboration with the Belgian authorities established beyond any reasonable doubt that they were responsible not only for that offence but also for sending letter bombs to prominent British politicians in 1946, which mercifully injured nobody. When Levstein was arrested he was in possession of another batch of letter bombs addressed to British ministers. The Belgian police had scanty knowledge of the Stern Gang and it was largely due to Wilkinson's briefing that the case was brought to a successful conclusion, in that Levstein and Knout were found guilty by a Belgian court of illegally importing explosives into the country and sentenced to eight months' and twelve months' imprisonment respectively.[7]

The threat from Jewish terrorists lingered on and in July 1948, Detective Superintendent G. G. Smith, widely known as 'Moonraker' on account of his pronounced Wiltshire accent,[8] received information from a contact suggesting that Irgun Zvai Leumi might be planning to sabotage RAF property. A Special Branch surveillance operation identified one of those involved in the conspiracy as Monti Harris, a Jewish grocer who ran his business from premises in Gravel Lane, in Aldgate. His shop was kept under continual observation by a team

---

6   James Barr, *A Line in the Sand: Britain, France and the Struggle that Shaped the Middle East* (London: Simon & Schuster, 2011), p. 337

7   George Wilkinson, *Special Branch Officer* (London: Odhams, 1956), pp. 204–21

8   Moonraker is a native of Wiltshire

of Special Branch officers for three weeks, as it was suspected he was storing explosives there. Commander Burt describes events leading up to his arrest:

> Harris was a hard man to follow – he was suspicious and sly. We managed to pounce on him one Saturday morning in a rather unconventional way. Five Special Branch officers and two women officers, dressed for a tennis tournament and chattering away about their prospects, jumped on a trolley bus that was taking Harris to his arsenal. There Detective Superintendent Smith arrested him.

(Note: Special Branch officers have never been lacking in innovative ideas.)

Large quantities of aluminium powder, detonators, fuses and other ingredients for making incendiary bombs were found in a search of his premises. On 14 October 1948, Harris was sentenced to seven years' imprisonment for offences under the Explosives Substances Act of 1883. He was released on 24 July 1950 on undertaking to leave the United Kingdom for Palestine. Burt commented that, had the Special Branch operation failed, 'there would have been a wave of incendiarism and sabotage in England'.[9]

KLAUS FUCHS

A t the end of the war, MI5's team of officers on loan from the CID lost these interrogators, with the exception of Jim Skardon, but remained responsible for counter-espionage. So it was that in 1950, Burt, now head of MPSB, found himself in the unaccustomed situation of having a case presented to him by MI5, almost completed, with a confession signed by the suspect, Dr Klaus Fuchs, who had been passing Britain's atomic secrets to the Russians from 1943 to 1947. All Burt had to do was to arrest Fuchs and present him at court; the

---

9   Burt, *Commander Burt of Scotland Yard*, p. 119

preparatory work had been carried out by his former colleague, Jim Skardon, who had elected to remain with the Security Service as their chief investigator, but no longer retained a power of arrest. Fuchs duly appeared in court in February 1950 and was sentenced to fourteen years' imprisonment.

Special Branch became involved in another case of espionage two years later when MI5's surveillance of a young Foreign Office cipher clerk led them to believe that he was passing classified information to a Soviet diplomat. As soon as the Branch was informed, a surveillance team under DCI Bill Hughes was set up and the young man, William Martin Marshall, kept under rigorous observation. It was not long before a clandestine meeting took place in a Wandsworth park with a man, who at that time was unknown to the watching officers. When they were arrested, Marshall had in his possession a top-secret document; the stranger, who claimed diplomatic immunity, was identified as a Soviet diplomat, Pavel Kuznetsov. He was told to leave the country within seven days. Marshall was sentenced to five years' imprisonment for unauthorised disclosure of classified information.[10]

From the Special Branch point of view, these were straightforward cases, but later breaches of the Official Secrets Acts were not all so easily dealt with; nevertheless the same procedure was followed in every instance. The 'Portland spy ring', MI5's own Michael Bettaney, John Vassall – all these cases were taken to court by Special Branch after the initial breach had been discovered by MI5. It was a system that worked well and depended for its successful operation upon close cooperation between the two services, which, in most cases, was achieved. This is not to suggest that when a case was handed to Special Branch the necessary evidence had already been secured and suspects identified; normally it was only after arrests were made that the Special Branch task began in earnest. In a big conspiracy such as the Portland case (see pp. 237–9), the business of interviewing witnesses, searching premises, preserving evidence, liaison with other agencies (frequently foreign) and a host of other tasks was labour-intensive and could keep a large section of the Branch busy for many weeks.

---

10   Allason, *The Branch*, pp. 130–31

THE IRA AGAIN

For fourteen years the British mainland was free of concerted IRA activity, but there have always been elements within that organisation determined to secure self-determination for Ireland, and in July 1953 a group of three republicans broke into a Junior Training Corps Armoury at Felstead School in Essex and made off with a quantity of arms and ammunition. The raid was a fiasco – initially they piled so many weapons onto their old van that it wouldn't move. When they did eventually get going, they lost their way and were stopped by a patrol car as they were travelling so slowly. The rest is history – the trio were arrested and sentenced to eight years' imprisonment. Had they been young, inexperienced Volunteers, their bungled efforts might have been understandable, but these were leading figures in the republican movement – Cathal Goulding later became leader of the IRA and Manus Canning had been a staunch republican for many years; Seán Mac Stíofáin was a unique republican, as he was English, born in Leytonstone, and his real name was John Edward Drayton Stephenson, but his mother and wife were Irish and he became absorbed in Irish affairs from an early age. He eventually became chief of staff of the Provisional IRA.

Following another abortive raid for arms in Omagh, information filtering though from informants made it apparent that the IRA was preparing for another campaign, either in Ireland or on the mainland. In London, Special Branch feared that it would be the latter and stepped up their monitoring of Sinn Féin activities in the capital, while alerting their provincial colleagues of the heightened threat. The problem facing the Branch was that there was no IRA organisation in London and the few informants that it had were merely Sinn Féin members, who were unlikely to be privy to details of IRA schemes.

Police fears were justified, as it was not long before the IRA struck again; this time their target was an REME training centre in Arborfield, Berkshire, the date: 13 August 1955. Despite warnings for increased security, which had been sent to all army bases in the country, the raiders easily overpowered the ill-prepared guards and made off in two vans with their booty: fifty-five sten guns, ten bren guns, an assortment of other firearms and more than 60,000 rounds of ammunition. One of the vans was stopped by police outside Ascot for speeding (unlike the Felsted trio, whose slow speed led to their downfall).

On searching the vehicle, the two constables, George Kerr and George Phillips, found a mass of arms and ammunition, not a consignment of batteries which the driver claimed they were delivering to an address in London. The two occupants gave their names as Joseph Doyle and Donal Murphy, although the Irish driving licences they produced gave their identities as Richard Wall and Robert Russell. The officers had not yet received news of the Arborfield raid, which was shortly afterwards broadcast to all patrol cars, and it was entirely due to their police training and perception, coupled with the Irishmen's carelessness and stupidity, that, yet again, the IRA's plans were foiled. The two men were arrested and escorted to Ascot police station, where they were searched and interrogated by Special Branch officers led by DCI Williams.

Although the men remained mute, a bill found on them indicated that they had recently stayed at the Bedford Hotel, Bloomsbury, together with six other Irishmen. Other documents in their possession led Special Branch officers to 16 Winkfield Road, Wood Green, where DI Leslie Garrett arrested James Andrew Mary Murphy, who admitted being a member of the IRA.[11] Extensive enquiries and persistent interrogation of the prisoners by Special Branch officers revealed that the contents of the second van had been unloaded at 237 Caledonian Road, N1. Detective Superintendent G. G. Smith led a large squad of men to this address, where surveillance was maintained during the next day in the hope that the rest of the team would return to collect their booty, which had been stored in the basement – but the birds had flown.[12]

The three men were tried at Berkshire Assizes in Reading and, on 5 October 1955, were each sentenced to life imprisonment for offences arising from the raid. The judge warmly commended all those, particularly PCs Kerr and Phillips,

11 Ibid., p. 133
12 Burt, *Commander Burt of Scotland Yard*, pp. 114–16

responsible for recovering the arms and bringing the prisoners to justice. The result was only a partial success for Special Branch since six of the gang had eluded them – Anthony Magan, Joseph Ryan, John Reynolds, James Garland, Pat Connor and William Roche. James Murphy only served three years of his sentence, as he escaped from Wakefield Prison in February 1959.

CHAPTER TWENTY

THE SPYING SEASON

OMMANDER BURT RETIRED in 1958 after a police career spanning forty-six years. He was succeeded by E. W. Jones, his deputy for much of his time as head of Special Branch. Jones was a tall, quietly spoken Welshman, a man of few words, which was just as well as he invariably spoke with a pipe in his mouth, rendering his speech incomprehensible to all but a small coterie of officers. New recruits were encouraged to learn the name of his favourite brand of tobacco, as a summons to his office invariably meant a trip to the nearest tobacconist for a fresh supply of Mick McQuaid Plug.

'Evan Willie', as he was disrespectfully referred to by 'the troops' (out of his hearing of course), controlled the Branch for eight years, a period that started uneventfully but later was packed with events that frequently dominated the headlines. All cases of espionage are important, but there had been none to catch the public imagination since 1950, when Klaus Fuchs was sent to prison for passing atomic secrets to the Russians.

Then in 1960, MI5, which had endured a torrid time in the 1950s with the exposure of the Cambridge spy ring (the majority of whom were their own employees) and were anxious to regain some of their former respectability, revealed to Jones that they wanted the help of Special Branch to ensnare a man whom they strongly believed to be a Soviet 'illegal' (an intelligence officer operating here under a false identity). What they wanted was a sight of the contents of a briefcase lodged in a safe deposit box at a branch of the Midland Bank; the Branch readily complied with their request and Superintendent G. G. Smith, armed with a warrant, was able to 'borrow' the briefcase while the owner, Gordon Lonsdale, was away on holiday. Although it contained what MI5 were seeking, evidence of espionage, the Service did not bring Special Branch fully into the picture until Lonsdale's contacts in this country had been identified. When eventually the Branch were entrusted with details of the case, some five months after Jones had initially been approached, they were given the particulars of five persons whom MI5 strongly suspected of complicity in espionage. Apart from Lonsdale, they were Harry Houghton and his girlfriend Ethel 'Bunty' Gee, who both worked at the Royal Navy Underwater Detection Establishment at Portland, and Peter and Helen Kroger, ostensibly antiquarian booksellers but who, like Lonsdale, were 'illegals'.

The Special Branch plan to arrest Lonsdale, Gee and Houghton worked perfectly. It was known that Houghton and his lover had regular afternoon meetings with Lonsdale near Waterloo Station on the first Saturday of every month. A large team of officers was warned for 'Special Enqs.' on Saturday 7 January 1961 to be briefed by 'Moonraker' Smith. The whole Branch was humming with curiosity but those 'in the know' remained silent.

Surveillance was maintained by Special Branch officers on Houghton and Gee after they arrived at Waterloo Station and they were followed on what appeared to be an innocuous afternoon's shopping expedition to East Street market on Walworth Road. When they returned to the station they met Lonsdale and papers were handed over, which later proved to be classified. It was at this moment that, in a dramatic swoop, all three were arrested by the surveillance teams led by G. G. Smith and taken into custody. Superintendents G. G. and Ferguson Smith, accompanied by DS Anne Winterbottom, went without delay to Ruislip and completed a satisfactory day's work with the arrest of the Krogers in their home. A bonus for the police and MI5 was the discovery by DS Winterbottom, in Helen Krogers's handbag, of a lengthy letter in Russian intended for encryption and conversion into a microdot.

The Krogers, who were suspected by the FBI of espionage in the USA under their true names, Morris and Lona Cohen, had been acting as the group's communication and technical support group. During a detailed and painstaking search of their home by Special Branch and MI5 officers, a vast amount of espionage paraphernalia was found. So well hidden were some of the items, particularly the radio transmitter, which was secreted under the kitchen floor, that it was several weeks before the search teams were satisfied that nothing had been missed. Apart from standard spy equipment – false passports, one-time pads and microdots – the house contained numerous innocent-looking items such as tins of talcum powder and cigarette lighters with concealed compartments, designed to hold microdots etc.[1]

In March 1961, the five spies were tried at the Central Criminal Court and convicted of offences under the Official Secrets Acts. Gordon Lonsdale, whose true name was Konon Trofimovich Molody, was sentenced to twenty-five years' imprisonment, the Krogers to twenty years each, Houghton and Gee to fifteen years each.

No sooner was the Portland spy case satisfactorily concluded than the Security Service was presented with intelligence of another security breach, this time the suspect was a member of the Secret Intelligence Service, namely George Blake, who had joined the SIS in 1944 and had been working for the KGB since 1951. On this occasion the arrest presented Superintendent 'Fergie' Smith and DCI Louis Gale with none of the problems that had confronted the police in the Lonsdale case, as he had already confessed his guilt to his MI5 interrogators and merely had to be taken into custody and conveyed to a police cell to await his trial the following month. The gravity of his offences can be gauged by the length of his sentence – forty-two years, a record.

There was no requirement for lengthy searches of Blake's accommodation, as there had been in the previous espionage case, as he had been living in Lebanon at the time of his summons to London by the SIS. Although he had been

---

1   Allason, *The Branch*, pp. 137-9; Andrew, *The Defence of the Realm*, pp. 483-7; and personal knowledge

told that his recall was for administrative reasons, the real purpose was for his employers to interrogate him. In the event he confessed without much of a fight and the case was handed over to the Branch who, with comparatively little investigation to be carried out, co-operated with the Director of Public Prosecutions to have the prosecution case prepared in time for proceedings at the Old Bailey, to be commenced on 3 May 1961.

Although preparation of the prosecution case against Blake presented Special Branch with no major difficulties and was no great drain on their resources, his later exploits certainly were, for on 22 October 1966 he made a well-planned escape from Wormwood Scrubs Prison and, after lying low for some time, made his way to East Berlin and on to his eventual home, Moscow. Blake's escape would not have been possible had it not been for the considerable assistance he had received from three of his former associates in prison, Michael Randle and Patrick Pottle, both leading members of the Committee of 100 (see p. 248), and Sean Bourke, a prominent Irish republican. Detective Chief Superintendent Tommy Butler, head of Scotland Yard's famous Flying Squad (the Sweeney), led the police inquiry into the escape and Special Branch were heavily involved in the many enquiries that had to be made and in extra vigilance at ports. It soon became apparent that Sean Bourke had assisted in the break-out, and DCI Arthur Cunningham from Special Branch visited the Irishman's home in Limerick, but his mother could not, or would not, assist the police enquiries. He surfaced in Moscow and later returned to the Republic of Ireland but attempts to extradite him were refused by the Dublin High Court on the grounds that any offence he may have committed was political.[2] Randle and Pottle's participation in the escape went undetected until 1989 when, following the example of Bourke, they published a detailed account of the episode; the following year Blake contributed his own version of the dramatic escape. The three narratives, which make interesting reading, describe how Blake, after lying low in north London for some weeks sheltered by Pottle, Randle and their friends, was driven by Ran-

2   Contemporaneous issues of the *Times* newspaper

dle in his Dormobile to East Berlin where he was reunited with Bourke, who accompanied him on the final lap of his journey to Moscow.[3]

Confronted with Pottle and Randle's admission of their complicity in the escape plot, police had little option but to prosecute; they duly appeared at the Old Bailey in June 1991, when they were acquitted by the jury despite the judge's summing up, which virtually directed them to convict.

Other espionage cases were to keep MI5 and the Branch busy for the rest of the decade and beyond. Lonsdale and his fellow conspirators had not long begun their prison sentences when the Security Service received intelligence from one of their agents which led them to investigate the activities of an Admiralty clerk, William John Christopher Vassall. The usual routine procedures – bugging of his flat, surveillance and a search of his desk at the Admiralty – failed to disclose any traces of espionage, but a clandestine search of his flat was more promising – two cameras and exposed film secreted in a purpose-built hiding place.[4] Having secured the evidence they were seeking, MI5 called in Special Branch and once more it was 'Moonraker' Smith who, on 12 September 1962, carried out the arrest. Like George Blake, Vassall made a full confession of his spying activities on behalf of the Russians and, on 22 October 1962, at the Central Criminal Court, pleaded guilty to offences under the Official Secrets Act, 1911, and was sentenced to eighteen years' imprisonment.

About this time Special Branch became reluctantly involved in what became known as 'the Profumo affair'. In the early part of 1963, a nineteen-year-old girl named Christine Keeler was due to appear as a prosecution witness in the case of a West Indian who had been charged with wounding and illegal possession of a firearm. When a CID sergeant called on her to serve a witness summons, she remarked that she had had an affair with the Secretary of State for War, John

---

3   The story of Blake's escape and subsequent evasion of discovery is told in *The Springing of George Blake* (Bourke); *The Blake Escape* (Randle & Pottle); and *No Other Choice* (Blake)

4   One is reminded of Detective Inspector Lestrade's rueful comment to Sherlock Holmes when the famous fictional detective has obtained some vital evidence after burgling a flat – 'We can't do these things in the Force, Mr Holmes. No wonder you get results that are beyond us.' Conan Doyle, 'The Adventure of the Bruce-Partington Plans' in *The Penguin Complete Sherlock Holmes* (London: Penguin, 2001), p. 928

Profumo, and was also 'friendly' with the Soviet naval attaché. Another of her many male acquaintances was Stephen Ward who, she alleged, had asked her on one occasion to obtain from Profumo 'the date on which certain atomic secrets were to be handed to West Germany by the Americans'.[5]

The CID passed on this information to Special Branch (DI Arthur Morgan), who in turn relayed it to MI5, who already had a record of Ward but denied there was any security or intelligence aspect to the case. Anxious not to get the Branch involved in a political scandal, Commander Jones instructed DI Morgan to cancel the appointment that he and Marylebone CID had made to see Christine Keeler on 1 February 1963. It was not long before rumours became rife that 'a minister' was in a relationship with Keeler. Soon the finger of suspicion was pointing unerringly at Profumo, who declared to the House of Commons, on 22 March, that there had been 'no impropriety whatsoever' between him and Keeler; he was subsequently forced to admit this was a lie and stood down as an MP.

At the same time, Marylebone CID were pursuing enquiries into allegations of sexual offences committed by Stephen Ward, as a result of which he was charged with living off the immoral earnings of prostitutes (Keeler and Mandy Rice-Davies). He was found guilty but committed suicide before sentence could be passed.

In the wake of Ward's conviction, questions were being asked in the press, in Parliament and elsewhere as to the roles played by police and the security services in the affair. Consequently Lord Denning, an experienced and respected judge, was appointed to make a thorough investigation of all aspects of the case, which he did in a remarkably short time, publishing his report in September 1963, the month following Ward's death. He completely exonerated MI5 from any blame but severely criticised the police, and particularly Special Branch, for not following up Christine Keeler's allegation that Stephen Ward was acting as a Soviet spy. He felt that this failure was due to 'an error in coordination' and not attributable to any individual.[6] His judgement has since been consistently

---

5   Allason, *The Branch*, p. 145

6   Ibid., pp. 144–5

questioned by 'conspiracy theorists' and others, principally Geoffrey Robert-
son QC in his book *Stephen Ward Was Innocent, OK*, who claim that Ward was
the victim of an Establishment plot and that the prosecution case against him
was seriously flawed.

Before the Profumo affair had reached its unfortunate conclusion, the Security Service presented the Branch with another case of what they perceived to
be espionage. For a number of months from August 1962, they had been con-
ducting investigations into the activities of Guiseppe Enrico Gilberto Martelli,
whom they strongly suspected of spying for the Russians. An unusual aspect of
the case was that the Italian, who was employed at the Culham laboratories of
the United Kingdom Atomic Energy Authority, had no access to classified information. However, a clandestine search of his home by MI5 uncovered items
typically used by spies, including a one-time pad, microfilm and a camera.

Martelli was arrested at Southend Airport on 26 April 1963 and the case taken
over by Special Branch (DCI David Stratton and DI 'Jock' Wilson). A small team
of Special Branch officers made the enquiries necessary for the case to be presented at the Old Bailey in July, when he was acquitted of nine charges, principally
of committing acts preparatory to the commission of offences under the Official
Secrets Acts. Unfortunately for the prosecution, his defence counsel convinced
the jury that there was an innocent explanation for his possession of the 'spy kit'.[7]

During the next four years a succession of espionage cases was uncovered
by the Security Services and presented to Special Branch for prosecution. The
first of these was that of Frank Clifton Bossard, who was employed at the Air
Ministry in the Research and Development Division. He was arrested by Detective Superintendent 'Jim' Wise on 15 March 1965, and on 10 May at the Central
Criminal Court was sentenced to twenty years' imprisonment for supplying
classified information to the Russians.[8]

Bossard was followed into the dock by Percy Sidney Allen, who in a separate

---

7   *The Times*, 16 July 1963; TNA CRIM 1/4133

8   TNA CRIM 1/4369; *The Times*, 6 April 1965

case was convicted of selling secret information, illicitly obtained from his employ-ers, the Ministry of Defence, to the Iraqis. Allen, a staff sergeant in the army, had been arrested on 16 March by DCI Wilson following surveillance by a team of Special Branch officers, who witnessed the soldier handing over classified infor-mation to an intelligence officer from the Iraqi embassy. MI5 had been monitoring Allen's activities for some months prior to handing the case to Special Branch, and were aware that he had been supplying the Iraqis with intelligence since 1961. He received a sentence of twenty-one years' imprisonment.[9]

One final case concluded the 1960s' plethora of prosecutions under the Official Secrets Acts. On 25 May 1967, Detective Superintendent 'Vic' Gilbert arrested separately both Helen Keenan and Norman Henry Blackburn on sus-picion of espionage. On 25 June Miss Keenan was sentenced to six months' imprisonment and Blackburn was jailed for five years. There was no romantic involvement between them, they both had steady partners, and they had met by chance in an Earls Court club. Blackburn, a surveyor, was a member of the South African Bureau of State Security and Keenan was employed as a shorthand typ-ist at the Cabinet Office. She was persuaded by Blackburn to obtain from her place of work some classified documents, which he intended to pass on to the Rhodesian Special Branch. MI5 discovered that she was in touch with Black-burn and passed this information on to Special Branch, who set up surveillance on the couple which led to their arrests.[10]

SURVEILLANCE

S urveillance as practised by MPSB in those days was a primitive art com-pared with the sophisticated science into which it developed. About this time (the late '60s) no electronic aids were available, although bulky personal

---

9   *The Times*, 11 May 1965

10   Richard Trahair and Robert Miller, *Encyclopaedia of Cold War Espionage, Spies and Secret Operations* (New York: Enigma, 2012), p. 185

radios would shortly be introduced, to be followed by made-to-measure ear pieces. Special Branch were the proud owners of 'an observation van', fondly referred to as the 'butcher's van' by those who had the misfortune to use it; it had previously belonged to a firm of butchers and had been sprayed to obscure the printing on the sides, which could still be clearly discerned underneath the thin film of paint. The van had no heating and, of course, no toilet facilities; narrow slits cut in the sides and rear of the van afforded only restricted vision; the sole ventilation consisted of the observation slits, through which cold blasts of air were directed in to the eyes of the beholders. At the end of a shift, the smoke-filled van (only smokers seemed to be picked for these jobs) would discharge its cargo of red-eyed, cold and thirsty officers outside the nearest pub where, not surprisingly, a dash for the toilet would take precedence over the need for a pint. Unmarked cars could also be used, but a vehicle containing a couple of big, young, fit-looking men which remained in the same area for any length of time would inevitably arouse suspicion, and often did. Not infrequently, embarrassing confrontations took place between surveillance officers and uniformed police summoned by worried, or curious, residents. Inevitably officers used their ingenuity to overcome these problems. Static observation posts (OPs) might be established in suitable buildings, either residential or commercial, if discreet enquiries established that the owner/occupier would be cooperative; one enterprising officer posing as a telephone engineer established his own temporary OP on the pavement outside a place of interest, in a canvas tent borrowed from the GPO; another, keeping watch on an IRA operative travelling on a train, posed as a restaurant-car attendant; a third, who knew his man would be travelling from a run-down area in west London to the City, started his stalking operation wearing a cloth cap and, at a suitable juncture, donned a bowler hat, which he produced from a carrier bag. The transformation was complete when he removed his thin anorak, stuffed it into the empty bag and continued his journey as a typical city gent resplendent in a dark suit and matching bowler. A junior member of the team was left to carry the anorak.

CHAPTER TWENTY-ONE

DEMONSTRATIONS
AND PUBLIC ORDER

T HE LATE '50S saw the start of a series of mass protests, not only in
Britain but throughout Europe and the rest of the world. Two controversial topics for demonstrations were the Vietnam War and nuclear
disarmament.

THE CAMPAIGN FOR NUCLEAR DISARMAMENT

I n Britain, the Campaign for Nuclear Disarmament (CND) was formed in
February 1958. Among its early leaders were the controversial philosopher
Bertrand Russell, the Labour politician Michael Foot and John Collins, a canon
of St Paul's Cathedral. It always aimed to pursue its main objective of banning
nuclear weapons through peaceful means and in this it was normally successful,
although one of its annual 'Aldermaston marches' in 1963 was marred by violence
caused by an anarchist minority. It is a phenomenon of large-scale demonstrations that extremists will frequently join the throng with the intention of causing
disruption, thereby gaining cheap publicity for themselves and aggravation for

their sworn enemy, the police. Special Branch devoted little time to covering the activities of the organisation or its individual members, but kept a watching brief on the Aldermaston marches, as the fringe elements were always likely to cause public order problems.

THE COMMITTEE OF 100[1]

O f more concern were offshoots of the CND, such as the Committee of 100, which was not so constrained by legal niceties. This organisation was formally established in October 1960, with a committee headed by Bertrand Russell and an original membership of 100, mostly former members of the CND, who, like Russell, felt that the latter organisation's embargo of any form of unlawful protest was ineffectual. Undoubtedly it was a clash of personalities between Russell and Canon Collins that accelerated the split. The Committee of 100 had similar aims as the CND, but it was their policy of non-violent direct action that distinguished the two organisations. From the start, conflicting views within the Committee about their conception of civil disobedience led to various factions emerging, from which, over the next two years, there developed an organisation with a pronounced anarchist philosophy.

Their first demonstration was held on 18 February 1961, outside the Ministry of Defence in Whitehall after a march from Marble Arch to Trafalgar Square. Several thousand people took part and generally complied with the organisers' instructions that no slogans be displayed or shouted, that there should be no provocation and no resistance if arrested. In the event, no arrests were made, which was remarkable as Whitehall was blocked to traffic for nearly three hours while the sit-down in the road was allowed to take place.

At the second protest in Parliament Square on 29 April, the police changed their tactics and made 826 arrests; simultaneously protests were held outside the

---

1   The following narrative is based on contemporaneous press reports and personal knowledge

US and Soviet embassies in London and at the Polaris submarine base in Scotland. Before the third such protest on 17 September, in an attempt to pre-empt a further mass demonstration, the police resorted to an ancient and little-used piece of legislation, the Justices of the Peace Act 1381. The 100 members of the Committee were summoned to court and bound over to be of good behaviour for one year. Thirty-two, including Bertrand Russell, refused to do so and were sent to prison. Undeterred, a mass of supporters, variously reported to be between 12,000 and 15,000, turned up to block the approaches to Trafalgar Square; 1,314 arrests were made.

After this, the Committee selected new sites for its protests. No longer were their sit-downs to be confined to public thoroughfares in London and other cities; in future they proposed to conduct their protests at locations where nuclear weapons would actually be stored. Their next demonstrations were planned for 9 December within the towns of Ruislip, Brize Norton, Cardiff and Wethersfield. But as the protests assumed a more sinister complexion, so the police adopted tougher tactics. Information supplied by MPSB led to the arrests of six of the Committee's principal organisers (Terry Chandler and others), who were charged with conspiracy to commit offences under the Official Secrets Acts and sentenced to terms of imprisonment ranging from twelve to eighteen months. Nevertheless, the Wethersfield demonstration went ahead, not entirely according to plan, as the original intention was to breach the perimeter fence and sit down on the runway but, in the light of intelligence received from Special Branch, the MoD hastily erected a barbed-wire barricade that kept the would-be invaders at bay. Estimates put the number of participants at 5,000, of whom 850 were arrested. They were confronted by some 3,000 civil and military police. The new tactic of targeting Royal Air Force bases was counter-productive, as the RAF joined forces with the civil police in sharing intelligence and defending MoD property – and they were not so inclined to wear kid gloves. There were also reports in the press that their civilian colleagues too were becoming more 'positive' in their treatment of the law breakers.

The Wethersfield event was a watershed in the history of the Committee of

100; support began to wane and, in March of the following year, Bertrand Russell found it difficult to persuade supporters to stage a sit-down in Parliament Square to protest against the imprisonment of Terry Chandler, Michael Randle, Patrick Pottle and their friends. All those who did attend, 1,172 in total, were arrested. Russell resigned from the organisation shortly afterwards and thereafter the Committee struggled to survive. It was decided to decentralise and thirteen regional committees were set up, of which the London Committee was by far the most active. The original theme of 'Ban the Bomb' was virtually abandoned as supporters turned their attention to more current issues, particularly the question of human rights in Greece, where the MP and peace activist Gregoris Lambrakis had been murdered in a climate of political unrest.

The visit to the UK in July 1963 of King Paul and Queen Frederica of the Hellenes was marked by violent demonstrations inspired by the anarchist fringe of the London Committee of 100, many of whom were arrested and sentenced to lengthy terms of imprisonment. Political tension in Greece again provoked a response from the Committee, when a military coup there in 1967 was followed by a 'peaceful invasion' of the Greek embassy in London on 28 April by a group of (mainly) Committee of 100 supporters, who barricaded themselves in the building before being ejected by the police. Forty-two were arrested and, in October, were dealt with at the Central Criminal Court for unlawful assembly, the sentences ranging from conditional discharge to, in the case of Terry Chandler, who had a string of convictions, fifteen months' imprisonment.

This was the Committee of 100's swan song and, in October 1968, the organisation was disbanded. During its comparatively brief lifetime, it had confronted the police with a rash of novel situations, not least of which was dealing appropriately with a mass of lifeless humanity and framing suitable charges for a mass invasion of an embassy. Special Branch, too, faced new challenges. Mass demonstrations, even if ostensibly peaceful, like the Aldermaston processions, always had the potential for violence, and it was the responsibility of Special Branch to furnish the Home Office with a faithful report of proceedings, including details of participating groups, inflammatory speeches and arrests. This would be expected by 10 a.m. on the day following the event, a formidable task when the report, including appendices, would frequently run into more than sixty pages. Particularly time-consuming was the task of compiling an accurate record, including previous convictions, of those arrested. It was fortunate that typists were extremely tolerant and efficient; they were regarded as an integral part of the reporting team.

THE VIETNAM SOLIDARITY CAMPAIGN

A contributory factor in the demise of the Committee of 100 was the rapid growth of popular protest against the war in Vietnam and the inevitable appeal of such a cause to 'Ban the Bomb' activists. They now threw in their lot with the Maoists, anarchists and Trotskyist organisations who, during the late '60s, as the Vietnam Solidarity Campaign (VSC), staged a series of mass protest demonstrations targeting the US embassy in Grosvenor Square. Their first large-scale demonstration took place in October 1967 and, although some 20,000, mainly young, individuals took part, it passed off comparatively peacefully. The same could not be said of the second demonstration organised by the charismatic Tariq Ali and his henchmen, which was held on 17 March 1968. On this occasion, approximately 30,000 demonstrators, which included some 100 members of the German SDS (an extreme youth movement), took part in events that were markedly more violent. Marbles were catapulted at the police horses and poles holding banners were used to batter policemen. The press reported instances of undisciplined retaliation by the police, who suffered numerous casualties, including one mounted inspector who was crippled when thrown from his horse. A total of eighty-six people were injured, of whom fifty (including twenty-five police) received hospital treatment. Eight police horses were also injured and almost 300 demonstrators were arrested.[2]

---

2   *The Times*, 18 March 1968

The VSC's next venture was planned for 27 October, and every indication was that it would be even bigger; widespread violence was predicted. The Commissioner was understandably concerned and on the day over 1,000 police paraded for duty. The march itself, via the Embankment, Fleet Street, Victoria Street, Whitehall, Oxford Street to Hyde Park, was reasonably peaceful. An amusing spectacle, which only a few SB observers could appreciate, was the sight of a senior SB officer mingling with the demonstrators, raising his fist as Scotland Yard was passed and joining his temporary comrades in a tirade of abuse. The anticipated violence occurred when a group of about 1,000 hardcore Maoists and anarchists broke away as the march passed Selfridges and rushed towards Grosvenor Square, where they encountered serried ranks of foot police reinforced by their mounted colleagues. Bottles, banners and other missiles were thrown at the police, but the human shield stood firm and, after about half an hour of violence, the militants rejoined their comrades in Hyde Park, licking their wounds – of which there were surprisingly few.

CREATION AND SUBSEQUENT DEVELOPMENT OF THE SPECIAL DEMONSTRATION SQUAD (SDS)

The police justifiably regarded their efforts to preserve the peace with some satisfaction, and some credit for this success is attributable to the advance intelligence supplied by Special Branch. After the lawlessness accompanying the demonstration in March, the Home Office, in consultation with the Commissioner, decided that better prior intelligence as to the likely course of events on that chaotic afternoon would probably have prevented many of the worst incidents. It was apparent that the comparatively small number of troublemakers had come prepared for a violent confrontation, the nature and severity of which had not been anticipated by the police. The Commissioner directed that a special section within MPSB should be created with the specific role of assimilating themselves with potential protesters and gathering intelligence on their likely tactics, the numbers expected on demonstrations and the identities of core militants. This initiative was supported by the Home Office, who provided direct and dedicated funding.

And so it was that, a few days after the Home Office had decided on the course of action to be taken, twelve bemused SB officers of various ranks (constable to chief inspector) were paraded by their chief, Commander 'Fergie' Smith, before the Assistant Commissioner for Crime, Peter Brodie. His message was simple: 'Find out what these people are planning for 27 October.' Back in his office, Fergie was unable to elaborate, except to warn his officers against acting as *agents provocateurs* and to take care not to become elected to office in any of the organisations they succeeded in joining. Detective Chief Inspector Conrad Dixon, a maverick and multi-talented officer, was appointed to take charge of the section, the Special Operations Squad (SOS), which later became officially known as the Special Demonstration Squad (SDS) and, unofficially, as 'the hairies'. In 1999, to reflect the widening scope of its remit, it was renamed the Special Duties Section, but those people 'in the know' continued to refer to it as the Special Demonstration Squad. The SDS functioned for two more years after the demise of Special Branch in 2006, but subsequent events dragged it out of its retirement and into the limelight when a former member of the SDS, Peter Francis, went public with a series of allegations about its activities. The matter was referred to the Independent Police Complaints Commission (IPCC), who directed that an investigation be carried out, codenamed Operation Herne. Some reference has been made to that operation in the following brief account of the SDS – brief because the true history of the section remains shrouded in secrecy.

The efficiency with which, in 1968, the newly formed unit fulfilled their role in the comparatively short time at their disposal went some way towards ensuring that, on 27 October, the front-line troops had a better appreciation of the probable tactics that the 'opposition' might employ and could react accordingly. After the protest, it was decided that the SDS should remain in existence, at least for the time being, and with the threat of violent mass demonstrations temporarily abated, Conrad Dixon had the opportunity to consolidate what had already been achieved.

By now, some members of the team had successfully infiltrated some of the more militant groupings on the left, while other members were obviously not suited to this type of work and were transferred to other duties. Over time, an office was allocated away from the Yard and 'safe houses' were acquired where members could relax and where supervising officers could visit them. Welfare was seen as of paramount importance, for it was appreciated that, to become accepted into an alien culture, an officer must adopt a totally different lifestyle from that of his choice, and family life would inevitably be subjected to unaccustomed stress. Senior officers paid frequent visits to 'the hairies' in safe houses and were always available for consultation; frequently one-to-one meetings took place out of ordinary office hours, at night, at weekends and on public holidays (SDS officers never knew such luxuries).[3]

As time went on, so the scope of SDS interests widened, for, as Operation Herne acknowledges, 'world political events dictated that the unit included groups covering the extreme right-wing and Animal Rights. [However] there was a continued focus towards all public disorder incidents.'[4] Over the forty years of its existence, both MI5 and the Home Office had cause to be grateful for the intelligence provided by the section and, again quoting Operation Herne:

> There is little doubt that the ability of police and public order command
> ers to deal with large scale disorder and protest was enhanced by the use
> of intelligence from undercover officers. Deployment of officers able to
> report upon such events was a key element in the protection of the pub
> lic and subsequent prosecution of offenders.[5]

3   Recollections of the writer

4   Operation Herne, Report No. 2 dated 2 March 2014 – 4.3

5   Ibid., 4.8

There is equally little doubt that the nature of the work performed by SDS officers exposed them to the risk of considerable personal danger in the event of their cover 'being blown', a fact that the public whom they were protecting could not appreciate because of the secrecy which, of necessity, surrounded the whole operation.

CHAPTER TWENTY-TWO

NEW CHALLENGES

THE '60S HAD been an eventful period in the history of the Branch, not least because of the appointment, in 1966, of a new head, who was to become a legend in his own time.

DEPUTY ASSISTANT COMMISSIONER 'FERGIE' SMITH

Ferguson George Donaldson Smith was born in 1914 and died in September 2013, a few days short of his ninety-ninth birthday. He joined the Metropolitan Police in 1935 and Special Branch a year later. During the war he volunteered to serve in the Royal Air Force and flew as a navigator in Lancaster bombers, emerging, bloodied but very much alive, with a Distinguished Flying Cross and bar to his credit. He rejoined the Branch and successfully dealt with a number of high-profile cases before his appointment, in 1966, as head of the Branch with the rank of commander. He had 300 men under his command, many of whom, like him, had served with distinction in the war and were accustomed to seeing action and making decisions. These qualities would stand the Branch in good stead in the difficult years to come.

In 1970, Commander Smith was promoted to Deputy Assistant Commissioner and three new posts of commander were created in Special Branch, reflecting not only its growth in establishment but also its increasing stature within the Metropolitan Police Force. A quietly spoken Scotsman, 'Fergie', as he was affectionately known to his troops, had a charismatic personality and was particularly concerned for the welfare of his younger officers. He retired in 1972; it is an indication of the regard that all ranks held for him that over 100 former members of Special Branch attended his funeral on 30 September 2013.

A NEW HOME

In 1967, the Branch moved into yet another home when the headquarters of the Metropolitan Police was transferred to a modern office block in Victoria Street; this was to be its final resting place. Special Branch was allocated the seventeenth and eighteenth floors in the taller of the two blocks that comprised the building – a far cry from its original accommodation in a dilapidated office situated above a public urinal. The move was much needed, for the frequent increases in establishment had led to overcrowding, although open-plan offices were not to everyone's liking. More office space enabled a training section to be set up, which included a lecture room – an essential provision, as MPSB had started a programme of training courses for officers from provincial forces who were setting up their own Special Branches.

FURTHER BREACHES OF THE OFFICIAL SECRETS ACTS

The '70s opened with two more espionage cases, both involving Czech intelligence officers. The first was unique in that, for the first time, a Member of Parliament was prosecuted for offences against the Official Secrets Acts. On 14 January 1970, Will Owen, Labour MP for Morpeth, was arrested by Detective

Superintendent 'Jock' Wilson acting on information supplied by MI5 that he had been in the pay of the Czech intelligence service for nearly ten years. In his trial lasting thirteen days, the prosecution alleged that Owen had been supplying the Czech intelligence service with classified information from 1961 and had received money from them between 1967 and 1969, but the jury believed his story that he had never passed classified material to the Czechs and he was acquitted on 6 May.[1]

The following year, Nicholas Anthony Prager, an electrical engineer from Rotherham, was arrested on 31 January by Detective Chief Superintendent Craig of the West Riding Constabulary. Although liaison was maintained with MPSB, it was the local force that dealt with the case throughout, a sign of the increasing independence of provincial Special Branches. Prager was sentenced to twelve years' imprisonment on two charges under the Official Secrets Act 1911.[2]

THE ANGRY BRIGADE AND ESTABLISHMENT OF THE 'BOMB SQUAD'

In August 1970, a small bomb was detonated at the home of the Commissioner, Sir John Waldron. The incident, although comparatively minor, led to significant developments in the Yard's response to terrorism. A time-honoured CID maxim, 'When in trouble or in doubt, form a squad and run about' – a paraphrase of a popular adage – was put into operation and a joint C1/SB unit, comprising a Detective Inspector, George Mould, two DSs from C1, two DSs from SB, Derek Brice and Tony Greenslade, and a SB DC, John Daniel, was put together without delay. The SB contingent busied themselves to learn about explosives and the principles of bomb-making, visiting the ICI Explosives Factory in Scotland, availing themselves of the knowledge and experience of Don Lidstone, a

---

1   *The Times*, 7 May 1970

2   Peter Rawlinson, *A Price Too High: An Autobiography* (London: Weidenfeld & Nicolson, 1989), p. 209

bomb expert at Woolwich Arsenal, and establishing a close rapport with the four explosives officers employed by the Metropolitan Police.

It was soon established that an anarchist group, styling itself 'the Angry Brigade' (hitherto unknown to Special Branch), was responsible for the explosion at the Commissioner's home and, later, for a series of small explosions, some twenty-five or so in total, which continued throughout 1971, commencing with one at the home of Robert Carr, at that time the Employment Secretary, on 12 January. This was to trigger immediate reaction from the police, who drafted in reinforcements to the 'Bomb Squad', which was to be controlled by a Commander, Ernie Bond. Under him were two sections: one, under Detective Chief Superintendent Roy Habershon, was staffed exclusively by mainstream CID officers and functioned as a prosecution unit; the other, comprising Special Branch officers headed by Conrad Dixon (now a chief superintendent), and including DCI Peter Curtis, three DIs and a number of DCs, would, hopefully, supply the prosecution unit with the information necessary to make arrests and secure convictions. A Special Branch chief inspector, Riby Wilson, was appointed to ensure effective liaison between the two sections.

It soon became apparent that there was little intelligence in SB records to assist in identifying the individuals responsible for the explosions and, in the absence of reliable informants in the anarchist fraternity, almost total reliance was placed on surveillance. An observation team, headed by Brice and Greenslade, used their own vehicles to carry out extensive surveillance in north London, which soon bore fruit. It was established that a group of anarchists was funding their terrorist activities through an extensive fraud operation involving stolen credit cards; a small joint C1/SB team pursued an investigation into their activities. The information that had pointed the surveillance team in the right direction was supplied by Jack Prescott, a prisoner in Albany Prison, who had boasted to a fellow prisoner of his connections with members of the Angry Brigade. Under intensive interrogation by Habershon and other members of the Bomb Squad, Prescott let slip information that led to the arrest of a total of twelve members of the Brigade, of whom five, including Prescott, were eventually convicted. Each one was sentenced to ten years' imprisonment (Prescott's original sentence of fifteen years was reduced to ten years on appeal), despite the traditional allegations of fabricated police statements and planted evidence.

The Bomb Squad had effectively put an end to this anti-establishment campaign, through efficient organisation and professional police work in which Special Branch had played a not insignificant role. This new arrangement, combining the investigative ability of the CID with the intelligence-gathering skills of Special Branch, was adapted to deal with other terrorist campaigns, notably the mainland activities of the IRA and, much later, of Islamist extremists. As 'the Anti-Terrorist Branch', it was to enjoy considerable success in bringing to justice scores of terrorists and served to establish an excellent bridge between the mainline CID and Special Branch.

In their efforts to establish the identities of the members of the Angry Brigade, and subsequently to monitor their movements, the Special Branch intelligence section of the Bomb Squad soon came to realise their poor expertise in the field of surveillance. The lack of adequate and suitable transport for this specialised form of detection was partially overcome by officers using their own cars, and this practice continued for several years. In other ways, too, this small section improved their techniques to such an extent that the team was retained as a unit to assist the various squads within SB as and when required. The need for a permanent surveillance squad was identified and so a much larger and more sophisticated unit developed.

MORE SPIES UNCOVERED

While the Bomb Squad was busy pursuing members of the Angry Brigade, other members of the Branch were busy investigating two more cases passed to them by MI5 as a result of the defection of Oleg Lyalin, a Soviet intelligence officer. The first related to two Greek Cypriot brothers-in-law, Kyriacos Costi and Constantinos Martianou, who were accused of various offences under the Official Secrets Acts. Although they had received training and spying paraphernalia from Lyalin, there was no evidence that they had passed any classified material to the Russians, they were merely required to pass on information received by them. On 7 December 1971, at the Old Bailey, they received sentences of four and six years' imprisonment respectively.[3]

The second involved a Malayan subject, Siroj Hussein Abdoolcader, who was convicted at the Central Criminal Court on 8 February 1972 of offences under the Official Secrets Acts; he had supplied the Russian intelligence services with details of cars in which they were interested, obtained by him through his employment with the vehicle registration authorities. The registration details that the Russians were interested in related to cars used by Special Branch and MI5 surveillance officers, which were stored in a special file at the Greater London Council. He was sentenced to three years' imprisonment. Both cases were handled by Detective Chief Inspector Gordon Fryer.[4]

Following Lyalin's defection, but not resulting from it, yet another espionage case surfaced in October 1971 with the arrest of Leonard Michael Hinchliffe, an FCO administration officer based at the British embassy in Algiers. Having confessed to his ambassador that he had been passing classified material to Soviet intelligence officers while stationed in Khartoum, he was ordered home and, shortly after his arrival in London, was detained by SB officers, taken to Bow Street Police Station and charged with offences under the Official Secrets Acts. He appeared at Bow Street Magistrates' Court the following day and was remanded in custody for a week, a procedure that was repeated regularly until 17 April 1972, when he pleaded guilty at the Old Bailey to a number of counts under the Official Secrets Acts and was sentenced to a total of ten years' imprisonment.

No prosecution under the Official Secrets Acts is simple, but this was a comparatively straightforward case as Hinchliffe had already acknowledged his guilt when interviewed by his superiors in Algiers. The offences occurred during

3   *Evening Standard*, 7 December 1971

4   *The Times*, 5 October 1971, 8 December 1971 and 9 February 1972; Rawlinson, *A Price Too High*, pp. 205–206

Hinchliffe's service at the British embassy in Khartoum, Sudan, between 1970 and 1971, when he was contacted by a Soviet intelligence officer named Andrei who threatened to inform Mrs Hinchliffe of a liaison he had had with a married woman in the Sudan some months earlier.

Although the accused did not contest the charges, there was a vast amount of enquiry work to be done by the inquiry team led by DCI Gordon Seage, assisted by DI Malcolm Moffatt (who carried out the principal interviews), DS Geoff Battye (shorthand writer), DS Geoff Craft (financial enquiries), DS Rod Bennett (legal matters) and DC Steve Cracknell (general factotum). A Foreign Office security official, who assisted in a liaison capacity, played an essential role in assessing the damage caused to British interests by Hinchliffe's treachery in passing classified material to the Russians. For once this was an espionage case in which MI5 played no part.

Despite Hinchliffe's confession, it was essential from an evidential point of view that every aspect of his admission be substantiated. This required statements to be taken from the staff at the embassies in Khartoum and Algiers. DI Moffatt and DS Battye welcomed this escape from winter in London to sunshine in the Middle East. As a consolation for those left behind, they brought back gifts of 'Khartoum Club' ties (black with small pictures of General Gordon astride a camel).

Every week Hinchliffe had to be escorted from Brixton Prison to Bow Street Magistrates' Court for a remand hearing. The trip was undertaken in a police car with four SB officers in attendance, normally a routine procedure, but one morning during the rush hour an incident occurred that illustrated that even the most mundane duties require thoughtful planning, constant vigilance and a degree of luck. Outside Brixton Underground Station, the car carrying Hinchliffe was hit by another vehicle. Fortunately nobody was hurt and uniformed police were quickly on the scene to take away the damaged car and convey prisoner and escort to the court, but had this been a contrived collision in an attempt to effect Hinchliffe's escape, or if the escorts had been seriously injured, enabling the prisoner to get away, an inevitable inquiry would have been held and undoubtedly undeserved criticism would have been levelled at the police driver, although the resulting police inquiry found him blameless.[5]

THE ONE THAT GOT AWAY

N ot all cases ended in success (for the Branch); The Hackney Arms Job, which was enacted late in 1971, was just such an operation. It foundered due to an unfortunate combination of factors, not least of which was the involvement of an informant, a species of the human race which, although indispensable in certain situations, is notoriously prone to mendacity.

John Parker had supplied SB with low-level information on Irish matters for a number of years and, in 1969, introduced a Branch officer operating under cover to a group of Irish nationalist supporters from Belfast living in the East End of London. According to Parker, the group intended to open a clothes shop at 257 Wick Road, Hackney, and send the profits to a relief fund for needy republicans in Northern Ireland. Special Branch believed that they were in fact members of the IRA and were planning to use their drapery business as a cover for clandestine IRA activities in Britain. Surveillance was set up in a convenient observation post and their telephone was tapped.

On the morning of 15 November 1971, premises in Sidcup used by the Kent Sea Cadets as an armoury were broken into and a small quantity of dummy rifles and eight bayonets were stolen. Suspicion fell on the group, two of whom flew home to Belfast the same afternoon; one of them, Martin Crawford, was promptly detained by the Royal Ulster Constabulary (RUC) Special Branch and made a statement in which he confessed to taking part in the raid, adding that 'Edward' Parker was also part of the raiding team. On 17 November, the remaining members of the group (Marjorie Allen, Edmund Pettigrew, Laurence McGrandles, Patrick O'Sullivan and Donal de Faoit), with the significant exception of Parker,

---

5   Rawlinson, *A Price Too High*, pp. 207–208; Recollections of DC Cracknell; *The Times*, 18 April 1972

were all arrested at their shop by a posse of armed police officers and charged with the illegal possession of firearms.

At their eventual trial at the Central Criminal Court in June 1972, the five were joined in the dock by Martin Crawford, who had been escorted back from Northern Ireland that day by SB officers. His appearance was a waste of time and expense for, at the outset of the day's proceedings, prosecuting counsel informed the Court, without giving a reason, that no evidence was being offered against him and he was discharged. The trial was marked by a further bizarre twist when, three days later, the Director of Public Prosecutions' representative made the dramatic announcement that, 'After considering the evidence over the weekend, it has been decided that it would not be proper for the prosecution to continue.' The police refused to comment other than to say that to do so 'would prejudice the interest of the state'. The prosecution also made no reply to accusations that the weapons had been planted by two police informants who had insinuated themselves into the group.[6]

---

6   Allason, *The Branch*, pp. 153–4; *The Times*, 9 November 1971 and 13 June 1972

CHAPTER TWENTY-THREE

A NEW WAVE OF IRA
TERROR IN ENGLAND

APART FROM THE two bungled attempts to steal arms in 1955, the IRA refrained from terrorist activities on the mainland from the end of their short, sharp campaign of 1939–40 until the beginning of the 1970s, but there were now ominous signs that they were again spoiling for a fight. Northern Ireland had once more become a theatre for their aggression as the Roman Catholics strove to assert their claims for equality and civil rights. However, not all republicans believed that they should completely abandon constitutional politics in this struggle and, at the movement's 1969 Ard Fheis (annual conference), the hardliners split from their more politically orientated Marxist colleagues to form the Provisional IRA (PIRA). The remainder became the Official IRA.

This, in itself, posed no problems to the security forces; but there were other factors that were to make the job of predicting the IRA's intentions on the mainland more difficult. There is no doubt that they had become more sophisticated and their Active Service Units (ASUs) more disciplined, but then, so had the police. The PIRA hierarchy realised at the start of their proposed new campaign, which was to plague England intermittently into the next century, that their operatives based on the mainland were too well known to Special Branch, which regularly monitored their movements and haunts, and were not considered capable of carrying out well-planned, military-style operations. The solution was to send over a succession of experienced and well-trained teams to carry out missions and return without delay to Ireland.

The IRA high command was justified in its assumption that MPSB was too well-informed about their supporters in the metropolis. In fact, there were very few members of the IRA based in London and they had no organisation here. It is true that their political wing, Sinn Féin, had organised groups (cumainn) named after Irish 'martyrs' (e.g. Wolfe Tone, Roger Casement, Kevin Barry etc.), which held regular meetings, but their activities were closely monitored by means of surveillance, technical resources and informants. Two agents in particular were well placed in the movement and supplied excellent information, but they began to quarrel with each other at meetings, for they were both anxious to be elected to office in order to have better access to intelligence and impress their handlers. At times they nearly came to blows, so it was decided, with some misgivings, that they should each be made aware of the other's role. The move was so successful that, far from arguing, they began to praise each other at meetings, with the result that they both became office holders; the downside was that they became drinking mates and would turn up for meetings drunk. The situation was resolved when one developed an ulcer and faded from the scene.

TWO FAILED IRA PLOTS –
TWO SPECIAL BRANCH SUCCESSES

The IRA's lack of confidence in their colleagues on this side of the water was justified, as was illustrated in an abortive attempt by a group of London-based IRA members to bomb a factory just outside London in 1970. Through informants, the MPSB became aware of the group's intentions and was able to set up an observation post in a house opposite the Irishmen's address in

Drakefield Road, Tooting, which enabled the surveillance officers to witness bombs being made and, with technical assistance, listen to their conversations. The team of six terrorists, led by a man well known to Special Branch, Brendan Magill, were all charged with offences under the Explosives Substances Act 1883. Magill was sentenced to two years' imprisonment for possession of explosives; James McGarrigle and James Monaghan each received sentences of three years for conspiracy to cause an explosion.[1]

In May 1971, MPSB received information that an IRA group led by Jack, aka 'Danny', McElduff, a defrocked priest, were planning a bank raid to finance the IRA activities of their compatriots in Northern Ireland. McElduff, who came from a family of dedicated republicans in County Tyrone, was based in Wellington Street, Colchester; the other three members of the group, Michael Gaughan, James Joseph Moore and Frank Golden, all lived in Mountview Road, Hornsey, London, but were temporarily staying with McElduff. Essex Special Branch was informed and established an observation post in a block of offices opposite the suspects' address, while surveillance of the rear entrance to the building was covered from a van; the flat had also been successfully bugged, enabling some of the conspirators' conversations to be heard. The surveillance extended over several days, during which time adrenalin ran high when the armed bank raiders did a dummy run to a bank in Hornsey but decided, for some reason known only to themselves, to abandon the venture for that day and return to Colchester, much to the chagrin of the waiting Flying Squad officers. The Special Branch surveillance team, which included John Bullard, Andy Patterson, Kevin Kindleysides, Nick Charles and Gary Atkinson, continued to watch the premises, although clear sight of the door was occasionally impaired by parked vehicles. It was apparent that during one of these periods the Irishmen had slipped out unobserved, for one afternoon they were seen returning to the house, carrying a case. Later that day the hidden listeners were surprised to hear snatches of conversation which made it apparent that the IRA team had successfully carried out their mission,

---

1   Recollections of the writer

as they could be heard counting out the proceeds of their raid, which turned out to be a paltry £530. Shortly afterwards, the four Irishmen left the flat and were followed to the station, where they caught a train to London and were arrested at Liverpool Street by Special Branch officers waiting with transport.

On 23 December 1971, at the Central Criminal Court, Moore and Gaughan were both convicted of armed robbery and of conspiracy to rob the Midland Bank and were each sentenced to seven years' imprisonment; Golden was acquitted of the robbery and conspiracy charges but sentenced to twelve months' imprisonment for illegal possession of a firearm without a certificate; Jack McElduff, who did not take part in the raid, was acquitted of conspiracy but was found guilty of dishonestly handling some of the stolen money and sent to prison for three years. Gaughan made the headlines again when he went on hunger strike while incarcerated in Parkhurst Prison on the Isle of Wight and died on 3 June 1974. On 8 June, thousands of mourners lined the streets of Kilburn as his coffin, flanked by a 'guard of honour', was borne to the Church of the Sacred Heart of Jesus for a requiem mass. Special Branch officers were present to identify members of the colour party and others and, as usual, a telephone message was sent to the Special Branch reserve room after the proceedings to report that everything had passed off peacefully. It caused some amusement, despite the gravity of the circumstances, when the officer taking the message recorded: 'The colour party all had blackberries on their heads' (instead of black berets)!

THE BOMB AT ALDERSHOT BARRACKS

I ronically, it was the Official IRA (OIRA), those who purported to seek a more constitutional path to their goal, who were to strike the first blow in the republicans' new assault on mainland Britain. Early in 1972, Special Branch had received intelligence that an OIRA ASU was on its way to carry out some form of atrocity in England; the intended location was not known. It was soon revealed as, on 22 February 1972, a powerful car bomb (200 lbs of gelignite) exploded at Aldershot army barracks outside the officers' mess of the Parachute Regiment, apparently in retaliation for the part played by that regiment in the so-called 'Bloody Sunday' demonstration three weeks earlier. The regiment was currently serving abroad, but the assassins succeeded in killing a Roman Catholic padre, five female cleaners and a civilian gardener as well as injuring eighteen other civilians.

The Hampshire Constabulary was in charge of the subsequent investigation but massive support was provided by adjacent forces, including Surrey, Thames Valley and members of the Bomb Squad from the Metropolitan Police. MPSB sent a sizeable contingent of officers experienced in dealing with Irish republican extremism, including DCI Des Winslow, DIs Brice and Graham Ison, DSs Peter Langley and Pat Thomas, DCs John Pascoe and Tom Robson. DS Geoff Battye played a tiring but vital role in taking shorthand notes of many of the interviews.[2] The day after the incident, two uniformed Metropolitan Police officers, PS Laidlaw and PC Pitches, stopped a man in the street for no other reason than that he was carrying a holdall and that their professional instinct prompted them to do so (policemen used to do that kind of thing). The holdall contained a gun, 280 rounds of ammunition and a quantity of IRA literature. At the police station he gave his name as Michael Duignan and his address a flat in nearby Amity Grove, Raynes Park. A search of the premises by a Special Branch sergeant, John Barnett, revealed nothing particularly significant. A more interesting development was the discovery by Hampshire CID of the cylinder block of the car used to conceal the bomb. From the serial number stamped on this it was a comparatively simple job for Special Branch to establish the last recorded owner of the vehicle as a car hire firm in north London, who had rented the car out to Francis Kissane of Victoria Rd, N4. Needless to say, Kissane was soon in custody. It must have been doubly satisfying to the police that Duignan admitted knowing him.[3]

However, Kissane and Duignan had played only minor parts in the ASU's

2   TNA J297/57 contains statements made by police, witnesses and the various suspects interviewed

3   Allason, *The Branch*, pp. 154–5

murderous scheme and police were employed round the clock interviewing hundreds of witnesses before, on 3 March, they finally confronted the leader of the team, Phillip Noel Jenkinson. Initially he was interviewed at his flat in St James's Lane, Muswell Hill, in north London by DCI Edwin Smith of the Hampshire Constabulary and DI Derek Brice MPSB, but he was noncommittal and it was the keen observation of another SB officer engaged in searching the premises that detected a vital clue, a rate demand from the local authority relating to a lock-up garage in the vicinity. This contained two sizeable gelignite bombs and a number of paratroopers' uniforms. Armed with this damning evidence, the police wheeled out the big guns in the shape of Commander Matthew Rodger MPSB, and Detective Chief Superintendent Cyril 'Tanky' Holdaway, head of Hampshire CID, who grilled Jenkinson in a more intimidating police environment.

The three men, the only members of the team ever arrested, were subsequently charged and convicted. Jenkinson faced seven counts of murder, for which he received a life sentence with a recommendation that he serve a minimum of thirty years, a qualification that proved unnecessary as he died four years later in Leicester Prison; Kissane was acquitted of murder but sentenced to two years' imprisonment for conspiracy to pervert the course of justice; Duignan was also convicted on the conspiracy charge and, additionally, illegal possession of a firearm; he was sentenced to three and a half years in jail.

SHANE PAUL O'DOHERTY AND THE LETTER BOMB CAMPAIGN

The Provisional IRA started their own campaign shortly afterwards. Towards the end of 1972, a nineteen-year-old IRA Volunteer from Londonderry, Shane Paul O'Doherty, whom the IRA regarded as one of their leading explosives experts, was sent to London to organise a series of letter bomb attacks on personalities and organisations whom the republicans bore a grudge against, such as prominent figures in the government, the military and the judiciary.[4] It was later learned that he returned to Londonderry the following year, constructed his vicious missiles there and had them posted in England by friendly messengers.

His final missive was delivered in September 1974, by which time he had sent twenty-four letter bombs (of which only ten exploded) and five parcel bombs and planted three time bombs. Although mercifully nobody had been killed, a number of people, principally secretaries and security guards, had been injured, some seriously. One of those receiving superficial injuries was Reginald Maudling MP, who was responsible for security arrangements for the 'Bloody Sunday' demonstration; other recipients included the Prime Minister, the Ministry of Defence, the Central Office of Information and the Conservative and Unionist Association. Compared with the tragic consequences of the Aldershot explosion, this letter bomb campaign was minor, but it involved Special Branch in a lot of work assisting the Bomb Squad in seeing witnesses, taking statements and, most importantly, liaising with the RUC. O'Doherty was originally arrested by the RUC in May 1975 for sending a letter bomb to a Londonderry solicitor and was kept in custody in Northern Ireland until the date of his trial; no evidence was offered by the prosecution and on his release he was rearrested on the steps of the court by Bomb Squad officers, who were not there by chance, and escorted back to England to face trial for the offences referred to above. On 10 September 1976, at the Central Criminal Court, O'Doherty was sentenced to life imprisonment; he was released in 1989.[5]

'THE LUTON THREE'

This was an extremely busy period for Special Branch's 'B' Squad (responsible for Irish matters). In 1973, information was received that a team of three Sinn

---

4   Shane Paul O'Doherty, *The Volunteer: A Former IRA Man's True Story* (London: Fount, 1993), p. 137

5   *The Times*, 11 September 1976

Féin members in Luton (Sean Campbell, Phillip Sheridan and Jeremiah Mealy) was planning to carry out an armed robbery; unusually, the name of the informant, Kenneth Joseph Lennon, was later made public through most unfortunate circumstances which will be unfolded later. Officers from the Branch maintained contact with Lennon and the force concerned, Luton and Bedfordshire, was informed. After one or two false starts, the Branch surveillance team, supplemented by local officers and a unit of No. 5 Regional Crime Squad, sighted the team of robbers on 9 August and monitored their movements for some hours until it became obvious that they were preparing their weapons for imminent action. This was the signal for the Branch, who were also armed, to move in and arrest them.

Even the tensest situations have their lighter moments, and this was no exception. The SB team, with prisoners on board, but on this occasion without local back-up, lost their way to the police station and had to stop a member of the public to ask for directions. Fortunately their weapons were out of sight. Once at the station, the local police went out to pick up a car that the prisoners had stolen and parked near the railway station to serve as a getaway vehicle. They would not have got very far, however, as it ran out of petrol within a few hundred yards. The case did not have a humorous ending, though, as far as 'the Luton Three' were concerned, for at St Albans Crown Court on 6 December they were each sentenced to ten years' imprisonment.[6] Although the result was a success for the Branch, it underlined once again the need for a permanent Special Branch team of dedicated surveillance officers with proper equipment. The team were still using their own cars and some of the officers involved had to be drawn from other duties, such as naturalisation enquiries, where expertise in the use of firearms was not a prime requirement! The officers concerned in this operation were: Tony Greenslade, Roger Williams, Jim Francke, Ken Carthew, Brian Woollard, John Daniels, Claude Jeal, Paul Croyden, Mick Couch, Keith Picken, and David McCarthy, of whom the last four named were required to give evidence in Court.[7]

6   *The Times*, 11 June 1974

7   Recollections of Paul Croyden

THE KENNETH LENNON ASSASSINATION[8]

Lennon's recruitment as a Special Branch informant began on 27 July 1973 when he telephoned Scotland Yard anonymously asking to speak to a Special Branch officer. In response, DCs Dwyer and Turner met the caller at St Pancras Station, where he revealed his identity and gave details of a PIRA plan to commit a robbery in the Luton area to finance the abduction and murder of a high-ranking British Army officer. Further contact was maintained between Lennon, Dwyer and DI Ron Wickens and, with the promise of financial reward for more detailed information, the Irishman provided the names of the three-man team, subsequently dubbed 'the Luton Three' and details of the premises they intended to rob – the Chrysler Working Men's Club.

Largely as a result of Lennon's cooperation with the police, the members of the gang were arrested and sentenced as described above, but the saga still had a long way to run. Having proved his reliability to the police, he was rewarded by the Luton and Bedfordshire Constabulary and authority was given for him to be paid £20 a month from the MPSB informants' fund. He continued to be seen on a weekly basis by DI Wickens and provided useful information on Irish republican extremist activities in Ireland and elsewhere. He became friendly with a republican named Patrick Joseph O'Brien to such an extent that the pair of them were arrested in suspicious circumstances and in possession of a legally held shotgun in the vicinity of Winson Green Prison, Birmingham, where 'the Luton Three' were being held on remand. At their subsequent trial on 8 April 1974, Lennon was acquitted and O'Brien found guilty, though the verdict on O'Brien was subsequently overturned on appeal, when the judge was told that Lennon was a police informant.

The day following the trial, Wickens and DS Harper debriefed Lennon at Euston and paid him some of the money owing to him. Shortly afterwards, the

---

8   This section is based on the contents of House of Commons paper 351, HMS.O., *Report to the Home Secretary from the Commissioner of Police for the Metropolis on the Actions of Police Officers Concerned with the Case of Kenneth Joseph Lennon*

Ulsterman called at the offices of the National Council of Civil Liberties and made a seventeen-page statement giving his version of his dealings with the police and expressing his fear that he might be murdered. Much of what he is alleged to have said tallies with the police account of their relationship. However, he stated that the police made the first move in recruiting him as an informant and thereafter exerted pressure on him; he also claimed that the police fixed the Birmingham trial so that he would be cleared.[9] Three days after his contact with the NCCL, his body was found face down in a ditch on Banstead Common; a single bullet had entered the back of his head.

As a result of the furore created by the case, the Police Commissioner Sir Robert Mark undertook to have a speedy report prepared concerning the involvement of SB officers in the Lennon affair. A team composed of three Metropolitan CID officers and three Special Branch officers, directed by the Deputy Commissioner James Starritt, was employed full-time producing this report, which was finally made public on 28 November 1974, although it had been completed in July. It concluded that the Special Branch officers involved had acted correctly throughout their dealings with Lennon; the Home Secretary endorsed these conclusions, adding, 'I see no grounds for further investigation into the actions of the police officers concerned.'[10] Apart from the SB officers engaged on the Starritt report, many others were kept busy assisting in the murder inquiry, which was never resolved.

'THE BELFAST TEN'

O'Doherty's letter-bomb campaign and the failed assassination plan of 'the Luton Three' were merely a foretaste of what was to come. Traditionally, the IRA has regarded publicity reaped from any successful operation on the

---

9   *The Times*, 17 April 1974

10   Ibid., 2 November 1974

mainland as many times more valuable than a similar act carried out in Ireland. Terrorist acts here are calculated to strike fear into the hearts of the public and to create a general feeling of insecurity, which in turn will translate into pressure on the government. It will be recalled that not until Fenian violence crossed the Irish Sea towards the end of the nineteenth century did the British government begin to take the threat posed by Irish nationalism seriously. The first blow in a fresh campaign was struck on the morning of 8 March 1973, not very successfully, thanks to the vigilance and prompt reaction of two members of the Special Patrol Group, PCs George Burrows and Stanley Conley. The two officers were on duty near New Scotland Yard when their suspicions were aroused by a Ford Corsair parked in Broadway; their professional instincts had not let them down, for the registration mark on the car proved to be false and closer examination revealed nearly 200 lbs of gelignite concealed under the seats. The Bomb Squad were very quickly summoned from their office across the road, Special Branch was alerted and a Metropolitan Police explosives officer successfully defused the bomb. The discovery had been made at 8.30 a.m. and within the hour SB officers at ports were aware of the situation.

It was as well that they were, for passengers at Heathrow Airport preparing for departure on the 10.45 flight to Belfast had not yet boarded the aircraft. SB officers subjected them all to close scrutiny and questioned those who could possibly be construed as likely terrorists. DS Nigel Somers became highly suspicious when he observed that one passenger, travelling under the name of Hugh Feeney, was carrying a substantial wad of five-pound notes. He was obviously friendly with two girls, who later turned out to be the infamous Price sisters, Dolours and Marian; they also were questioned closely and another officer, DC Alan Mallett, noticed that their tickets all bore the same lettering. Examination of the other passengers' tickets by DS Denis Welch revealed that three others had tickets bearing similar markings. Enquiries of the airline revealed that all these tickets were part of a block booking. Seven potential travellers in total found their travel plans abruptly changed and, instead of flying to Belfast courtesy of BEA, they found themselves at Ealing Police Station courtesy of the Metropolitan Police. They were later reunited there with three more of their team, who became known collectively as 'the Belfast Ten'. The arrest of this hardened team of PIRA murderers, whose actions on that day led to the death of one elderly man and injuries to 228 other individuals, highlights the value of the unsung heroes of Special Branch, who every day unobtrusively cast their perceptive eyes over thousands of passengers at seaports and airports throughout the country.

In total, four bombs had been planted by the team during the morning; two were defused, including the one opposite New Scotland Yard, but two others, outside the Old Bailey and an Army Recruiting Office in Great Scotland Yard, caused extensive damage and injuries, including one fatality. Anonymous telephone calls giving imprecise details of the numbers and locations of the cars holding the bombs were made to the *Times* newspaper but, in the case of the Old Bailey and Army Recruiting Office, too late for the areas to be properly evacuated or the bombs rendered harmless.[11]

Preparing the case for presentation at court involved both the Bomb Squad and Special Branch in a tremendous amount of work, interrogating other suspects, interviewing witnesses and taking statements, preparing exhibits and a hundred and one other tasks. Among these other tasks, liaison with the Royal Ulster Constabulary in Northern Ireland and An Garda Síochána in the south was of paramount importance, and over the years the three services came respectively to appreciate the particular problems faced by their colleagues across the water. The police in Northern Ireland were particularly helpful and the Branch was frequently the beneficiary of vital information leading to the arrest of Irish terrorists or, even more importantly, of forewarnings of impending attacks in this country. There was also close cooperation with An Garda Síochána Special Branch, who were always anxious to help but whose hands were tied by their political masters. Even so, by the time the Branch had been deprived of their lead role against Irish republican extremism in 1992, the cooperation that existed between the two departments had never been closer.

11   Ibid., 9 March 1973

In the case of 'the Belfast Ten', the RUC had warned the Branch that an ASU was on its way to England but were unable to provide specific details. While regretting the injuries inflicted by the gang, they were as delighted as MPSB over the loss of nine of their residents, who were sentenced at Winchester Assizes on 14 November to life imprisonment (later commuted to twenty years); they were Dolours and Marian Price, Martin Brady, Gerald Kelly, Hugh Feeney, Paul Holmes, William McLarnon, Robert Walsh, William Armstrong and Roisin McNearney. The last named, who had assisted police in their investigations, was acquitted.

THE CONTINUING CAMPAIGN

Over the next three decades England was subjected to a series of PIRA bombings and shootings targeted at military personnel and establishments, the judiciary, politicians, high-profile events, shopping malls and any place where people gathered together in large numbers. In the course of these operations, the terrorists claimed the lives of 175 human beings, including a number of women and children, and injured thousands more; they also slaughtered large numbers of animals. But they had lost many of their own personnel too, mainly to imprisonment for long periods, but also a few to defection or 'misadventure'.

During this period, the establishment of the Branch's 'B' Squad grew to over eighty, although double this number would have been required to cope with the demands made of it. Like all the other operational squads in MPSB, it was not exempt from the requirement to provide personnel for Official Secret Acts prosecutions; reserve duties; training courses; summer relief duty at ports and lines of route on state and other vulnerable occasions. Personal protection of visiting heads of state and politicians and of other personalities assessed to be 'high risk' was a continual drain on resources. However, when PIRA activity in London was particularly rampant, the Irish section would be temporarily boosted with officers drafted in from other squads.

There follow details of the most publicised incidents, but scores of other acts of terrorism, less newsworthy but equally traumatic to the victims, were perpetrated. According to *The Times*, the IRA had planted forty-three time bombs, mostly in London, in the first year of the campaign.[12] In many cases, telephoned warnings, identified as genuine by the use of a code, were given, but frequently information about the location was incorrect or misleading or allowed insufficient time to clear the area of people before the bomb detonated. Special Branch officers played an active part in the investigation of those incidents that took place in London and provided liaison and assistance where requested in other areas. The reception of information from and dissemination to provincial forces and other relevant organisations was a particularly important part of their function.

1974 was only a few weeks old when five bombs were planted during one weekend at high-profile targets in the London area, causing thousands of pounds worth of damage but fortunately no injuries. Three exploded – at Madame Tussauds; at the International Boat Show at Earl's Court; and at the home of the general officer commanding London district. Two others, at the premises of a manufacturer of anti-terrorist devices and at the home of another high-ranking soldier, were defused by one of the extremely courageous police explosives experts, Major Biddle, who yet again saved lives, prevented crippling injuries, avoided serious damage to property and preserved valuable evidence. A year later, one of his colleagues, Roger Goad, was killed while defusing a device in Kensington, and in 1981 Kenneth Howorth gave his own life while saving others in Oxford Street.

THE M62 COACH BOMB

Shortly afterwards, a coach travelling on the M62 near Batley was ripped apart when a bomb that had been secreted in the luggage compartment exploded. On 4 February 1974, servicemen and their families returning to married quarters

---

12   Ibid., 25 October 1974

at military bases in the north were devastated by the blast, which killed twelve of the occupants, including women and two children. The solitary claim for the atrocity was made by an anonymous male with an Irish accent, who acknowledged that it was the work of Saor Eire (Free Ireland), a little-known militant Irish republican group with pronounced left-wing views. This is highly improbable, although no other group admitted responsibility.

The hunt for the killers was led by Detective Chief Superintendent George Oldfield of West Yorkshire Police, who arrested Judith Ward, aged twenty-four. She apparently belonged to no Irish extremist group, although professing pronounced republican sympathies. In the light of her confession and other incriminating evidence, she was convicted and sentenced to eighteen years' imprisonment, although she was known to be suffering from a severe mental disorder. She was released in 1992 after the Court of Appeal found her conviction to be unsafe. DI Graham Ison and others from MPSB played an active role in the investigation, taking statements, assisting with their extensive knowledge of the Irish political scene, particularly of the IRA and its members, and liaising with the RUC.

BOMBS IN GUILDFORD, WOOLWICH AND BIRMINGHAM

L ater in the year, the IRA hit two prestigious targets, the Houses of Parliament on 17 June, slightly injuring eleven people and causing considerable damage, and the Tower of London a month later, when they succeeded in killing one person and injuring forty-one. They also created an explosion at Brooks's Club, a favourite resort of many establishment figures and retired army officers; nobody was seriously injured. But the two most shocking atrocities of 1974 were staged in the closing months of the year, in Guildford (5 October) and Birmingham (21 November).

Two public houses in Guildford popular with soldiers from neighbouring army bases were attacked on the same evening. The first bomb, at the Horse and

Groom, resulted in the deaths of four soldiers and a civilian and injuries to sixty-five others. Nearly an hour later a second explosion severely damaged the Seven Stars public house; mercifully no deaths resulted, but eleven people were injured. A massive police investigation followed, involving 170 officers from the Surrey Constabulary, backed up by officers from the Metropolitan Police Bomb Squad and Special Branch, who were not there merely 'to make up the numbers' but carried out interrogation of suspects and, among other things, provided invaluable liaison with the RUC. On 16 December 1974, four persons – Paul Hill, Patrick Armstrong, Gerard Conlon and Carole Richardson (the 'Guildford Four') – were charged with murder and possession of explosives; they were similarly charged in relation to another incident that had taken place on 7 November 1974 in Woolwich. On that occasion, a bomb, packed with nails calculated to cause widespread injuries, was thrown into the bar of the King's Arms public house adjacent to the Royal Artillery Barracks. As this was situated in the Metropolitan Police District, the Bomb Squad and Special Branch led the investigation, which soon revealed that those responsible had also bombed the Guildford pubs. In a separate trial, a group who became known as the 'Maguire Seven' were charged with handling explosives used in making the bombs – they were the Maguire family, Anne, Patrick (her husband), Patrick and Vincent (their sons), Sean Smyth (Anne's brother), Patrick Conlon (Anne's brother-in-law) and Patrick O'Neill (a family friend).

In the trial of the 'Guildford Four', which took place at the Old Bailey in September 1975, all four defendants were sentenced to life imprisonment. Sentences on the 'Maguire Seven' were announced on the same day – Anne Maguire and her husband received fourteen years' imprisonment; Sean Smyth, Patrick O'Neill and Patrick Conlon, twelve years; Vincent Maguire, five years' imprisonment; his brother Patrick, four years. In every case the convictions were quashed on appeal, in 1989 and 1991 respectively. Three Surrey police officers were subsequently charged with 'conspiracy to pervert the course of justice' by allegedly tampering with statements. They were each found not guilty.

The bombing of the Mulberry Bush and the Tavern in the Town public houses in Birmingham was not directed at military targets but against civilian members of the public. A total of twenty-one, mainly young, people were killed and nearly 200 injured in distressing circumstances. Fewer than thirty minutes before the two explosions, a coded warning was telephoned to two Birmingham newspaper offices, but there was insufficient time for the police to clear the buildings. The Serious Crimes Squad of the newly created West Midlands Police conducted the ensuing investigation with extensive support from the Bomb Squad and MPSB.

On 15 August 1975, six men (the 'Birmingham Six') were sentenced to life for murder and for conspiracy to cause eleven other explosions in the Midlands; they were Patrick Hill, Gerry Hunter, William Power, John Walker, Hugh Callaghan and Richard McIlkenny. They had been arrested by Special Branch officers on 24 November when about to board the Heysham ferry to return to Ireland. Charged with them were James Kelly, who received a nominal sentence for possession of explosives, Michael Sheehan, who received a total of nine years' imprisonment for conspiracy to cause explosions and possession of explosives, and Michael Murray, who was jailed for nine years for conspiracy. As in the cases of the Guilford Four and the Maguire Seven, their convictions were squashed.

The government's response to this callous act was to introduce the Prevention of Terrorism (Temporary Provisions) Act 1974 (PoT Act), in effect a revision of the Prevention of Violence Act 1939, which had been allowed to relapse in 1953. Among other things, it provided the police with wider powers of arrest in relation to persons suspected of being involved with Irish terrorism, and extended the period for which such a person could be detained before being charged with an offence. It was replaced by the Terrorism Act of 2000, which gave way to the Prevention of Terrorism Act of 2005. At the same time, an office, the National Joint Unit, staffed by a mix of MPSB and provincial police officers under the administration of a Special Branch chief inspector, was set up within the Special Branch complex at New Scotland Yard to provide a 24-hour service to port officers requesting advice about procedures under the PoT Act, for searches in records on persons detained under the Act and to provide the Home Office with statistics and other intelligence concerning the day-to-day operation of the Act.

Another pub frequented by soldiers from a neighbouring army base was the

Caterham Arms in Caterham, which was devastated by an IRA bomb on 27 August 1975. It had all the hallmarks of the Guildford bombs, with the potentially lethal package having been left under a seat in the public bar. Thirty-three persons, mostly soldiers, were injured, eight of them seriously. Detective Chief Superintendent Simmonds, head of Surrey CID, with the recently formed Surrey Bomb Squad at his disposal and the Metropolitan Police Bomb Squad and Special Branch to assist, took charge of the investigation. Those responsible for the attack were convicted at the Old Bailey in February 1977 of this and nineteen other atrocities (see below).

THE BALCOMBE STREET SIEGE[13]

The IRA's bloodthirsty campaign of terror that had gripped London and the suburbs for over fourteen months finally came to an end on 6 December 1975, when four members of an ASU were cornered in a Marylebone cul-de-sac and held an elderly couple hostage in their first-floor flat in a siege lasting six days, while they bargained with police for their release. The men, Harry Duggan, Joe O'Connell, Eddie Butler and Hugh Doherty, were convicted at the Old Bailey in February 1977 of seven murders, conspiring to cause explosions and falsely imprisoning Mr and Mrs Matthews. They each received multiple life sentences with whole-life tariffs but were released in 1999 under the Good Friday Agreement. Other members of the gang, Brendan Dowd and Liam Quinn, were later arrested for other offences, imprisoned and, like their confederates, were released under the Good Friday Agreement.

Although the Balcombe Street gang were only charged with seven murders, they undoubtedly committed many more during the forty or more bomb attacks and shootings that had taken place in London and its environs during 1974 and 1975. The most recent of these, on 27 November, was the cold-blooded assassination of Ross

---

13   The following narrative is based on conversations with Lord Imbert and David Waghorn and on the excellent account of the event contained in Steven Moysey's book *The Road to Balcombe Street* (London: Routledge, 2008)

McWhirter, co-founder of *The Guinness Book of Records*, Conservative Party activist and outspoken critic of the IRA. They also claimed, although they were never charged, to have carried out the Guildford and Woolwich pub bombings, which resulted in the controversial convictions and subsequent acquittals of seventeen individuals.

The events leading up to the siege were dramatic in the extreme. Towards the end of 1975, the IRA had been bombing, with increasing frequency, top-class restaurants in Mayfair and the West End of London to such an extent that celebrity diners were tending to stay away from these establishments. Places such as Scott's and Trattoria Fiori in Mount Street, the Hilton Hotel and the Ritz all became targets and then the terrorists turned from bombs to firearms, when they murdered Ross McWhirter on his own doorstep.

At this time, David Waghorn, a detective sergeant who had been serving in the Bomb Squad since February and was employed full time in the operations room, realised that the attacks fell into a predictable pattern based on timing, weather, location and a number of other factors. He reasoned that if a sufficient number of officers were stationed at appropriate points to form a rough cordon round the terrorists' hunting ground at a time when they usually struck, then, with luck, they might fall into the ambush. He prepared a report based on his observations and submitted it to his line managers, Detective Chief Inspector Graham Ison and Detective Superintendent Peter Imbert, Special Branch officers on attachment to the Bomb Squad, who were suitably impressed and recommended that nothing was to be lost by implementing it. Approval was given by the senior management team for the go-ahead and plans were put in place for the scheme, codenamed 'Operation Combo', to begin in the week commencing 22 November. But it was not to be, for shortly after the final briefing took place the *Evening Standard* devoted its front page to exposing details of the secret plan. Everyone privy to the operation was furious, not only that a colleague had leaked the information and the newspaper had been irresponsible enough to publish it, but that hopes of trapping the murderers and ending the carnage had been shattered. Understandably, it was decided to postpone Combo – some thought it should be cancelled – and it was decided to try again at the beginning of December, though with diminished expectations of success. Nevertheless, on the evening of 6 December, some 250 pairs of officers in plain clothes took up their freezing evening vigil in the West End. They were unarmed to avoid the possibility of officers opening fire on their colleagues but armed back-up was provided by units of the Special Patrol Group stationed in their vehicles outside the cordon.

Just after 9 p.m., Duggan and his cronies drove slowly past Scott's in Mount Street in a stolen Ford Cortina and fired shots into the restaurant. Two patrolling police officers who witnessed the attack immediately radioed the information to the Yard and within minutes the bored and frozen players in the Combo drama were galvanised into action. DI John Purnell and DS Phil McVeigh in Portman Street were the next to spot the stolen Cortina; they commandeered a taxi and pursued it towards Regent's Park, but the car chase finished abruptly when the Irishmen found themselves in a dead-end, Alpha Close, and abandoned the vehicle. The action continued on foot and the gunmen opened fire, but the police officers continued following them. By this time more police had joined their two colleagues, three Flying Squad officers led by DI Henry Dowsell and a unit of armed Special Patrol Group (SPG) officers who exchanged fire with their quarry. The chase finally reached its conclusion in Balcombe Street, when the four terrorists broke into a council flat occupied by an elderly couple, Mr and Mrs Matthews; they were held as hostages for the next six days, during which time Detective Chief Superintendent Jim Nevill, deputy head of the Bomb Squad, and Peter Imbert skilfully led negotiations which concluded with the two hostages released, shaken but otherwise unharmed, and the four PIRA operatives, prisoners of the police.

Jim Nevill was shortly afterwards promoted to Commander and assumed command of the Bomb Squad; Peter Imbert later became Commissioner of the Metropolitan Police and subsequently Lord Lieutenant of Greater London. John Purnell was awarded the George Medal for bravery and most of the other officers involved and shot at in the pursuit to Balcombe Street received decorations. David Waghorn received £250 from the Bow Street Fund and was highly commended by the Commissioner for devising the plan leading to Operation Combo (it is ironic that Ross McWhirter, just before his murder, had offered

£50,000 for information leading to the arrest of the London bombers). David's other reward was to be transferred shortly afterwards to Special Branch.

THE CHRISTMAS 1978 CAMPAIGN

The PIRA were intent on keeping their name on the front pages of British newspapers. In the year following the trial of the Balcombe Street gang, the streets of London were again reverberating with the sound of IRA bombs exploding. During the night of 17/18 December 1978, a bomb went off in a car left in the underground car park of the YMCA building in Great Russell Street, Holborn; one man was slightly injured. About the same time, another car bomb was detonated outside the Oasis swimming pool and sports complex in Holborn, causing a number of minor injuries to members of staff and shattering windows on most of the eight floors of the building. There were a number of small bombs planted in shops in London and four other cities during the same night but no serious injuries were reported. In the New Year unsuccessful attempts were made to blow up a gas works in Greenwich and an oil depot on Canvey Island. One of the main suspects for this mini-campaign was Gerard (Gerry) Tuite, whose name was to become familiar to most Special Branch officers over the course of the next few years.

OPERATION OTIS, AN UNSUCCESSFUL PIRA ATTEMPT TO RESCUE ONE OF THEIR MEMBERS FROM BRIXTON PRISON[14]

During the 1970s, the Provisional IRA organised many bombing attacks on the British mainland, which resulted in multiple deaths. Brian Pascal

---

14   The following account has been compiled from the recollections of members of the Special Branch teams
       involved in 'Operation Otis' and from contemporaneous press reports

Keenan, a very senior member of the PIRA, was suspected of organising many of these attacks and, on 20 March 1979, he was arrested by the RUC in Belfast for his involvement in the 1974 and 1975 bombing campaigns on the mainland, which included the 'Balcombe Street Siege'. He was transported to London and appeared at Bow Street Magistrates' Court on 26 March 1979, charged with conspiring to cause explosions. He was remanded in custody in Brixton Prison, where he remained until June 1980, when he was sentenced to eighteen years' imprisonment at the Old Bailey.

Keenan is without doubt the most important member of the PIRA ever to have been arrested and convicted of terrorist offences in this country. He had been a leading and active terrorist throughout the 1970s and at the time of his arrest he was almost certainly 'PIRA Director of Operations'. His value to the PIRA hierarchy was such that, late in the summer of 1979, the PIRA embarked on a plan to enable his escape from Brixton Prison – a plan that was not only auda-cious in its conception but one that, had it succeeded, would have boosted the PIRA's morale immeasurably and would have been a source of embarrassment to the British authorities equal only to the escape of spy George Blake in 1966.

The PIRA plan was to deploy a four-man ASU, comprising Robert Camp-bell, Richard Glenholmes and later Robert Storey and Gerry Tuite, to effect the escape of Keenan from Brixton Prison, by lifting him out of the exercise yard, known as 'The Cage', using a helicopter. In the event, all the persons actively involved in the plot were arrested on the day before the first trial helicopter flight was due to take place.

The PIRA team had no reason to suspect that the British Police would closely monitor their activities for over eight weeks – virtually from the outset of their scheme until the mass arrests. In fact, Campbell and Glenholmes arrived in Lon-don in the September of 1979 but police were not aware of their presence here until early October. Initially the two men stayed with Campbell's cousin, Mar-garet Parratt in Southgate and later with two girls in Notting Hill. It was later discovered that the route in and out of England was via the Belfast–Liverpool ferry, when, with the assistance of a crew member, they were enabled to use the crew gangway using a crew-pass, subsequently staying at the address of a relative of Campbell's in Liverpool.

Prior to police becoming aware of their movements, both Campbell and Glenholmes returned to Dublin to liaise with the PIRA hierarchy and discuss details of their plans, including selection of the two additional members of the team. While in Dublin, the two men took the opportunity to have their wives join them – just as well, seeing that it would be some considerable time before they could once more enjoy the pleasures of conjugal bliss. However, it can only be presumed that neither of the men disclosed to their wives their extra-marital activities with their lady friends in London.

On 12 October 1979, the RUC informed MPSB of Campbell's return to England. They had learned that Campbell's wife had telephoned the Liverpool relatives and told them to 'expect a visitor'. The Liverpool surveillance team spotted him and the next morning followed him on to the train to Euston. The MPSB surveillance team then took over and heard Campbell purchasing a Tube ticket to New Southgate. The surveillance team had a difficult time following their suspect, as the walk to Campbell's destination in Woodland Way led through open ground and round a boating lake at Grovelands Park. Campbell felt he was safely ensconced in Woodland Way, which was the address of his cousin, Margaret Parratt, secretary to the manager of Barclays bank, Dalston, in east London, a position she used to provide the ASU with references when renting premises and booking the helicopter. The same evening, Parratt drove Campbell to the Underground station to pick up Glenholmes; it was obvious to the surveillance team that Parratt was employing basic anti-surveillance moves during the journey.

An OP was soon set up in a suitable premises near to Parratt's address and the observation continued smoothly for just over a week, during which time the two men made frequent trips into central London, seeking suitable flats to rent and also meeting Christine 'Chrissie' Keenan after prison visits to her husband.

On 20 October, they moved in with one Jackie O'Malley and a female friend in her flat in Wilsham Street, Notting Hill, and a week later drove to Liverpool in a car hired by O'Malley. Travelling as crew members, they sailed on the night

ferry to Belfast for further discussions with the PIRA's top officials. An unfore-
seen problem had arisen, as Keenan had been switched to a different wing of
the prison with a different exercise yard. However, the conspirators had extensive knowledge of the prison system and layout as information was being passed
from Keenan to his wife during her frequent visits to him. While enjoying a
welcoming passionate kiss, the prisoner would deliver into her mouth a tightly
rolled piece of paper (known as 'The Dog') containing the necessary information. The farewell kiss enabled Chrissie Keenan to return the compliment with
further instructions from the PIRA. Once this stratagem was discovered by the
prison authorities, they stopped visitors from having physical contact with those
they had come to see.

On Campbell's return to Liverpool he spotted a man he suspected was a police
surveillance officer. He panicked and spent the night at the safe house in Merseyside, but the following morning, obviously rattled, he contacted O'Malley, who then
took charge of the situation, hired another car and directed him to take a taxi and
meet her at a pre-selected hotel in Knutsford, Cheshire. Surveillance was virtually
withdrawn but the pair were seen to enter O'Malley's address at about midnight.

Up until now, MPSB were in the dark about the aim of the conspiracy, but
about this time they received information that in fact the object was to spring
Keenan from captivity. Immediate and extensive checks were made at the prison
for signs of tunnelling and the RAF agreed to over-fly the site at very high level
with sophisticated equipment capable of detecting soil disturbance many metres
down. This involved closing Heathrow Airport for an hour while the RAF was
carrying out this operation. No evidence of tunnelling was discovered.

For the next three weeks Campbell and O'Malley busied themselves enquiring
about radio-controlled equipment and negotiating for flats to rent. On 3 December,
using references from Margaret Parratt, they entered into an agreement to rent a
top-floor flat in Holland Park. At the same time, they chartered a helicopter from
Alan Mann Helicopters of Chobham, Surrey, to fly a party from Battersea Heli-
port to the Great Danes Hotel, near Maidstone, on 13 December at a cost of £251.

On the evening of Saturday 8 December, Campbell, Glenholmes and a third man, later identified as Gerry Tuite, a PIRA explosives expert already wanted by police for his part in the 1978 'Christmas campaign' (see p. 287), moved into the Holland Park flat. The following morning they were joined by Robert Storey, a known PIRA gunman who had apparently stayed overnight with O'Malley in her Wilsham Street flat nearby.

It was apparent that the ASU was now in place and ready to strike; senior Metropolitan Police officers were fully aware of the situation and decided that to let the operation continue would represent a serious threat to the public, prison staff at Brixton, the helicopter pilot and police themselves. So it was that, at 4 a.m. on Wednesday 12 December, a large contingent of armed police stormed the Holland Park flat, although no shots were fired. Inside were found the four members of the ASU, two Browning pistols and ammunition, a map of the interior of Brixton Prison, about £3,000 in cash and a quantity of other incriminating evidence.

As with all such long-running operations, the difficulties encountered, especially with setting up and maintaining OPs and mobile surveillance, were considerable. Support provided by the Home Office in the form of CCTV, installed by the Metropolitan Police C7 Department, was of inestimable value as it enabled staff and senior officers to view the three main sites of interest – Woodland Way, Wilsham Street and the conspirators' base in Holland Park – in the Operations Room at New Scotland Yard. This facility was particularly helpful to the surveillance teams as they could position themselves at a discreet distance from the target addresses in the knowledge that any imminent move on the part of the terrorists would be reported to them from the Operations Room. Campbell and his confederates would invariably check that the coast was clear before venturing into the street.

Unwittingly the suspects themselves and their contacts assisted police knowledge of their activities by lax discipline on the telephone. It was also a bonus to the watchers that the main players normally went out together, so that only one team of surveillance personnel was needed at a time. Nevertheless, a minimum of twenty-four officers was required to provide full-time mobile cover, with a further thirty personnel employed in manning the Operations Room, OPs and on follow-up enquiries.

Operation 'Otis' was undoubtedly one of success, a triumph of team work – without the long-term intelligence-gathering operations carried out by the RUC and An Garda Síochána, and their readiness to impart their intelligence to their counterparts on the mainland, this intelligence-led operation would never have got off the ground. Of equal importance was the unstinting co-operation of the provincial forces involved and those members of the public who readily agreed to allow their premises to be used as OPs or for the installation of CCTV. Finally, there were the roles played by various branches of the Metropolitan Police – the Anti-Terrorist Branch, the Firearms Branch (D.11), C7 (for the CCTV), the uniform branch and, last but not least, the Special Branch.

On 17 March 1981, at the Old Bailey, Glenholmes and Campbell were each sentenced to ten years' imprisonment for conspiring to effect Keenan's escape and possession of firearms; Keenan, who had supplied the conspirators with accurate plans of the prison which he had drawn himself, had three years added to the eighteen he was already serving; Parratt and O'Malley, who both pleaded guilty, were each fined £1,000 and were given suspended prison sentences, eighteen months in the case of O'Malley, twelve months for Parratt; after a retrial, Storey was acquitted of being involved in the escape plot and possession of firearms. As he was released from custody he was rearrested and an exclusion order applied for under the Prevention of Terrorism Act. Gerry Tuite (see below) did not appear in the dock with his fellow conspirators as he had escaped from Brixton Prison while in custody. Christine Keenan had been acquitted at an earlier court appearance.[15]

GERARD (GERRY) TUITE – A HISTORIC CASE

Police were delighted when Gerry Tuite was rounded up with the other conspirators, for he was already wanted in connection with explosions over the

15   *Daily Telegraph*, 18 March 1981

Christmas period in 1978. However, he did not appear in the dock with his confederates, for, on 16 December 1980, together with two other prisoners, he tunnelled out of the maximum-security wing of Brixton Prison while on remand and contrived to make his way back to Ireland.[16] He remained at liberty until 4 March 1982, when An Garda Síochána arrested him at Drogheda, in the Republic of Ireland, and held him in custody under the Offences Against the State Act while the British authorities deliberated as to whether to apply for his extradition.[17] It was considered unlikely that any such application would be successful, as the case would be viewed in the Republic as political and Irish courts normally refused such requests. The British Director of Public Prosecutions (DPP), however, decided on a different course of action by asking his opposite number in Dublin to have Tuite tried in the Irish courts on a charge of possessing explosives with intent to endanger life and property between July 1978 and March 1979.

This would be the first occasion for an Irish citizen to be tried in an Irish court for a terrorist offence committed in Britain and police in London and in Dublin were apprehensive about the practicalities of preparing the evidence in a manner acceptable to the Irish court. Commander William Hucklesby, head of the Anti-Terrorist Branch, had productive discussions with top brass from An Garda Síochána to discuss the feasibility of this sensitive operation. Later, in order to familiarise himself with Irish court procedure and to discuss the evidence with senior officers from An Garda Síochána, DCS Philip Corbett, Hucklesby's deputy, accompanied by DCS Ray Wilson from MPSB, travelled to Dublin, where productive talks were held at the Phoenix Park headquarters of the Republic's police force. In the event, the DPP's initiative paid off for, on 13 July 1982, at Dublin's Special Criminal Court Tuite was found guilty of possessing bomb-making equipment in London four years previously and sentenced to ten years' imprisonment. His subsequent appeal against conviction was unsuccessful.[18]

16   *The Times*, 17 December 1980

17   Ibid., 5 March 1982

18   Personal recollections of the writer

After the 1978 series of bomb attacks, in which Tuite had played a leading role, the '70s was to see one final example of Irish republican terrorism. On 30 March 1979, Airey Neave MP was killed when his car was blown up by a tilt bomb as he drove up the ramp leading from the Palace of Westminster's car park. The Irish National Liberation Army (INLA), which had split from the IRA many years before, claimed responsibility for the killing, but no one was ever convicted for the offence.

CHAPTER TWENTY-FOUR

THE DIVERSITY OF SPECIAL BRANCH WORK

T HE FOLLOWING CHAPTER describes a selection of some of the more unusual situations with which the Branch has been called upon to deal.

PORT DUTY

L ittle has been written in this history, with the notable exception of the arrest of 'the Belfast Ten', about the vital role played in the effective functioning of Special Branch by those officers performing duty at port. Virtually every Special Branch section, not to mention other agencies, benefited from their unobtrusive yet thoroughly efficient methods in assisting their colleagues to deal with protection, counter-terrorism, foreign and domestic extremism. Other branches of the police service have also been grateful for their assistance in, for example, the apprehension of wanted criminals and, in some cases, the detection of crimes committed by passengers in transit.

THE CASE OF ABDELKEBIR EL-HAKKAOUI AND OTHERS

On 29 December 1973, an attractive Californian teenager, Allison Thompson, arrived at Heathrow Airport from America with the unlikely story that, although she only had £10 in cash on her, she was here for a month's holiday. Immigration officials asked customs officers to search her baggage, a large trunk adorned with a flamboyant black and white chequered design. It was discovered that the box had a false bottom, which concealed five handguns and 150 rounds of ammunition. Thompson, seemingly unaware of its contents, claimed that she had been asked by her boyfriend, later identified as Abdelkebir El-Hakkaoui, a Moroccan, to bring the trunk to London, where she would be met by a man she did not know, who would identify her by her distinctive trunk.

At this stage, Metropolitan Police from Ealing were called in and one of them spotted a likely candidate for her unknown contact lurking in the shadows near the arrival hall. In fact, he was known to Thompson, he was her boyfriend, El-Hakkaoui. As the case began to assume the characteristics of a terrorist plot, the senior Special Branch officer at the airport, Detective Superintendent Don Ginn, was informed. Ginn, unusually for a senior Special Branch officer, had a wealth of operational CID experience and decided that Special Branch would deal with the case. SB airport officers did not normally handle their own cases and DS Dewi Jones, DC Cracknell and others welcomed the opportunity to be actively involved rather than act as 'agents' for the CID. Within two days of El-Hakkaoui's and Thompson's detention, a third member of what transpired to be a conspiracy arrived at Heathrow Airport to be promptly arrested by SB officers; he was a Pakistani student named Ather Naseem.

After extensive questioning by Ginn and his team, it emerged that El-Hakkaoui, a supporter of a Moroccan anti-royalist organisation, UMFP, dedicated to the 'liberation' of the country, needed the firearms, which would be transferred to France at a later date, where they would be used to carry out a plot to kidnap a senior French government official as a hostage for the release of thirty Moroccan political prisoners. The scheme was the brainchild of El-Hakkaoui, who persuaded Naseem to assist him and duped another girl, Giulia McCartney, to accompany him to the airport to collect the case from Thompson.

On 17 May 1974, the three appeared at the Old Bailey, when El-Hakkaoui was sentenced to three years' imprisonment and Naseem to twelve months for the unlawful possession of firearms. The two men both supported Allison Thompson when she denied any knowledge of the contents of her trunk; she was acquitted on a similar charge but was detained for questioning by the FBI on her return to the USA, together with others in connection with the same conspiracy.

This case was unusual in that Special Branch involvement was limited to those officers employed at the airport, but it illustrated the excellent relations that existed between HM Customs, Immigration and the local police, a rapport that had been built up over many years working together. This culture was not confined to Heathrow Airport; at sea and airports throughout the country it was the ability to operate harmoniously with other agencies that epitomised Special Branch work and was an important ingredient of its success.[1]

THE CONTROVERSIAL VISIT OF ALEXANDER SHELEPIN

E very protection assignment presents its own particular problems, never more so than the visit of Alexander Shelepin in March 1975. Shelepin, a member of the Politburo, chairman of the USSR's central trade union council and former head of the KGB, was visiting Britain at the invitation of the Trade Union Congress in furtherance of attempts to open lines of communication with 'trade union organisations' in the Soviet Union. He was scarcely an ideal figure to head a 'goodwill' visit, as he was vilified by thousands of Jews in this country for alleged ill-treatment of Soviet Jewry in the USSR; he was also the target for the wrath of masses of Ukrainian, Lithuanian and other Soviet ethnic minorities

---

1   Recollections of Dewi Jones and Steve Cracknell; *Daily* Express, 18 May 1974; Contemporaneous editions of *The Times*

in Britain who held him responsible, while head of the KGB, for the assassination of their leader, Stepan Bandera, and many other dissident members of the
Soviet community. It was anticipated that there would be violent protests during
the visit and appropriate police measures, based on Special Branch risk assessments, were prepared to guarantee Shelepin's personal safety.

An early problem encountered by the SB personal protection team was that
the trade union officials responsible for organising the visit had no experience
of managing such a task, particularly one fraught with the likelihood of violent
demonstrations. Arrangements for state and official government-sponsored visits are always in the very capable hands of the Lord Chamberlain's office and
the Government Hospitality Fund respectively, everybody knows what they are
doing and timing is of the essence. In this case, however, with only a few days to
go, only a provisional programme had been drafted and, for example, no thought
had been given to transport arrangements for the visitors, which, the organisers
naively believed, would be handled by the police. Another hurdle to overcome
was convincing the Russian embassy that the visiting protection officers would,
under no circumstances, be allowed to carry weapons.

However, these and other administrative difficulties were finally sorted out,
although it was with some apprehension that, on the afternoon of 31 March 1975, a
team of SB personal protection officers awaited the arrival of the Soviet visitors at
Heathrow Airport's north extension, the specialist VIP reception unit. Earlier in
the day there had been a rowdy demonstration of some 3,000 protestors, mainly
Ukrainians, outside the Soviet embassy in London, but there were few spectators to
witness Mr Shelepin's arrival at the airport. Nevertheless, no risks were being taken
by the police – there was a very obvious uniformed presence at the airport and, in
addition to Special Branch, a heavy police escort accompanied the Russian and his
entourage to the embassy in Kensington Palace Gardens. The first day of the visit
ended peacefully with a dinner there attended by the Soviet ambassador Nikolai
Lunkov, general secretary of the TUC Len Murray and other trade union officials.

The following day was more eventful. Although details of the visit had not
been widely publicised, early the next morning a sizeable and vociferous crowd

gathered outside Congress House, headquarters of the TUC, where it was generally (and correctly) anticipated he would be having talks with leading members of the Council. Some of the protection team, sent on in advance, reported that it would be inadvisable for Mr Shelepin to enter the building by the main door in Great Russell Street, so it was decided that he would go in through a rear entrance while a decoy car went to the front to distract the demonstrators momentarily. The plan worked, for while the advance car and its occupants were subjected to a torrent of abuse and a hail of leaflets and missiles, including a bottle of milk, on leaving the embassy and on arriving at Congress House, the car carrying Mr Shelepin safely negotiated a back street and delivered its passengers to their destination without mishap, thus averting what could have been an 'international incident'. When the protestors realised that their prey had eluded them, there were ugly scenes and Special Branch officers assisted their uniformed colleagues in preventing a forced entry to the building. A large crowd of noisy protestors remained outside the building all day and when the day's proceedings were completed many of them walked in an orderly fashion to the embassy, occasionally shouting 'Ukrainian blood on your hands!' or 'We want Shelepin dead!'

The third day of the visit was more to the Russians' liking. In the morning a flight in an Aeroflot aircraft took the delegation and protection officers to Scotland, far from the hostile demonstrations of London. A hastily arranged visit to a manufacturing company at Kilmarnock was followed by a quick lunch in Glasgow before a premature departure for Moscow. As a goodwill visit, this could scarcely be called a success, but from the Special Branch point of view it was a useful operation, drawing grateful thanks from Len Murray for averting what could have been a disaster at Congress House and from Mr Shelepin who expressed his personal thanks for what he called 'a good job of work'. The Russians can never understand why public protests are allowed in this country; it is always the same when a Russian VIP visits; they insist 'no demonstrations' and wonder why we do not lock up all potential troublemakers for the duration of a visit![2]

2   Personal reminiscences of the writer

THE VISIT OF ANDREY A. GROMYKO, SOVIET MINISTER OF FOREIGN AFFAIRS

The following year, the Soviet Foreign Minister, Andrey Gromyko, visited Britain from 22 to 25 March, an event that failed to create much interest except among protest groups espousing the causes of Jewish prisoners of conscience and Soviet dissidents. The demonstrators, many of whom posed as prisoners, wearing pyjamas and shackled with chains, were markedly less rowdy than those enlivening the previous year's visit. However, on the second day of the visit, a member of the SB protection team, Stephen Cracknell, noticed a young man behaving in a furtive manner near the ambassadors' door of the Foreign and Commonwealth Office shortly before Mr Gromyko was due to leave after talks with our Foreign Minister. The perceptive officer, realising that he was wearing a blue and yellow scarf, the colours of the Ukrainian national flag, decided to question him. When searched, the youth – Keith Stephen Bomok from Slough, his place of birth – was found to have a hammer and anti-Soviet literature concealed beneath his coat; he was quietly arrested and given into the custody of a uniformed officer from Cannon Row Police Station, where he was charged with 'being in possession of an offensive weapon'.[3]

THE 'STOP THE SEVENTY TOUR' CAMPAIGN (STST)

Towards the end of 1969, it became public knowledge that the Cricket Council, the governing body of English cricket, had invited the South African Cricket Association to send a team to England in the summer to play a series of Test matches. At the time, the South African rugby team, the Springboks, was playing matches against English teams in a tour that was marked by violent demonstrations against the apartheid regime in South Africa. Frequent clashes

---

3   Personal reminiscence of the writer and DC Steve Cracknell

with the police resulted in hundreds of arrests. This was part of a wider campaign directed by the Anti-Apartheid Movement (AAM) against any sporting event featuring South African players. The intention was to focus attention on South Africa's anti-apartheid policy by denying white South Africa any sporting outlets beyond their own country.

The 'Stop the Seventy Tour' campaign (STST) was formed in September 1969 by a small group of activists led by Peter Hain, the son of South African communists, and himself a young man of extreme political views. Soon after its formation, it became apparent that the STST was intent on preventing or at least seriously disrupting the South African projected cricket tour. Although it was not scheduled to start until 2 June, the Home Office began drawing up contingency plans in December 1969 by writing to relevant Chief Constables and emphasising that it was their responsibility to 'make appropriate arrangements'. A month later, a meeting of interested parties took place at the Home Office at which the Home Secretary pointed out that the function of the police should be (i) to allow matches to be played and (ii) to deal with any threat to law and order. There was no question at this stage that the government would intervene to have the tour cancelled. The greater part of the ensuing proceedings was taken up with discussing the numbers of police likely to be required and the cost – how much and who would pay.

While these discussions were going on, the police were facing reality and preparing their own contingency plans. A central factor in formulating police strategies to counter any breaches of the peace contemplated by the militants was intelligence supplied by Special Branch in the form of regular reports to A.8 Department (responsible for the preservation of public order) and to the Home Office. These reports were prepared by DI Gerry Donker, an officer with comprehensive knowledge of South African politics, and were based on information supplied by a source close to the leadership of the STST Committee, which was supplemented by Special Branch's coverage of STST's meetings and rallies and by surveillance.

Regular meetings of ministers and their civil service advisers continued to be held throughout May and there was a constant flow of memoranda between departments reflecting their consternation and indecision. Throughout this period, Prime Minister Harold Wilson maintained that the government would not force the organisers to cancel the tour but, after a ministerial meeting on 21 May, the Home Secretary James Callaghan wrote to the Cricket Council asking them to withdraw the invitation to the South African touring team. The reasons given for this request at such a late hour (the touring party was due to arrive the following week) were three-fold. If the tour went ahead, (i) the burden on the police would be intolerable, (ii) a number of African countries were threatening to withdraw from the forthcoming Commonwealth games to be held in Edinburgh, and (iii) trade, and relations in general with South Africa, would suffer as a result of the extensive public disorder that would be caused.[4]

The tour was cancelled and as a consequence the STST Committee was disbanded, but the AAM, hoping to benefit from the public support that the campaign had attracted, planned a comprehensive programme of action directed at firms trading with South Africa. However, it failed to capitalise on a private South African amateur cricket tour of London and the Home Counties by a team named the Penguins, which took place from 4 June to 6 July. It was sponsored by Barclays Bank DCO and the team was accompanied throughout by two Special Branch officers, whose function was to liaise with local police and advise of any likely demonstrations. In the event there were no incidents marring the tour; this was one of the less demanding protection commitments undertaken by the Branch![5]

THE ABC TRIAL

A nother issue involving MPSB was the highly controversial prosecution of two journalists and a former member of the Intelligence Corps on various

---

4   TNA FCO 45/728

5   Personal recollection of David Yeadel

charges under the Official Secrets Acts, a case which became known as the ABC Trial, an acronym for the names of the defendants, Crispin Aubrey, John Berry and Duncan Campbell. The prosecution had its origins in the simultaneous deportation in 1977 of two American citizens, Mark Hosenball, an investigative journalist, and Philip Agee, a former CIA agent working in this country. Hosenball's eviction resulted from his participation in the publication in *Time Out* magazine in 1975 of an article dealing with the hitherto unmentionable GCHQ and other government electronic 'listening posts' throughout Britain and the rest of the world. In a separate case, Agee was wanted by the American authorities for exposing alleged malpractices by the CIA in his book *Inside the Company: CIA Diary*, published in 1975.[6]

Co-author of the article, entitled 'Eavesdroppers', which led to Hosenball's deportation was an investigative journalist named Duncan Campbell; together with a fellow writer, Crispin Aubrey, he was prominent in a campaign that endeavoured to overturn the deportation orders against Agee and Hosenball. Among the many free thinkers aroused by the controversy was a former corporal in the British Army, John Berry, who had been employed in the Intelligence Corps, where he dealt with SIGINT[7] material. Berry was anxious to meet Aubrey and Campbell as he wanted to give them intelligence recalled from his days as an analyst in the Intelligence Corps, which he thought they might be able to utilise. A meeting between the three took place on 18 February 1977, which was tape-recorded by Aubrey. Following the publication of the 'Eavesdroppers' article, MI5 and Special Branch had been maintaining surveillance on Campbell and were aware of this meeting; an SB team led by DCS Harry Nicholls arrested all three men soon afterwards. A subsequent search of Campbell's flat revealed a vast quantity of correspondence relating to communications, SIGINT and telephone interception, also photographs of defence establishments.

In the absence of any evidence of communication with foreign intelligence

---

6   Philip Agee, *Inside the Company: CIA Diary* (London: Allen Lane, 1975)

7   SIGINT – Signals intelligence obtained through the interception of communications

services, the men were initially charged with offences under Section 2 of the Official Secrets Act of 1911, of communicating classified information to an unauthorised person (in the case of Berry) and of the unauthorised reception of classified information (in the case of Campbell and Aubrey). In May and June more serious charges under Section 1 of the Act were added, but these were quickly withdrawn. Sifting through the documents and photographs found in Campbell's flat, evaluating the information contained on the tape recording and interviewing witnesses was a time-consuming task for the Special Branch team and, while this was going on, frantic discussions were taking place between the directors of Army, Naval and RAF Security, the permanent under secretary at the Home Office and the FCO, the Cabinet Secretary, Security Service Legal Adviser and other high-ranking officials. Their concerns were two-fold. The first problem concerned the likelihood of an appearance in open court of a responsible officer from SIGINT and what evidence he could give (the very existence of SIGINT had always been a closely guarded secret); of particular concern was the effect it would have on UK/US intelligence cooperation if 'details of our SIGINT activities were bandied about in open court'.[8]

The second issue related to the suitability of Section 2 of the Official Secrets Act to deal with cases such as this. Over the years there had been much public debate over the unfair restrictions that the Section imposed upon the freedom of the press; Lord Hutchinson QC, counsel for Duncan Campbell, gave voice to these misgivings when he addressed the Court before sentence was passed, referring to 'the doubts and confusions surrounding Section 2 of the Official Secrets Act, in the shadow of which reputable and hard-working journalists had to do their work'.[9] (NOTE: Section 2 was eventually replaced by the Official Secrets Act of 1989, which contained 'provisions protecting more limited classes of official information'.)

The first trial of the three men at the Old Bailey commenced on 5 September

---

8   TNA DEFE 47/34 E22

9   *The Times*, 18 November 1978

1978 but had to be abandoned due to the indisposition of the judge, and it was not until 17 November that sentencing was completed – the deliberations of the jury alone lasted for sixty-eight hours. The accused were all found guilty, but none of them received custodial sentences; for such serious offences they were extremely leniently dealt with, a reflection of the judge's unease at the use of the Official Secrets Act in this case. Berry was sentenced to six months' imprisonment, suspended for two years, and ordered to pay £250 defence costs; Campbell was conditionally discharged for three years and ordered to pay £2,200 towards the prosecution costs and £2,500 towards his defence; Aubrey was also conditionally discharged for three years, ordered to pay £2,500 towards the prosecution costs and a third of his own (unlike the others, he was not legally aided).

The trial provoked a lot of criticism from the public, which the media was not slow to encourage, for it was seen as an attempt to curb the freedom of the press and, particularly, investigative journalism. Those involved in the framing of the charges, the decision to prosecute and the presentation of the evidence were themselves concerned at the outcome of the trial and, judging from the plethora of memoranda passing between the FCO, the Security Service, Cabinet Office, Home Office and others, which apparently did not involve the police, a scapegoat was sought for the disappointing climax to their endeavours. It would appear that the police (i.e. the Special Branch) had very little influence on the management of the case, for a Ministry of Defence memorandum dated 20 June 1977 clearly stated 'the case is being handled by the Security Service' and elsewhere in the same document 'both the Attorney General and the Security Service are anxious [...] to secure a successful prosecution'. The Director of Public Prosecutions would have been involved before any charges were brought and the Attorney General's fiat would have been granted before the case was brought to court. And yet, in a letter from the Secretary to the Cabinet (Sir John Hunt) to the permanent under secretary to the Home Office (Sir Robert Armstrong), dated 27 November 1978, Sir John refers to an earlier conversation between them in which they agreed that 'the police ought to be very sure of their ground before blundering into something which could backfire', and he comments 'and what a backfire it has been!' It is strange that, although the matter was 'being handled by the Security Service',[10] Christopher Andrew, in his history of MI5, *The Defence of the Realm*, makes no mention of the case.

THE GRUNWICK DISPUTE

B etween 1976 and 1978, a long-running industrial dispute at the Grunwick Film Processing Laboratories in Willesden, north-west London became a severe drain on police resources, involving as it did thousands of demonstrators (mainly trade unionists) confronted by hundreds of police. During that period the frequently violent day's events on the picket lines normally dominated the headlines in the national press, and national television news programmes.

Grunwick's was making vast profits from its business of photographic processing and finishing, which it conducted on a postal basis, receiving undeveloped films and payment by mail and returning the finished product by the same means. A large number of the firm's workforce consisted of east African women who allegedly worked long hours in poor conditions and on comparatively low pay. In August 1976, a young Asian man was sacked and three others walked out in protest; later the same day Mrs Jayaben Desai was involved in an argument with the same manager and she too stopped work, together with her son. The following week they began picketing outside the factory gates, where they were joined by another fifty employees. Not long afterwards, they joined a trade union, APEX.

Shortly afterwards all the strikers were sacked and the strike developed into a bitter dispute between the trade unions and management, who refused to entertain any approaches from APEX to discuss reinstatement of the dismissed workers. From the spring of the following year, the local Trades Council in Brent became increasingly active in raising support for the strikers from other Trades Councils, Labour organisations and trade unions. In June, the Strike Committee led by

10   TNA DEFE 47/34

Mrs Desai organised a mass picket, which became violent and saw eighty women arrested. The strike and the picket continued to escalate, with postal workers refusing to handle the company's mail and sporadic picketing taking place outside shops doing business with Grunwick's. Other large-scale pickets followed, including the famous occasion on 11 July when the miners' leader, Arthur Scargill, brought hundreds of his supporters to the picket lines and, in the process, was arrested. It is estimated that over 500 arrests were made during the two years of the picketing.

Two more similar shows of worker solidarity took place in the autumn, but the industrial action gradually petered out after a Court of Inquiry, headed by Lord Scarman, condemned the mass picketing and unofficial postal blockade but recommended that Grunwick's should recognise the trade union APEX and reinstate the sacked workers, which the firm refused to do (so much for Courts of Inquiry!). The strike was called off in July the following year.

Special Branch played an important role in police endeavours to preserve the peace. As always, the various extremist organisations, in this case particularly the Socialist Workers' Party, strove to turn what was intended to be a peaceful picket into a confrontation with the police. In this instance it was extremely difficult to assess numbers and tactics of the demonstrators (because this is what they were) since the extremists were not cooperating with the Strike Committee any more than with the police and were changing their battle order from day to day. It was the much-maligned Special Demonstration Squad that was able to supply the uniform branch with up-to-date information on what they were likely to encounter. On most days an early-morning telephone call was made from the senior officer of the SDS to the Deputy Assistant Commissioner of 'A' Department, responsible for public order, giving him the latest available intelligence on the extremists' plans for the day.

MIDDLE EAST TERRORISM

It would be wrong to imagine that the IRA represented the only terrorist threat to this country. From the beginning of the '70s, an overspill of the

Arab–Israeli conflict had begun to manifest itself in London. In December 1971, a Special Branch report, based on information from a reliable source, warned that terrorists from the Popular Front for the Liberation of Palestine (PFLP) had arrived in London with the intention of assassinating members of the Jordanian royal family or hijacking a plane. The intelligence was not far off the mark for, on 15 December, the car carrying Zaid al-Rifai, the Jordanian ambassador, was attacked by a young man firing a Sten gun; the ambassador escaped with minor injuries to his hand. In the next few years further reflections of the desperate, schismatic struggle in the Middle East emerged in the metropolis, most notable of which was the shooting at his St John's Wood home in 1973 of Joseph Edward Sieff, a former chairman of Marks & Spencer and a leading British Zionist. Strongly suspected, but never charged with the offence, was Ilich Ramírez Sánchez (Carlos the Jackal), who was later imprisoned by the French for other terrorist offences.

From 1977 onwards, the Middle East conflict on the streets of London intensified and by the end of 1978 there had been at least eight assassinations and numerous attempts on the lives of Arabs living in the capital. The man responsible for many of these atrocities was Abu Nidal, who had broken away from the comparatively moderate Palestine Liberation Organisation (PLO) led by Yasser Arafat to form his own, more violent group, Black September. But there were several other extreme factions, such as the PFLP, which, like Abu Nidal, could not agree on a settlement with Israel and were quite prepared to seek a solution to their problems through murder.

A catalogue of their appalling crimes is extensive; the more notorious include:

10 April 1977: Abdullah al-Hajri, former Prime Minister of North Yemen, his wife and a minister at the embassy were shot dead outside the Lancaster Hotel, Bayswater. Information supplied by a Special Branch informant named Zohair Akache as one of the gunmen. It was later learned that he had slipped out of the country soon after the assassination and later perished at Mogadishu, Somalia, in October 1977 during the hijacking by the PFLP of a Lufthansa airliner.

31 December 1977: Two Syrians were killed in a car bomb attack in Mayfair.

4 April 1978: Said Hammami, the London representative of the PLO, was assassinated in his London office by Abu Nidal supporters.

10 July 1978: General Abdul Razak al-Naif, former premier of Iraq, was fatally wounded in an armed attack outside the Intercontinental Hotel in Mayfair. Two men, one an Iraqi, the other a citizen of Bahrain, were later charged with the killing.

28 July 1978: Taha Ahmed Al-Dawood, the Iraqi ambassador, escaped injury when a grenade was thrown under his car outside the embassy. Khouloud Moghrabi, a female Lebanese student, and Mahmoud Abu Naami, an Algerian mechanic, were later arrested for the attack.

21 August 1978: Two people died and nine were seriously injured when terrorists bombed and machine-gunned a coach carrying El Al aircrew in central London. An Arab, Fahad Mihyi, was subsequently charged with murder.[11]

This list is far from comprehensive but it illustrates the callousness and bravado displayed by terrorists involved in the seemingly insoluble Middle East crisis. Inevitably the police, particularly the Anti-Terrorist Branch and Special Branch, were engulfed in the spin-off from the violence that was unfolding on the streets of London. For their part, Special Branch were obtaining excellent intelligence from informants about the identities of the perpetrators of the crimes after they had been committed, but, regrettably, because of the complexity of the situation, with so many factions involved, each with its own particular axe to grind, it was virtually impossible to gain advance information about the terrorists' plans. After the bombing of the El Al coach, the bitter clashes between Abu Nidal's violent group of terrorists, the more moderate, though none the less dangerous, Palestine Liberation Organisation and other Palestinian factions entered a quieter phase after intervention by the Algerian ambassador to the Lebanon, Muhammad Yazid.

---

11   The above details are taken from contemporaneous editions of *The Times*

CONTRASTING EXAMPLES OF ESPIONAGE

Often, like buses, breaches of the Official Secrets Acts have a habit of coming along in groups after a long period without any. Such was the case in 1982/83, when no fewer than five individuals were sent to jail for offences against the Official Secrets Acts – Geoffrey Prime was sentenced to thirty-eight years' imprisonment on 10 November 1982 and Lance Corporal Philip Aldridge four years on 18 January 1983. The remaining three instances were dealt with by MPSB and are described in more detail below. Detective Superintendent Peter Westcott was the officer in charge of each case and they clearly illustrate how much espionage cases can differ both in character and in seriousness.

Miss Rhona Jane McIntyre Ritchie was employed at the British embassy in Tel Aviv from July 1981 as a second secretary and, from March 1982, as a first secretary. From the latter date the Security Service were receiving reports of an ongoing affair between Miss Ritchie and her opposite number at the Egyptian embassy, Rifaat al Ansari, during which she had been regularly passing secret documents to him. She was recalled to London on 14 March and immediately interviewed by MI5, to whom she confessed that she had indeed disclosed classified information to the Egyptians. As there was clear evidence of an offence under Section 2 of the Official Secrets Act of 1911, the case was handed over to Special Branch for further investigation with a view to prosecution.[12]

Unlike most breaches of the Official Secrets Acts, this was a comparatively straightforward investigation; after arrest by Westcott, Miss Ritchie was conveyed to Rochester Row Police Station where she was interrogated by the superintendent and DS Don Adams, to whom she admitted having passed confidential telegrams to her lover, Ansari. It was considered that disclosure of the documents, classified as confidential, did not represent a threat to national security but were rather an embarrassment to effective diplomatic relations. The prosecution relied

---

12   Hansard, 28 July 1983

for evidence entirely on her own admissions and the interviewing of witnesses was accordingly kept to a minimum.[13]

On 29 November 1982, at the Central Criminal Court, Miss Ritchie pleaded guilty to a specimen count of wrongful communication of information contrary to Section 2 (1)(a) of the Official Secrets Act of 1911. She was sentenced to nine months' imprisonment which was suspended for twelve months.

A stark contrast is provided by the case involving Professor Hugh ('Hugo') George Hambleton, a lecturer at a Canadian university who spied for the Russian Intelligence Service for over thirty years from 1952. Hambleton was arrested by Peter Westcott at the Royal Overseas League in the West End of London on 25 June 1982, while ostensibly en route to France for a holiday. The circumstances leading up to his arrest, and subsequently, are bizarre in the extreme.

Hambleton's secret life as a spy for the Russian Intelligence Services was revealed to officers of the American Federal Bureau of Investigation in 1977 after they arrested a key RIS agent employed in the USA who handled a number of spies working for the Russians. This man, Rudi Hermann, faced with the prospect of a lengthy spell in prison, agreed to co-operate with the authorities in return for immunity from prosecution. During an exhaustive debriefing he revealed the names of a number of agents he ran, including one Hugh Hambleton, who lived and worked in Canada. When, some months later, the Royal Canadian Mounted Police (RCMP) were informed of this coup, two of their representatives flew to the States to question Hermann. On their return to Canada, the RCMP carried out extensive enquiries into Hambleton's life and background but it was not until November 1979 that they took positive action.

Early in the morning on 4 November, RCMP officers called at his apartment in Quebec with a search warrant and for the next eight hours carried out a rigorous examination of his home; a similar operation was performed at his Ottawa property. They took away a large quantity of documents, a radio, a decoder and other spying equipment. He was not arrested but told they would be back the

---

13   This information was supplied by former Detective Superintendent Peter Westcott

following day to carry out a full interview. Over the next eighteen months the RCMP constantly harried him and interviewed him on no fewer than thirteen occasions. These interviews were carried out in a seemingly friendly fashion and Hambleton spoke at length about his contacts with the RIS, although initially the period before 1962 was almost totally ignored; he created the false impression of a modest, pleasant, frugally living professor.

The RCMP were anxious to arrest and charge him but, to their frustration, the Canadian solicitor general offered him immunity from prosecution in exchange for cooperation with the security services. He readily agreed. In taking the decision to make the offer, the Liberal government, which had just ousted the Conservatives, had apparently decided that there was insufficient evidence to take action under the Official Secrets Act. The decision not to prosecute provoked heated discussion in the Canadian Parliament and although the government claimed that the decision was made on the grounds of national security, it was generally considered that the most likely reason was political.

From this point onwards, Hambleton, reassured by the promise of immunity from prosecution, spoke more freely about his cooperation with the RIS, which covered the period from 1956 when he was working for NATO in Paris and had access to 'top secret' material. In June 1982, Hambleton told his tormentors from the RCMP that he proposed to take his son on holiday to Europe and would be staying overnight in London on the night of the twenty-second; he was repeatedly advised by the RCMP that he might be arrested if he travelled to the UK, but this advice was ignored.[14] The RCMP dispatched their dossier on the case to MI5, MPSB was informed and Westcott was duly handed a hot potato.[15]

When Hambleton arrived at Heathrow Airport, there was some confusion as to what should be done with him but he was eventually allowed to proceed to his

---

14   The first part of this account of the Hambleton case is based on reports in the *New York Times, The Times* and on extracts from the book written by his friend, Leo Heaps, *Thirty Years With the KGB: The Double Life of Hugh Hambleton* (London: Methuen, 1984)

15   The remainder of the account is based on D. Supt. Westcott's recollections of the case and on contemporaneous press reports

hotel, the Royal Overseas League in Mayfair, where Westcott met him for the first time in his bedroom the following morning and arrested him. He was conveyed to Rochester Row Police Station where he was charged and, over the course of the next three days, under interrogation by Westcott and DS Adams, made a full confession of his spying activities in a statement running to over 270 pages.

Having been interrogated so many times by the RCMP, his confession was well-rehearsed and his answers to the two officers' questions varied little from what he had already repeated many times over in Canada. His father was British but he was born in Canada and therefore had dual nationality. He was educated in the United Kingdom and Canada and spent part of his childhood in France, where his father was a press reporter. According to his statement, from 1944 he served variously with the Free French Army in Algiers, with the United States Army and with the Intelligence Branch of the Canadian Army (at his subsequent trial Sir Michael Havers, the Attorney General, completely debunked these claims).

Westcott carefully took him through the next part of his narrative, for this was at the core of his spying activities. After studying economics at the Sorbonne until 1956, he began working for the North Atlantic Treaty Organisation in Paris; he was employed there for five years, during which time he sent regular supplies of classified information, ranging from 'confidential' to 'top secret', to his Russian handlers. Every Friday he turned on his radio to receive messages in Morse code from Moscow. He would remove documents from his office, photograph them and clandestinely hand the film over to Russian agents at night in darkened streets or on the Métro. One lighter side of an otherwise tedious interrogation was Hambleton's reference to one of his coded messages from Moscow; he found decoding a lengthy and complicated process and was not overjoyed after grappling with one particularly irksome message to discover it was merely wishing him a 'Happy Birthday'. During one interview, Hambleton remarked, 'There is a sense of excitement, there is a sense of camaraderie with the person who is looking after you.'

When he left Paris in 1961, he came to London to study for a PhD at the London School of Economics and, in 1964, complete with doctorate, he became a professor

of economics at Laval University in Quebec. From that time onwards he appeared
to have acted as a talent-spotter for the Russians. His role as a spy was brought
to an abrupt end with the arrest by the FBI of his supervisor, Rudolph Hermann,
and the beginning of the RCMP's investigation into his life of espionage. The
Canadian police had mixed feelings about his insistence on travelling to England
and risking prosecution; on the one hand they wanted him brought to justice for
what he had done but on the other hand, after all the time they had spent on the
case, they wanted to do it themselves. They repeatedly warned Hambleton that
if he travelled to England he might be arrested – but he did, and he was. Their
Inspector Frank Pratt who, with Sergeant Robert McIlroy, had carried out all the
interrogations of Hambleton in Canada, co-operated fully with the Metropolitan
Police and expressed himself delighted with the ultimate outcome.

At the trial at the Old Bailey in December 1982, Westcott was questioned at
length about his interviews with the accused, but Inspector Pratt was not required
to give evidence. This was a high-profile case; apart from Pratt, other persons
attending court were a representative from the French Directorate of Territo-
rial Security (DST), to refute Hambleton's claim that he had been a French
double agent, and the Director General of the Canadian Security Service, as
well as members of the British Security Service. On 7 December 1982, Hambleton was sentenced to ten years' imprisonment for passing top-secret NATO
documents to the RIS, contrary to Section 1 of the Official Secrets Act of 1911.
Another charge of obtaining information likely to be useful to an enemy between
1956 and 1979 was not proceeded with. He served part of his sentence in Gartree
top-security prison, Leicester, and was transferred to a Canadian prison in 1986.
He was finally released under supervision in March 1989.

Michael Bettaney, born in 1950, was a member of MI5 who demonstrated
that it is easier to get employment with the domestic security services than it
is to enter the intelligence network of Russia as a spy. He became a member of
MI5 in 1974 after graduating from Pembroke College, Oxford, where he had
already appeared to disqualify himself from employment in any form of classified work through his public declarations of admiration for Adolf Hitler, his

penchant for singing pro-Nazi songs, a conviction for drunkenness, fare-dodging on the railway, heavy drinking and various other displays of character defects. The Bettaney case was as much an indictment of MI5 management as it was an espionage investigation.[16]

Nevertheless, these failings did not seem to hinder his progress in the Service and, by 1983, he had steadily achieved an average level of advancement and was now employed on the Russian desk. In hindsight and to the average 'man in the street', his behaviour was of a most bizarre character and when information of a leak from within the Security Service was received from the much-trusted defector, Oleg Gordievsky, it was not difficult for the investigators to focus their attention on Bettaney.

Bettaney's treachery began in April 1983 when this highly unpredictable intelligence officer pushed through the letter box of the Holland Park residence of Arkadi Guk, head of the KGB station in London, an envelope containing secret documents, the offer of further classified information and instructions on how to contact him. The Russian, believing it to be a provocation designed to trap him, did not respond. When the Security Service learned, through an informant within the embassy, that a second package had been delivered to Guk, it became obvious that the source was within the Security Service and soon the search for the culprit was confined to 'K' Branch, in which Bettaney was employed. By August, his behaviour, even more bizarre than usual, had convinced the MI5 hierarchy that he was the traitor in their midst. Without sufficient evidence for a successful prosecution, it was decided to confront Bettaney with the case against him and hope for a confession, which came after nearly two days of questioning. As soon as he indicated that he wished to make a confession, MPSB were informed and Detective Superintendent Westcott, accompanied by DS Adams, arrived at MI5's Gower Street headquarters to arrest Bettaney and convey him to Rochester Row Police Station – this was on 16 September 1983.[17]

---

16 Hansard, 17 January 1989

17 The Bettaney Case, prior to arrest – Andrew, *The Defence of the Realm*, pp. 714–21

The investigation team was faced with a relatively straightforward task in obtaining sufficient evidence to charge him with having committed offences under the Official Secrets Act of 1911. He seemed only too willing to confess that on more than one occasion he had posted classified documents through the letterbox at the KGB resident's address in Holland Park. The team charged with the task of searching his house in Cousldon, Surrey, could not have had an easier task, as he told them exactly where to find a number of secret documents, which were hidden precisely where he had indicated. This was useful information as it rebutted any possible suggestion by his defence that they had been 'planted'. During his comparatively brief interrogation (compared with, for example, that of Hambleton), he spoke at some length, and with some obvious conceit, about his use of tradecraft, for example leaving chalk marks at Underground stations and hiding film of secret material in the cisterns in public conveniences.

Those Special Branch officers with whom he came into contact could not understand how such an apparently insecure and confused individual, with an obvious alcohol problem, could have been engaged in such sensitive employment for so long. What puzzled them particularly was what motivation he had for carrying out his acts of treachery. MI5 were just as mystified and Bettaney himself said little to solve the mystery. He is reported to have told his Security Service interrogators before his arrest: 'There was no simple motive, it was a cumulative process [...] I have put the Service in a bloody position but it wasn't my intention.'[18]

On 16 April 1984, at the Old Bailey, Bettaney was convicted on ten counts under the Official Secrets Act of 1911 and sentenced to twenty-three years' imprisonment; much of the evidence during the trial was heard in camera. He was released in May 1998.[19]

---

18   Andrew, *The Defence of the Realm*, p. 720

19   The Bettaney case, post arrest, is based on Det. Supt. Westcott's recollections

CHANGES AT THE YARD

During the '70s and '80s a lot of changes in structure and personnel, many of which affected Special Branch, took place at New Scotland Yard. In 1977, Sir Robert Mark was replaced as Commissioner by Sir David McNee, Chief Constable of Strathclyde; another Scotsman, 'Jock' Wilson, a former chief superintendent in Special Branch, was shifted from the post of Assistant Commissioner (Crime) to AC (Traffic). In the same year, Deputy Assistant Commissioner Vic Gilbert left the Met to be Chief Constable of Norfolk and DAC 'Bob' Bryan became head of Special Branch, a post he held for the next four years before DAC Colin Hewett was transferred from 'A' Department to replace him, a novel appointment since never before had an officer been transferred from another police department to head the Branch. Hewett had only two commanders under him – Operations (Rollo Watts) and Administration, including protection (Philip Saunders); the post of Commander Ports had disappeared in 1978 when provincial forces assumed responsibility for a Special Branch presence at those ports within their jurisdiction. Under the commanders, seven chief superintendents managed the squads: 'A' – protection and general administrative matters; 'B' – Irish extremists; 'C' – domestic extremists; 'D' – Naturalisation; 'E' – foreign extremists; 'P' – Ports; 'S' – embracing the special demonstration squad, photographic, surveillance and European liaison sections. Within these squads, smaller specialist sections were continually springing up like so many mushrooms. For example, a European liaison section under a superintendent reflected the increasing interaction between MPSB and its equivalent police departments on the Continent; this section, staffed by officers with linguistic ability, also provided assistance to other branches in the Metropolitan Police and provincial forces. A training section ran courses for new recruits to the rapidly increasing number of provincial Special Branches and for officers performing duty at ports.

By 1980, the strength of the Branch stood at an all-time high of over 400 men with the return of a number of officers from the Anti-Terrorist Branch (formerly the Bomb Squad). The establishment now included ten women officers, a great asset, especially in the fields of surveillance and protection. Another development in the Branch's history took place in the early part of 1978 when the newly installed Commissioner, Sir David McNee, withdrew MPSB officers from all ports with the exception of Heathrow Airport and the Port of London. Coverage of the *Night Ferry* continued until 31 October 1980, when the service was terminated; no longer was it possible to board a train in London and alight in France, with only the slightest of breaks in the journey across the Channel, but already plans were afoot to replace the *Golden Arrow* (*Flèche d'Or*) with what was to become the Eurostar, Channel Tunnel service.

SPECIAL BRANCH REGISTRY

During DAC Bryan's period at the helm, a transformation of seismic proportions was taking place in Special Branch Registry. A time-consuming process of back-record conversion was undertaken as part of the computerisation of all the Yard's specialist records. When completed, the new system permitted instant access on visual display units installed in SB offices at the Yard and at Heathrow Airport to all the Branch's records, formerly stored on bulky files and accessed through equally bulky card indices. Appropriate security measures were installed to ensure that only suitably vetted personnel could access the more sensitive records. There is no doubt that the new computerised system was a tremendous improvement on the archaic methods it replaced, both in speed and in versatility. Special Branch Registry was now a highly professional, integral section of MPSB, run by a senior executive officer and staffed by civilians, predominantly female, who were all positively vetted and had their own career structure. Following the publication of the Radcliffe Report in 1962, it became a requirement, broadly speaking, for anyone in a position allowing access to classified material to be positively vetted.

A section comprising four inspectors was set up in Special Branch to carry out this function.

CHAPTER TWENTY-FIVE

A VERY STRESSFUL PERIOD

THE BRIEF RESPITE from Middle East violence which London enjoyed during 1979 was shattered in most spectacular fashion on 30 April 1980 when a group of Arab separatists stormed the Iranian embassy in Knightsbridge and held the occupants hostage in a siege that lasted six days. This was the first of a whole series of major incidents which were to keep the Branch at full stretch over the next five years. In October 1981, there were two particularly unpleasant IRA bomb attacks, at Chelsea Barracks and at a Wimpy Bar in Oxford Street, in which another courageous explosives officer, Kenneth Howorth, lost his life saving others. Then, the following year, the Israeli ambassador was shot, but not fatally, while leaving a function at the Dorchester Hotel; his protection officer shot the would-be assassin, who miraculously survived; three men were later arrested. Later in the year, a more peaceful event took place when Pope John Paul II paid a pastoral visit to the UK, but violence soon returned to the capital with twin atrocities committed on the same day in London's Hyde and Regent's Parks, which saw the slaughter of soldiers and their horses. In November 1982, in a comparatively minor incident, a letter bomb from the 'Animal Rights Militia' addressed to Margaret Thatcher was delivered to 10 Downing Street and injured one of the staff. Although not a major event, it was a grim reminder of the potential and ever-present threat posed by the various animal rights movements. On 17 December 1983, one of the most devastating of the IRA's long list of 'achievements' was the detonation of a bomb in Harrods department store, which was packed with Christmas shoppers. The death toll amounted to six, which included three police officers attempting to clear the store before the fatal explosion; a police dog was blown to pieces and ninety civilians were injured. Almost a year later, five people were killed and many injured, some seriously, when the IRA achieved a major coup in detonating a bomb at the Grand Hotel, Brighton, where the Prime Minister was staying during the Conservative Party's annual conference.

THE IRANIAN EMBASSY SIEGE

On 30 April 1980, people, not only of London, but of the rest of Britain and indeed the democratic world, were stunned by the news that a group of gunmen had illegally entered the Iranian embassy in Princes Gate, London, and were holding hostage the staff and other people who happened to be in the embassy at the time, including Trevor Lock, the armed member of the Diplomatic Protection Group who had been on duty at the door. The terrorists were members of an organisation operating under the title Democratic Revolutionary Front for the Liberation of Arabistan (DRFLA), which was campaigning for Arab national sovereignty in the southern part of Khüzestän province (otherwise known as Arabistan); they were demanding the release of Arab prisoners from jails in Khüzestän and their own safe passage out of the United Kingdom, demands that were promptly refused.

After six days of nerve-racking negotiations, which gained valuable time for the SAS to make preparations for the storming of the building, should that course of action be required, the terrorists shot dead one of the hostages and threatened to kill the rest within thirty minutes if their demands were not met. The

Commissioner promptly asked the Home Secretary, Willie Whitelaw, for permission to hand over control of the situation to the army; after the Prime Minister had agreed to this, the army began their final preparations for the assault while the police negotiator at this vital stage, Ray Tucker, kept Oan talking in order to distract him and prevent him from giving orders for more killings. This was Oan Ali Mohammed, aged twenty-seven, from Khüzestän, the leader of the group, who conducted negotiations with police via a field telephone which had been put through one of the windows.

Only one hostage lost his life during the ensuing action, while nineteen were rescued comparatively unharmed. Five had already been released. Of the six terrorists, five were killed and the sixth, Fowsi Nejad, was later sentenced to life imprisonment but released after twenty-seven years.

The soldiers who had rescued the hostages from probable death while risking their own lives were later accused of wilful killing but at the subsequent inquest were rightly cleared of any wrongdoing.

DAC John Dellow was in overall charge of the response force, which included, apart from the SAS, a psychiatrist, an interpreter, a contingent of police marksmen (D.11), technical experts managing the surveillance equipment, officers from the Anti-Terrorist Branch and Special Branch officers who had little part to play in the drama, apart from the important role performed by Detective Inspector, later Detective Chief Superinendent, Ray Tucker, one of the police negotiators. Although the SAS team deserve every bit of praise lavished upon them for their extremely courageous actions in seizing the embassy and freeing the hostages with only one loss, there were other unsung heroes who played a vital role in securing an almost perfect conclusion to the six-day drama. These were the police negotiators who established some kind of rapport with Oan, which enabled them to make him see reason occasionally and probably prevented more of the hostages losing their lives. But the undisputed hero was PC Trevor Lock, who remained cool throughout the six days and was seen as the epitome of everything that is expected of the British bobby. He was awarded the George Medal for his behaviour under great stress during the siege, during which he managed to conceal his gun until the SAS arrived.

THE ATTEMPTED ASSASSINATION OF THE ISRAELI AMBASSADOR, SHLOMO ARGOV

On the evening of 3 June 1982, an incident unique in the history of the Metropolitan Police Special Branch took place in London's fashionable Mayfair, when the Israeli ambassador, Shlomo Argov, was shot in the head by Hussein Ghassan Said, a member of an Abu Nidal assassination squad. The event was unique since this was the sole occasion on which a person receiving Special Branch protection had been injured; it was doubly unique as this was the first and only time when an SB officer has fired a shot 'in anger'.

The following narrative of the event is based upon Detective Constable Colin Simpson's first-hand account of this tragedy, which cut short the career of a brilliant diplomat who was generally recognised as one of the stabilising influences in the Arab–Israeli conflict. On the fateful evening, Argov attended the annual De La Rue Diplomatic Corps Dinner held at the Dorchester Hotel, Park Lane. Colin Simpson was the only protection officer accompanying him and none of the other guests had Special Branch protection; moreover, only one armed officer from the Diplomatic Protection Group (DPG) was on duty outside the hotel. DC Simpson had been to the venue in the afternoon and ensured that the banqueting hall had been searched by 'explosives' dogs, but he was unhappy about the proposed low level of DPG presence outside and expressed his disquiet to their control room. He was told they had no one else available.

At about 10.45 p.m. the ambassador was leaving the hotel by way of the ballroom entrance in Park Lane; the driver, Michael Silver, was standing with the car about twenty yards away and as Simpson stood by the open rear door a figure suddenly rushed by and shot Mr Argov through the head as he stooped to enter the vehicle. Colin directed Silver to radio for urgent assistance and, as others were caring for Mr Argov, he pursued the assailant, who was still in sight. The chase continued into a side street but Said continued running when called upon to stop, turned and fired at the pursuing officer but missed. Colin returned his fire and wounded him in the neck. By now the DPG officer had arrived on the scene and was left with the assailant while Simpson returned to Mr Argov to find the Assistant Commissioner (Crime) Gilbert Kelland with him, while the Commissioner, Sir David McNee, was directing traffic! They had both been guests at the banquet.

Subsequent examination of the gunman's weapon revealed that it had jammed after the two shots, one at the ambassador and one at Simpson, had been discharged. The officer's day did not end with the departure of the seriously injured Mr Argov to hospital; Commanders Wilson (Operations) and Bicknell (Protection) and the head of the DPG were put in the picture and a brief statement was prepared for the Anti-Terrorist Branch. After that, the dedicated officer visited Mrs Argov at home, where another SB officer was already in attendance – it was now after 3 a.m. The following day he made a further, more detailed, statement, collected a fresh firearm and ammunition and underwent his first course of what he refers to as 'post-traumatic stress counselling – a few beers'.

Said, a Jordanian student, was arrested at the scene, his two accomplices were arrested by the crew of an area car on Southwark Bridge; an observant security guard at the Dorchester Hotel had informed the police of their suspicious behaviour outside the hotel and given their car registration number to police. They were Marwan al-Banna and Nawaf al-Rosan, both of whom, like Said, were members of the Abu Nidal organisation. At the Old Bailey in March of the following year the three men received a total of ninety-five years' imprisonment.

Mr Argov remained hospitalised until his death on 23 February 2003. DC Simpson continued protection duties with Yoav Biran, the acting ambassador, and with Mrs Argov for about six months. He was later Highly Commended by the Commissioner and received a cheque from the Bow Street Fund but the subsequent recommendation for a bravery award was not approved by the Home Secretary Leon Brittan.

A RESUMPTION OF IRA BOMBING IN BRITAIN

SULLOM VOE

After a brief respite from IRA violence, Great Britain once again became a target for Irish terrorist activity in May 1981, when an incident that could have been a prestigious success for the PIRA in fact scarcely received a mention in English newspapers. Sullom Voe on the Shetland Islands is the site of one of the largest oil terminals in Europe. On 9 May, HM Queen Elizabeth, the King of Norway and many other VIPs were there for its official opening ceremony. As the proceedings were about to begin, a distant explosion was heard, dismissed by the experts as an electrical fault. In fact it was a bomb that had exploded in a building some 500 yards away, causing no casualties and only superficial damage. An officer from MPSB was dispatched to the scene and his enquiries established that among the workforce on the site were a number of Irishmen with pronounced republican views, one of whom had recently received a parcel posted from Ireland. It was believed this contained the bomb; there was consternation when it was learned that he had expected a second bomb before he fled without collecting his pay. Further investigation revealed that this second parcel arrived after his departure and eventually made its way back to Ireland, where it failed to be delivered to his address and was collected by an RUC officer from the post office. It contained a small bomb and a twelve-day timing device. Although the PIRA's hopes for a 'spectacular' did not materialise, they boasted that they had breached the Queen's security. This was merely a prelude to the bloody events that were to follow. The good co-operation that existed between the RUC and MPSB was invaluable in unravelling this case.

CHELSEA BARRACKS

On 10 October 1981, the PIRA resumed their bombing campaign on mainland Britain when a nail bomb exploded outside Chelsea Barracks, which, significantly, was the London base of the Irish Guards. The bomb, concealed in a

laundry van parked overnight in Ebury Bridge Road and moved in the morning to a spot about fifty yards from the barrack gates, comprised about 30 lbs of
high explosives packed with some 1,000 or more six-inch nails, bent in order
to cause maximum injury. It was detonated by a member of the ASU by remote
control, using 300 feet of command wire running to a vantage point where he
could observe the target coach just before it turned into the barracks. Although
frequently employed in Northern Ireland, this was the first occasion on which
this method of detonation had been used on the mainland. The blast killed
two civilians and caused more than fifty casualties, including twenty-two of the
twenty-three Irish Guardsmen on board the coach. It was justifiably described
by the Prime Minister, Margaret Thatcher, after visiting some of the injured in
hospital, as a 'cold, callous, brutal and sub-human thing'.

Some idea of the horrific results of the attack can best be described in the
words of one of the victims, former Lance Corporal John Radley:

> When I eventually came around and woke up, it was like a scene from the
> Crimean War. People with bits of metal material stuck out of their faces
> and all kinds of things. Some of the nails they [the bombers] bent in half
> to act like a boomerang so when the explosion happened, the blast would
> make them spin through the air to try to cause maximum damage and car-
> nage. A lot of us had nails pierce our bodies. When I went to hospital they
> actually took four six-inch nails out of my mouth. The top of my nose was
> hanging off – a bit like a boiled egg.

A six-inch nail also went into Mr Radley's neck and was stuck half way into his
back. Another lodged in his forehead. At the time of writing he still had wires
in his left hand, which he used to try to shield his face from the blast. He estimates that he has had more than 6,000 stitches in his body, says he is in pain
every day and has had extensive surgery to his ear.[1] No one was arrested at the

---

1   http://www.bbc.co.uk/news/uk-northern-ireland-22747968 Retrieved 27 September 2014

time but Paul Kavanagh and Thomas Quigley, experienced IRA bombers, were subsequently arrested and sentenced for these and other murders (see below).

SIR STEUART PRINGLE

The team's next target, once more a military one, was the Commandant-General of the Royal Marines, Lieutenant General Sir Steuart Pringle. On 17 October, the general sustained extensive injuries, including the loss of his lower leg, when a bomb exploded as he drove away from his house. The gang displayed their versatility in bombing techniques, for this time they attached magnetic explosives underneath the officer's car while it was parked outside his home in Dulwich. Surprisingly, Sir Steuart, who was well aware of the need for security precautions in view of his position, failed to spot the bomb, which was attached to the underside of the wheel arch of his VW Passat.

BOMBS IN OXFORD STREET

The ASU (it was now correctly assumed that the same individuals were responsible for all these attacks) soon struck again. On 26 October, two bombs were discovered within a short space of time in Oxford Street in the West End of London; the first of these, triggered by a booby trap, went off in the toilets at a Wimpy Bar, killing Kenneth Howorth, the Metropolitan Police explosives officer who was in the process of defusing it. A thirty-minute warning had been given and the area cleared, so mercifully nobody else was injured. Warning had also been given of a second bomb planted in Debenhams department store, but on this occasion an equally brave, but more fortunate, explosives officer rendered the device harmless and nobody was injured.

SIR MICHAEL HAVERS

The following month, the PIRA chose a member of the judiciary as their next target. On this occasion it was Sir Michael Havers, the Attorney General who had led the prosecution in a number of trials of PIRA members, who became the focus of the terrorist gang's attention. On 13 November, the back of his house in Wimbledon was severely damaged by a bomb; although the premises had a uniformed constable guarding the front of the house, the rear was unprotected and the bomber would have been able to approach unobserved across an open field. Fortunately, Sir Michael and his wife were away on holiday. Had they been at home, they would probably have been killed or seriously injured, as the explosion virtually demolished their bedroom.

THE END OF THE AFFAIR

The sequel to this bloodthirsty campaign was enacted at the Central Criminal Court in March 1985 when justice, which they had eluded for so long, finally caught up with Paul Kavanagh and Thomas Quigley and they were sentenced to long terms of imprisonment. It was the chance discovery of an explosives cache at Pangbourne near Reading in 1983 that led to the identification of the two men; advanced technology enabled their fingerprints to be detected on some of the items contained in the store and the RUC quickly identified them in their records. It was not long before Quigley was arrested in Belfast and escorted to London, where he appeared in court on 8 December 1983 charged with conspiracy to cause explosions, but six months elapsed before Kavanagh joined him in the dock. They were both convicted of the two murders outside Chelsea Barracks and of Kenneth Howorth in Oxford Street; they were also convicted of numerous other offences in relation to their participation in the Chelsea Barracks explosion, the two Oxford Street bombs, the attempted murder of Sir Steuart Pringle and the explosion at Sir Michael Havers's home in Wimbledon. In addition, they were both found guilty of the possession of arms and explosives which were discovered in the huge cache at Pangbourne two years after their bombing campaign in London. The discovery by police of two more stores of arms and explosives at Salcey Forest in Northamptonshire and Annesley Forest in Nottinghamshire the following year led to further charges against Kavanagh and the ASU's quartermaster, Natalino Vella from Dublin. Kavanagh and Quigley were each jailed for a recommended minimum of thirty-five years; Vella was sentenced to a term of fifteen years' imprisonment. They were all released under the terms of the 1998 agreement and Kavanagh became a 'special adviser' to Martin McGuinness, deputy first minister in the Stormont government.

It should be stressed that the excellent liaison that existed between An Garda Síochána, the RUC and Metropolitan Police Special Branches played a big part in enabling this case eventually to reach a successful conclusion in the imprisonment of the three men. The discovery of the stores of arms and ammunition at Salcey and Annesley Forests was due to the good work of the Special Branch surveillance team and will be described later.

CARNAGE IN HYDE PARK AND REGENT'S PARK

In terms of publicity, the next two bombing incidents probably ranked with anything that the PIRA had achieved up to this point, but in fact they had a negative impact on public support for the organisation, particularly in the USA, which was an important source of IRA funding. On 20 July 1982, the terrorists returned to their favourite target, the military, in a day of carnage enacted in two of London's Royal Parks.

The first incident took place at 10.40 a.m., when a nail bomb stowed in the boot of a Morris Marina motor car, parked in the South Carriage Drive near to Hyde Park Corner, exploded as a contingent of the Household Cavalry was passing on its way to take part in the daily ceremony of changing the guard at Horse Guards Parade. Four soldiers were killed and many badly wounded. Seven of their mounts were killed instantaneously or had to be put down subsequently.

In the second attack two hours later, a bomb exploded underneath the grandstand in Regent's Park where the Royal Green Jackets Band was playing to an audience of over 100. Seven bandsmen were killed and the remaining twenty-three injured, while at least eight members of the audience were injured. Those are the bald facts of the incidents that so horrified the public and prompted Margaret Thatcher to remark, 'These callous and cowardly crimes have been committed by evil, brutal men who know nothing of democracy. We shall not rest until they are brought to justice.'

Two of the perpetrators were brought to justice, British justice, which allowed them to go free again because of the Good Friday Agreement. In 1987, Danny McNamee, the bomb maker, was convicted for his part in the bombings, sentenced to twenty-five years' imprisonment and released in 1998 under the terms of the Agreement. Shortly after the murders, Special Branch had received information, passed on to the Anti-Terrorist Branch, that another of those involved was John Anthony (Sean) Downey, who had fled to the Republic of Ireland shortly after the incidents. For many years he lay low in County Donegal where the RUC could not touch him, although they were aware that the Metropolitan Police Anti-Terrorist Branch had a warrant for his arrest and were constantly reminded of this by Special Branch. However, in 2007, the Police Service of Northern Ireland sent him and 186 other 'on-the-run' IRA suspects a letter giving them an assurance that they were no longer wanted by any police force in the UK. Consequently, after 2007, Downey freely travelled in and out of the United Kingdom[2]. On 19 May 2013, however, he was arrested at Gatwick Airport en route to Greece and charged with murder; he subsequently appeared at the Old Bailey charged with four murders and intending to cause an explosion likely to endanger life. The trial collapsed, as the judge ruled that Downey had been misled by the letter of 2007 and prosecuting him would be an abuse of power.[3]

SUSPECTED PLOT TO BOMB WEETON BARRACKS, LANCASHIRE

In 1983, the police experienced a set-back in their constant pursuit of PIRA terrorists when prolonged and difficult surveillance of two suspected

2   *The Guardian*, 26 February 2014

3   BBC News, 25 February 2014

PIRA members ended in frustration as the quarry, at last realising they were being followed, took evasive action and returned to Ireland. The surveillance had been set up in March 1983, following the receipt by Lancashire Police of information from MPSB that intelligence from An Garda Síochána suggested that a Blackpool man was in touch with the IRA and was worth watching. As a result, police surveillance teams kept a close watch on two men, later identified as Patrick Murray and Patrick Magee, for nearly two weeks – no easy task. The two men were showing unusual interest in Weeton Army Barracks, near Blackpool, and were often seen drinking in the Eagle and Child public house, which was frequently used by soldiers from the neighbouring barracks. It was assumed from the surveillance and information from other sources that they may be preparing for some form of attack on the barracks. On the final day of the surveillance it became increasingly apparent that the pair were preparing to collect the means to carry out their attack as they set off in a hired car towards the south. It was hoped that they would lead police to their cache of arms and explosives but it was not to be; suddenly accelerating as they entered Preston, they shook off the pursuing police cars and abandoned their vehicle outside the railway station, leaving the doors open and the windscreen wipers working. Despite an extensive search of the area, their pursuers did not see them again.

MURDER AT HARRODS DEPARTMENT STORE, DECEMBER 1983

For nearly eighteen months after the incidents in the Royal Parks, London was free of major IRA violence. Intelligence suggested that IRA plans to carry out a campaign had been disrupted to a certain extent by the discovery in October of some of their arms and explosives buried in fields near Pangbourne, Berkshire, earlier in the year, but, on 10 December 1983, the peace was broken when a bomb exploded outside Woolwich Barracks, slightly injuring four soldiers and a civilian. This was followed three days later by the discovery of four small bombs in Phillimore Gardens, Kensington, which were disarmed by explosives officers from the Anti-Terrorist Squad. However, worse was to follow – much worse.

On Saturday 17 December 1983, Mohamed Al-Fayed's prestigious department store, Harrods, in Knightsbridge, was crowded with families doing last-minute Christmas shopping. At 12.41 p.m. a telephone message purporting to come from the IRA was received at the central London office of the Samaritans; the message, giving a hitherto unused code word, stated that two bombs had been placed in Harrods and another two at stores in Oxford Street. Earlier that day, twenty-two false alarms had been received by police and nothing suspicious was found in Oxford Street. The information about Harrods was vague and in part misleading; there was, in fact, only one bomb discovered. These facts are relevant when considering subsequent allegations that the police had not acted promptly or efficiently in clearing the area. The bomb, with an estimated weight of 25 lbs, had been left in a car parked in Hans Crescent at the side of Harrods; it was detonated using a timing device.

This incident, even by IRA standards, was totally callous. Although the IRA could claim that it was aimed at an economic target, their feeble excuses that they did not intend to cause civilian casualties failed to dispel public abhorrence at the attack, which killed six people (three police officers and three civilians), injured ninety (including fourteen police officers) and killed a police dog. In addition, thousands of pounds worth of property was destroyed. In a statement to the House of Commons condemning the violence, the Home Secretary, Leon Brittan, said:

> The IRA made a statement last night in Dublin in which it admitted responsibility for the attack as well as for the bomb outside Woolwich Barracks ten days ago. It also claimed that the attack was unauthorised and would not be repeated, and regretted the civilian casualties. As I have said elsewhere, I find the disclaimer of responsibility utterly contemptible. Those who place a bomb of this size in a street crowded with Christmas shoppers cannot evade responsibility in that way. Moreover, the bomb was timed to go off just at the moment when those investigating the situation were likely to be approaching it. [...] What has happened

is that the action taken by its members has caused universal revulsion and condemnation.

Intelligence suggests that the IRA leadership was indeed concerned about the public revulsion at the wilful carnage. Evidence of their embarrassment was demonstrated when the president of Sinn Féin, Gerry Adams, speaking after the atrocity, stated that his organisation never condoned civilian casualties but added that it was 'an example of an operation that had not gone right' and that the bombing had not been authorised by the [IRA] 'army council'.[4] When Natalino Vella, described as an IRA quartermaster, was later arrested for a separate, but related, offence, he explained to Commander Hucklesby, head of the Anti-Terrorist Branch, that some of the IRA hierarchy were very angry at the fact that innocent shoppers were among those killed. He reiterated what Adams had said, 'The unit had stepped outside its limits. There was a lot of trouble about Harrods. We didn't want all those people killed.' So troubled were the Provisional Army Council by the atrocity, which had been carried out without their permission, that they sent Vella to England on a two-fold mission – to find out why Harrods had been bombed and to tell the unit responsible to return to Ireland.[5]

CACHES OF ARMS AND BOMB-MAKING EQUIPMENT IN SALCEY FOREST AND ANNESLEY FOREST

But there was another reason for Vella's mission – the discovery of PIRA caches of arms and explosives at Pangbourne on 26 and 27 October 1983. As an IRA quartermaster he needed to know the disposition and availability of arms and explosives in this country and it was to acquire that knowledge that his visit was made. One day in January 1984, a telephone message was received in Special Branch from An Garda Síochána, informing them that an IRA operative,

---

4   *The Times*, 20 December 1983

5   Ibid., 8 March 1985

Natalino Vella, from Dublin was flying to London on 15 January. No further details were given but it was assumed that some importance should be attached to the information, as it was unusual for the Garda, who were quite properly always very circumspect even in scrambled telephone messages, to be so specific on the phone.[6]

The SB surveillance team under DI Matt Dwyer was briefed to follow Vella wherever he went and to note particularly any contacts he made. He duly arrived at Heathrow Airport, was followed to central London, where he did some shopping of no consequence, and on to an address in the Earls Court area, where he stayed the night. When the surveillance was resumed, he was tailed on the Underground to Euston Station, where he boarded a train for Northampton; there he was met by two (possibly three) persons, not known to the surveillance team, who led him to a white Rover car. There followed a short journey to Salcey Forest, where the Rover pulled up in a lay-by and two of the occupants, Vella and a man later identified as Paul Kavanagh, got out and walked into the wood. They were away for some time, possibly half an hour, but were not obviously carrying anything either when entering or leaving the forest.

The pursuit continued on the M1 motorway into Nottinghamshire, where a second halt was made in a lay-by. What could have been an embarrassing, or worse, situation then arose, as sometimes used to happen before Special Branch had its own dedicated radio channel; the local Regional Crime Squad surveillance team was operating in the vicinity and had been monitoring the SB transmissions. However, no harm was done; the two teams met and the RCS team even offered to lend a hand if needed, but this was politely declined. Meanwhile, as before, Vella and Kavanagh had alighted from the car and entered the wood (Annesley Forest); again they were not observed to be carrying anything. On this occasion one of the SB officers, John Daniels, followed the couple into the wood in an attempt to see what they were doing, a typically brave action as he was unarmed; however, nothing significant was observed. On returning to the M1, the driver

---

6   Personal recollection

of the Rover began to carry out anti-surveillance manoeuvres and to increase speed; to continue the chase would have been dangerous and, since none of the quarry was known to be wanted and they had not been observed to be breaking the law, the surveillance was discontinued. Had Kavanagh been identified at the time, the operation would have run a different course, as he was wanted for the 1981 series of PIRA atrocities. However, the surveillance operation was by no means a waste of time, for it was later ascertained that on their forays into Salcey and Annesley Forests Kavanagh and Vella were in fact inspecting PIRA arms caches hidden there, which a thorough police search uncovered shortly afterwards. Officers on the surveillance team were able to give useful evidence in court when Vella and Kavanagh were convicted of, among other offences, possession of the arms and ammunition hidden in the forests.[7]

THE BOMB AT THE GRAND HOTEL, BRIGHTON[8]

The next instalment in this particular series of bombings was the most alarming and the most spectacular. It took place in Brighton at the aptly named Grand Hotel, where the Prime Minister Margaret Thatcher, her Cabinet, their spouses and many of the other delegates were staying during the annual Conservative Party conference. At about 2.45 a.m. on 12 October 1984, a bomb exploded in Room 629, where it had been placed about three weeks previously behind a panel surrounding the bath; the device weighing about 20 lbs was detonated by means of a long-delay timer, only the second occasion on which the IRA had used such a means of detonation in this country (the first was at Sullom Voe). Special Branch had received intelligence beforehand from the RUC that there was a heightened risk of an incident during the conference, although there was no specific threat. A letter to this effect was sent to chief constables. MPSB worked hard to secure a safe venue for the conference, under the prevailing strictures, and in the weeks

---

7   Recollection of DI Matt Dwyer

8   The following account is based on the recollections of Commander Bicknell, DCS Greenslade and contemporary newspaper reports

leading up to the event Commander David Bicknell, the Special Branch officer with overall responsibility for ministerial and VIP security, had several times met with senior officers from the Sussex Constabulary who would be responsible for security at the conference. Bicknell's deputy, Detective Chief Superintendent Tony Greenslade, who had specific responsibility for protection matters, had also been to Brighton for discussions on the personal protection of ministers, of whom there would be eight receiving close protection. However, Roger Birch, later Sir Roger, Chief Constable of Sussex Constabulary, exercised his right of office when discussing security with Commander Bicknell, telling him in no uncertain terms that, 'The security of the conference was his responsibility and apart from doing their protection duty, MPSB could leave it to him and his force.' On visiting his officers at the hotel on the day before the explosion, Bicknell was struck by the lack of proper security there; the swarms of journalists in Brighton to cover the week's proceedings had left bags and photographic equipment scattered about haphazardly in the entrance lobby and people were wandering in and out through the front door unhindered, for the hotel was still open for normal business.

Within minutes of the detonation Commander Bicknell was on his way to Brighton, having been alerted by Detective Superintendent Ray Parker, who was in charge of the Prime Minister's personal protection. Bicknell himself spoke to Deputy Assistant Commissioner Colin Hewett, head of the Branch, and soon senior Metropolitan Police officers who needed to know had been informed. To Bicknell's surprise, Birch had immediately accepted the offer of assistance from the Anti-Terrorist Branch, who had great experience in dealing with similar incidents, whereas Sussex had virtually none. Once in Brighton, courtesy of a speedy Metropolitan Police traffic patrol car and driver, Commander Bicknell made his way to Brighton Town Police Station, where he met up with Tony Greenslade and was relieved to hear that all the protection teams were accounted for and had survived safely; the only casualty among them was one officer who had lost his shoes and had scratched his feet in the debris, but he was saved by Denis Thatcher, who lent him a spare pair. The delegates had not fared so well;

five died and two members of the Cabinet, Norman Tebbit and John Wakeham, sustained serious injuries. Members of the Cabinet, accompanied by their protection officers, had assembled at the Police Training School, where an impromptu Cabinet meeting was held to decide what they should do. It must have been one of the strangest Cabinet meetings ever, but there was no hesitation over their next move. Margaret Thatcher was determined that the conference should carry on as planned and she would give her end-of-conference speech, which she did in her usual forthright style.

In the wake of the disaster, the obligatory 'post mortem' was held, which was attended by representatives of all government security departments and an MI5 officer, who directed thinly veiled criticism at the Branch, demanding to know 'What changes are the Metropolitan Police going to make now to ensure the security of government ministers?'

Commander Bicknell, who had far more experience of personal protection than his interrogator, replied, 'We are not going to make any!' He went on to explain that there were certain aspects of the arrangements over which the police had no control and that, according to government rules, the conference was a Conservative Party function and the Prime Minister was attending in her capacity as leader of the party and not as the Prime Minister. Ideally the hotel should have been closed for two days before the gathering started in order that the police could conduct a proper security check with explosives officers and sniffer dogs, but neither the government nor the Conservative Party was prepared to foot the bill for this to be done. Only limited screening in ministers' rooms and places such as the restaurant could be carried out. Bicknell referred to the highly vulnerable Middle East Peace Talks that were held in the summer of 1978 at Leeds Castle in Kent, which was closed to the public for the police to make a thorough search of the castle and grounds, after which admittance was strictly controlled. It was the Americans who paid for the venue to be closed to the public. The meeting agreed that in future the police should be allocated time and money and given government backing to close down venues such as the Grand Hotel when such conferences took place. Special Branch derived some satisfaction from a subsequent inquiry conducted by the deputy chief constable of Hampshire, John Hoddinott, into why the lapse in security had occurred, which found that the MPSB was in no way to blame.

Some changes, however, were made to the administration of Special Branch personal protection. A Ministerial Liaison Office run by a detective inspector was set up which would have close contact with the private offices of all Cabinet ministers. Not all ministers would be afforded personal protection, but if a non-protected minister were scheduled to attend a function in circumstances that indicated a heightened risk, then protection could be provided through the new liaison office. Another innovation, which highlighted the advance of technology, was the provision of BT pagers to all protection teams for the first time (see Chapter 28).

Officers from the Sussex Police had the mammoth task of tracing all the guests who had stayed at the hotel in the weeks preceding the incident; they were assisted in their investigations by the MPSB and the Anti-Terrorist Branch. Eventually the only person not satisfactorily identified was a guest registered as Roy Walsh, who had stayed there some three to four weeks earlier. A palm print on his hotel registration card matched a print taken by police in Norwich many years earlier from a youthful Patrick Magee, who over the years had become a hardened PIRA terrorist. He was now a wanted man and was arrested in Glasgow the following year, together with other members of an ASU who were planning further atrocities.

MAGEE'S CONTINUING TERRORIST ACTIVITIES

In June 1985, police finally caught up with Patrick 'Chancer' Magee in a highly successful operation involving MPSB, Strathclyde Police and the Royal Ulster Constabulary, which netted a team of dedicated, hardened and ruthless PIRA murderers who were all jailed for life the following year. In June, the RUC informed the MPSB that they were maintaining surveillance on an active member of PIRA, Peter Sherry, who had travelled from County Tyrone and was now on his way by ferry to the mainland, closely followed by an RUC observation team of five under Detective Superintendent Phoenix. Once in Glasgow, the RUC officers linked up with the Strathclyde Police and informed MPSB, who immediately dispatched a surveillance team to the north. Sherry stayed the night in Glasgow and the following day, 22 June, caught a train to Carlisle, where he met Pat Magee off the train from Euston and returned with him to Glasgow. The local police wanted to arrest the pair immediately but the wise counsel of Phoenix prevailed and they were allowed to carry on their way. They caught a bus to Shawlands in the city suburbs and were followed to a ground-floor flat at 236 Landside Road. Once there, they sat down with the other three occupants to a meal of steak and chips but scarcely had they begun when there was a knock at the front door; Magee answered it and was roughly seized as twenty to thirty armed police officers burst into the apartment. The speed and efficiency with which the police, a mixture of RUC, Strathclyde and Metropolitan Police Special Branch, carried out the raid left the terrorists no time to draw their own weapons and within a short space of time the prisoners were bundled into police vans and transported to Craigie Street Divisional Police Headquarters, leaving police forensic, photographic and explosives experts to search for evidence – of which they found plenty.[9]

One of the addresses found in correspondence at the flat, in James Gray Street, Glasgow, was 'visited' and found to contain a vast amount of arms, ammunition and explosives hidden under the floorboards. Another document convinced police that a room at the Rubens Hotel, opposite the Royal Mews, in Buckingham Palace Road, London, contained an explosive device; after a three-hour search, an unprimed bomb was indeed discovered there. It was established that Magee had stayed at the hotel about a week before. The bombers' flat contained, among other items, a handbag holding over £1,000 sterling in notes, a loaded Browning automatic pistol and a passport belonging to Martina Anderson but bearing a false name, a vast quantity of maps, timetables and addresses and miscellaneous

9   Jack Holland and Susan Phoenix, *Phoenix: Policing the Shadows* (London: Coronet, 1997), pp. 182–3

firearms and ammunition.[10] It was apparent from other documents seized that the team had planned to bomb four hotels in London and twelve holiday resorts, including the seaside towns of Ramsgate, Margate, Dover and Great Yarmouth.

The five were tried at the Central Criminal Court in June 1986, when Ella O'Dwyer, Martina Anderson, Gerry 'Bute' McDonnell and Peter Sherry were each sentenced to thirty-five years' imprisonment for plotting to cause explosions; Patrick Magee received a sentence of a minimum of thirty-five years in jail for five murders plus associated offences in Brighton and for his part in the Glasgow conspiracy. They were all released under the terms of the Good Friday Agreement. A year after his release in 1999, Magee met the daughter of one of his victims at Brighton; together with this woman, Jo Berry, he now runs an organisation 'promoting peace and conflict resolution throughout the world'.[11] It is interesting to conjecture whether Magee, a serial killer, would have been allowed to go free if he had succeeded in his aim of killing the British Prime Minister.

ANOTHER PIRA OPERATION THWARTED[12]

The year after Magee and his team were sentenced, the RUC informed MPSB that the PIRA was continuing to plan attacks on the mainland and a reconnaissance team for an ASU would shortly arrive here. It comprised Liam McCotter, a bomb maker, and Patrick McLaughlin, a marksman.

Once the pair had arrived, the Special Branch surveillance team followed them to a hotel opposite Finchley Park, where an observation post was set up in the park keeper's lodge. However, it was soon realised that the birds had already flown to a flat in north London but were making periodic trips to Manchester, where a base in another flat was established. Their frequent journeys north caused their pursuers a number of problems; the surveillance team split their resources, with some

---

10   *Glasgow Herald*, 3 June 1986

11   http://theforgivenessproject.com, retrieved on 7 October 2014

12   This section is based on the recollections of DC Gerard Hancock, who was involved in the surveillance

members travelling on the train with the terrorists and the remainder by road; the squad's motorcycle was transported in the guard's van. An element of excitement spiced up the journeys to Manchester – would those travelling by train arrive before or after their colleagues on the road? Invariably it was the latter and it is conceivable that money changed hands over the results of the 'races'.

McCotter and McLaughlin purchased a car that was advertised in the magazine *Loot* and their behaviour was so suspicious that the young man selling it informed the police that he thought he'd sold his vehicle to a terrorist (little did he know!). The job of following was not made easier by this acquisition of transport, for the car was prone to break down on the motorway, and there are no convenient hiding places on the M1. The surveillance team were obliged to take turns in 'breaking down' themselves and parking on the hard shoulder with their bonnet up within sight of their quarry, while taking the precaution of advising traffic patrols from local forces to ignore them.

Later the pair bought a van and their intentions became clearer when they went on a shopping spree to buy shovels, dustbins and bin liners. Their next trip was to Macclesfield and Delamere Forests, where the last vestige of doubt about their plans was removed as they applied themselves to digging holes in which to stow the dustbins. There was only one thing missing – something to fill the dustbins. All was revealed when McCotter's and McLaughlin's later sortie took them to Cemaes Bay in Anglesey, which boasts a natural sheltered harbour facing the Irish Sea. Under cover of darkness they met a fishing boat and unloaded a number of bundles, which were swiftly stowed away in their vehicle. A decision now had to be made as to whether to arrest the two Irishmen together with the crew of the fishing boat or to let the operation run in the hope of catching the remaining members of the ASU when they arrived; it was decided to go with the latter option and continue with the surveillance on McCotter and McLaughlin. As anticipated, they lost no time in driving to the forests they had visited earlier, which were no great distance away, and depositing their load in the hides they had constructed a few days earlier. When the contents of the bundles were later checked they proved to be, as expected, arms and explosives (nearly 200 lbs of high explosives and other bomb-making materials, three automatic rifles, two handguns and ammunition). Back at Scotland Yard, a decision was taken that it was too risky to allow the terrorists to remain at liberty any longer and, much to the disappointment of the officers involved, the operation was handed over to the Anti-Terrorist Branch with a view to arrests being made. The participation in the operation of MPSB surveillance officers extended over six weeks and at times exposed them to considerable personal risks and discomfort, not least of which was an occasion in Macclesfield Forest when a member of the team concealed in undergrowth was almost drenched as one of the terrorists decided to relieve himself in the vicinity of the officer's hideout. On their return to headquarters the members of the surveillance team were personally congratulated by the Commissioner on what was a truly professional piece of work.

On 19 February 1987, McCotter and McLaughlin were arrested in Manchester by armed officers from the Anti-Terrorist Branch working alongside officers from Greater Manchester Police. In June 1988, the pair were sentenced to seventeen years' and twenty years' imprisonment respectively for conspiring to cause explosions; the longer term reflecting McLaughlin's earlier convictions for riotous behaviour in 1971 and unlawful possession of a firearm in 1974. In September 1994, McCotter was one of a group mainly comprising IRA prisoners who escaped from Whitemoor maximum security prison in Cambridgeshire; his taste of freedom was short-lived, however, as he was captured in the prison grounds.

LIBYAN TERRORISM

While 'B' Squad was fully occupied grappling with the seemingly endless series of PIRA bombings and successfully warding off further PIRA attacks, 'E' Squad (responsible for monitoring foreign extremist activity in London) had problems of its own in the form of escalating confrontations between

Libyan 'revolutionary committees' loyal to the Gaddafi regime and dissident members of the Libyan National Salvation Front (LNSF). During the early '80s, it was not unusual for Libyans opposed to Colonel Gaddifi's regime to be beaten up in the streets by Libyan government supporters. On occasions, dissidents were killed by Gaddafi's henchmen. In April 1980, journalist Muhammad Ramadan was shot by two gunmen,[13] while later the same month a Libyan lawyer, Mahmoud Nafa, was killed in his office; in both cases the assassins were sentenced to life imprisonment.[14] No further incidents of note occurred until March 1983, when a number of newsagent's shops and news kiosks in London and Manchester selling Arabic newspapers were subjected to bomb attacks in which some twenty-five people were injured. Nine Libyan suspects were arrested. Throughout this troublesome period, officers from 'E' Squad were constantly calling on potential targets to give security advice and, where necessary, to offer personal protection.

According to the Security Service, the Libyan embassy in London, using the title 'Libyan People's Bureau', was directing these operations against the dissidents. This made it difficult for Special Branch to obtain sufficient evidence against suspects to bring them before the courts, despite extensive use of surveillance and enquiries based on intelligence supplied by the Security Service. Early in 1984, it was learned that Gaddafi had ordered that action against dissidents should be increased, which led to MPSB and MI5 redoubling their efforts to counter any escalation of violence. According to intelligence received by the Branch from an informant in April, an anti-Gaddafi group planned to hold a demonstration outside the People's Bureau in St James's Square on 17 April. Uniformed police were informed and made the necessary arrangements to ensure that the demonstration passed off peaceably, which initially seemed to be the case, a contingent of about thirty officers keeping the seventy or more noisy protesters under control. However, at about 10.15 a.m., shots

---

13   *The Times*, 12 April 1980

14   Ibid., 26 April 1980

from an automatic weapon (later identified as a Sterling sub-machine-gun) were fired from a window in the People's Bureau. Eleven people were injured including, tragically, Police Constable Yvonne Fletcher, who died within the hour at Westminster Hospital.

Armed police surrounded the building, which, according to international convention, they could not enter without permission,[15] and for the next eleven days the People's Bureau was effectively under siege. Gaddafi retaliated by subjecting the British embassy in Tripoli to similar treatment; the impasse was resolved after eleven days when the Libyans were allowed to leave and were promptly expelled from the country. Six British subjects were imprisoned in Libya for nine months as 'political hostages'. Nobody has been charged with Yvonne Fletcher's murder, despite vigorous efforts by the Anti-Terrorist Branch to carry out a proper investigation; in 2013 it was announced that officers from the Metropolitan Police would be allowed to visit Libya again to pursue their enquiries into her murder and the investigation.[16]

THE DESTRUCTION OF PAN AM FLIGHT 103 OVER LOCKERBIE

Nearly five years later, on 21 December 1988, the world was again shocked by a horrendous act of Libyan terrorism, when a Pan Am flight that had just left Heathrow Airport for the USA exploded in the air over Lockerbie, Scotland, causing the death of 270 individuals. After an extremely complicated and protracted investigation run by Strathclyde Police assisted by, among other agencies, the Metropolitan Police Anti-Terrorist Branch and the Security Service, a suspected Libyan intelligence officer, Abdelbaset al-Megrahi, was convicted of murder at a specially convened Scottish Court in Holland in January 2001. He

---

15 In the wake of the shooting in St James's Square, the Diplomatic and Consular Premises Act of 1987 was passed, which gave limited right of entry

16 *The Guardian*, 31 January 2013

was sentenced to life imprisonment but was released in 2009 on compassionate grounds as he was allegedly dying of cancer. He died in 2012. MPSB played only a minor role in the investigation.

CHAPTER TWENTY-SIX

NON-IRISH ACTIVITIES

PASTORAL VISIT OF POPE JOHN PAUL II TO THE UNITED KINGDOM

On 2 June 1982, in stark contrast to the latest stage in the Arab–Israeli conflict (the murderous attack on the Israeli Prime Minister by Arab terrorists the following day), Pope John Paul II returned to his home in the Vatican after a six-day visit marked by remarkable demonstrations of love and reconciliation between Roman Catholic and Protestant leaders.

The Pope's visit was possibly the most unusual VIP protection responsibility that had ever been undertaken by the Branch and caused six days of headaches for Detective Chief Superintendent Geoff Craft, who was head of the Special Branch team responsible for the Pope's well-being during the visit and who has provided most of the details for the following narrative.

Pope John Paul II was a contentious figure, having been a catalyst in the breakup of the Soviet Empire; he had been the victim of an assassination attempt the previous year, following which there were concerns that his poor health might cause the visit to be cancelled. The ongoing Falklands War between Britain and Argentina presented another obstacle to overcome. But overcome it was, together with numerous other problems which necessitated frequent changes to the itinerary. Instead of the usual immaculately prepared programme presented to all the interested parties before official or state visits, the Special Branch protection team was provided with what Geoff Craft refers to as 'Draft Itinerary No.40a with manuscript amendments' just before His Holiness arrived at Gatwick Airport.

Security problems were compounded by the fact that this was a 'pastoral' visit, as distinct from a 'state' or 'official' visit which would come under the auspices of the Lord Chamberlain's Office or the Protocol Department of the Foreign and Commonwealth Office. They were accustomed to organising such events according to a tried and tested procedure, at the conclusion of which an official printed programme would be produced in which all those involved would have their roles clearly defined. In this case it was the Roman Catholic Church, which had comparatively little experience of such matters, particularly one of such enormity, upon whom the onerous task of organisation fell. The only people involved in the numerous planning consultations who had any experience in delivering and safeguarding such occasions were the Metropolitan Police, specifically Special Branch and 'A' Department. The Special Branch Technical Protection Unit (TPU), formed in 1979, performed a discreet but vital role in security arrangements; it played a major part, together with the manufacturers and engineers, in the development of the four armoured vehicles (including the so-called 'Popemobile') used at the outdoor events attended by the Pope and also the bullet-resistant lectern employed at Westminster and Southwark Cathedrals, when he would have been particularly vulnerable. All official cars were driven by police drivers from 'B' Department, who had all passed the stringent police driving tests. Apart from its personal protection role, Special Branch was also responsible for overall transport arrangements and, in conjunction with the army, venue bomb searching. Detective Superintendent Colin Colson (head of the TPU) rode as 'motorcade supervisor' in a smaller version of the 'Popemobile'. (The development and role of the TPU is described in detail in Chapter 27.)

The visit was extremely wide-ranging and included not only Roman Catholic locations but also Canterbury Cathedral, as well as non-secular sites in England, Wales and Scotland. The Pope met HM Queen Elizabeth II; the Prince of Wales; the leader of the Roman Catholic Church in this country, Cardinal Basil Hume; the Archbishop of Canterbury, Robert Runcie; and the Chief Rabbi of the United Kingdom, Sir Immanuel Jakobovits. Apart from a few small, perfunctory protests by supporters of the late Rev. Ian Paisley, the visit was well received and passed off with no major problem. That is, except for one amusing interlude which occurred in Roehampton at a gathering of the local religious community – nuns, brothers and priests. Geoff Craft recalls:

> We had been warned in advance by Archbishop Marcinkus, who organised papal visits, 'to be careful of a phalanx of flying nuns'. Everything went fine until we'd got him into the papal vehicle at the end, whereupon we had a phalanx of flying nuns led by a tiny contemplative nun. She was kicking the shins of my biggest protection officer while desperately trying to get on the Popemobile.

The overall policing arrangements were the subject of highly favourable comments in the official Vatican Annals for 1982, and the Home Secretary, William Whitelaw, wrote to the Commissioner afterwards:

> Now that the Pope has left Great Britain after his visit, I wanted to express to you my admiration for the professionalism and coolness with which your officers provided his personal protection. We often say that our police are the best in the world but it is not always easy to prove it. Television has now provided a basis for direct comparison of the methods of protection employed during the Pope's visits all over the world in the last three or four years. My impression is that no other country has achieved such a good balance between safety and accessibility. The protection was always in place but never unnecessarily obtrusive.

ESTABLISHMENT OF THE 'PORT' OF WATERLOO

On 14 November 1994, Eurostar rail services began operating between Waterloo International Station in London, Gare du Nord in Paris and (later) Brussels-South Station in Brussels. This event was the culmination of years of planning (since the early '80s), involving not only the operating companies of the countries involved but, on the British side, the Home Office, HM Immigration, HM Customs, British Transport Police, Metropolitan Police, Kent Police and numerous other interested parties.

The original intention was to run a roll-on/roll-off car ferry service via the Channel Tunnel (completed in 1993), but European Passenger Services (EPS) soon decided to utilise the tunnel for passenger-only services as well. This meant that a new purpose-built terminal at Waterloo International would see thousands of passengers a day passing through immigration controls and naturally a sizeable Special Branch presence would be required. DCI Peter Gardner was delegated to safeguard Special Branch interests throughout the discussion period and was able to influence the committee on a number of factors that would affect the Branch.[1]

A feature of the negotiations was the manner in which the various parties involved seemed anxious to co-operate with each other, which made a complex task less difficult. It should be pointed out that there were two services under discussion, both using the Channel Tunnel: the roll-on/roll-off car ferry from Cheriton in Kent to the Continent and the passenger-only service from Waterloo and Ashford (Kent) to Frethun (Calais), Gare du Nord (Paris), Lille and, later, Brussels. The Kent Special Branch would have responsibility for coverage of the car ferry at Cheriton and the passenger trains at Ashford International Railway Station.

EPS were anxious for checks on passengers to be carried out on board the moving trains before it was realised that at some point under the Channel police

---

1   I am indebted to Peter Gardner for his helpful account of the establishment of a Special Branch unit to cover the new Eurostar service

officers, whether French or English, would be outside their jurisdiction. Foreign Office legal advisers were now brought in to the discussions and, together with their French counterparts, devised an ingenious plan in which a 'control zone' was proposed, in which police officers could act as if in their own country. The 'control zone' was construed as including the Eurostar train, the lines it stood on when stationary, the platform at which it stopped, the police authority's office and the direct route to it. This clause was written into the appropriate British, French and Belgian law.

Another problem to be overcome, and was, concerned the necessity for some provision for facilities when police/immigration officers were operating controls on the moving train. EPS undertook to provide necessary facilities for all three countries concerned, both on the train and at stations. This included, in the case of MPSB, sizeable office space sufficient to accommodate sixty-four officers, which was the initial establishment, proposed by Gardner and approved, of the Waterloo port unit.

TWO ESPIONAGE CASES: ERWIN VAN HAARLEM AND MICHAEL SMITH

Although it attracted most of the headlines, the investigation of terrorism represented only a minor part of Special Branch work. Another aspect of the department's activities that always aroused the public's interest, but not so frequently, was its involvement in investigation of breaches of the Official Secrets Acts. Although the Security Service has traditionally been responsible for detecting cases of espionage, its officers have no power of arrest and it has always been the Special Branch who 'merely arrested and questioned spies at the request of MI5, when the latter organisation, which had detected them, considered that the time for arrest had arrived'.[2] It is doubtful whether

---

2   Andrew, *The Defence of the Realm*, citing a document apparently written by Holt-Wilson, DDG of MI5, p. 117

SB officers involved in some OSA cases would agree that the adverb 'merely' accurately defines the bringing of a case of espionage to court – as the two cases described below illustrate.

ERWIN VAN HAARLEM

Erwin Van Haarlem first attracted the attention of the Security Service quite fortuitously during their surveillance of a suspected GRU (Soviet military intelligence) agent on Hampstead Heath in April 1986. This man, a member of the Soviet Trade Delegation, was 'behaving in a generally furtive manner' before entering the Old Bull and Bush public house. About half an hour later, a second man appeared to be searching an area of ground before he too entered the public house. On leaving the premises, the second individual was followed to an address in Friern Barnet which proved to be his home; he was identified as a forty-year-old Dutch national named Erwin Van Haarlem. Investigations proved him to be an illegal (an agent working under deep cover) who had assumed the identity of one Erwin Van Haarlem, the illegitimate son of a Dutch mother and a German soldier. He was a self-employed art dealer, an occupation that was merely a cover for his espionage activities, which consisted of providing his controllers with intelligence about British supporters of the Jewish 'refuseniks' who were prevented from emigrating from the Soviet Union to Israel. After extensive investigations, MI5 concluded that the Czech intelligence services, who controlled his activities, passed to the Russians all the information he gave them, although he himself had no direct contact with the KGB.[3]

This was the information that was passed to the MPSB with a request that he should, if possible, be caught in the act of transmitting information and sufficient evidence produced to prosecute him. This was achieved, although it was by no means a matter of 'merely arresting and questioning'. The following narrative

---

3   Andrew, *The Defence of the Realm*, pp. 727–8.

has been provided by Kevin Kindleysides, who was the Special Branch exhibits officer in the case.

It is important to appreciate that the timing of entry to Van Haarlem's flat at 35 Silver Birch Court, Friern Barnet, north London was of the essence to catch him in the act of receiving a transmission from his Czech controllers. It was known that transmissions were made openly in Morse code on shortwave radio on Wednesday evenings and Saturday mornings. After transmission, the message would be repeated until a new message superseded it; the repetition was made to allow the recipient to check his Morse transcription.

On Saturday 2 April 1988, the transmission commenced at 8 a.m. and finished at 8.27 a.m. It was essential that the whole transmission had been received before attempting entry to the premises, so, at 8.26 a.m., a Gallini hydraulic door opener was put in place and at 8.27 a.m. precisely the door to the flat swung open without a sound, allowing the Special Branch team of some seven officers led by Detective Superintendent Nigel Somers to take the occupant by surprise. In the kitchen, perched on a stool at the breakfast bar, sat a man wearing pyjamas with, in one ear, an earpiece connected to a high-quality radio from which sounds of Morse code were being emitted. The man, Van Haarlem, was seized by Detective Inspector 'Dickie' Bird and his pulse taken; this was done as experienced operators are known to be able to control their nerves and, consequently, their pulse rate. His pulse quickened when he was first seized but quickly slowed down as he controlled his breathing and calmed down, indicating that here was a seasoned campaigner.

Having been shown the search warrant, he watched quietly as officers with sophisticated search equipment including high-powered drills and fibre optic cameras began to go through the flat; he even assumed a co-operative attitude, handing one of the searchers a bar of soap still in a wrapper which, when cut open, revealed a one-time pad. It was unused and obviously had been produced as a red herring, as the one currently in use was soon discovered concealed with other unused ones in a recess behind a kitchen cupboard. Some of the first items seized were those which Van Haarlem had been using when the flat had been entered – the radio, the earpiece, a sheet of paper with groups of numbers written on it and a piece of glass on which the paper was resting to prevent any traceable impressions of the message being left on any underlying surface. A simple, yet virtually foolproof method of encryption was used, employing letters, numbers, a unique 'buzzword' known only to the agent and his controller and one-time pads (destroyed after use). It was later learned that, in the thirteen years of his work as a spy, Van Haarlem had received over 200 messages using this method. After an initial search and preliminary questions verifying his name etc., Van Haarlem was formally arrested and cautioned and a thorough search of the premises was begun – a search that would continue throughout the next seven days. But, before this commenced, the photographers took pictures of everything in the flat for possible use as evidence. While this activity was taking place in the prisoner's apartment, Royal Navy ships and a land station had obtained a directional fix on the source of the transmissions – situated in a suburb of Prague.

In subsequent interrogation, Van Haarlem revealed the following details of his life. He claimed to be the son of a Jewish Dutch woman, Joanna Van Haarlem, who had had an intimate relationship with a German soldier in occupied Holland towards the end of World War Two. The father died in fighting at Caen and the mother passed the baby, Erwin, to the Red Cross for adoption. That was the last she saw of him. Thirty years later 'Erwin Van Haarlem', who had taken on the identity of her son and was travelling on a Dutch passport, arrived in England and secured work at the Kensington Hilton Hotel, where he was employed for ten years, latterly as the purchasing manager. He was not without a sense of humour and on leaving the job declared that he was going to work in a 'spice shop' (a 'spy shop'). In fact, he set up business as an art dealer. When the investigating officers had his books examined by an accountant, it was discovered that over £70,000 had been moved through these accounts in the course of the previous two years, allegedly through the sale of some miniatures, which in fact had never left his possession, being found in the course of the search of his home. It was assumed, though never proved, that many of his other 'art transactions' were hypothetical.

From the time of his arrest until his return to Czechoslovakia in 1993, 'Van Haarlem' did not reveal his true identity, although it has since been established that he was in fact Vaclav Jelinek, a lieutenant colonel in the Czech intelligence service, STB (Statni Tajna Bezpecnost), who was given the identity of Van Haarlem, which entitled him to a Dutch passport by virtue of the nationality of Joanna, his fictitious mother. During his residence in this country he contacted this lady, who came to visit him several times in London and was convinced that he was her long-lost son, although he was careful not to allow the relationship to become too close. Special Branch officers travelled to Holland in order to obtain samples of her blood, which was compared with that of the prisoner. This proved that the chances of Van Haarlem being her son were at least a million to one against.[4]

On 3 March 1989, at the Old Bailey, he was convicted of offences against the Official Secrets Acts and sentenced to ten years' imprisonment with a recommendation for deportation. In 1993, when the Soviet 'empire' had collapsed and relations between Britain and Czechoslovakia had improved, Van Haarlem was released from prison and deported to Prague. He had never revealed the nature of his spying although, at his trial, Stella Rimington, the Deputy Director General of MI5, stated that it was unlikely that an intelligence officer of his rank would have been posted here merely to report on refusenik support groups but would probably have been a 'sleeper' intended for a more important role in the event of an East–West crisis or other event that prevented embassies operating normally.[5]

It was later ascertained that he did not transmit messages to Prague but used 'secret writing' methods when he needed to send reports back to control. He would use invisible chemicals to write in the pages of UK magazines, which were sent to friendly addresses in Czechoslovakia and subjected to chemical treatment to bring up the invisible writing.

---

4   Recollections of DS Kevin Kindleysides

5   Andrew, *The Defence of the Realm*, p. 728

MICHAEL JOHN SMITH

In September 1993, one of the biggest Official Secrets Act trials in recent years went before a jury at the Old Bailey. The case was remarkable as much for the alleged 1970s espionage activities that the defendant, Michael John Smith, was *not* tried for, as his subsequent acts of treachery in the early 1990s that earned him twenty-five years' imprisonment (later reduced on appeal to twenty years). The trial lasted eight weeks, parts of which were heard in camera. Full details of the case history, including testimony from a large number of highly qualified expert witnesses in the fields of physics and materials science, defence experts, MI5 officers, police witnesses (including over eleven hours of taped interviews at Paddington Green Police Station) and, what must be unprecedented in terms of public disclosure, hitherto secret MI5 debriefing notes from two former KGB officers, are now in the public domain and available online.[6]

On 25 July 1992, Viktor Oschenko, a senior SVR (formerly KGB) officer attached to the Russian embassy in Paris, approached British intelligence and asked for political asylum in Britain. In return, he agreed to provide MI5 with a detailed account of his espionage activities while serving as a Line X[7] officer at the Soviet embassy in London from 1974–79. Oschenko provided vital intelligence about the identity of an agent whom he claimed to have recruited in 1975 and ran successfully until 1979. This agent was Michael John Smith, a graduate in electronic and electrical engineering from Surrey University and a member of the Communist Party of Great Britain, who resided in Surrey. They initially met at a trade union meeting in Kingston in 1975 and as part of the KGB grooming process there followed regular monthly meetings, during which Smith confided to Oschenko that he was disillusioned with life and could see no future in his employment.

During these meetings, Oschenko suggested he could offer Smith a 'more adventurous' lifestyle and as the grooming went on he encouraged him to join

---

6   En.wikipedia.org/wiki/Michael_John_Smith(espionage)

7   Line X is the science and technology section within the Russian Intelligence Service

a tennis club and even gifted him a tennis racquet. He was also advised to distance himself from his Communist Party and trade union contacts and that he should change his daily newspaper to the *Daily Telegraph*. He was in effect being encouraged to adopt an overt bourgeois lifestyle.

After about twelve months, Oschenko suggested that he should consider getting himself a better job and together they drew up a shortlist of companies that Smith should write to. The list included Thorn-EMI Defence Research Establishment at Feltham, Middlesex. To the surprise of the Russians, Smith was offered a position as a test engineer in their quality assurance department but, as the salary was less than what he was earning at his previous employment, the Russians offered to compensate him for the difference. Smith commenced employment with Thorn-EMI in July 1976 and the KGB rewarded him with an additional £1,000 for securing the position.

Thorn-EMI was a List X company contracted to the Ministry of Defence to carry out secret defence research projects and was a designated 'Prohibited Place' under the Official Secrets Act, requiring all employees to sign the OSA declaration. After some months, Smith was moved to the highly sensitive XN-715 defence project on the development and design of radar fuses for the British free-fall nuclear bomb. As a quality control engineer, it was his job to test the fuses. Disclosure of any information relating to this project would have been highly damaging to British national security and would have enabled the Russians to jam or otherwise interfere with the operation of the WE-177 bomb in time of conflict. Oschenko alleged that Smith supplied him with information relating to this project. There is no suggestion that coercion played a part in Smith's recruitment and all the indications are that he was a willing and compliant recruit for the KGB.

Yuri Andropov, the then head of the KGB who later became the President of the USSR, had concerns about Smith's recruitment and the possibility that he may have been under MI5 control. It was decided to put Smith through a lie detector test and the KGB made elaborate arrangements for him to visit Vienna, where he was to be tested. As a further test of his commitment, he was asked to bring with him to the meeting copies of classified information from Thorn-EMI. Smith allegedly obliged but it is not known if the information he produced on this occasion related to the XN-715 project or if it was passed over on another occasion. He passed the lie detector test.[8]

Oschenko also gave details of how, on another occasion, Smith travelled to Oporto, Portugal, to take part in a KGB training exercise for clearing 'dead letter boxes' (DLBs), which he carried out to the KGB's satisfaction. At that time Portugal was a location favoured by the KGB for this type of exercise, as they were not subject to the same level of monitoring by the Portuguese intelligence authorities as was the case in Britain and other parts of Western Europe. When Smith's address was searched after his arrest, tourist maps with various markings of Oporto were found.

By the late 1970s, British and US intelligence became aware that the Russians had knowledge of the XN-715 fuse technology, compromising the integrity of the nuclear free-fall bomb. Extensive investigations were mounted on both sides of the Atlantic and the source of the leak was eventually identified as the Thorn-EMI Research Establishment at Feltham. MI5 compiled a list of 150 potential suspects, which was eventually narrowed down to around twenty-five, including Smith. Due to the commonness of his surname, MI5 had difficulty in positively identifying Smith and, improbable as it may sound, there were in fact two Michael John Smiths who were members of the Kingston Branch of the CPGB at that time. As there was insufficient intelligence to positively link the Michael John Smith at Thorn-EMI to the leaked secrets and, to avoid alerting him to their suspicions, Thorn-EMI managements removed him from his post and promoted him to a position in the Medical Research Division at another site out of harm's way. According to Oschenko, even in his new post Smith continued to provide him with company information, albeit unclassified and in the public domain, such was his enthusiasm to please his KGB masters. Later

---

8   The drop link MI5/Oschenkodebriefing notes contains details of the elaborate arrangements the KGB put into this meeting

on, when Smith reapplied for a position back in his old department, he became aware that his previous security clearance had been withdrawn at the time of his promotion and transfer.

Keen to establish the reason behind the decision, holding to the view that 'attack was the best form of defence' and the unlikelihood that a guilty person would deem to question such a decision, the KGB encouraged him to pursue the matter with Thorn-EMI management. In January 1980, prior to a meeting with a Ministry of Defence Procurement Executive officer, Smith completed a questionnaire inviting him to state whether he had ever been a member of a 'communist, Trotskyist or fascist organisation'. He denied that he had. In a further interview in June of that year with an MI5 officer (using MoD cover), he again made a false declaration that he had never been a member of the Communist Party and only admitted it after being confronted with the evidence. The KGB still had doubts about Smith and suggested that he should write to the then Prime Minister Margaret Thatcher to protest his innocence while taking the opportunity to criticise Thorn-EMI's lax security. The letter was never sent, and was only discovered during the search of Smith's flat following his arrest. The experience surrounding the withdrawal of his vetting clearance had an unsettling effect on Smith and left him paranoid that he was from time to time placed under surveillance; he even admitted as much during the interviews.

For MI5, who had been investigating the leaked information on the XN-715 project for over fifteen years, the Oschenko defection and his allegations implicating Smith was the confirmation they needed that Smith was the source of the leak.

Against this background, two senior MI5 officers attended New Scotland Yard on 6 August 1992 for a Special Branch briefing chaired by Commander Don Buchanan. The two officers confirmed that the allegations were of a historical nature and that MI5 had no information that Smith was still working for Russian intelligence. They did, however, express concerns that Smith, who had been made redundant the previous week, was making preparations to emigrate to New Zealand. Smith had been employed as a quality control manager at the GEC research laboratory, the Hirst Research Centre (HRC) at Wembley since 1985.

Detective Superintendent Malcolm MacLeod was assigned to the case and, together with his deputy, DCI Martin Gray, put an operational plan in place. Arrest and search warrants were obtained for Smith, his flat and his car and surveillance was mounted on his address with immediate effect.

On Saturday 8 August 1992, as a precursor to Michael's Smith's arrest and to test his knowledge and understanding of KGB tradecraft, a sting operation was put in place. An MI5 officer, using the nom de guerre 'George' and effecting a strong Eastern European accent, made a subterfuge telephone call to Smith's home number purporting to be 'a friend of Viktor' and requested an urgent meeting. Smith acknowledged 'George' and didn't question him when he gave instructions to go to a local telephone box to await further directions. A short while later, Smith was observed leaving his home address closely followed by the Special Branch surveillance and arrest teams. Due to a communications hitch, Smith missed the follow-up call at the kiosk and the default arrest plan was implemented. As he returned to his address he was arrested by the late Detective Inspector Martin Nicholson. Simultaneously, Smith's wife Pamela was detained at their flat.

The post-arrest operational plan was for Smith and his wife to be taken separately to the high-security wing at Paddington Green Police Station. After being cautioned and told the reason for his arrest, Smith was being driven in the back of the nondescript Special Branch car, handcuffed to one of the three arresting officers, when events took an unexpected turn. Realising that he was not being driven towards the local police station at Kingston, he panicked and became violent in the back of the car, struggling and shouting that he was being 'kidnapped' and that he knew who 'they' – the arresting officers – were. The arrest team was forced to make an emergency stop in Kingston High Street to call for urgent uniformed police assistance. To the bemusement of the early-morning shoppers outside John Lewis's store, Smith was unceremoniously transferred to a marked police van and, escorted by a police traffic car, continued the journey in convoy to Paddington Green. In the grand scheme of things, this incident would not ordinarily merit mention and its significance wasn't immediately apparent, but as the investigation progressed, the relevance of Smith's erratic behaviour became clear. What no one in MI5 knew at the time was that, two years previously, Smith, a 'sleeper agent', had been reactivated and was still spying for the Russians. His imagined 'kidnappers' must have been the Russians.

By the time MacLeod and Detective Sergeant Steve Beels embarked on the interviews late on the Saturday afternoon, they believed they were dealing with events that occurred seventeen years previously and rated the likelihood of obtaining evidence against Smith to be negligible. This notwithstanding, MacLeod instructed the arresting officers to advise Smith to make use of the free legal advice services provided by the duty solicitor, which he took up. The duty solicitor, Richard Jefferies of Tucker & Co., was present throughout the interviews. In the initial interviews MacLeod didn't have much in the way of evidence to put to Smith other than asking him to account for his movements just prior to his arrest. From the outset, Smith adopted a belligerent attitude, fudging questions and being generally aggressive. He denied receiving a telephone call that morning and it was only when he was presented with the taped telephone conversation with 'George' and the photographic evidence from the surveillance operation showing him on his morning jaunt to and from the local telephone kiosk that the seriousness of his situation registered with him.

During the four days of interviews that were to follow, Smith repeatedly lied and obfuscated as details emerged that he had in fact been actively engaged in espionage activities for the Russians from 1990 to the time of his arrest, evidence which was substantiated by the plethora of incriminating items discovered in the course of the search of his flat and car. In the boot of his car the search team found plastic bags with numerous documents and electrical components, all relating to projects being carried out by GEC's Hirst Research Centre at Wembley. Like Thorn-EMI, GEC was also a List X firm contracted to the Ministry of Defence and a designated 'Prohibited Place' under the Official Secrets Act. Late in the evening of Sunday 9 August, DCI Gray and DI Nicholson requested an urgent meeting with Dr Stephen Cundy, the Director of the Hirst Research Centre. He was shown all the exhibits seized from Smith's car and his initial assessment was that there had been a systematic attempt to obtain details of manufacturing procedures and parts to delay lines for the Rapier missile; similar efforts were made in respect of surface wave acoustics devices. The collection of documents included stolen material classified 'restricted' and an effort had been made to summarise the objectives and aims of company confidential projects.

At that time the British Rapier missile system was still in service with the British military and had been deployed in the previous year in the First Gulf War.

Also in the car the searchers found a single sheet of lined notepaper with a handwritten list of technical subjects which Dr Cundy identified as project work in progress at HRC. This sheet of paper, which was in a transparent plastic sheath, was secreted under a mat in the footwell of the car and was described by the prosecution as a 'shopping list' and proof that Smith was 'spying to order' for the Russians. When asked in the interviews about this particular document and why it was planted under the footwell mat, Smith initially evaded the question, rubbishing the notes and then, to the incredulity of MacLeod and Beels, he admitted that he had placed it under the mat to 'stop a leak'.

Further incriminating evidence was found during the search of Smith's flat including, in a lingerie drawer in the master bedroom:

- a handwritten letter postmarked 24 September 1990, addressed to Smith and signed 'Williams', seeking to re-establish a relationship that Smith would have been aware of. This letter was held up at the trial as evidence that Smith had been re-activated by the Russian Intelligence Service.

- a sheet of paper bearing handwritten notes and cryptic symbols relating to covert meetings and specifically to a meeting at St Mary's churchyard at Harrow on the Hill on 5 August, three days before his arrest.

- an invoice for a £10,000 music synthesiser computer purchased by Smith.

- £2,000 cash in bundles of new £50 notes.

Smith's finances were examined by DC Jonathan Say, a qualified financial investigator, who established that Smith had not used his bank accounts for cash withdrawals or to pay food retailers from mid-1991, suggesting that Smith had cash access to resources to the tune of £20,000 between 1991 and '92.

Before DC Say had an opportunity to question Smith about his financial affairs, the latter announced that there was something he wanted to clear up. What came next was tantamount to a qualified admission, not of espionage, but of 'industrial espionage'. He claimed that in early 1990 he received a telephone call out of the blue at work from an 'Englishman' named 'Harry' who, in brief, offered to pay for information relating to projects being worked on by GEC. 'Harry' explained that this offer came from one of GEC's competitors. Over the next two years (until April 1992), according to Smith's highly improbable narrative, he provided 'Harry' with what he described as 'worthless' and 'dated' information for which he was paid varying sums of money. MacLeod had little doubt that 'Harry' and the equally mysterious 'Williams' were one and the same person – probably with an address at 6/7 Kensington Palace Gardens (the Russian embassy). Smith in his naivety had hoped that admitting to 'industrial espionage' would somehow mitigate his treachery.

Having obtained a partial admission of guilt, MacLeod focused on Smith's movements on Thursday 6 August, the date on the tradecraft note found at his address which suggested a meeting was to have taken place at or near St Mary's Churchyard at Harrow on the Hill. Playing on Smith's paranoia about surveillance, he was taken through the day from the time he left home for a pre-employment induction presentation at a company in Basingstoke, to which he had applied for a job, to his subsequent detour mid-day to Harrow town centre to purchase a magazine (which he could have purchased nearer to his home). Labouring under the mistaken assumption that he had been under surveillance that day and, obviously unaware that MacLeod was in possession of the tradecraft note, he admitted to having visited St Mary's Churchyard at Harrow on the

Hill. His highly implausible reason for visiting the area that day was to purchase a computer magazine from WH Smith's in Harrow and, as his wife wasn't going to be home until late afternoon and it was a 'nice summer's day', he decided 'to kill time' in the area.

What Smith didn't know was that when his recruiter and mentor Viktor Oschenko defected the previous week, the Russian embassy in London contacted the Foreign Office, who confirmed that Oschenko had indeed defected and was seeking political asylum in Britain. The Russians immediately aborted the planned meeting at Harrow on the Hill and the hapless Smith was dropped like a hot potato; disastrous for him but fortuitous for the police. When Macleod put the evidence to Smith, culminating in the aborted meeting at Harrow on the Hill with his handler, in characteristic arrogance he mocked MacLeod, saying, 'They'll laugh you out of court.' An hour later, Smith was charged with espionage. Had Oschenko delayed his defection by only a few days, the documents and components in the boot of his car would have been handed over to his SVR handler and the Smiths would have been free to proceed with their plans to emigrate to New Zealand. His wife, Pamela Smith, was eliminated from the investigation and released from custody after three days.

MacLeod, recently promoted to Detective Chief Superintendent, interviewed Oschenko at an MI5 location. The Russian appeared a broken man and, perhaps not surprisingly, declined to make a statement supporting his allegations against Smith. Consequently it was not possible to charge Smith with the alleged espionage offences while he was employed at Thorn-EMI. There was, however, sufficient evidence to charge him with the most recent spying offences at GEC between 1990 and 1992.

Smith was arraigned before Justice Blofeld at the Old Bailey in September 1993 on four counts of espionage under Section 1 of the Official Secrets Act 1911 relating to his spying activities at GEC between 1990 and 1992. The prosecution was led by the Solicitor General, Sir Derek Spencer QC MP, supported by Sir John Nutting QC and John Kelsey-Fry QC. Smith was represented by Rock Tansey QC and Gary Summers. During the eight-week trial, evidence was taken from a large number of witnesses, many of whom were leading subject-matter experts in their own particular fields of science and technology. On 18 November, the jury returned verdicts of guilty on three out of the four counts of espionage. Smith was sentenced to twenty-five years' imprisonment.

In 1995, the Court of Appeal varied the sentence to twenty years. In his summing up, the Lord Chief Justice (the late Lord Taylor) spelt out his views on espionage, concluding with the words, 'Treachery is treachery. It must be deterred and it must be punished.' Smith made three further appeals, two to the Criminal Cases Review Commission to have his case referred back to the Court of Appeal and, in 1997, to the European Court of Human Rights. All these applications were rejected. A subsequent Security Review Commission's report on the case criticised MI5's handling of Smith's vetting and classified the alleged damage to national security from Smith's disclosures as 'serious'.[9]

At various times during the pre-trial hearings and the trial, the defence counsel criticised DCS MacLeod's 'aggressive' interviewing techniques, but Justice Blofeld in his post-sentencing comments dismissed the criticism, referring to the defendant's persistent lying throughout the interviews, and commended MacLeod on the manner in which the lengthy interviews were conducted. It was as well that MacLeod had insisted before he and Beels commenced the interviews that Smith should be legally represented, for at no time did his solicitor raise any concerns about Smith's treatment.

The successful conclusion of the case was the culmination of weeks of investigation by the dedicated team of Special Branch detectives and the two MI5 liaison officers who supported the team at Paddington Green Police Station.

Despite the rejection of his judicial appeals, Smith has consistently used his blog to lampoon the credibility of a large number of people involved in his case, ranging from the trial judge, through the prosecution and defence teams to the many highly qualified and reputable witnesses who appeared for the prosecution. MacLeod did not escape his wrath and found some of his rants outrageously

---

9   http://cryptome.org/michael-smith.htm

libellous; he chose not to take any action lest it should provide Smith with the oxygen of publicity that he craved.

Smith is a complex character; his egocentricity made him a willing and pliant recruit for the KGB as he relished the thrill of spying and the notoriety of being a convicted spy, while at the same time denying his treachery. His motives for his espionage have been described as ideological and financial but while the financial incentive was clear, the ideological motive may not have been as strong as he's been given credit for. In his first interview with the late DI Nicholson he gave his reason for joining the Communist Party as an opportunity 'to meet women for sex'.

Of one thing there is no doubt – his guilt. In his closing speech to the jury, Sir Derek Spencer QC, the Solicitor General, declared that Smith's guilt 'ran like a silver thread from the alpha to the omega'.

CHAPTER TWENTY-SEVEN

PROTECTION[1]

WHILE THEIR COLLEAGUES were engaged in the never-ending fight against espionage and terrorism, other officers were pursuing their careers in the less dramatic, yet equally vital business of protection. In an earlier part of this book reference is made to the role played by the Branch since its establishment in the provision of personal protection for VIPs and other vulnerable individuals. In this chapter, it is proposed to examine more closely how this role developed to contend with the increased threat from the PIRA and non-UK terrorist organisations.

Ministerial protection in the UK prior to the 1970s was essentially limited to the Prime Minister, the Foreign Secretary and the Home Secretary, these being the three ministers of state, or their equivalents, whom the Hague Conventions stipulated were entitled to personal protection when visiting the countries of fellow signatories. Also, of course, heads of state of any signatory would be provided with protection. Throughout the UK this close protection was the sole responsibility of MPSB. When principals travelled outside London, local police provided support to the Metropolitan Police Special Branch close protection officers.

---

1   I am indebted to Colin Colson and Peter Smither for providing the information on which this section is based

In the UK, the provision of protection officers to former ministers in the above categories, or indeed to any other politician or VIP, was determined by threat assessments undertaken by the Home Secretary based on input from both Security Services and MPSB. The length of time and also the form of this protection were subject to regular review. Similar assessments were prepared in relation to visiting dignitaries who might be under threat but did not fall within the four categories mentioned above who were automatically entitled to protection. When residents in the UK receiving Special Branch protection travelled abroad, accompanying MPSB officers acted only in a liaison and advisory role, full responsibility for the safety of the 'principal' resting with the host country, usually in the hands of their equivalent to the Metropolitan Police Special Branch.

Throughout the 1970s, with the resurgence of the PIRA and also the growing threat posed by non-UK terrorist organisations to UK diplomats and politicians, one aspect of protection was increasingly causing concern to the SB teams involved in their security. Essentially, the problem was that there existed no central government department to assess, approve, authorise and regulate the expenditure on any close-protection security equipment and, in particular, measures relating to the protection of the private homes of politicians and other VIPs assessed as being under threat. The physical and electronic measures provided and also the very critical advice given to staff, spouses and families varied greatly throughout the UK depending, to a large extent, on the policies, priorities and commitments of the respective chief constables. In most cases, ministers' own private offices would arrange directly for HMG Property Services Agency (PSA) alarm engineers and building construction experts to survey the private home of their own boss, make recommendations and, if so agreed, carry out the necessary measures. Whether the recommendations were acted upon depended very much on the particular department's budget and the whim of the minister and his Principal Private Secretary (PPS).

There was no central reference point to standardise or approve expenditure on basic equipment for personal protection teams, including such items as ministerial vehicle protection and communication equipment and personal radios for individual officers. British protection officers viewed with envy the resources and equipment available to their American and European counterparts, which highlighted the inadequacies of their own equipment, research and training.

A significant improvement in the status quo was the establishment, in the latter months of 1978, of the 'Standing Cabinet Office Committee on Ministerial Protection' (the CMP as it was referred to), which directed that all surveys of ministers' homes would henceforward be carried out by technical experts from the PSA accompanied by an officer from MPSB. Significantly, it was the Special Branch officer who would be responsible for compiling a report listing their recommendations, sending this to the appropriate PPS and, where necessary, discussing the findings with the principal. Any disagreements between the three parties concerned, i.e. SB, PPS and principal, would be referred to the CMP.

A further important step forward was achieved in the spring of 1979, when a small Special Branch Technical Protection Unit (TPU) under a detective superintendent, Colin Colson, was formed within the Special Branch complex at New Scotland Yard. Its role was to implement CMP directives and within the next few years it developed into a virtual property management agency. It was a great asset to the TPU that Colson had studied building technology, had previously been involved in Special Branch technical operations and, by virtue of three years' protection duty with the Prime Minister, was familiar with routines and staff at No. 10 and government offices in Whitehall. The efficiency of the unit was also boosted by the unstinting support it received from the PSA technical officers, from the Metropolitan Police engineering department, from other government agencies and from private commercial companies.

The TPU became responsible for the installation, care and maintenance of security measures at some forty or more properties varying from small flats in Westminster to large estates in Cornwall, farms in Sussex, an ancient listed moated building in Norfolk and castles in Scotland – the private residences of 'vulnerable' VIPs, many of whom received SB close protection too. The unit also served as a point of contact for the families and households of principals seeking advice and reassurance about the intrusion of protective measures into their daily lives, often for the first time.

At the same time, the process of assessing the vulnerability of ministers was formalised into a system which placed them within one of five levels of threat, from one (being the highest) to five. In 1985, a standard package of building protection facilities was notionally allocated to each threat level, although a number of other factors was taken into consideration when deciding the package actually provided. TPU staff were closely involved in the nature and extent of the physical protection provided and often needed to explain directly to the individual the appropriateness of all their recommendations – occasionally this would result in protracted negotiations with the principal and his or her PPS, which would normally result in an amicable agreement.

With its increasing expertise and proven competence, the advice of the TPU was frequently sought about the development of security equipment and its assistance requested for an increasing variety of one-off tasks in addition to its basic property security role. Some of the more noteworthy events in its history were:

June 1979 – the compilation of a pocket book on personal security (the 'Blue Book'), adapted from the RUC's more comprehensive version. Initially issued to Members of both Houses of Parliament, the booklet was so much in demand that distribution was extended to virtually all senior civil servants, the judiciary and senior officers of the three armed forces. It was packed with sound advice on 'measures to improve personal security', chief of which must be: 'Regardless of what assistance is provided by police, in the final analysis personal security is the responsibility of the individual.' Following the IRA bombing of the Grand Hotel in Brighton and at the instigation of the Home Secretary, a 'Brown Book' on meetings' security in the style of the 'Blue Book', but also covering wider aspects of security, was produced by the TPU for distribution to all MPs and lower echelons of political workers, e.g. constituency staff.

In 1980 – the development of an attaché case portable radio intrusion detection system which could be used when a protected VIP stayed overnight away from his or her normal place of residence in a hotel or private residence with inadequate security. This enabled the SB team to set up a secure perimeter quickly and also provide a 'personal attack' alarm to assist venue security; this was often provided at very short notice by local police.

29 July 1981 – on that day over 700 million TV viewers worldwide watched the wedding of the Prince of Wales and Lady Diana Spencer; over ninety-seven armed SB officers didn't. They were engaged in protecting the monarchs, heads of state and other dignitaries attending the event. The TPU manned an SB control room which, among other functions, ensured that the forty-three teams protecting them 'got them to the church on time' and in the right protocol order. The TPU control also endeavoured not to 'lose' any VIP during the ensuing celebrations at the Palace and the Hyde Park firework display.

In the period leading up to the big day, the TPU installed their portable alarm systems (see above) in several suites in major London hotels which would be the temporary homes of some of the guests. Thanks to a system installed at the Hilton Hotel in Park Lane, the one and only arrest by protection officers was made – a hotel thief was caught attempting to sneak up the back stairs in the hope that everyone would be watching TV!

13 November 1981 – a bomb planted by the IRA badly damaged the rented home of Sir Michael Havers, the Attorney General. At first sight it appeared that the PSA-installed and subsequently TPU-approved system had failed, but a closer examination of the scene revealed that the bomber had gained access to the rear of the property through the adjacent garden, which belonged to Sir Michael's landlady, and he (Sir Michael) had refused permission for a beam system to be installed there. He had evidently not read his 'Blue Book' or chosen to ignore the advice about personal security being, in the final analysis, the responsibility of the individual.

28 May to 2 June 1982 – the pastoral visit of Pope John Paul II to the UK (see Chapter 26) saw the close involvement of the TPU from approximately six months before the pontiff's arrival until three days after his departure. The early start was due to the frequent meetings with the Catholic Church to keep up with the continual changes in the programme and the complex logistics involved in moving both officers and four specialist papal vehicles about the UK.

The unit was particularly involved with all matters concerning transport security and took particular care to ensure that effective communication systems were available to all SB close protection officers. They also had to ensure that officers were aware that, at that time, ballistic-resistant armour, both glass and panelling, extended only to forty-eight inches from the floor in the rear compartments of all vehicles, so it might be necessary to duck down swiftly or get behind a papal figure in the event of an attack. SB protection officers normally occupy the front passenger seat.

As was the case at the royal wedding in July of the previous year, a control room was manned by TPU officers to assist all SB officers involved in the operation, motorcades, venues and lines of route surveillance.

12 October 1984 – the IRA bomb at the Grand Hotel in Brighton (see Chapter 25) was to have significant effects upon the future of the Special Branch Technical Protection Unit. Following completion of an inquiry into the lax security arrangements made for the 1984 Conservative Party conference, the Home Secretary announced the setting up of a committee chaired by the Home Office and including Police, Security Services and the Army. The intention was to plan a course for the training in search techniques of police officers from all mainland police forces. The TPU was directed by DACSB to represent the Branch in all future committee meetings and to attend the Royal School of Military Engineering, Rochester, to assist in the design of the initial POLSA (Police Search Adviser) courses to be held in April and again later in 1985. As this was a long-term commitment, DI Smither, Colson's deputy in the TPU and earmarked to succeed Colson on the latter's retirement in a year's time, was appointed to take full responsibility for all aspects of police involvement in the POLSA courses. Colin Colson duly retired in 1986 and was awarded the MBE for services to the security of the state.

Due in no small measure to his outstanding achievements with POLSA, Smither was seconded to the Home Office in September 1987 and attached as the first Police Liaison Officer (with temporary rank of DCI) to the Royal School of Military Engineering (RSME). He became a key figure in the growth of police

search training throughout the UK, and was closely involved in the establishment of the first National Search Training Centre. He retired nine years later,
in April 1996, with the rank of detective superintendent. In 1994, he had been
awarded the Queen's Police Medal for his 'distinguished service'.

What started as a single residential course in 1985, with thirty police students
of sergeant to chief inspector rank, developed into full-time ongoing courses at
three levels carried out both at RSME and within all GB police services, by one
HQ team and two fully equipped mobile teams of police and Royal Engineer
staff, comprising some eight police officers, seven Royal Engineer personnel
and a number of civilian support staff managed by a detective superintendent.

Among the more personal and rewarding tasks successfully carried out by
the TPU after the Brighton bomb, was the design of communication equipment
attached to the motorised wheelchair of Mrs Tebbit, who was severely injured
in the blast, enabling her to move freely around unaided but always in contact
with both security and care staff. The adaptation of special protective measures and alarm systems at both the Tebbits' London and country residences
also demanded several unique adoptions of other equipment. The team also
designed the security system at the new Dulwich home of the Prime Minister,
Margaret Thatcher, and her husband Denis, a job made most enjoyable by the
active assistance of the latter; always accompanied by his offer of very expert
suggestions and gin and tonics.

In 2006, when Special Branch lost its identity, management of the Technical
Protection Unit was taken over by the Home Office.

CHAPTER TWENTY-EIGHT

THE PERENNIAL IRISH PROBLEM AND TRANSFER OF THE LEAD ROLE AGAINST THE IRA TO THE SECURITY SERVICE

A FTER THE CONVICTION in June 1986 of PIRA's ace bomber Magee and other key operatives, the PIRA took time to regroup, which left the mainland comparatively free of Irish terrorism for a few years. The peace was abruptly shattered on 22 September 1989 when the Royal Marines barracks at Deal in Kent was subjected to a murderous attack. The precise target, the regiment's School of Music, was extensively damaged by the terrorists' bomb, which killed eleven bandsmen and wounded another twenty-one (one died later). Approximately 15 lbs of explosive charge was used in the manufacture of the device, which was detonated by a timing mechanism.

Within a few days of this atrocity, the attention of the counter-terrorism services was directed to South Wales. Codenamed Operation Pebble, the narrative begins with the receipt in Special Branch Reserve Room of a message from the Anti-Terrorist Branch relaying information received from Dyfed-Powys Police. In brief, the information related to a discovery by workmen re-setting a signpost on the Pembrokeshire coastal path of a quantity of electric wires and circuit boards. Unaware of the significance of the find, they loaded it into the back of their truck, where it remained over the weekend until they handed it in to the local police station at Haverfordwest. While uniformed police were investigating the site where the material had been buried, they were approached by a bird watcher, who mentioned that there was also some disturbed ground in a disused quarry some 300 yards away. The police quickly discovered the 'disturbed ground', which was in fact a massive store of arms and ammunition covered by a tarpaulin hidden by cut bracken and gorse.

After receiving this information, officers from the Anti-Terrorist Branch and MPSB, joined later by their surveillance team, were quickly on the scene to attend a conference chaired by the Assistant Chief Constable, at which it was decided to set up an OP about 200 yards from the hide to be manned by Metropolitan Police officers and the local armed response unit. SB surveillance officers inevitably drew the short straw – they were set the unenviable task of concealing themselves near the hide in atrocious conditions and remaining *in situ* initially in three-day shifts, reduced to two days when they showed signs of physical exhaustion (they were medically examined after each changeover). The stakeout lasted over seven weeks, when, to the relief of all concerned, not least the frozen watchers, two PIRA members arrived to retrieve some of the equipment and were promptly arrested.

A shrewd move by Commander George Churchill-Coleman, in charge of the operation, was to call a conference during the surveillance assuring the press, who already sensed that something was in the air, that they would get their story when the action was finished, providing they maintained silence until then. Not a word appeared in the newspapers until after the arrests and they got their story.

In December 1990, Damien McComb and Liam O'Duibhir were each sentenced to thirty years' imprisonment for conspiracy to cause explosions. This operation could not have succeeded had it not been for the excellence of the teamwork displayed by the three agencies concerned, the Anti-Terrorist Branch, MPSB and, particularly, Dyfed-Powys Police. But, above all, the stoicism and tenacity of the surveillance teams were outstanding and deserving of the utmost praise.

Regrettably, other arsenals were available to the PIRA and there followed a wave of PIRA bomb attacks throughout England which continued until April 1997, nearly three years before the 'Belfast Agreement' came into effect. The vast majority of these occurred within the Metropolitan Police District, but one notable exception was the murder of Ian Gow MP, who was killed on 30 July 1990 by a car bomb outside his Sussex home. Ian Gow, a popular member of the House of Commons and at one time Margaret Thatcher's parliamentary private secretary, was killed when a 4.5 lb Semtex bomb, which had been affixed under his car during the night, exploded as he reversed out of his driveway. He received grievous wounds to his lower body and died ten minutes later. He was a close personal friend of the Prime Minister and an outspoken opponent of the IRA. In admitting responsibility for his death, the IRA stated, 'He was targeted because he was a close personal associate of Margaret Thatcher and due to his role in developing British policy on Northern Ireland.'[1] Despite being an obvious target for the IRA, he chose to ignore security advice, parked his car on the drive and even had his telephone number recorded in the local telephone directory. Although the incident took place within the jurisdiction of the Sussex Police, Commander George Churchill-Coleman, head of the Metropolitan Police Anti-Terrorist Branch, immediately went to the scene to offer assistance, and MPSB also rendered support. No one was arrested for the crime, which was undoubtedly carried out by an IRA cell responsible for many other incidents during the current campaign.

As a direct result of the politician's assassination, enhanced physical and technical protection measures (over and above those dealt with in Chapter 27)

---

1   sussexhistoryforum.co.uk, accessed on 17 November 2014

were introduced for figures who were assessed by Special Branch to be at the greatest risk from the IRA. A scheme, codenamed Operation Octavian, provided for increased patrols around targets considered particularly vulnerable. Each of the eight areas within the Metropolitan Police District was allocated an Armed Response Vehicle crewed by a traffic patrol driver and two authorised firearms officers, which visited each of the potential targets twice within every eight-hour shift. As in Operation Neon (see below), no terrorists were arrested, but hopefully the scheme went some way towards preventing further atrocities. The cost of the scheme was to be financed out of the public purse.

The difficulty of providing protection for vulnerable personalities, particularly those who courageously or negligently failed to take basic security precautions, was further illustrated in September 1990, when Air Chief Marshal Sir Peter Terry, who was Governor of Gibraltar at the time of the controversial shooting there by the SAS of a team of would-be PIRA killers, was seriously wounded at his Staffordshire home by a lone gunman. The failed assassination by a member of the PIRA was seen as retaliation for the deaths of the three terrorists on the Rock. Like Sir Ian Gow, Sir Peter adopted a cavalier approach to his personal security, declined personal protection and kept his name in the local telephone directory and in *Who's Who*.

Another provincial atrocity that provoked a storm of bitter public condemnation took place in the centre of Warrington when an IRA bomb exploded, killing two children and wounding many other people out shopping. Once again, the Metropolitan Police Special Branch and Anti-Terrorist Branch rendered what assistance they could to the provincial police who were in charge of the investigation, but no one has ever been prosecuted for the offence.

In London, many of the early targets were military, including easily accessible premises like the Army Recruiting Centre in Wembley, where Sergeant Charles Chapman of the Queen's Regiment was killed. In an attempt to forestall this particular type of attack, Operation Neon was drawn up by Assistant Commissioner Bill Taylor, head of Special Operations. It involved the mounting of intensive surveillance for a restricted period of time on every military recruiting office in

England. A briefing organised by SB, to which senior officers from every Constabulary in the country were invited, took place at New Scotland Yard; following this, every force was encouraged to make its own contingency plans. In London alone there were at least twelve centres requiring surveillance, each of which was to be covered, front and rear, by an OP; each site was allocated an armed response vehicle with a tactical firearms team on standby. A dedicated unit was set up at Scotland Yard to monitor the operation, which dealt separately and discreetly with reports from the OPs of unrelated criminal activity. The whole scheme, a tremendous drain on resources, was shrouded in secrecy and it is to the credit of all those involved that no leakages of information appeared in the press until many years later. Regrettably, no terrorists were captured or identified through Operation Neon, although several burglars and would-be car thieves were arrested through reports from the OPs.

In the first five years of the campaign, hundreds of bombs were detonated, resulting in the loss of many lives, hundreds of injuries and damage to property amounting to millions of pounds. It is not proposed to catalogue all these events, but a number of incidents in London stand out: the attacks on Downing Street (1991), the Baltic Exchange (1992), Harrods (1993) and Bishopsgate (1993).

The mortar attack on Downing Street was probably the most audacious and, had it been successful, the most devastating of any of the IRA's attacks on the mainland. On 7 February 1991, a hired Transit van was parked in Horse Guards Avenue near the junction with Whitehall by an IRA member, who quickly left the scene on a waiting motorcycle. The van contained a rocket launcher and a number of mortar shells, each four-and-a-half-feet long and carrying a pay load of 40 lbs of Semtex. The device was aimed at the rear of 10 Downing Street but, when fired, only one shell exploded, uncomfortably close to where a Cabinet meeting was in progress some thirty yards away. Four people were injured but no members of the Cabinet were hurt. The politicians may have escaped unscathed but the incident dealt a mortal blow to Special Branch in their already doomed attempt to retain their primacy in mainland operations against Irish republicans.

From the earliest days of the establishment of MI5 in 1909, there was rivalry between the Metropolitan Police Special Branch, which had already been in existence for twenty-five years, and the new organisation. Christopher Andrew, in his history of MI5, makes frequent reference to this rivalry, which intensified in 1913 with the appointment of the flamboyant Basil Thomson to the post of Assistant Commissioner (Crime) with overall responsibility for Special Branch. He soon crossed swords with Vernon Kell, head of MO5(g), forerunner of MI5, and by 1916 had earned 'the collective enmity of most of MI5'.[2] This 'enmity' flourished over the years and Andrew refers to a 1920 document probably written by Eric Holt-Wilson, Kell's deputy until 1940, who shared his chief's distaste for Sir Basil and Special Branch:

> Sir Basil Thomson's existing higher staff consists mainly of ex-officers of MI5 not considered sufficiently able for retention by that Department. The Army Council are not satisfied with their ability to perform the necessary duties under Sir Basil Thomson's direction and they are satisfied that detective officers alone, without direction from above, are unfitted for the work.

Reference has already been made in Chapter 8 to MI5's low opinion of Special Branch, which Andrew attributes to the deep animosity of senior staff in the Security Service towards Sir Basil Thomson and resentment towards those who had jumped ship from MI5.[3]

In 1929, MPSB suffered a grievous blow to its pride when two of its officers were dismissed from the police service after being found guilty by a disciplinary board of supplying information to 'an unauthorised person'. Undoubtedly this had some influence on the Home Office's decision in June 1931 to transfer responsibility for countering domestic subversion to MI5. Vernon Kell was delighted and for the ensuing sixty years MI5 had its eyes firmly fixed on the

---

2   Andrew, *The Defence of the Realm*, pp. 81–3

3   Ibid., pp. 117–18

next goal, the lead role in countering Irish republican terrorism on the mainland. Andrew refers to the reluctance of the Security Service leadership in 1981 'to provoke a conflict with the Met by claiming the lead intelligence role against Irish republican terrorism on the mainland [...] despite its private criticism of the MPSB'.[4] This ill-concealed ambition is further illustrated by Andrew when he asserts that Stella Rimington, who became their Director General in 1992, 'argued that the aftermath of the Brighton bombing would have been the moment for the Security Service to claim from the MPSB the lead intelligence role in combating Irish republican terrorism in Britain'. Rimington blamed senior management who had not wanted to take on the responsibility because they were afraid of criticism if they failed. Andrew adds his own comment that the 'ineffectiveness of PIRA mainland operations after the Brighton bombing also lessened what pressure there was for a radical reorganisation of counter-terrorism'.[5] He neglects to mention that this 'ineffectiveness' was due, in no small measure, to the major role played by MPSB in forestalling the planned PIRA series of bombing attacks in London and holiday resorts in 1985, described earlier.

For many years, MI5 confined discussion of their aspirations to the higher echelons of the Service, but although they kept MPSB in the dark about their ultimate intentions, it was common knowledge among the senior ranks of 'C' Department at New Scotland Yard that the Security Service would dearly love to add the Irish lead role to their repertoire. However, early in 1991, the Service abandoned its previous hesitancy in bidding for that role with a whole series of measures. Impetus was given to their efforts by what must have seemed to them a gift from the gods, the 1991 PIRA mortar-bomb attack on 10 Downing Street, which Stella Rimington saw as 'strengthening the case for Service primacy over MPSB in mainland operations against Irish republicans'.[6]

---

4   Ibid., p. 696

5   Ibid., p. 734

6   Stella Rimington, *Open Secret* (London: Hutchinson, 2001), p. 220

Having already set up a new 'T' Branch to deal with its existing Irish counter-terrorist responsibilities, MI5 secured ministerial approval in April 1991 for increased counter-terrorist resources. By June, it had begun preparing a detailed case for the transfer of the lead intelligence role against Irish terrorism from MPSB. In July 1991, Sir Gerry Warner, described by Andrew as 'the most influential Whitehall supporter of the Service case', was appointed Intelligence Co-ordinator. This sounded the death knell for any hopes that the MPSB had for retaining its lead responsibilities, for Warner was to play a significant role in influencing the future of counter-terrorism on the mainland.

Soon after his appointment, Warner persuaded the chairman of the Joint Intelligence Committee, Sir Percy Cradock, to visit the Service for briefings. It was no great surprise that within days the Director General of the Security Service and Sir Percy met the Cabinet Secretary for discussions about a hypothetical takeover. The Security Service's plans were sent to Sir Robin Butler, the Cabinet Secretary, at which point the transfer of responsibilities was a fait accompli. Within a week, the Cabinet Secretary told a meeting attended by the Director General, Warner, Cradock and the Permanent Under-Secretary at the Home Office that the benefits accruing from a transfer of responsibility now outweighed the possible disruption that the change would involve. The Prime Minister, John Major, agreed but, due to the complexities involved, first sought a review and report, which was to be undertaken by Ian Burns, Deputy Under-Secretary at the Home Office.

While the above negotiations were proceeding with indecent haste, MPSB was not formally consulted and, although general rumours existed, the scale and knowledge of the Security Service's political manoeuvrings were confined to a very select audience.

Burns subsequently met the police side, represented by Assistant Commissioner Specialist Operations Bill Taylor; DAC John Howley, Head of MPSB, and Commander Operations Don Buchanan. He explained that his remit was to review how the resources of MPSB and the Security Service could be best structured and directed in the future to deal with PIRA terrorism on the mainland,

and make recommendations. After individual meetings had taken place, the Metropolitan Police was invited to prepare a paper setting out its proposals. The submission articulated a powerful case for MPSB to retain the lead responsibility within a broader structure, embracing the Security Service's extensive technical resources and manpower. The police case stressed the intelligence/evidential interface through liaison with the Anti-Terrorist Branch, the positive embedded relationships with the RUC and An Garda Síochána, the comprehensive Special Branch Records system, expertise in criminal law and court procedure and their familiarity and knowledge of the Irish scene based on over 100 years of intelligence-gathering and investigations. Burns accepted that this report highlighted a number of important issues which, hitherto, had not been considered or acknowledged by the Security Service, but he also sought the views of selected provincial chief constables and heads of Special Branches; unhelpfully (to the Branch) some of the latter, at best, were lukewarm in their support for MPSB.

Unsurprisingly, Burns recommended that the lead responsibility for combating Irish republican terrorism on the mainland be transferred from MPSB to the Security Service. Shortly afterwards, there was a series of meetings at the Security Service to discuss arrangements for the handover. Representing the Security Service were Stephen Lander, Eliza Manningham-Buller and Jonathan Evans – the principals behind the successful bid – who were, in due course, destined to become successive Directors General of the Service. These meetings were fractious affairs. The Security Service team displayed breathtaking arrogance and demanded that the transfer take place forthwith, as they were fully prepared and organised for their new role. MPSB pointed out that, to maintain continuity, minimise disruption and avoid compromising existing investigations, the handover must be carried out incrementally within a structured plan. The Security Service reluctantly accepted this approach after being apprised of the scale and complexities involved.

The reason for their haste was abundantly obvious. The end of the Cold War, the collapse of the Soviet bloc and the disintegration of the Soviet Union meant a rapid de-escalation in the subversive and espionage threat to this country.[7] The large number of officers dealing with those matters thus became virtually redundant and Operation Ascribe was as much a means of securing new work for them as its advertised intention of providing a more professional approach to the threat posed by Irish republican terrorism.

The decision to remove the lead role from MPSB was announced to the House of Commons on 8 May 1992 and there followed five months of fraught negotiations between the two services before the official handover from MPSB to the Security Service took place on 1 October 1992.[8]

THE CONTINUING PIRA CAMPAIGN

Blissfully ignorant of the internecine struggle that was exercising the minds of the security services, the PIRA pressed on with their campaign and now turned their eyes towards the City of London for their next target. The bomb that extensively damaged the Baltic Exchange on 10 April 1992 was devastating to British commercial trading, as the Exchange was at the hub of world shipping interests and had been since the middle of the eighteenth century. The device that created the explosion weighed one ton and comprised homemade explosive wrapped in 100 lbs of Semtex. It killed three people and injured nearly 100.[9] The event marked a shift in the PIRA's targeting policy and the beginning of a potentially crippling offensive against the City of London, at that time the commercial capital of the world. Christopher Andrew cites a Whitehall report which states: 'The cost of four or five similar explosions [to the Baltic Exchange] would have been equivalent to the contingency reserve for a financial year.' Andrew

7   Andrew, *The Defence of the Realm*, p. 771

8   The above section relies to a large extent on details contained in *The Defence of the Realm* and on conversations with the head of MPSB at the time, DAC John Howley, and his Commander Operations, Don Buchanan

9   A. R. Oppenheimer, *The Bombs and the Bullets: A History of Deadly Ingenuity* (Dublin: Irish Academy Press, 2009), p. 124

comments, 'The Service's role in preventing a series of City bombings on the scale of that at the Baltic Exchange made an important and perhaps crucial difference to the struggle against PIRA.'[10]

Nevertheless, the Service was unable to prevent the PIRA from detonating a bomb, similar in size and composition, at the NatWest Tower in Bishopsgate on 24 April 1993, killing one person, inflicting injuries on thirty more and causing damage estimated at £350 million. However, a sophisticated Security Service operation, in which Special Branch (as well as many other agencies) played a crucial role, helped to forestall an extension of the offensive. This operation, which the Security Service initiated with surveillance on a senior member of the IRA, Robert 'Rab' Fryers, revealed that Fryers intended to elude the 'ring of steel' that police had placed round the City of London by carrying a bomb on a bus, as he believed only private motor vehicles were being stopped. He had confided to a confederate, Hugh Jack, that he would drive from Scotland to the Scratchwood Service Station on the M1 and, after a rest, would continue his drive to Neasden, where he proposed to catch a bus into the City. Unbeknown to Fryers, he was tracked by MI5 surveillance teams to Scratchwood, where MPSB surveillance officers took up the chase early in the morning of 14 July 1993 and arrested him in Neasden after he had parked his car. At the time of his arrest he was in possession of a timer and power unit (TPU), 2 lbs of Semtex explosive and half a gallon of petrol in a plastic container. His accomplice, Jack, together with some friends and relatives, was arrested by Central Scotland Police shortly afterwards; this led to the discovery in local woods of sufficient Semtex, TPUs and detonators to construct six car bombs for use in a continuance of the City of London campaign. At their Old Bailey trial on 20 January 1995, Fryers was jailed for twenty-five years and Jack for twenty years. This success was some compensation to the Security Service for their failure to prevent the Bishopsgate bomb, which Stephen Lander described as 'one of the low points in his career'.[11]

---

10   Andrew, *The Defence of the Realm*, p. 782

11   Ibid., p. 783, citing 'Recollections of Stephen Lander'

On 13 May 1994, two Englishmen, Patrick Hayes and Jan Taylor, were each sentenced to thirty years' imprisonment for their part in a number of the incidents that took place during the recent campaign and for possession of explosives and firearms. This was an atypical example of Irish republican terrorism, for not only were the two principal protagonists English, but their political antecedents did not suggest that they were hardened terrorists. However, the pair were both known to Special Branch: Jan Taylor had a 1984 conviction for selling Sinn Féin literature in a Hammersmith public house and Hayes was heavily involved with Red Action, an extreme left-wing/anarchic organisation that strongly supported the Irish republican movement, but was essentially a violent anti-fascist organisation.

The pair were caught on CCTV outside Harrods on 28 January 1993, when Hayes was seen to drop a package, later proved to be a bomb containing about 1lb of Semtex, into a metal litter bin. Approximately half an hour later, at 9.40 a.m., the bomb exploded, slightly injuring four people and causing extensive damage to a window display. It was not until a month later that an experienced and perceptive Special Branch officer, examining images from the video, identified Hayes. Not long afterwards, armed police burst into Hayes's basement flat in Stoke Newington and arrested him and Taylor. The flat contained damning evidence against the pair – 22 lbs of Semtex, hand guns and ammunition, detonators, timing devices and the keys to Pandora's box: a lock-up garage in Muswell Hill which was a store-house for a large quantity of explosives. It was apparent that the attack on Harrods was not an isolated incident and forensic evidence linked them both with a recent attack on a train in Kent and Hayes along with several large lorry bombs similar to the ones used at the Baltic Exchange and Bishopsgate.[12]

While Hayes and Taylor were awaiting trial, MPSB played a vital role in another successful MI5-led operation which prevented further carnage being perpetrated by the IRA. In January 1994, Security Service watchers commenced

12   *The Independent*, 14 May 1994

a protracted surveillance operation on Feilim Hamill (Feilim O'Hadhmaill), a lecturer at the University of Central Lancashire in Preston. After weeks of patient surveillance, the watchers followed him by a tortuous trail to a South Mimms motorway service station where he entered a Datsun motor car, which MI5 intelligence suggested contained bomb-making equipment. Hamill drove the car home to Accrington, where he had begun dismantling it in the garage when he was surprised in the act by armed Special Branch personnel in company with MI5 officers storming in to arrest him. A vast array of detonators, Semtex, magnetic booby trap bombs, a pistol and ammunition and TPUs was recovered, which led to his conviction in November 1994 and a sentence of twenty-five years' imprisonment.[13]

There followed a temporary lull in the IRA's terrorist activities as the so-called 'Peace Process' teetered towards its eventual conclusion; Loyalist bombings and shootings, however, continued regardless. This fragile truce was shattered on 9 February 1996, when the PIRA detonated a massive truck bomb near the Docklands Light Railway in the Canary Wharf complex, killing two people, injuring many others and causing extensive damage to commercial buildings and railway property. Following an exhaustive investigation by MPSB and Anti-Terrorist Branch officers, James McArdle was arrested, convicted of conspiracy to cause explosions and, on 25 June 1998, sentenced to twenty-five years' imprisonment.[14] He served only a tiny fraction of this term, as he was released under the terms of the Good Friday Agreement in 2000. Other PIRA members responsible for this incident had been arrested in South Armagh in April 1997.

Before this peace pact came into effect, the PIRA made a final effort to mount a large-scale campaign on the mainland. That they failed in their mission was due to a superhuman response by the security forces, who not only prevented the terrorists carrying out their plans but in the process netted a number of the

---

13   Tony Geraghty, *The Irish War: The Hidden Conflict Between the IRA and British Intelligence* (London: Harper Collins,1998), pp. 149–51

14   *The Independent*, 25 June 1998

PIRA's top operatives. Special Branch played a not insignificant role in two major operations codenamed 'Airlines' and 'Tinnitus', alongside officers from the Security Service, Metropolitan Police Firearms Unit, the Anti-Terrorist and Criminal Intelligence Branches.

But, prior to these operations taking place, a massive search, unique in the history of the war against the IRA terrorist campaign in mainland Britain, struck the PIRA in their supposedly impregnable fortress of South Armagh, which intelligence clearly indicated was linked, either through personnel or direction, to most of the recent Irish atrocities in this country. In June 1996, Commander John Grieve, recently appointed head of the Anti-Terrorist Branch, led a contingent of officers from his department, reinforced by an MPSB presence supplying critically vital intelligence, into this PIRA stronghold, seeking, among other things, evidence for the Docklands bombing. According to Toby Harnden, more than 1,000 soldiers from British regiments sealed off Mullaghbawn and Forkhill while ninety officers from the Metropolitan Police were flown in. Several vehicles were airlifted back to England for forensic examination but, although there were arrests, no convictions followed. What was most important from a police viewpoint was the deep psychological impact the raid had on the PIRA; to quote John Grieve, 'It makes life much more difficult for [them] in the future.'[15]

Undeterred, in June 1996 a team of known members of the PIRA began actively plotting to bring chaos to London and the south-east of England by blowing up pylons and electricity sub-stations in the area. In July, a massive surveillance operation, which included electronic eavesdropping, was mounted by the security forces. Members of the terrorist cell were seen reconnoitring power stations over a wide area from Amersham in the north to Canterbury in the south; they were followed as they conducted research in public libraries where they obtained information about the National Grid and they were known to have acquired ladders for scaling the perimeter fences round their targets.

---

15   Toby Harnden, 'Bandit Country': The IRA and South Armagh (London: Hodder & Stoughton, 2000), pp. 247–8

On 15 July, the three addresses used by the conspirators were raided by MI5 officers and teams of police, some armed, who took possession of thirty-seven bombs already made up, together with false documents, money and plans for future PIRA operations.[16]

At the end of their Old Bailey trial on 2 July 1997, the six members of the team, Donal Gannon, John Crawley, Gerard Hanratty, Robert Morrow, Patrick Martin and Francis Rafferty, were each sentenced to thirty-five years' imprisonment for conspiracy to cause explosions. Two others, Clive Brampton and Martin Murphy, were acquitted.[17]

In Operation Tinnitus, four members of a second PIRA team plotting to cause massive explosions in England in September 1996 were arrested after weeks of a sophisticated surveillance operation involving the combined forces of the Anti-Terrorist Branch, Special Branch and MI5. At the Old Bailey in December 1997, Brian McHugh, leader of the group, was sentenced to twenty-five years' imprisonment, Patrick Kelly, twenty years, James Murphy, seventeen years, and a fourth member of the ASU was acquitted; Diarmuid O'Neill was shot dead in the raid on his Hammersmith flat, the first member of the IRA to lose his life at the hands of 'the enemy' in this country, although a number died of self-inflicted wounds.

Between June 2000 and November 2001, the Real IRA (RIRA; a maverick group who did not recognise the Good Friday Agreement) carried out a number of comparatively minor attacks chiefly on the SIS headquarters at Vauxhall (with an RPG-22 rocket), outside the BBC TV Centre in west London and at Ealing Broadway, where seven people were injured. Later, four RIRA members were sentenced to terms of imprisonment ranging from twenty to twenty-two years while a fourth, on account of his age, was ordered to be detained for twenty-one years.

There were no further Irish republican attacks on the mainland before

---

16   Andrew, *The Defence of the Realm*, pp. 795–7

17   *The Independent*, 3 July 1997

2006, when Special Branch (SO12) as an entity ceased to exist, ending a tradition that had been proudly upheld for over 120 years. It is something of a paradox that after the Security Service took the lead role in countering Irish republican terrorism the Branch's primary focus became more Irish-orientated, with the bulk of surveillance, technical and operational support being targeted against PIRA – tasks that its officers, despite the disappointment of losing the lead on Irish republican terrorism, undertook with typical professionalism, dedication and probity. In the final years of its existence, the establishment of 'B' Squad rose to a record level of 150 or more officers, thirty of whom comprised an intelligence cell concentrating on maintaining and improving the already excellent links with An Garda Síochána and the RUC, the source of some of the vital leads resulting in many of the successful operations against the terrorists.

Meanwhile, other traditional roles that the Branch had successfully performed over the years – naturalisation, protection, prosecution of espionage offenders and the monitoring of anarchists, among others – continued to be carried out quietly and efficiently. It is a tribute to the calibre of Special Branch personnel that no fewer than seven of its members were selected to become chief officers of other police forces – Brian Hayes (Kent); Victor Gilbert (Cambridgeshire); Michael Fuller (Kent); Ben Gunn (Cambridgeshire); Hugh Annesley (RUC) – while Peter Imbert eventually became Commissioner of the Metropolitan Police.

•   •   •

I t is a measure of the regard that former members of the Branch hold for their old department and the camaraderie that was forged through many years' involvement in pursuing a common and, one felt, worthy cause – the defence of the realm – that over 300 one-time colleagues keep in touch through membership of an 'old boys' association and regular social gatherings, some of which attract up to sixty rapidly ageing pensioners. They are proud of the history and

tradition of the Branch and it is hoped that this book will go some way to preserving that history.

BIBLIOGRAPHY

Adams, Ian, *Fenian Folly: The Story of the Clerkenwell Explosion on Friday 13 December, 1867*, Spiker Publications, Titchfield, 2006.

Adams, Ian, *The Sabotage Plan*, Spiker Publications, Titchfield, 2011.

Agee, Philip, *Inside the Company: CIA Diary*, Allen Lane, London, 1975.

Allason, Rupert, *The Branch: A History of the Metropolitan Police Special Branch 1883–1983*, Secker & Warburg, London, 1983.

Anderson, Gerald D., *Fascists, Communists and the National Government: Civil Liberties in Great Britain, 1931–1937*, University of Missouri Press, Columbia, 1983.

Anderson, Robert, *The Lighter Side of My Official Life*, Hodder & Stoughton, London, 1910.

Andrew, Christopher, *Secret Service: The Making of the British Intelligence Community*, Hodder & Stoughton, London, 1986.

Andrew, Christopher, *The Defence of the Realm: The Authorized History of MI5*, Allen Lane, London, 2009.

Ascoli, David, *The Queen's Peace*, Hamish Hamilton, London, 1979.

Barnes, James J. and Patience B. Barnes, *Nazis in Pre-War London 1930–1939: The Fate and Role of German Party Members and British Sympathizers*, Sussex Academic Press, Brighton, 2005.

Barr, James, *A Line in the Sand: Britain, France and the Struggle that Shaped the Middle East*, Simon & Schuster, London, 2011.

Barrington, Mary A. (ed.), *The Irish Independence Movement on Tyneside 1919–1921*, Dun Laoghaire Genealogical Society, 1999.

Behan, Brendan, *Borstal Boy*, Avon, New York, 1955.

Bennett, Gill, *History Notes: A Most Extraordinary and Mysterious Business: The Zinoviev Letter of 1924*, Foreign and Commonwealth Office, London, 1999.

Bennett, Gill, *Churchill's Man of Mystery: Desmond Morton and the World of Intelligence*, Routledge, London, 2007.

Bennett, Richard, *The Black and Tans*, Hulton, London, 1959.

Bew, Paul, *Land and the National Question in Ireland, 1858–82*, Gill & Macmillan, Dublin, 1978.

Blake, George, *No Other Choice: An Autobiography*, Jonathan Cape, London, 1990.

Boghardt, Thomas, *Spies of the Kaiser: German Covert Operations in Great Britain During the First World War Era*, Palgrave Macmillan, Basingstoke, 2004.

Bourke, Sean, *The Springing of George Blake*, Cassell, London, 1990.

Brady, Edward, *The Irish Secret Service in England, 1919–21*, Payot, Paris, 1933.

Brust, Harold, *I Guarded Kings: The Memoirs of a Political Police Officer*, Stanley Paul & Co., London, 1935.

Burt, Leonard, *Commander Burt of Scotland Yard*, Pan Books, London, 1962.

Childs, Sir Wyndham, *Episodes and Reflections: being some records from the life of Major-General Sir Wyndham Childs, K.C.M.G., K.B.E., C.B.*, Cassell & Co., London, 1930.

Churchill, Sir Winston, *The Gathering Storm: The Second World War, Vol. 1*, Cassell, London, 1948.

Conrad, Joseph, *The Secret Agent*, Vintage Books, London, 2007.

Coogan, T. P., *The IRA*, Fontana Books, London, 1980.

Cook, Andrew, *M: MI5's First Spymaster*, Tempus, Stroud, 2004.

Critchley, T. A., *A History of Police in England and Wales, 900–1966*, Constable, London, 1967.

Cronin, Sean, *The McGarrity Papers*, Anvil, Tralee, Ireland, 1977.

Denieffe, Joseph, *A Personal Narrative of the Irish Revolutionary Brotherhood*, Irish University Press, Shannon, 1969.

Dickens, Charles, 'The Detective Police' in *The Uncommercial Traveller and Reprinted Pieces etc.*, Oxford University Press, London, 1958 (first published in 1868).

Dipaola, Petro, *Italian Anarchists in London, 1870–1914*, University of London, London, 2004.

Doherty, Shane Paul, *The Volunteer: A Former IRA Man's True Story*, Fount, London, 1993.

Dorril, Stephen, *Blackshirt: Sir Oswald Mosley and British Fascism*, Penguin, London, 2007.

Doyle, Conan, 'The Adventure of the Bruce Partington Plans' in *The Penguin Complete Sherlock Holmes*, Penguin, London, 2001.

Eatwell, Roger, *Fascism: A History*, Chatto & Windus, London, 1995.

Emsley, Clive, *Crime and Society in England, 1750–1900*, 2nd edition, Addison Wesley Longman, Harlow, Essex, 1996.

Emsley, Clive, *The English Police: A Political and Social History*, 2nd edition, Addison Wesley Longman, Harlow, Essex, 1996.

Enno, Stephan, *Spies in Ireland*, MacDonald, London, 1963.

Fairfield, Letitia (ed.), *The Trial of Peter Barnes and others: The IRA Coventry Explosion of 1939*, Hodge, London, 1953.

Fitch, Herbert, *Memoirs of a Royal Detective*, Hurst & Blackett, London, 1933.

Fitch, Herbert, *Traitors Within*, Hurst & Blackett, London, 1933.

Geraghty, Tony, *The Irish War: The Hidden Conflict Between the IRA and British Intelligence*, Harper Collins, London, 1998.

Goodway, David, *London Chartism, 1838–1848*, Cambridge University Press, Cambridge, 1982.

Gray, Tony, *Ireland This Century*, Little, Brown, London, 1994.

Griffiths, Richard, *Patriotism Perverted: Captain Ramsay, the Right Club and British Anti-Semitism, 1939-1940*, Constable, London, 1998.

Harnden, Toby, *Bandit Country: The IRA and South Armagh*, Hodder & Stoughton, London, 2000.

Heaps, Leo, *Thirty Years with the KGB: The Double Life of Hugh Hambleton*, Methuen, London, 1984.

Holland, Jack and Susan Phoenix, *Phoenix: Policing the Shadows*, Coronet, London, 1997.

Jeffery, Keith, *MI6: The History of the Secret Intelligence Service, 1909-1949*, Bloomsbury, London, 2010.

Jeyes, S. H. and F. D. How, *The Life of Sir Howard Vincent*, George Allen, London, 1912.

Kee, Robert, *Ireland: A History*, Sphere Books, London, 1982.

Kee, Robert, *The Bold Fenian Men*, Penguin, London, 1989.

Kitchener, R. *The Memoirs of an Old Detective, 1910-37*, Unpublished.

Le Caron, Henri, *Twenty-Five Years in the Secret Service: The Recollections of a Spy*, EP Publishing, Wakefield, 1972.

Ledger, Sally and Roger Luckhurst, *The Fin de Siècle: A Reader in Cultural History c. 1880-1900*, OUP, Oxford, 2000.

Littlechild, John, *The Reminiscences of Chief Inspector Littlechild*, Leadenhall Press, London, 1894.

Lyons, F. S. L., *Ireland since the Famine*, Weidenfeld & Nicolson, London, 1971

Madeira, Victor, 'Moscow's Interwar Infiltration of British Intelligence', in *The Historical Journal 46*, Cambridge University Press, December 2003.

Matthews, L. Harrison and Maxwell Knight, *The Senses of Animals*, Methuen, London, 1963.

Morton, James, *Spies of the First World War*, National Archives, London, 2010.

Moysey, Steven P., *The Road to Balcombe Street: the IRA Reign of Terror in London*, Routledge, London, 2009.

Murphy, James, H., *Ireland: A Social, Cultural and Literary History, 1791-1891*, Four Courts Press, Dublin, 2003.

O'Brien, R. Barry, *The Life of Charles Stewart Parnell*, two volumes, Smith, Elder & Co., London, 1898.

O'Brien, William and Desmond Ryan, eds, *Devoy's Post Bag: 1871–1928*, vol. 2: *1880–1928*, Irish Academy Press, Dublin, 1953.

Oppenheimer, A. R. *The Bombs and the Bullets: A History of Deadly Ingenuity*, Irish Academy Press, Dublin, 2009.

Pankhurst, Sylvia, *The Suffragette Movement: An Intimate Account of Persons and Ideals,* Virago, London, 1977.

Porter, Bernard, *Plots and Paranoia*, Unwin, London, 1986.

Porter, Bernard, *The Origins of the Vigilant State*, Weidenfeld & Nicolson, London, 1987.

Randle, Michael and Patrick Pottle, *The Blake Escape: How We Freed George Blake – and Why*, Harrap, London, 1989.

Rawlinson, Peter, *A Price Too High: An Autobiography*, Weidenfeld & Nicolson, London, 1989.

Rimington, Stella, *Open Secret*, Hutchinson, London, 2001.

Rushdie, Salman, *Joseph Anton: A Memoir,* Jonathan Cape, London, 2012.

Saikia, Robin (ed.), *The Red Book: The Membership List of the Right Club, 1939*, Foxley Books, London, 2010.

Saunders, Hilary St George, and Denis Richards, *Royal Air Force 1939–45, Vol. III: The Fight is Won*, Her Majesty's Stationery Office, London, 1955

Sellers, Leonard, *Shot in the Tower: The Story of the Spies Executed in the Tower of London During the First World War,* Leo Cooper, London, 1997.

Short, K. R. M., *The Dynamite War*, Gill & Macmillan, Dublin, 1979.

Sillitoe, Percy, *Cloak Without Dagger*, Cassell & Co., London, 1955.

Smith, Philip Thurmond, *Policing Victorian London: Political Policing, Public Order and the London Metropolitan Police,* Greenwood Press, Connecticut, 1985.

Srebrnik, Henry Felix, *London Jews and British Communism,* Vallentine Mitchell, Ilford, 1995.

Sweeney, John, *At Scotland Yard: Being the Experiences During Twenty-Seven*

Years' Service of John Sweeney, Reproduction by Harvard Law School Library, Grant Richards, London, 1904.

Templewood, Viscount, *Nine Troubled Years*, Collins, London, 1954.

Thompson, W. H., *I Was Churchill's Shadow*, C. Johnson, London, 1951

Thurlow, Richard, *The Secret State, British Internal Security in the Twentieth Century*, Blackwell, Oxford, 1994.

Trahair, Richard and Robert Miller, *Encyclopaedia of Cold War Espionage, Spies and Secret Operations*, Enigma, New York, 2012.

Watts, W. H., 'Records of an Old Police Court' in *St James's Magazine*, 12, 1865.

West, Nigel, *MI5: British Security Service Operations, 1909–45*, The Bodley Head, London, 1981

West, Nigel, *A Matter of Trust: MI5, 1945–72*, Weidenfeld & Nicolson, London, 1982.

Wilkinson, George, *Special Branch Officer*, Odhams, London, 1956.

Woodhall, Edwin T., *Spies of the Great War*, John Long, London, 1936.

Young, Sarah J., *Russians in London* (sarahjyoung.com/site/2011/01/16/).

NEWSPAPERS, JOURNALS & PERIODICALS

An Phoblacht

An t'Óglách

Criminal Law Review

Daily Express

Daily Herald

Daily Telegraph

Evening Standard

Fun

Glasgow Herald

The Guardian

Hansard

The Independent

Irish Exile

Irish Nation

Irish World

Pall Mall Gazette

Police Orders

Punch

The Times

ABBREVIATIONS

TNA: The National Archives, Kew

ADM: Admiralty

CAB: Cabinet Office

FO: Foreign Office

HO: Home Office

KV: Security Service

MEPO: Metropolitan Police

WO: War Office

WVHP: Harcourt papers, Bodleian Library, Oxford

INDEX